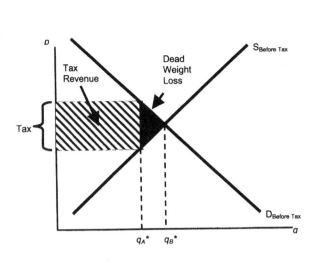

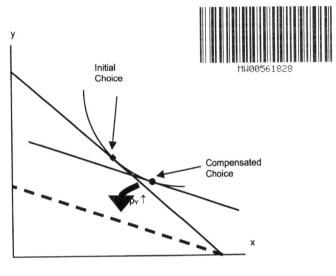

Introduction to Economic Analysis

by

R. Preston McAfee

J. Stanley Johnson Professor of Business, Economics & Management

California Institute of Technology

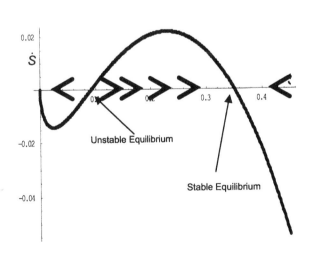

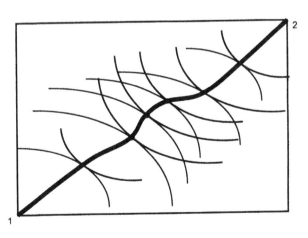

Dedication to this edition:

For Sophie. Perhaps by the time she goes to university, we'll have won the war against the publishers.

Disclaimer:

This is the third draft. Please point out typos, errors or poor exposition, preferably by email to intro@mcafee.cc. Your assistance matters.

In preparing this manuscript, I have received assistance from many people, including Michael Bernstein, Steve Bisset, Grant Chang-Chien, Lauren Feiler, Alex Fogel, Ben Golub, George Hines, Richard Jones, Jorge Martínez, Joshua Moses, Dr. John Ryan, and Wei Eileen Xie. I am especially indebted to Anthony B. Williams for a careful, detailed reading of the manuscript yielding hundreds of improvements.

Introduction to Economic Analysis
Version 2.0

by

R. Preston McAfee

J. Stanley Johnson Professor of Business, Economics & Management

California Institute of Technology

Begun: June 24, 2004
This Draft: July 24, 2006

This book presents introductory economics ("principles") material using standard mathematical tools, including calculus. It is designed for a relatively sophisticated undergraduate who has not taken a basic university course in economics. It also contains the standard intermediate microeconomics material and some material that ought to be standard but is not. The book can easily serve as an intermediate microeconomics text. The focus of this book is on the conceptual tools and not on fluff. Most microeconomics texts are mostly fluff and the fluff market is exceedingly over-served by $100+ texts. In contrast, this book reflects the approach actually adopted by the majority of economists for understanding economic activity. There are lots of models and equations and no pictures of economists.

Table of Contents

1 What is Economics?

Economics studies the allocation of scarce resources among people – examining what goods and services wind up in the hands of which people. Why scarce resources? Absent scarcity, there is no significant allocation issue. All practical, and many impractical, means of allocating scarce resources are studied by economists. Markets are an important means of allocating resources, so economists study markets. Markets include stock markets like the New York Stock Exchange, commodities markets like the Chicago Mercantile, but also farmer's markets, auction markets like Christie's or Sotheby's (made famous in movies by people scratching their noses and inadvertently purchasing a Ming vase) or eBay, or more ephemeral markets, such as the market for music CDs in your neighborhood. In addition, goods and services (which are scarce resources) are allocated by governments, using taxation as a means of acquiring the items. Governments may be controlled by a political process, and the study of allocation by the politics, which is known as political economy, is a significant branch of economics. Goods are allocated by certain means, like theft, deemed illegal by the government, and such allocation methods nevertheless fall within the domain of economic analysis; the market for marijuana remains vibrant despite interdiction by the governments of most nations. Other allocation methods include gifts and charity, lotteries and gambling, and cooperative societies and clubs, all of which are studied by economists.

Some markets involve a physical marketplace. Traders on the New York Stock Exchange get together in a trading pit. Traders on eBay come together in an electronic marketplace. Other markets, which are more familiar to most of us, involve physical stores that may or may not be next door to each other, and customers who search among the stores, purchasing when the customer finds an appropriate item at an acceptable price. When we buy bananas, we don't typically go to a banana market and purchase from one of a dozen or more banana sellers, but instead go to a grocery store. Nevertheless, in buying bananas, the grocery stores compete in a market for our banana patronage, attempting to attract customers to their stores and inducing them to purchase bananas.

Price – exchange of goods and services for money – is an important allocation means, but price is hardly the only factor even in market exchanges. Other terms, such as convenience, credit terms, reliability, and trustworthiness are also valuable to the participants in a transaction. In some markets such as 36 inch Sony WEGA televisions, one ounce bags of Cheetos, or Ford Autolite spark plugs, the products offered by distinct sellers are identical, and for such products, price is usually the primary factor considered by buyers, although delivery and other aspects of the transaction may still matter. For other products, like restaurant meals, camcorders by different manufacturers, or air travel on distinct airlines, the products differ to some degree, and thus the qualities of the product are factors in the decision to purchase. Nevertheless, different products may be considered to be in a single market if the products are reasonable substitutes, and we can consider a "quality-adjusted" price for these different goods.

Economic analysis is used in many situations. When British Petroleum sets the price for its Alaskan crude oil, it uses an estimated demand model, both for gasoline consumers and also for the refineries to which BP sells. The demand for oil by refineries is governed by a complex economic model used by the refineries and BP estimates the demand by refineries by estimating the economic model used by refineries. Economic analysis was used by experts in the antitrust suit brought by the U.S. Department of Justice both to understand Microsoft's incentive to foreclose (eliminate from the market) rival Netscape and consumer behavior in the face of alleged foreclosure. Stock market analysts use economic models to forecast the profits of companies in order to predict the price of their stocks. When the government forecasts the budget deficit or considers a change in environmental regulations, it uses a variety of economic models. This book presents the building blocks of the models in common use by an army of economists thousands of times per day.

1.1.1 Normative and Positive Theories

Economic analysis is used for two main purposes. The first is a scientific understanding of how allocations of goods and services – scarce resources – are actually determined. This is a *positive* analysis, analogous to the study of electromagnetism or molecular biology, and involves only the attempt to understand the world around us. The development of this positive theory, however, suggests other uses for economics. Economic analysis suggests how distinct changes in laws, rules and other government interventions in markets will affect people, and in some cases, one can draw a conclusion that a rule change is, on balance, socially beneficial. Such analyses combine positive analysis – predicting the effects of changes in rules – with value judgments, and are known as *normative* analyses. For example, a gasoline tax used to build highways harms gasoline buyers (who pay higher prices), but helps drivers (who face fewer potholes and less congestion). Since drivers and gasoline buyers are generally the same people, a normative analysis may suggest that everyone will benefit. This type of outcome, where everyone is made better off by a change, is relatively uncontroversial.

In contrast, *cost-benefit analysis* weighs the gains and losses to different individuals and suggests carrying out changes that provide greater benefits than harm. For example, a property tax used to build a local park creates a benefit to those who use the park, but harms those who own property (although, by increasing property values, even non-users obtain some benefits). Since some of the taxpayers won't use the park, it won't be the case that everyone benefits on balance. Cost-benefit analysis weighs the costs against the benefits. In the case of the park, the costs are readily monetized (turned into dollars), because the costs to the tax-payers are just the amount of the tax. In contrast, the benefits are much more challenging to estimate. Conceptually, the benefits are the amount the park users would be willing to pay to use the park if the park charged admission. However, if the park doesn't charge admission, we would have to estimate willingness-to-pay. In principle, the park provides greater benefits than costs if the benefits to the users exceed the losses to the taxpayers. However, the park also involves transfers from one group to another.

Welfare analysis provides another approach to evaluating government intervention into markets. Welfare analysis posits social preferences and goals, like helping the poor. Generally a welfare analysis involves performing a cost-benefit analysis taking account not just of the overall gains and losses, but also weighting those gains and losses by their effects on other social goals. For example, a property tax used to subsidize the opera might provide more value than costs, but the bulk of property taxes are paid by lower and middle income people, while the majority of opera-goers are rich. Thus, the opera subsidy represents a transfer from relatively low income people to richer people, which is not consistent with societal goals of equalization. In contrast, elimination of sales taxes on basic food items like milk and bread generally has a relatively greater benefit to the poor, who spend a much larger percentage of their income on food, than to the rich. Thus, such schemes may be considered desirable not so much for their overall effects but for their redistribution effects. Economics is helpful not just in providing methods for determining the overall effects of taxes and programs, but also the *incidence* of these taxes and programs, that is, who pays, and who benefits. What economics can't do, however, is say who ought to benefit. That is a matter for society at large to decide.

1.1.2 Opportunity Cost

Economists use the idea of cost in a slightly quirky way that makes sense once you think about it, and we use the term *opportunity cost* to remind you occasionally of our idiosyncratic notion of cost. For an economist, the cost of something is not just the cash payment, but all of the value given up in the process of acquiring the thing. For example, the cost of a university education involves tuition, and text book purchases, and also the wages that would have been earned during the time at university, but were not. Indeed, the value of the time spent in acquiring the education – how much enjoyment was lost – is part of the cost of education. However, some "costs" are not opportunity costs. Room and board would not generally be a cost because, after all, you are going to be living and eating whether you are in university or not. Room and board are part of the cost of an education only insofar as they are more expensive than they would be otherwise. Similarly, the expenditures on things you would have otherwise done – hang-gliding lessons, a trip to Europe – represent savings. However, the value of these activities has been lost while you are busy reading this book.

The concept of opportunity cost can be summarized by a definition:

The opportunity cost is the value of the best foregone alternative.

This definition captures the idea that the cost of something is not just its monetary cost but also the value of what you didn't get. The opportunity cost of spending $17 on a CD is what you would have done with the $17 instead, and perhaps the value of the time spent shopping. The opportunity cost of a puppy includes not just the purchase price of the puppy, but also the food, veterinary bills, carpet cleaning, and the value of the time spent dealing with the puppy. A puppy is a good example, because often the purchase price is a negligible portion of the total cost of ownership. Yet people acquire puppies all the time, in spite of their high cost of ownership. Why? The economic view of the world is that people acquire puppies because the value they expect to get exceeds the opportunity cost. That is, they acquire a puppy when the value of a puppy is higher than the value of what is foregone by the acquisition of a puppy.

Even though opportunity costs include lots of non-monetary costs, we will often monetize opportunity costs, translating the costs into dollar terms for comparison purposes. Monetizing opportunity costs is clearly valuable, because it gives a means of comparison. What is the opportunity cost of 30 days in jail? It used to be that judges occasionally sentenced convicted defendants to "thirty days or thirty dollars," letting the defendant choose the sentence. Conceptually, we can use the same idea to find out the value of 30 days in jail. Suppose you would choose to pay a fine of $750 to avoid the thirty days in jail, but wouldn't pay $1,000 and instead would choose time in the slammer. Then the value of the thirty day sentence is somewhere between $750 and $1000. In principle, there exists a price where at that price you pay the fine, and at a penny more you go to jail. That price – at which you are just indifferent to the choice – is the monetized or dollar cost of the jail sentence.

The same idea as choosing the jail sentence or the fine justifies monetizing opportunity costs in other contexts. For example, a gamble has a *certainty equivalent*, which is the amount of money that makes one indifferent to choosing the gamble versus the certain amount. Indeed, companies buy and sell risk, and much of the field of *risk management* involves buying or selling risky items to reduce overall risk. In the process, risk is valued, and riskier stocks and assets must sell for a lower price (or, equivalently, earn a higher average return). This differential is known as a *risk premium*, and it represents a monetization of the risk portion of a risky gamble.

Home buyers considering various available houses are presented with a variety of options, such as one or two story, building materials like brick or wood, roofing materials, flooring materials like wood or carpet, presence or absence of swimming pools, views, proximity to parks, and so on. The approach taken to valuing these items is known as *hedonic pricing*, and corresponds to valuing each item separately – what does a pool add to value on average? – and then summing the value of the components. The same approach is used to value old cars, making adjustments to a base value for the presence of options like leather interior, CD changer, and so on. Again, such a valuation approach converts a bundle of disparate attributes into a monetary value.

The conversion of costs into dollars is occasionally controversial, and nowhere is it more controversial than in valuing human life. How much is your life worth? Can it be converted into dollars? A certain amount of insight into this question can be gleaned by thinking about risks. Wearing seatbelts and buying optional safety equipment reduce the risk of death by a small but measurable amount. Suppose a $400 airbag option reduces the overall risk of death by 0.01%. If you are indifferent to buying the option, you have implicitly valued the probability of death at $400 per 0.01%, or $40,000 per 1%, or around $4,000,000 per life. Of course, you may feel quite differently about a 0.01% chance of death than a risk ten thousand times greater, which would be a certainty. But such an approach provides one means of estimating the value of the risk of death – an examination what people will, and will not, pay to reduce that risk.

Opportunity cost – the value of the best foregone alternative – is a basic building block of economic analysis. The conversion of costs into dollar terms, while sometimes controversial, provides a convenient means of comparing costs.

1.1.3 Economic Reasoning and Analysis

What this country needs is some one-armed economists.
-Harry S Truman

Economic reasoning is rather easy to satirize. One might want to know, for instance, what the effect of a policy change – a government program to educate unemployed workers, an increase in military spending, or an enhanced environmental regulation – will be on people and their ability to purchase the goods and services they desire. Unfortunately, a single change may have multiple effects. As an absurd and tortured example, government production of helium for (allegedly) military purposes reduces the cost of children's birthday balloons, causing substitution away from party hats and hired clowns. The reduction in demand for clowns reduces clowns' wages and thus reduces the costs of running a circus. This cost reduction increases the number of circuses, thereby forcing zoos to lower admission fees to compete with circuses. Thus, were the government to stop subsidizing the manufacture of helium, the admission fee of zoos would likely rise, even though zoos use no helium. This example is superficially reasonable, although the effects are miniscule.

To make any sense at all of the effects of a change in economic conditions, it is helpful to divide up the effect into pieces. Thus, we will often look at the effects of a change "other things equal," that is, assuming nothing else changed. This isolates the effect of the change. In some cases, however, a single change can lead to multiple effects; even so, we will still focus on each effect individually. A gobbledygook way of saying "other things equal" is to use Latin and say "*ceteris paribus.*" Part of your job as a student is to learn economic jargon, and that is an example. Fortunately, there isn't too much jargon.

We will make a number of assumptions that you may not find very easy to believe. Not all of the assumptions are required for the analysis, and instead merely simplify the analysis. Some, however, are required but deserve an explanation. There is a frequent assumption that the people we will talk about seem exceedingly selfish relative to most people we know. We model the choices that people make, assuming that they make the choice that is best for them. Such people – the people in the models as opposed to real people – are known occasionally as "homo economicus." Real people are indubitably more altruistic than homo economicus, because they couldn't be less: homo economicus is entirely selfish. (The technical term is acting in one's *self-interest*.) That doesn't necessarily invalidate the conclusions drawn from the theory, however, for at least four reasons:

- People often make decisions as families or households rather than individuals, and it may be sensible to consider the household as the "consumer." That households are fairly selfish is more plausible perhaps than individuals being selfish.
- Economics is pretty much silent on *why* consumers want things. You may want to make a lot of money so that you can build a hospital or endow a library, which would be altruistic things to do. Such motives are broadly consistent with self-interested behavior.
- Corporations are often required to serve their shareholders by maximizing the share value, inducing self-interested behavior on the part of the corporation. Even if corporations had no legal responsibility to act in the financial interest of

their shareholders, capital markets may force them to act in the self-interest of the shareholders in order to raise capital. That is, people choosing investments that generate a high return will tend to force corporations to seek a high return.

- There are many good, and some not-so-good, consequences of people acting in their own self-interest, which may be another reason to focus on self-interested behavior.

Thus, while there are limits to the applicability of the theory of self-interested behavior, it is a reasonable methodology for attempting a science of human behavior.

Self-interested behavior will often be described as "maximizing behavior," where consumers maximize the value they obtain from their purchases, and firms maximize their profits. One objection to the economic methodology is that people rarely carry out the calculations necessary to literally maximize anything. However, that is not a sensible objection to the methodology. People don't carry out the physics calculations to throw a baseball or thread a needle, either, and yet they accomplish these tasks. Economists often consider that people act "as if" they maximize an objective, even though no calculations are carried out. Some corporations in fact use elaborate computer programs to minimize costs or maximize their profits, and the entire field of operations research is used to create and implement such maximization programs. Thus, while individuals don't carry out the calculations, some companies do.

A good example of economic reasoning is the sunk cost fallacy. Once one has made a significant non-recoverable investment, there is a psychological tendency to invest more even when the return on the subsequent investment isn't worthwhile. France and Britain continued to invest in the Concorde (a supersonic aircraft no longer in production) long after it became clear that the project would generate little return. If you watch a movie to the end, long after you become convinced that it stinks, you have exhibited the sunk cost fallacy. The fallacy is the result of an attempt to make an investment that has gone bad turn out to be good, even when it probably won't. The popular phrase associated with the sunk cost fallacy is "throwing good money after bad." The fallacy of sunk costs arises because of a psychological tendency to try to make an investment pay off when something happens to render it obsolete. It is a mistake in many circumstances.

The fallacy of sunk costs is often thought to be an advantage of casinos. People who lose a bit of money gambling hope to recover their losses by gambling more, with the sunk "investment" in gambling inducing an attempt to make the investment pay off. The nature of most casino gambling is that the house wins on average, which means the average gambler (and even the most skilled slot machine or craps player) loses on average. Thus, for most, trying to win back losses is to lose more on average.

The way economics is performed is by a proliferation of mathematical models, and this proliferation is reflected in this book. Economists reason with models. Models help by removing extraneous details from a problem or issue, letting one analyze what remains more readily. In some cases the models are relatively simple, like supply and demand. In other cases, the models are relatively complex (e.g. the over-fishing model of Section 6.3.6). In all cases, the models are the simplest model that lets us understand the question or phenomenon at hand. The purpose of the model is to illuminate connections between ideas. A typical implication of a model is "when A increases, B falls." This "*comparative static*" prediction lets us see how A affects B, and why, at least in the context of the model. The real world is always much more complex than the models we use to understand the world. That doesn't make the model useless, indeed, exactly the opposite. By stripping out extraneous detail, the model represents a lens to isolate and understand aspects of the real world.

Finally, one last introductory warning before we get started. A parody of economists talking is to add the word *marginal* before every word. Marginal is just economist's jargon for "the derivative of." For example, marginal cost is the derivative of cost; marginal value is the derivative of value. Because introductory economics is usually taught to students who have not yet studied calculus or can't be trusted to remember even the most basic elements of it, economists tend to avoid using derivatives and instead talk about the value of the next unit purchased, or the cost of the next unit, and describe that as the marginal value or cost. This book uses the term marginal frequently because one of the purposes of the book is to introduce the necessary jargon so that you can read more advanced texts or take more advanced classes. For an economics student not to know the word marginal would be akin to a physics student not knowing the word mass. The book minimizes jargon where possible, but part of the job of a principles student is to learn the jargon, and there is no getting around that.

2 Supply and Demand

Supply and demand are the most fundamental tools of economic analysis. Most applications of economic reasoning involve supply and demand in one form or another. When prices for home heating oil rise in the winter, usually the reason is that the weather is colder than normal and as a result, demand is higher than usual. Similarly, a break in an oil pipeline creates a short-lived gasoline shortage, as occurred in the Midwest in the year 2000, which is a reduction in supply. The price of DRAM, or dynamic random access memory, used in personal computers falls when new manufacturing facilities begin production, increasing the supply of memory.

This chapter sets out the basics of supply and demand, introduces equilibrium analysis, and considers some of the factors that influence supply and demand and the effects of those factors. In addition, quantification is introduced in the form of elasticities. Dynamics are not considered, however, until Chapter 4, which focuses on production, and Chapter 5 introduces a more fundamental analysis of demand, including a variety of topics such as risk. In essence, this is the economics "quickstart" guide, and we will look more deeply in the subsequent chapters.

2.1 *Supply and Demand*

2.1.1 Demand and Consumer Surplus

Eating a French fry makes most people a little bit happier, and we are willing to give up something of value – a small amount of money, a little bit of time – to eat one. What we are willing to give up measures the value – our personal value – of the French fry. That value, expressed in dollars, is the *willingness to pay* for French fries. That is, if you are willing to give up three cents for a single French fry, your willingness to pay is three cents. If you pay a penny for the French fry, you've obtained a net of two cents in value. Those two cents – the difference between your willingness to pay and the amount you do pay – is known as *consumer surplus*. Consumer surplus is the value to a consumer of consumption of a good, minus the price paid.

The value of items – French fries, eyeglasses, violins – is not necessarily close to what one has to pay for them. For people with bad vision, eyeglasses might be worth ten thousand dollars or more, in the sense that if eyeglasses and contacts cost $10,000 at all stores, that is what one would be willing to pay for vision correction. That one doesn't have to pay nearly that amount means that the consumer surplus associated with eyeglasses is enormous. Similarly, an order of French fries might be worth $3 to a consumer, but because French fries are available for around $1, the consumer obtains a surplus of $2 in the purchase.

How much is a second order of French fries worth? For most of us, that first order is worth more than the second one. If a second order is worth $2, we would still gain from buying it. Eating a third order of fries is worth less still, and at some point we're unable or unwilling to eat any more fries even when they are free, which implies that at some point the value of additional French fries is zero.
We will measure consumption generally as units per period of time, e.g. French fries consumed per month.

Many, but not all, goods have this feature of *diminishing marginal value* – the value of the last unit consumed declines as the number consumed rises. If we consume a quantity q, it implies the marginal value $v(q)$ falls as the number of units rise.[1] An example is illustrated in Figure 2-1. Here the value is a straight line, declining in the number of units.

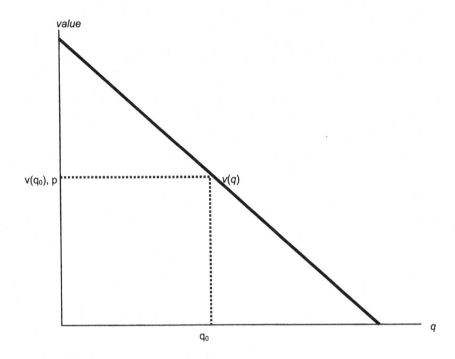

Figure 2-1: The Demand Curve

Demand need not be a straight line, and indeed could be any downward-sloping curve. Contrary to the usual convention, demand gives the quantity chosen for any given price off the horizontal axis, that is, given the value p on the vertical axis, the corresponding value q_0 on the horizontal axis is the quantity the consumer will purchase.

It is often important to distinguish the demand curve itself – the entire relationship between price and quantity demanded – from the quantity demanded. Typically, "demand" refers to the entire curve, while "quantity demanded" is a point on the curve.

Given a price p, a consumer will buy those units with $v(q)>p$, since those units are worth more than they cost. Similarly, a consumer should not buy units for which $v(q)<p$. Thus, the quantity q_0 that solves the equation $v(q_0)=p$ gives the quantity of units the consumer will buy. This value is also illustrated in Figure 2-1.[2] Another way of

---

[1] When diminishing marginal value fails, which sometimes is said to occur with beer consumption, constructing demand takes some additional effort, which isn't of a great deal of consequence. Buyers will still choose to buy a quantity where marginal value is decreasing.

[2] We will treat units as continuous, even though in reality they are discrete units. The reason for treating them as continuous is only to simplify the mathematics; with discrete units, the consumer buys those units with value exceeding the price, and doesn't buy those with value less than the price, just as before. However, since the value function isn't continuous, much less differentiable, it would be an accident for

summarizing this insight is that the *marginal value* curve is the inverse of demand function, where the demand function gives the quantity demanded for any given price. Formally, if $x(p)$ is the quantity a consumer buys given a price of p, then $v(x(p)) = p$.

But what is the marginal value curve? Suppose the total value of consumption of the product, in dollar value, is given by $u(q)$. That is, a consumer who pays $u(q)$ for the quantity q is just indifferent to getting nothing and paying nothing. For each quantity, there should exist one and only one price that exactly makes the consumer indifferent between purchasing it and getting nothing at all, because if the consumer is just willing to pay $u(q)$, any greater amount is more than the consumer should be willing to pay.

The consumer facing a price p gets a net value or consumer surplus of $CS = u(q) - pq$ from consuming q units. In order to obtain the maximal benefit, the consumer would then choose the level of q to maximize $u(q) - pq$. When the function CS is maximized, its derivative is zero, which implies that, at the quantity that maximizes the consumer's net value

$$0 = \frac{d}{dq}(u(q) - pq) = u'(q) - p.$$

Thus we see that $v(q) = u'(q)$, that is, the *marginal value* of the good is the derivative of the total value.

Consumer surplus is the value of the consumption minus the amount paid, and represents the net value of the purchase to the consumer. Formally, it is $u(q)-pq$. A graphical form of the consumer surplus is generated by the following identity.

$$CS = \max_{q}(u(q) - pq) = u(q_0) - pq_0 = \int_0^{q_0}(u'(x) - p)dx = \int_0^{q_0}(v(x) - p)dx.$$

This expression shows that consumer surplus can be represented as the area below the demand curve and above the price, as is illustrated in Figure 2-2. The consumer surplus represents the consumer's gains from trade, the value of consumption to the consumer net of the price paid.

---

marginal value to equal price. It isn't particularly arduous to handle discreteness of the products, but it doesn't lead to any significant insight either, so we won't consider it here.

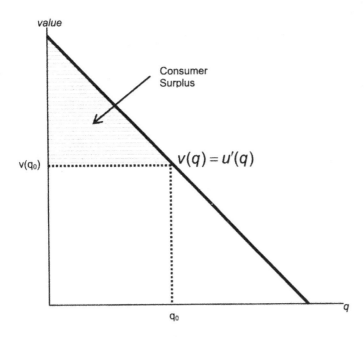

Figure 2-2: Consumer Surplus

The consumer surplus can also be expressed using the demand curve, by integrating from the price up. In this case, if $x(p)$ is the demand, we have

$$CS = \int_{p}^{\infty} x(y)dy.$$

When you buy your first car, you experience an increase in demand for gasoline because gasoline is pretty useful for cars and not so much for other things. An imminent hurricane increases the demand for plywood (to protect windows), batteries, candles, and bottled water. An increase in demand is represented by a movement of the entire curve to the northeast (up and to the right), which represents an increase in the marginal value v (movement up) for any given unit, or an increase in the number of units demanded for any given price (movement to the right). Figure 2-3 illustrates a shift in demand.

Similarly, the reverse movement represents a decrease in demand. The beauty of the connection between demand and marginal value is that an increase in demand could in principle have meant either more units demanded at a given price, or a higher willingness to pay for each unit, but those are in fact the same concept – both create a movement up and to the right.

For many goods, an increase in income increases the demand for the good. Porsche automobiles, yachts, and Beverly Hills homes are mostly purchased by people with high incomes. Few billionaires ride the bus. Economists aptly named goods whose demand doesn't increase with income *inferior* goods, with the idea that people substitute to better quality, more expensive goods as their incomes rise. When demand for a good increases with income, the good is called *normal*. It would have been better to call such goods superior, but it is too late to change such a widely accepted convention.

value

Figure 2-3: An Increase in Demand

Another factor that influences demand is the price of related goods. The dramatic fall in the price of computers over the past twenty years has significantly increased the demand for printers, monitors and internet access. Such goods are examples of *complements*. Formally, for a given good X, a complement is a good whose consumption increases the value of X. Thus, the use of computers increases the value of peripheral devices like printers and monitors. The consumption of coffee increases the demand for cream for many people. Spaghetti and tomato sauce, national parks and hiking boots, air travel and hotel rooms, tables and chairs, movies and popcorn, bathing suits and sun tan lotion, candy and dentistry are all examples of complements for most people – consumption of one increases the value of the other. The complementarity relationship is symmetric – if consumption of X increases the value of Y, then consumption of Y must increase the value of X.[3] There are many complementary goods and changes in the prices of complementary goods have predictable effects on the demand of their complements. Such predictable effects represent the heart of economic analysis.

The opposite case of a complement is a *substitute*. Colas and root beer are substitutes, and a fall in the price of root beer (resulting in an increase in the consumption of root beer) will tend to decrease the demand for colas. Pasta and ramen, computers and typewriters, movies (in theaters) and sporting events, restaurants and dining at home, spring break in Florida versus spring break in Mexico, marijuana and beer, economics

---

[3] The basis for this insight can be seen by denoting the total value in dollars of consuming goods x and y as $u(x, y)$. Then the demand for x is given by the partial $\partial u / \partial x$. The statement that y is a complement is the statement that the demand for x rises as y increases, that is, $\partial^2 u / \partial x \partial y > 0$. But then with a continuous second derivative, $\partial^2 u / \partial y \partial x > 0$, which means the demand for y, $\partial u / \partial y$, increases with x.

courses and psychology courses, driving and bicycling are all examples of substitutes for most people. An increase in the price of a substitute *increases* the demand for a good, and conversely, a decrease in the price of a substitute decreases demand for a good. Thus, increased enforcement of the drug laws, which tends to increase the price of marijuana, leads to an increase in the demand for beer.

Much of demand is merely idiosyncratic to the individual – some people like plaids, some like solid colors. People like what they like. Often people are influenced by others – tattoos are increasingly common not because the price has fallen but because of an increased acceptance of body art. Popular clothing styles change, not because of income and prices but for other reasons. While there has been a modest attempt to link clothing style popularity to economic factors,[4] by and large there is no coherent theory determining fads and fashions beyond the observation that change is inevitable. As a result, this course, and economics more generally, will accept preferences for what they are without questioning why people like what they like. While it may be interesting to understand the increasing social acceptance of tattoos, it is beyond the scope of this text and indeed beyond most, but not all, economic analyses. We will, however, account for some of the effects of the increasing acceptance of tattoos through changes in the number of firms offering tattooing, changes in the variety of products offered, and so on.

2.1.1.1 (Exercise)   A *reservation price* is the maximum willingness to pay for a good that most people buy one unit of, like cars or computers. Graph the demand curve for a consumer with a reservation price of $30 for a unit of a good.

2.1.1.2 (Exercise)   Suppose the demand curve is given by $x(p) = 1 - p$. The consumer's expenditure is $px(p) = p(1 - p)$. Graph the expenditure. What price maximizes the consumer's expenditure?

2.1.1.3 (Exercise)   For demand $x(p) = 1 - p$, compute the consumer surplus function as a function of p.

2.1.1.4 (Exercise)   For demand $x(p) = p^{-\varepsilon}$, for $\varepsilon > 1$, find the consumer surplus as a function of p. (Hint: recall that the consumer surplus can be expressed as

$$CS = \int_{p}^{\infty} x(y)dy .)$$

2.1.2 Supply

The supply curve gives the number of units, represented on the horizontal axis, as a function of the price on the vertical axis, which will be supplied for sale to the market. An example is illustrated in Figure 2-4. Generally supply is upward-sloping, because if it is a good deal for a seller to sell 50 units of a product at a price of $10, then it remains a good deal to supply those same 50 at a price of $11. The seller might choose to sell

---

[4] Skirts are allegedly shorter during economic booms and lengthen during recessions.

more than 50, but if the first 50 weren't worth keeping at a price of $10, that remains true at $11.[5]

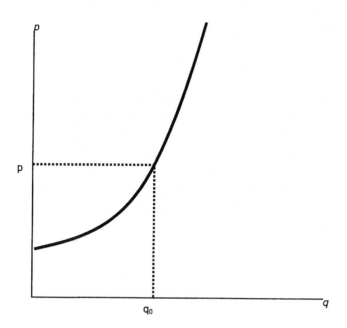

Figure 2-4: The Supply Curve

The seller who has a cost $c(q)$ for selling q units obtains a profit, at price p per unit, of $pq - c(q)$. The quantity which maximizes profit for the seller is the quantity q^* satisfying

$$0 = \frac{d}{dq} pq - c(q) = p - c'(q^*).$$

Thus, price equals marginal cost is a characteristic of profit maximization; the seller sells all the units whose cost is less than price, and doesn't sell the units whose cost exceeds price. In constructing the demand curve, we saw that the demand curve was the inverse of the marginal value. There is an analogous property of supply: *the supply curve is the inverse function of marginal cost.* Graphed with the quantity supplied on the horizontal axis and price on the vertical axis, the supply curve is the marginal cost curve, with marginal cost on the vertical axis.

Exactly in parallel to consumer surplus with demand, profit is given by the difference of the price and marginal cost

---

[5] This is a good point to remind the reader that the economists' familiar assumption of "other things equal" is still in effect. If the increased price is an indication that prices might rise still further, or a consequence of some other change that affects the sellers' value of items, then of course the higher price might not justify sale of the items. We hold other things equal to focus on the effects of price alone, and then will consider other changes separately. The pure effect of an increased price should be to increase the quantity offered, while the effect of increased expectations may be to decrease the quantity offered.

$$\text{Profit} = \max_{q} pq - c(q) = pq^* - c(q^*) = \int_{0}^{q^*} (p - c'(x))dx.$$

This area is shaded in Figure 2-5.

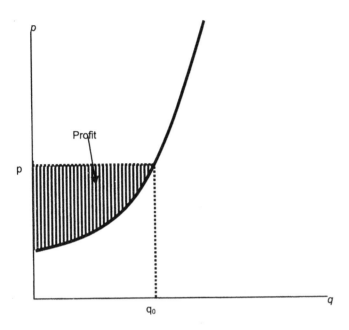

Figure 2-5: Supplier Profits

The relationship of demand and marginal value exactly parallels the relationship of supply and marginal cost, for a somewhat hidden reason. Supply is just negative demand, that is, a supplier is just the possessor of a good who doesn't keep it but instead offers it to the market for sale. For example, when the price of housing goes up, one of the ways people demand less is by offering to rent a room in their house, that is, by supplying some of their housing to the market. Similarly, the marginal cost of supplying a good already produced is the loss of not having the good, that is, the marginal value of the good. Thus, with exchange, it is possible to provide the theory of supply and demand entirely as a theory of *net* demand, where sellers are negative demanders. There is some mathematical economy in this approach, and it fits certain circumstances better than separating supply and demand. For example, when the price of electricity rose very high in the western United States in 2003, several aluminum smelters resold electricity they had purchased in long-term contracts, that is, demanders became suppliers.

However, the "net demand" approach obscures the likely outcomes in instances where the sellers are mostly different people, or companies, than the buyers. Moreover, while there is a theory of complements and substitutes for supply that is exactly parallel to the equivalent theory for demand, the nature of these complements and substitutes tends to be different. For these reasons, and also for the purpose of being consistent with common economic usage, we will distinguish supply and demand.

An *increase in supply* refers to either more units available at a given price, or a lower price for the supply of the same number of units. Thus, an increase in supply is graphically represented by a curve that is lower or to the right, or both, that is, to the south-east. This is illustrated in Figure 2-6. A decrease in supply is the reverse case, a shift to the northwest.

Figure 2-6: An Increase in Supply

Anything that increases costs of production will tend to increase marginal cost and thus reduce the supply. For example, as wages rise, the supply of goods and services is reduced, because wages are the input price of labor. Labor accounts for about two-thirds of all input costs, and thus wage increases create supply reductions (a higher price is necessary to provide the same quantity) for most goods and services. Costs of materials of course increase the price of goods using those materials. For example, the most important input into the manufacture of gasoline is crude oil, and an increase of $1 in the price of a 42 gallon barrel of oil increases the price of gasoline about two cents – almost one-for-one by volume. Another significant input in many industries is capital, and as we will see, interest is cost of capital. Thus, increases in interest rates increase the cost of production, and thus tend to decrease the supply of goods.

Parallel to complements in demand, a *complement in supply* to a good X is a good Y such that an increase in the price of Y increases the supply of X. Complements in supply are usually goods that are jointly produced. In producing lumber (sawn boards), a large quantity of wood chips and sawdust are also produced as a by-product. These wood chips and saw dust are useful in the manufacture of paper. An increase in the price of lumber tends to increase the quantity of trees sawn into boards, thereby increasing the supply of wood chips. Thus, lumber and wood chips are complements in supply.

It turns out that copper and gold are often found in the same kinds of rock – the conditions that give rise to gold compounds also give rise to copper compounds. Thus, an increase in the price of gold tends to increase the number of people prospecting for gold, and in the process increases not just the quantity of gold supplied to the market, but also the quantity of copper. Thus, copper and gold are complements in supply.

The classic supply-complement is beef and leather – an increase in the price of beef increases the slaughter of cows, thereby increasing the supply of leather.

The opposite of a complement in supply is a *substitute in supply*. Military and civilian aircraft are substitutes in supply – an increase in the price of military aircraft will tend to divert resources used in the manufacture of aircraft toward military aircraft and away from civilian aircraft, thus reducing the supply of civilian aircraft. Wheat and corn are also substitutes in supply. An increase in the price of wheat will lead farmers whose land is reasonably well-suited to producing either wheat or corn to substitute wheat for corn, increasing the quantity of wheat and decreasing the quantity of corn. Agricultural goods grown on the same type of land usually are substitutes. Similarly, cars and trucks, tables and desks, sweaters and sweatshirts, horror movies and romantic comedies are examples of substitutes in supply.

Complements and substitutes are important because they are common and have predictable effects on demand and supply. Changes in one market spill over to the other market, through the mechanism of complements or substitutes.

2.1.2.1 (Exercise)   A typist charges $30/hr and types 15 pages per hour. Graph the supply of typed pages.

2.1.2.2 (Exercise)   An owner of an oil well has two technologies for extracting oil. With one technology, the oil can be pumped out and transported for $5,000 per day, and 1,000 barrels per day are produced. With the other technology, which involves injecting natural gas into the well, the owner spends $10,000 per day and $5 per barrel produced, but 2,000 barrels per day are produced. What is the supply? Graph it.

(Hint: Compute the profits, as a function of the price, for each of the technologies. At what price would the producer switch from one technology to the other? At what price would the producer shut down and spend nothing?)

2.1.2.3 (Exercise)   An entrepreneur has a factory the produces L^α widgets, where $\alpha < 1$, when L hours of labor is used. The cost of labor (wage and benefits) is w per hour. If the entrepreneur maximizes profit, what is the supply curve for widgets?

Hint: The entrepreneur's profit, as a function of the price, is $pL^\alpha - wL$. The entrepreneur chooses the amount of labor to maximize profit. Find the amount of labor that maximizes, which is a function of p, w and α. The supply is the amount of output produced, which is L^α.

2.1.2.4 (Exercise)   In the above exercise, suppose now that more than 40 hours entails a higher cost of labor (overtime pay). Let w be \$20/hr for under 40 hours, and \$30/hr for each hour over 40 hours, and $\alpha = \frac{1}{2}$. Find the supply curve.

Hint: Let $L(w, p)$ be the labor demand when the wage is w (no overtime pay) and the price is p. Now show that, if $L(20,p) < 40$, the entrepreneur uses $L(20,p)$ hours. This is shown by verifying that profits are higher at $L(20,p)$ than at $L(30,p)$. If $L(30,p) > 40$, the entrepreneur uses $L(30,p)$ hours. Finally, if $L(20,p) > 40 > L(30,p)$, the entrepreneur uses 40 hours. Labor translates into supply via L^{α}.

2.1.2.5 (Exercise)   In the previous exercise, for what range of prices does employment equal 40 hours? Graph the labor demanded by the entrepreneur.

Hint: The answer involves $\sqrt{10}$.

2.1.2.6 (Exercise)   Suppose marginal cost, as a function of the quantity q produced, is mq. Find the producer's profit as a function of the price p.

2.2 *The Market*

Individuals with their own supply or demand trade in a market, which is where prices are determined. Markets can be specific or virtual locations – the farmer's market, the New York Stock Exchange, eBay – or may be an informal or more amorphous market, such as the market for restaurant meals in Billings, Montana or the market for roof repair in Schenectady, New York.

2.2.1 Market Demand and Supply

Individual demand gives the quantity purchased for each price. Analogously, the *market demand* gives the quantity purchased by all the market participants – the sum of the individual demands – for each price. This is sometimes called a "horizontal sum" because the summation is over the quantities for each price. An example is illustrated in Figure 2-7. For a given price p, the quantity q_1 demanded by one consumer, and the quantity q_2 demanded by a second consumer are illustrated. The sum of these quantities represents the market demand, if the market has just those two-participants. Since the consumer with subscript 2 has a positive quantity demanded for high prices, while the consumer with subscript 1 does not, the market demand coincides with consumer 2's demand when the price is sufficiently high. As the price falls, consumer 1 begins purchasing, and the market quantity demanded is larger than either individual participant's quantity, and is the sum of the two quantities.

Example: If the demand of buyer 1 is given by $q = \max \{0, 10 - p\}$, and the demand of buyer 2 is given by $q = \max \{0, 20 - 4p\}$, what is market demand for the two-participants?

Solution: First, note that buyer 1 buys zero at a price 10 or higher, while buyer 2 buys zero at a price of 5 or higher. For a price above 10, market demand is zero. For a price between 5 and 10, market demand is buyer 1's demand, or $10 - p$. Finally, for a price between zero and 5, the market quantity demanded is $10 - p + 20 - 4p = 30 - 5p$.

Market supply is similarly constructed – the market supply is the horizontal (quantity) sum of all the individual supply curves.

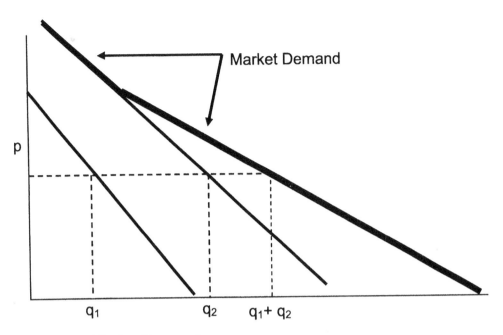

Figure 2-7: Market Demand

Example: If the supply of firm 1 is given by $q = 2p$, and the supply of firm 2 is given by $q = \max\{0, 5p - 10\}$, what is market supply for the two-participants?

Solution: First, note that firm 1 is in the market at any price, but firm 2 is in the market only if price exceeds 2. Thus, for a price between zero and 2, market supply is firm 1's supply, or $2p$. For $p>2$, market supply is $5p - 10 + 2p = 7p - 10$.

2.2.1.1 (Exercise)   Is the consumer surplus for market demand the sum of the consumer surpluses for the individual demands? Why or why not? Illustrate your conclusion with a figure like Figure 2-7.

2.2.1.2 (Exercise)   Suppose the supply of firm i is $\alpha_i\, p$, when the price is p, where i takes on the values 1, 2, 3, ... n. What is the market supply of these n firms?

2.2.1.3 (Exercise)   Suppose consumers in a small town choose between two restaurants, A and B. Each consumer has a value v_A for A and a value v_B for B, each of which is a uniform random draw from the [0,1] interval. Consumers buy whichever product offers the higher consumer surplus. The price of B is 0.2. In the square associated with the possible value types, identify which consumers buy from firm A. Find the demand (which is the area of the set of consumers who buy from A in the picture below). Hint: Consumers have three choices: Buy nothing (value 0), buy from A (value $v_A - p_A$) and buy from B, (value $v_B - p_B$

$= v_B - 0.2$). Draw the lines illustrating which choice has the highest value for the consumer.

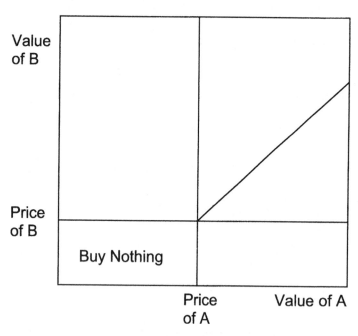

2.2.2 Equilibrium

Economists use the term *equilibrium* in the same way as the word is used in physics, to represent a steady state in which opposing forces are balanced, so that the current state of the system tends to persist. In the context of supply and demand, equilibrium refers to a condition where the pressure for higher prices is exactly balanced by a pressure for lower prices, and thus that the current state of exchange between buyers and sellers can be expected to persist.

When the price is such that the quantity supplied of a good or service exceeds the quantity demanded, some sellers are unable to sell because fewer units are purchased than are offered. This condition is called a *surplus*. The sellers who fail to sell have an incentive to offer their good at a slightly lower price – a penny less – in order to succeed in selling. Such price cuts put downward pressure on prices, and prices tend to fall. The fall in prices generally reduces the quantity supplied and increases the quantity demanded, eliminating the surplus. That is, a surplus encourages price cutting, which reduces the surplus, a process that ends only when the quantity supplied equals the quantity demanded.

Similarly, when the price is low enough that the quantity demanded exceeds the quantity supplied, a *shortage* exists. In this case, some buyers fail to purchase, and these buyers have an incentive to accept a slightly higher price in order to be able to trade. Sellers are obviously happy to get the higher price as well, which tends to put upward pressure on prices, and prices rise. The increase in price tends to reduce the quantity demanded and increase the quantity supplied, thereby eliminating the shortage. Again, the process stops when the quantity supplied equals the quantity demanded.

Figure 2-8: Equilibration

This logic, which is illustrated in Figure 2-8, justifies the conclusion that the only equilibrium price is the price in which the quantity supplied equals the quantity demanded. Any other price will tend to rise in a shortage, or fall in a surplus, until supply and demand are balanced. In Figure 2-8, a surplus arises at any price above the equilibrium price p^*, because the quantity supplied q^s is larger than the quantity demanded q^d. The effect of the surplus – leading to sellers with excess inventory – induces price cutting which is illustrated with three arrows pointing down.

Similarly, when the price is below p^*, the quantity supplied q^s is less than the quantity demanded q^d. This causes some buyers to fail to find goods, leading to higher asking prices and higher bid prices by buyers. The tendency for the price to rise is illustrated with the arrows pointing up. The only price which doesn't lead to price changes is p^*, the *equilibrium price in which the quantity supplied equals the quantity demanded*.

The logic of equilibrium in supply and demand is played out daily in markets all over the world, from stock, bond and commodity markets with traders yelling to buy or sell, to Barcelona fish markets where an auctioneer helps the market find a price, to Istanbul gold markets, to Los Angeles real estate markets.

2.2.2.1 (Exercise)   If demand is given by $q^d(p) = a - bp$, and supply is given by $q^s(p) = cp$, solve for the equilibrium price and quantity. Find the consumer surplus and producer profits.

2.2.2.2 (Exercise) If demand is given by $q^d(p) = ap^{-\varepsilon}$, and supply is given by $q^s(p) = bp^\eta$, where all parameters are positive numbers, solve for the equilibrium price and quantity.

2.2.3 Efficiency of Equilibrium

The equilibrium of supply and demand balances the quantity demanded and the quantity supplied, so that there is no excess of either. Would it be desirable, from a social perspective, to force more trade, or to restrain trade below this level?

There are circumstances where the equilibrium level of trade has harmful consequences, and such circumstances are considered in Chapter 6. However, provided that the only people affected by a transaction are the buyer and seller, *the equilibrium of supply and demand maximizes the total gains from trade.*

This proposition is quite easy to see. To maximize the gains from trade, clearly the highest value buyers must get the goods. Otherwise, if there is a potential buyer that doesn't get the good with higher value than one who does, the gains from trade rise just by diverting the good to the higher value buyer. Similarly, the lowest cost sellers must supply those goods; otherwise we can increase the gains from trade by replacing a higher cost seller with a lower cost seller. Thus, the only question is how many goods should be traded to maximize the gains from trade, since it will involve the lowest cost sellers selling to the highest value buyers. Adding a trade increases the total gains from trade when that trade involves a buyer with value higher than the seller's cost. Thus, the gains from trade are maximized by the set of transactions to the left of the equilibrium, with the high value buyers buying from the low cost sellers.

In the economist's language, the equilibrium is *efficient*, in that it maximizes the gains from trade, under the assumption that the only people affected by any given transaction are the buyers and seller.

2.3 Changes in Supply and Demand

2.3.1 Changes in Demand

What are the effects of an increase in demand? As the population of California has grown, the demand for housing has risen. This has pushed the price of housing up, and also spurred additional development, increasing the quantity of housing supplied as well. We see such a demand increase illustrated in Figure 2-9, which represents an increase in the demand. In this figure, supply and demand have been abbreviated S and D. Demand starts at D_1 and is increased to D_2. Supply remains the same. The equilibrium price increases from p_1^* to p_2^*, and the quantity rises from q_1^* to q_2^*.

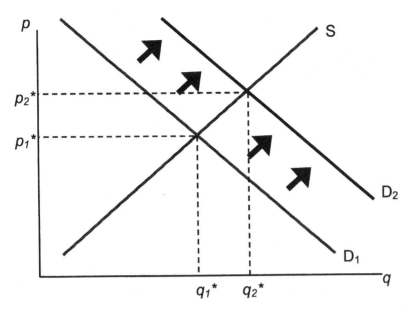

Figure 2-9: An Increase in Demand

A decrease in demand – such as occurred for typewriters with the advent of computers, or buggy whips as cars replaced horses as the major method of transportation – has the reverse effect of an increase, and implies a fall in both the price and the quantity traded. Examples of decreases in demand include products replaced by other products – VHS tapes were replaced by DVDs, vinyl records replaced by CDs, cassette tapes replaced by CDs, floppy disks (oddly named because the 1.44 MB "floppy," a physically hard product, replaced the 720KB, 5 ¼ inch soft floppy disk) replaced by CDs and flash memory drives, and so on. Even personal computers experienced a fall in demand as the market was saturated in the year 2001.

2.3.2 Changes in Supply

An increase in supply comes about from a fall in the marginal cost – recall that the supply curve is just the marginal cost of production. Consequently, an increased supply is represented by a curve that is lower and to the right on the supply/demand graph, which is an endless source of confusion for many students. The reasoning – lower costs and greater supply are the same thing – is too easily forgotten. The effects of an increase in supply are illustrated in Figure 2-10. The supply curve goes from S_1 to S_2, which represents a lower marginal cost. In this case, the quantity traded rises from q_1^* to q_2^* and price falls from p_1^* to p_2^*.

Computer equipment provides dramatic examples of increases in supply. Consider Dynamic Random Access Memory, or DRAM. DRAMs are the chips in computers and many other devices that store information on a temporary basis.[6] Their cost has fallen dramatically, which is illustrated in Figure 2-11.[7] Note that the prices in this figure reflect a logarithmic scale, so that a fixed percentage decrease is illustrated by a straight line. Prices of DRAMs fell to close to 1/1000th of their 1990 level by 2004. The means

---

[6] Information that will be stored on a longer term basis is generally embedded in flash memory or on a hard disk. Neither of these products lose their information when power is turned off, unlike DRAM.
[7] Used with permission of computer storage expert Dr. Edward Grochowski.

by which these prices have fallen are themselves quite interesting. The main reasons are shrinking the size of the chip (a "die shrink"), so that more chips fit on each silicon disk, and increasing the size of the disk itself, so that more chips fit on a disk. The combination of these two, each of which required the solutions to thousands of engineering and chemistry problems, has led to dramatic reductions in marginal costs and consequent increases in supply. The effect has been that prices fell dramatically and quantities traded rose dramatically.

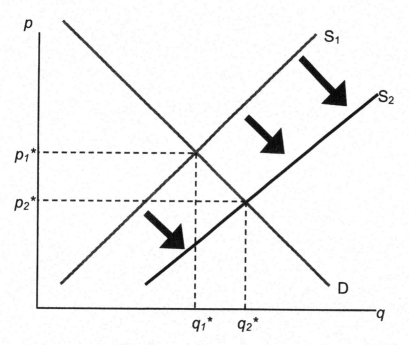

Figure 2-10: An Increase in Supply

An important source of supply and demand changes are changes in the markets of complements. A decrease in the price of a demand-complement increases the demand for a product, and similarly, an increase in the price of a demand-substitute increases demand for a product. This gives two mechanisms to trace through effects from external markets to a particular market via the linkage of demand substitutes or complements. For example, when the price of gasoline falls, the demand for automobiles (a complement) overall should increase. As the price of automobiles rises, the demand for bicycles (a substitute in some circumstances) should rise. When the price of computers falls, the demand for operating systems (a complement) should rise. This gives an operating system seller like Microsoft an incentive to encourage technical progress in the computer market, in order to make the operating system more valuable.

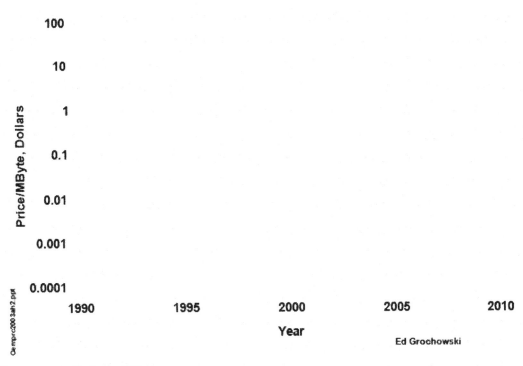

Figure 2-11: Price of Storage

An increase in the price of a supply-substitute reduces the supply of a good (by making the alternative good more attractive to suppliers), and similarly, a decrease in the price of a supply complement reduces the supply of a good. By making the by-product less valuable, the returns to investing in a good are reduced. Thus, an increase in the price of DVD-R discs (used for recording DVDs) discourages investment in the manufacture of CD-Rs, which are a substitute in supply, leading to a decrease in the supply of CD-Rs. This tends to increase the price of CD-Rs, other things equal. Similarly, an increase in the price of oil increases exploration for oil, tending to increase the supply of natural gas, which is a complement in supply. However, since natural gas is also a demand substitute for oil (both are used for heating homes), an increase in the price of oil also tends to increase the demand for natural gas. Thus, an increase in the price of oil increases both the demand and the supply of natural gas. Both changes increase the quantity traded, but the increase in demand tends to increase the price, while the increase in supply tends to decrease the price. Without knowing more, it is impossible to determine whether the net effect is an increase or decrease in the price.

2.3.2.1 (Exercise)   Video games and music CDs are substitutes in demand. What is the effect of an increase in supply of video games on the price and quantity traded of music CDs? Illustrate your answer with diagrams for both markets.

2.3.2.2 (Exercise)   Electricity is a major input into the production of aluminum, and aluminum is a substitute in supply for steel. What is the effect of an increase in price of electricity on the steel market?

2.3.2.3 (Exercise)   Concerns about terrorism reduced demand for air travel, and
         induced consumers to travel by car more often. What should happen to the
         price of Hawaiian hotel rooms?

When the price of gasoline goes up, people curtail their driving to some extent, but don't immediately scrap their SUVs and rush out and buy more fuel-efficient automobiles or electric cars. Similarly, when the price of electricity rises, people don't replace their air conditioners and refrigerators with the most modern, energy-saving models right away. There are three significant issues raised by this kind of example. First, such changes may be transitory or permanent, and people reasonably react differently to temporary changes than to permanent changes. The effect of uncertainty is a very important topic and will be considered in section 5.2.6, but only in a rudimentary way for this introductory text. Second, energy is a modest portion of the cost of owning and operating an automobile or refrigerator, so it doesn't make sense to scrap a large capital investment over a small permanent increase in cost. Thus people rationally continue operating "obsolete" devices until their useful life is over, even when they wouldn't buy an exact copy of that device, an effect with the gobbledygook name of *hysteresis*. Third, a permanent increase in energy prices leads people to buy more fuel efficient cars, and to replace the old gas guzzlers more quickly. That is, the effects of a change are larger over a larger time interval, which economists tend to call the *long-run*.

A striking example of such delay arose when oil quadrupled in price in 1973-4, caused by a reduction in sales by the cartel of oil-producing nations, OPEC, which stands for the Organization of Petroleum Exporting Countries. The increased price of oil (and consequent increase in gasoline prices) caused people to drive less and to lower their thermostats in the winter, thus reducing the quantity of oil demanded. Over time, however, they bought more fuel efficient cars and insulated their homes more effectively, significantly reducing the quantity demanded still further. At the same time, the increased prices for oil attracted new investment into oil production in Alaska, the North Sea between Britain and Norway, Mexico and other areas. Both of these effects (long-run substitution away from energy, and long-run supply expansion) caused the price to fall over the longer term, undoing the supply reduction created by OPEC. In 1981, OPEC further reduced output, sending prices still higher, but again, additional investment in production, combined with energy-saving investment, reduced prices until they fell back to 1973 levels (adjusted for inflation) in 1986. Prices continued to fall until 1990, when they were at all-time low levels and Iraq's invasion of Kuwait and the resulting first Iraqi war sent them higher again.

Short-run and long-run effects represent a theme of economics, with the major conclusion of the theme that substitution doesn't occur instantaneously, which leads to predictable patterns of prices and quantities over time.

It turns out that direct estimates of demand and supply are less useful as quantifications than notions of percentage changes, which have the advantage of being unit-free. This observation gives rise to the concept of elasticity, the next topic.

2.4 Elasticities

2.4.1 Elasticity of Demand

Let $x(p)$ represent the quantity purchased when the price is p, so that the function x represents demand. How responsive is demand to price changes? One might be tempted to use the derivative x' to measure the responsiveness of demand, since it measures directly how much the quantity demanded changes in response to a small change in price. However, this measure has two problems. First, it is sensitive to a change in units. If I measure the quantity of candy in kilograms rather than pounds, the derivative of demand for candy with respect to price changes even when demand itself has remained the same. Second, if I change price units, converting from one currency to another, again the derivative of demand will change. So the derivative is unsatisfactory as a measure of responsiveness because it depends on units of measure. A common way of establishing a unit-free measure is to use percentages, and that suggests considering the responsiveness of demand in percentage terms to a small percentage change in price. This is the notion of *elasticity of demand*.[8] The elasticity of demand is the percentage decrease in quantity that results from a small percentage increase in price. Formally, the elasticity of demand, which is generally denoted with the Greek letter epsilon ε (chosen to mnemonically suggest elasticity) is

$$\varepsilon = -\frac{dx/x}{dp/p} = -\frac{p}{x}\frac{dx}{dp} = -\frac{px'(p)}{x(p)}.$$

The minus sign is included to make the elasticity a positive number, since demand is decreasing. First, let's verify that the elasticity is in fact unit free. A change in the measurement of x cancels because the proportionality factor appears in both the numerator and denominator. Similarly, if we change the units of measurement of price to replace the price p with $r=ap$, $x(p)$ is replaced with $x(r/a)$. Thus, the elasticity is

$$\varepsilon = -\frac{r\dfrac{d}{dr}x(r/a)}{x(r/a)} = -\frac{rx'(r/a)\dfrac{1}{a}}{x(r/a)} = -\frac{px'(p)}{x(p)},$$

which is independent of a, and therefore not affected by the change in units.

How does a consumer's expenditure, also known as (individual) total revenue, react to a change in price? The consumer buys $x(p)$ at a price of p, and thus expenditure is $TR = px(p)$. Thus

$$\frac{d}{dp}px(p) = x(p) + px'(p) = x(p)\left(1 + \frac{px'(p)}{x(p)}\right) = x(p)(1-\varepsilon).$$

Therefore,

---

[8] The concept of elasticity was invented by Alfred Marshall, 1842-1924, in 1881 while sitting on his roof.

$$\frac{\frac{d}{dp}TR}{\frac{1}{p}TR} = 1 - \varepsilon.$$

Table 2-1: Various Demand Elasticities[9]

Product	ε
Salt	0.1
Matches	0.1
Toothpicks	0.1
Airline travel, short-run	0.1
Residential natural gas, short-run	0.1
Gasoline, short-run	0.2
Automobiles, long-run	0.2
Coffee	0.25
Legal services, short-run	0.4
Tobacco products, short-run	0.45
Residential natural gas, long-run	0.5
Fish (cod) consumed at home	0.5
Physician services	0.6
Taxi, short-run	0.6
Gasoline, long-run	0.7
Movies	0.9
Shellfish, consumed at home	0.9
Tires, short-run	0.9
Oysters, consumed at home	1.1
Private education	1.1
Housing, owner occupied, long-run	1.2
Tires, long-run	1.2
Radio and television receivers	1.2
Automobiles, short-run	1.2-1.5
Restaurant meals	2.3
Airline travel, long-run	2.4
Fresh green peas	2.8
Foreign travel, long-run	4.0
Chevrolet automobiles	4.0
Fresh tomatoes	4.6

---

[9] From http://www.mackinac.org/archives/1997/s1997-04.pdf; cited sources: *Economics: Private and Public Choice*, James D. Gwartney and Richard L. Stroup, eighth edition 1997, seventh edition 1995; Hendrick S. Houthakker and Lester D. Taylor, *Consumer Demand in the United States*, 1929-1970 (Cambridge: Harvard University Press, 1966,1970); Douglas R. Bohi, *Analyzing Demand Behavior* (Baltimore: Johns Hopkins University Press, 1981); Hsaing-tai Cheng and Oral Capps, Jr., "Demand for Fish" *American Journal of Agricultural Economics*, August 1988; and U.S. Department of Agriculture.

In words, the percentage change of total revenue resulting from a one percent change in price is one minus the elasticity of demand. Thus, a one percent increase in price will increase total revenue when the elasticity of demand is less than one, which is defined as an *inelastic* demand. A price increase will decrease total revenue when the elasticity of demand is greater than one, which is defined as an *elastic* demand. The case of elasticity equal to one is called *unitary elasticity*, and total revenue is unchanged by a small price change. Moreover, that percentage increase in price will increase revenue by approximately 1-ε percent. Because it is often possible to estimate the elasticity of demand, the formulae can be readily used in practice

Table 2-1 provides estimates on demand elasticities for a variety of products.

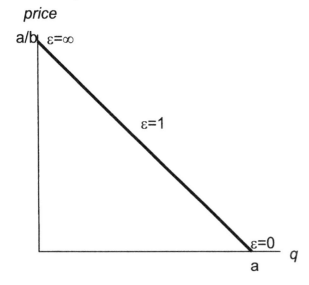

Figure 2-12: Elasticities for Linear Demand

When demand is linear, $x(p)=a-bp$, the elasticity of demand has the form

$$\varepsilon = \frac{bp}{a-bp} = \frac{p}{a/b - p}.$$

This case is illustrated in Figure 2-12.

If demand takes the form $x(p)=ap^{-\varepsilon}$, then demand has *constant elasticity*, and the elasticity is equal to ε.

2.4.1.1 (Exercise)   Suppose a consumer has a constant elasticity of demand ε, and demand is *elastic* (ε > 1). Show that expenditure increases as price decreases.

2.4.1.2 (Exercise)   Suppose a consumer has a constant elasticity of demand ε, and demand is inelastic (ε < 1). What price makes expenditure the greatest?

2.4.1.3 (Exercise)   For a consumer with constant elasticity of demand $\varepsilon > 1$, compute the consumer surplus.

2.4.2 Elasticity of Supply

The elasticity of supply is analogous to the elasticity of demand, in that it is a unit-free measure of the responsiveness of supply to a price change, and is defined as the percentage increase in quantity supplied resulting from a small percentage increase in price. Formally, if $s(p)$ gives the quantity supplied for each price p, the elasticity of supply, denoted η (the Greek letter "eta", chosen because epsilon was already taken) is

$$\eta = \frac{ds/s}{dp/p} = \frac{p}{s}\frac{ds}{dp} = \frac{ps'(p)}{s(p)}.$$

Again similar to demand, if supply takes the form $s(p)=ap^\eta$, then supply has *constant elasticity*, and the elasticity is equal to η. A special case of this form is linear supply, which occurs when the elasticity equals one.

2.4.2.1 (Exercise)   For a producer with constant elasticity of supply, compute the producer profits.

2.5 *Comparative Statics*

When something changes – the price of a complement, the demand for a good – what happens to the equilibrium? Such questions are answered by *comparative statics*, which are the changes in equilibrium variables when other things change. The use of the term "static" suggests that such changes are considered without respect to dynamic adjustment, but instead just focus on the changes in the equilibrium level. Elasticities will help us quantify these changes.

2.5.1 Supply and Demand Changes

How much do the price and quantity traded change in response to a change in demand? We begin by considering the constant elasticity case, which will let us draw conclusions for small changes in more general demand functions. We will denote the demand function by $q_d(p)=ap^{-\varepsilon}$ and supply function by $q_s(p)=bp^\eta$. The equilibrium price p^* is given by the quantity supplied equal to the quantity demanded, or the solution to the equation:

$$q_d(p^*) = q_s(p^*).$$

Substituting the constant elasticity formulae,

$$ap^{*-\varepsilon} = q_d(p^*) = q_s(p^*) = bp^{*\eta}.$$

Thus,

$$\frac{a}{b} = p*^{\varepsilon+\eta},$$

or

$$p* = \left(\frac{a}{b}\right)^{1/\varepsilon+\eta}.$$

The quantity traded, $q*$, can be obtained from either supply or demand and the price:

$$q* = q_S(p*) = bp*^{\eta} = b\left(\frac{a}{b}\right)^{\eta/\varepsilon+\eta} = a^{\eta/\varepsilon+\eta}b^{\varepsilon/\varepsilon+\eta}.$$

There is one sense in which this gives an answer to the question of what happens when demand increases. An increase in demand, holding the elasticity constant, corresponds to an increase in the parameter a. Suppose we increase a by a fixed percentage, replacing a by $a(1+\Delta)$. Then price goes up by the multiplicative factor $(1+\Delta)^{1/\varepsilon+\eta}$ and the change in price, as a proportion of the price, is

$$\frac{\Delta p*}{p*} = (1+\Delta)^{1/\varepsilon+\eta} - 1.$$

Similarly, quantity rises by

$$\frac{\Delta q*}{q*} = (1+\Delta)^{\eta/\varepsilon+\eta} - 1.$$

These formulae are problematic for two reasons. First, they are specific to the case of constant elasticity. Second, they are moderately complicated. Both of these issues can be addressed by considering small changes, that is, a small value of Δ. We make use of a trick to simplify the formula. The trick is that, for small Δ,

$$(1+\Delta)^r \approx 1 + r\Delta.$$

The squiggly equals sign $\approx$ should be read "approximately equal to."[10] Applying this insight, we have that:

---

[10] The more precise meaning of $\approx$ is that, as Δ gets small, the size of the error of the formula is small even relative to Δ. That is, $(1+\Delta)^r \approx 1 + r\Delta$. means $\frac{(1+\Delta)^r - (1+r\Delta)}{\Delta} \xrightarrow{\Delta \to 0} 0.$

For a small percentage increase Δ in demand, quantity rises by approximately $\eta\Delta/(\varepsilon+\eta)$ percent and price rises by approximately $\Delta/(\varepsilon+\eta)$ percent.

The beauty of this claim is that it holds even when demand and supply do not have constant elasticities, because the effect considered is local, and locally, the elasticity is approximately constant if the demand is "smooth."

2.5.1.1 (Exercise) Show that for a small percentage increase Δ in supply, quantity rises by approximately $\varepsilon\Delta/(\varepsilon+\eta)$ percent and price falls by approximately $\Delta/(\varepsilon+\eta)$ percent.

2.5.1.2 (Exercise) If demand is perfectly inelastic, what is the effect of a decrease in supply? Apply the formula and then graph the solution.

2.6 Trade

Supply and demand offers one approach to understanding trade, and it represents the most important and powerful concept in the toolbox of economists. However, for some issues, especially those of international trade, another related tool is very useful: the production possibilities frontier. Analysis using the production possibilities frontier was made famous by the "guns and butter" discussions of World War II. From an economic perspective, there is a tradeoff between guns and butter – if a society wants more guns, it must give up something, and one thing to give up is butter. That getting more guns might entail less butter often seems mysterious, because butter, after all, is made with cows, and indirectly with land and hay. But the manufacture of butter also involves steel containers, tractors to turn the soil, transportation equipment, and labor, all of which either can be directly used (steel, labor) or require inputs that could be used (tractors, transportation) to manufacture guns. From a production standpoint, more guns entail less butter (or other things).

2.6.1 Production Possibilities Frontier

Formally, the set of production possibilities is the collection of "feasible outputs" of an individual, group or society or country. You could spend your time cleaning your apartment, or you could study. The more of your time you devote to studying, the higher your grades will be, but the dirtier your apartment will be. This is illustrated, for a hypothetical student, in Figure 2-13.

The production possibilities set embodies the feasible alternatives. If you spend all your time studying, you would obtain a 4.0 (perfect) grade point average (GPA). Spending an hour cleaning reduces the GPA, but not by much; the second hour reduces by a bit more, and so on.

The boundary of the production possibilities set is known as the *production possibilities frontier*. This is the most important part of the production possibilities set, because at any point strictly inside the production possibilities set, it is possible to have more of everything, and usually we would choose to have more.[11] The slope of the production possibilities frontier reflects opportunity cost, because it describes what must be given up in order to acquire more of a good. Thus, to get a cleaner apartment, more time, or capital, or both, must be spent on cleaning, which reduces the amount of other goods and services that can be had. For the two-good case in Figure 2-13, diverting time to cleaning reduces studying, which lowers the GPA. The slope dictates how much lost GPA there is for each unit of cleaning.

Grades

Cleanliness

Figure 2-13: The Production Possibilities Frontier

One important feature of production possibilities frontiers is illustrated in the Figure 2-13: they are concave toward the origin. While this feature need not be universally true, it is a common feature, and there is a reason for it that we can see in the application. If you are only going to spend an hour studying, you spend that hour doing the most important studying that can be done in an hour, and thus get a lot of grades for the hour's work. The second hour of studying produces less value than the first, and the third hour less than the second. This is the principle of *diminishing marginal returns*. Diminishing marginal returns are like picking apples. If you are only going to pick apples for a few minutes, you don't need a ladder because the fruit is low on the tree; the more time spent, the fewer apples per hour you will pick.

---

[11] To be clear, we are considering an example with two goods, cleanliness and GPA. Generally there are lots of activities, like sleeping, eating, teeth-brushing, and the production possibilities frontier encompasses all of these goods. Spending all your time sleeping, studying and cleaning would still represent a point on a three-dimensional frontier.

Consider two people, Ann and Bob, getting ready for a party. One is cutting up vegetables, the other is making hors d'oeuvres. Ann can cut up two ounces of vegetables per minute, or make one hors d'oeuvre in a minute. Bob, somewhat inept with a knife, can cut up one ounce of vegetables per minute, or make two hors d'oeuvres per minute. Ann's and Bob's production possibilities frontiers are illustrated in the Figure 2-14, given that they have an hour to work.

Since Ann can produce two ounces of chopped vegetables in a minute, if she spends her entire hour on vegetables, she can produce 120 ounces. Similarly, if she devotes all her time to hors d'oeuvres, she produces 60 of them. The constant translation between the two means that her production possibilities frontier is a straight line, which is illustrated in the left side of Figure 2-14. Bob's is the reverse – he produces 60 ounces of vegetables, or 120 hors d'oeuvres, or something on the line in between.

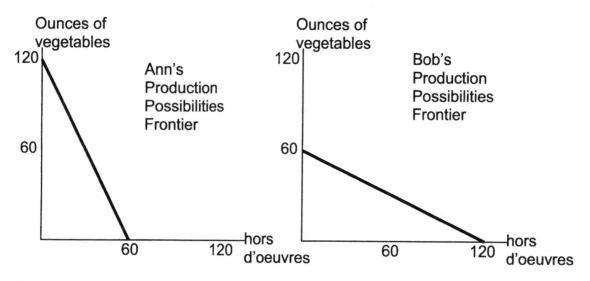

Figure 2-14: Two Production Possibilities Frontiers

For Ann, the opportunity cost of an ounce of vegetables is half of one hors d'oeuvre – to get one extra ounce of vegetable, she must spend 30 extra seconds on vegetables. Similarly, the cost of one hors d'oeuvres for Ann is two ounces of vegetables. Bob's costs are the inverse of Ann – an ounce of vegetables costs him two hors d'oeuvres.

What can Bob and Ann accomplish together? The important insight is that they should use the low cost person in the manufacture of each good, when possible. This means that if fewer than 120 ounces of vegetables will be made, Ann makes them all. Similarly, if fewer than 120 hors d'oeuvres are made, Bob makes them all. This gives a joint production possibilities frontier illustrated in the Figure 2-15. Together, they can make 180 of one and none of the other. If Bob makes only hors d'oeuvres, and Ann makes only chopped vegetables, they will have 120 of each. With fewer than 120 ounces of vegetables, the opportunity cost of vegetables is Ann's, and is thus half an hors d'oeuvre, but if more than 120 are needed, then the opportunity cost jumps to two.

Now change the hypothetical slightly – suppose that Bob and Ann are putting on separate dinner parties, each of which will feature chopped vegetables and hors d'oeuvres in equal portions. By herself, Ann can only produce 40 ounces of vegetables and 40 hors d'oeuvres if she must produce equal portions. She accomplishes this by spending 20 minutes on vegetables and 40 minutes on hors d'oeuvres. Similarly, Bob can produce 40 of each, but using the reverse allocation of time.

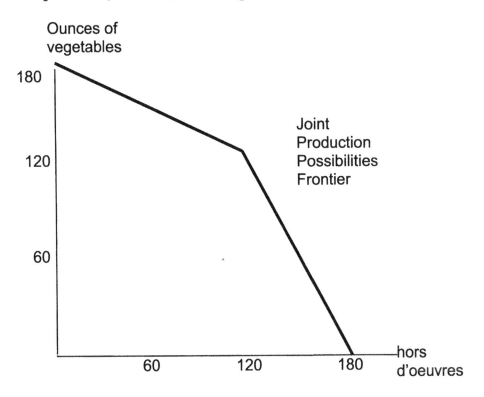

Figure 2-15: Joint PPF

By working together, they can collectively have more of both goods. Ann specializes in producing vegetables, and Bob specializes in producing hors d'oeuvres. This yields 120 units of each, which they can split equally, to have 60 of each. By specializing in the activity in which they have lower cost, Bob and Ann can jointly produce more of each good.

Moreover, Bob and Ann can accomplish this by trading. At a "one for one" price, Bob can produce 120 hors d'oeuvres, and trade 60 of them for 60 ounces of vegetables. This is better than producing the vegetables himself, which netted him only 40 of each. Similarly, Ann produces 120 ounces of vegetables, and trades 60 of them for 60 hors d'oeuvres. This trading makes them both better off.

The gains from specialization are potentially enormous. The grandfather of economics, Adam Smith, writes about specialization in the manufacture of pins:

> "...One man draws out the wire; another straights it; a third cuts it; a
> fourth points it; a fifth grinds it at the top for receiving the head; to make
> the head requires two or three distinct operations ; to put it on is a peculiar
> business; to whiten the pins is another ; it is even a trade by itself to put
> them into the paper ; and the important business of making a pin is, in this

manner, divided into about eighteen distinct operations, which, in some manufactories, are all performed by distinct hands, though in others the same man will sometimes perform two or three of them."[12]

Smith goes on to say that skilled individuals could produce at most twenty pins per day acting alone, but that with specialization, ten people can produce 48,000 pins per day, 240 times as many pins.

2.6.1.1 (Exercise)   The Manning Company has two factories, one that makes roof trusses, and one that makes cabinets. With m workers, the roof factory produces $\sqrt{m}$ trusses per day. With n workers, the cabinet plant produces $5\sqrt{n}$. The Manning Company has 400 workers to use in the two factories. Graph the production possibilities frontier. (Hint: Let T be the number of trusses produced. How many workers are used making trusses?)

2.6.1.2 (Exercise)   Alarm & Tint, Inc., has 10 workers working a total of 400 hours per week. Tinting takes 2 hours per car. Alarm installation is complicated, however, and performing A alarm installations requires A^2 hours of labor. Graph Alarm & Tint's production possibilities frontier for a week.

2.6.2 Comparative and Absolute Advantage

Ann produces chopped vegetables because her opportunity cost of producing vegetables, at ½ of one hors d'oeuvre, is lower than Bob's. A lower opportunity cost is said to create a *comparative advantage*. That is, Ann gives up less to produce chopped vegetables than Bob, so in comparison to hors d'oeuvres, she has an advantage in the production of vegetables. Since the cost of one good is the amount of another good foregone, a comparative advantage in one good implies a *comparative disadvantage* in another. If you are better at producing butter, you are necessarily worse at something else, and in particular the thing you give up less of to get more butter.

To illustrate this point, let's consider another party planner. Charlie can produce one hors d'oeuvre, or one ounce of chopped vegetables, per minute. His production is strictly less than Ann's, that is, his production possibilities frontier lies inside of Ann's. However, he has a comparative advantage over Ann in the production of hors d'oeuvres, because he gives up only one ounce of vegetables to produce a hors d'oeuvre, while Ann must give up two ounces of vegetables. Thus, Ann and Charlie can still benefit from trade if Bob isn't around.

2.6.2.1 (Exercise)   Graph the joint production possibilities frontier for Ann and Charlie, and show that collectively they can produce 80 of each if they need the same number of each product. Hint: First show that Ann will produce some of both goods, by showing that if Ann specializes, there are too many ounces of vegetables. Then show, if Ann devotes x minutes to hors d'oeuvres, that

$$60 + x = 2(60 - x).$$

---

[12] Adam Smith, "An Inquiry into the Nature and Causes of the Wealth of Nations," originally published 1776, released by the Gutenberg project, 2002.

When one production possibilities frontier lies outside another, the larger is said to have an absolute advantage – more total things are possible. In this case, Ann has an absolute advantage over Charlie – she can, by herself, have more – but not over Bob. Bob has an absolute advantage over Charlie, too, but again, not over Ann.

Diminishing marginal returns implies that the more of a good that a person produces, the higher is the cost (in terms of the good given up). That is to say, diminishing marginal returns means that supply curves slope upward; the marginal cost of producing more is increasing in the amount produced.

Trade permits specialization in activities in which one has a comparative advantage. Moreover, whenever opportunity costs differ, potential gains from trade exist. If person 1 has an opportunity cost of c_1 of producing good X (in terms of Y, that is, for each unit of X that person 1 produces, person 1 gives up c_1 units of Y), and person 2 has an opportunity cost of c_2, then there are gains from trade whenever c_1 is not equal to c_2 and neither party has specialized.[13] Suppose $c_1 < c_2$. Then by having person 1 increase the production of X by Δ, $c_1 \Delta$ less of the good Y is produced. Let person 2 reduce the production of X by Δ, so that the production of X is the same. Then there is $c_2 \Delta$ units of Y made available, for a net increase of $(c_2 - c_1) \Delta$. The net changes are summarized in Table 2-2.

Table 2-2: Construction of the Gains From Trade

	1	2	Net Change
Change in X	$+\Delta$	$-\Delta$	0
Change in Y	$-c_1 \Delta$	$c_2 \Delta$	$(c_2 - c_1) \Delta$

Whenever opportunity costs differ, there are gains from re-allocating production from one producer to another, gains which are created by having the low cost producers produce more, in exchange for greater production of the other good by the other producer, who is the low cost producer of this other good. An important aspect of this re-allocation is that it permits production of more of all goods. This means there is little ambiguity about whether it is a good thing to re-allocate production – it just means we have more of everything we want.[14]

How can we guide the reallocation of production to produce more goods and services? It turns out that under some circumstances, the price system does a superb job of creating efficient production. The price system posits a price for each good or service, and anyone can sell at the common price. The insight is that such a price induces efficient production. To see this, suppose we have a price p which is the number of units

---

[13] If a party specialized in one product, it is a useful convention to say that the marginal cost of that product is now infinite, since no more can be produced.

[14] If you are worried that more production means more pollution or other bad things, rest assured. Pollution is a bad, so we enter the negative of pollution (or environmental cleanliness) as one of the goods we would like to have more of. The reallocation dictated by differences in marginal costs produces more of all goods. Now with this said, we have no reason to believe that the reallocation will benefit everyone – there may be winners and losers.

of Y one has to give to get a unit of X. (Usually prices are in currency, but we can think of them as denominated in goods, too.) If I have a cost c of producing X, which is the number of units of Y that I lose to obtain a unit of X, I will find it worthwhile to sell X if $p > c$, because the sale of a unit of X, nets me $p - c$ units of Y, which I can either consume or resell for something else I want. Similarly, if $c > p$, I would rather buy X (producing Y to pay for it). Either way, only producers with costs less than p will produce X, and those with costs greater than p will purchase X, paying for it with Y, which they can produce more cheaply than its price. (The price of Y is $1/p$ – that is the amount of X one must give to get a unit of Y.)

Thus, a price system, with appropriate prices, will guide the allocation of production to insure the low cost producers are the ones who produce, in the sense that there is no way of re-allocating production to obtain more goods and services.

2.6.2.2 (Exercise)   Using Manning's production possibilities frontier in 2.6.1.1
        (Exercise), compute the marginal cost of trusses in terms of cabinets.

2.6.2.3 (Exercise)   Using Alarm & Tint's production possibilities frontier in 2.6.1.2
        (Exercise), compute the marginal cost of alarms in terms of window tints.

2.6.3 Factors and Production

Production possibilities frontiers provide the basis for a rudimentary theory of international trade. To understand the theory, it is first necessary to consider that there are fixed and mobile factors. *Factors of production* are jargon for inputs to the production process. Labor is generally considered a fixed factor, because most countries don't have borders wide open to immigration, although of course some labor moves across international borders. Temperature, weather, and land are also fixed – Canada is a high-cost citrus grower because of its weather. There are other endowments that could be exported, but are expensive to export because of transportation costs, including water and coal. Hydropower – electricity generated from the movement of water – is cheap and abundant in the Pacific Northwest, and as a result, a lot of aluminum is smelted there, because aluminum smelting requires lots of electricity. Electricity can be transported, but only with losses (higher costs), which gives other regions a disadvantage in the smelting of aluminum. Capital is generally considered a mobile factor, because plants can be built anywhere, although investment is easier in some environments than in others. For example, reliable electricity and other inputs are necessary for most factories. Moreover, comparative advantage may arise from the presence of a functioning legal system, the enforcement of contracts, and the absence of bribery, because enforcement of contracts increases the return on investment by increasing the probability the economic return to investment isn't taken by others.

Fixed factors of production give particular regions a comparative advantage in the production of some kinds of goods, and not in others. Europe, the United States and Japan have a relative abundance of highly skilled labor, and have a comparative advantage in goods requiring high skills, like computers, automobiles and electronics. Taiwan, South Korea, Singapore and Hong Kong have increased the available labor skills, and now manufacture more complicated goods like VCRs, computer parts and the like. Mexico has a relative abundance of middle-level skills, and a large number of assembly plants operate there, as well as clothing and shoe manufacturers. Lower skilled Chinese workers manufacture the majority of the world's toys. The skill levels of China are rising rapidly.

The basic model of international trade was first described by David Ricardo (1772-1823), and suggests that nations, responding to price incentives, will specialize in the production of goods in which they have a comparative advantage, and purchase the goods in which they have a comparative disadvantage. In Ricardo's description, England has a comparative advantage of manufacturing cloth, and Portugal in producing wine, leading to gains from trade from specialization.

The Ricardian theory suggests that the United States, Canada, Australia and Argentina should export agricultural goods, especially grains that require a large land area for the value generated (they do). It suggests that complex technical goods should be produced in developed nations (they are) and that simpler products and natural resources should be exported by the lesser developed nations (they are). It also suggests that there should be more trade between developed and underdeveloped nations than between developed and other developed nations. The theory falters on this prediction – the vast majority of trade is between developed nations. There is no consensus for the reasons for this, and politics plays a role – the North American Free Trade Act vastly increased the volume of trade between the United States and Mexico, for example, suggesting that trade barriers may account for some of the lack of trade between the developed and the underdeveloped world. Trade barriers don't account for the volume of trade between similar nations, which the theory suggests should be unnecessary. Developed nations sell each other mustard and tires and cell phones, exchanging distinct varieties of goods they all produce.

2.6.4 International Trade

The Ricardian theory emphasizes that the relative abundance of particular factors of production determines comparative advantage in output, but there is more to the theory. When the United States exports a computer to Mexico, American labor, in the form of a physical product, has been sold abroad. When the United States exports soybeans to Japan, American land (or at least the use of American land for a time) has been exported to Japan. Similarly, when the United States buys car parts from Mexico, Mexican labor has been sold to the United States, and similarly when the Americans buy Japanese televisions, Japanese labor has been purchased. The goods that are traded internationally embody the factors of production of the producing nations, and it is useful to think of international trade as directly trading the inputs through the incorporation of inputs into products.

If the set of traded goods is broad enough, the value of factors of production should be equalized through trade. The United States has a lot of land, relative to Japan, but by selling agricultural goods to Japan, it is as if Japan had more land, by way of access to US land. Similarly, by buying automobiles from Japan, it is as if a portion of the Japanese factories were present in the United States. With inexpensive transportation, the trade equalizes the values of factories in the United States and Japan, and also equalizes the value of agricultural land. One can reasonably think that soybeans are soybeans, wherever they are produced, and that trade in soybeans at a common price forces the costs of the factors involved in producing soybeans to be equalized across the producing nations. The purchase of soybeans by Japanese drives up the value of American land, and drives down the value of Japanese land by giving an alternative to its output, leading toward equalization of the value of the land across the nations.

This prediction, known as *factor price equalization,* of modern international trade theory was first developed by Paul Samuelson (1915 –) and generalized by Eli Heckscher (1879 – 1952) and Bertil Ohlin (1899 – 1979). It has powerful predictions, including the equalization of wages of equally skilled people after free trade between the United States and Mexico. Thus, free trade in physical goods should equalize the price of haircuts, and land, and economic consulting, in Mexico City and New York. Equalization of wages is a direct consequence of factor price equalization because labor is a factor of production. If economic consulting is cheap in Mexico, trade in goods embodying economic consulting – boring reports, perhaps – will bid up the wages in the low wage area, and reduce the quantity in the high wage area.

An even stronger prediction of the theory is that the price of water in New Mexico should be the same as in Minnesota. If water is cheaper in Minnesota, trade in goods that heavily use water – e.g. paper – will tend to bid up the value of Minnesota water, while reducing the premium on scarce New Mexico water.

It is fair to say that if factor price equalization works fully in practice, it works very, very slowly. Differences in taxes, tariffs and other distortions make it a challenge to test the theory across nations. On the other hand, within the United States, where we have full factor mobility and product mobility, we still have different factor prices – electricity is cheaper in the Pacific Northwest. Nevertheless, nations with a relative abundance of capital and skilled labor export goods that use these intensively, nations with a relative abundance of land export land-intensive goods like food, nations with a relative abundance of natural resources export these resources, and nations with an abundance of low-skilled labor export goods that make intensive use of this labor. The reduction of trade barriers between such nations works like Ann and Bob's joint production of party platters: by specializing in the goods in which they have a comparative advantage, there is more for all.

3 The US Economy

An important aspect of economics is economic statistics, and an army of economists collect and analyze these statistics. This chapter presents an overview of the economic activity of the United States. How much do you need to know about these statistics? It would be ridiculous to memorize them. At the same time, it would be undesirable to be ignorant of how we are changing, and how we are not.[15]

3.1.1 Basic Demographics

There are about three hundred million people in the United States, up from 76 million in 1900.

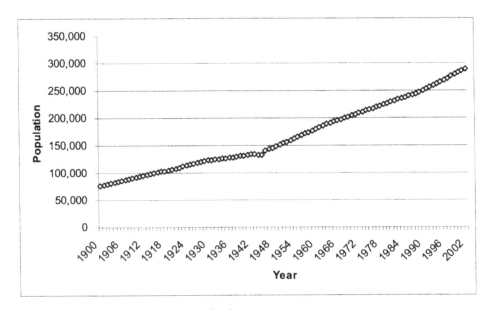

Figure 3-1: US Resident Population

During the last century, the US population has become primarily an urban population, growing from 40% to 80% urban. The population is primarily white, with 12-13% African-American and 4% classified as other. These proportions are relatively stable over the century, with the white population falling from 89% to 83%. The census is thought to understate minority populations because of greater difficulties in contacting minorities. The census does not attempt to classify people but instead accepts people's description of their own race.

---

[15] I apologize to those using the book in foreign countries; this chapter is about the US not because it is more important but because I know it better. Encourage your professor to write a chapter on your country! All of the statistics in this chapter come from Fedstats, http://www.fedstats.gov/, from FRED, http://research.stlouisfed.org/fred2/, and from the NBER, http://www.nber.org/.

Figure 3-2: US Urban and White Population

The United States population has been aging significantly, with the proportion of seniors (over 65 years old) tripling over the past century, and the proportion of young people dropping by over a third. Indeed, the proportion of children between zero and five years old has dropped from 12.1% of the population to under 7%.

Figure 3-3: Population Proportions by Age Group

The baby boom – a dramatic increase in births for the years 1946-1964, is visible in the Figure 3-3 as the population in the 0-24 age group begins increasing in 1950, peaking in 1970 and then declining significantly as the baby boom moves into the 25-44 year old bracket. There is a slight "echo" of the baby boom, most readily seen by looking at the 0-5 age bracket, as in Figure 3-4.

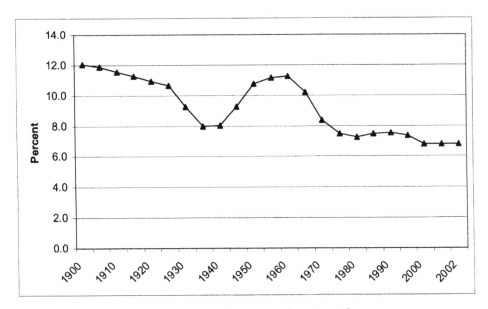

Figure 3-4: Proportion of Population under Age Five

The aging of the American population is a consequence of greater life expectancy. When social security was created in 1935, the average American male lived to be slightly less than sixty years old. The social security benefits, which didn't start until age 65, thus were not being paid to a substantial portion of the population.

Figure 3-5 shows life expectancy at birth, thus including infant mortality. The significant drop in life expectancy in 1918 – to nearly 30 years old for non-whites – is primarily a consequence of the great influenza, which killed about 2.5% of the people who contracted it and killed more Americans in 1918 than did World War I. The Great Depression (1932-39) also reduced life expectancy. The steady increase in life expectancy is also visible, with white females now living eighty years on average.

Figure 3-5: US Life Expectancy at Birth

It is said that the United States is a country of immigrants, and a large fraction of the population had ancestors that came from elsewhere. Immigration into this United States, however, has been increasing after a long decline, and the fraction of the population that were born in foreign countries is about 11% -- one in nine.

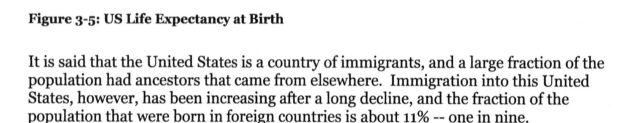

Figure 3-6: US Immigrant Population, in Percent, by Continent of Origin

The majority of immigrants during this century came from Europe, but immigration from Europe has been declining for most of the century, while immigration from Asia and Latin America has grown substantially. Figure 3-7 aggregates the total country of origin data over the century, to identify the major sources of immigrants.

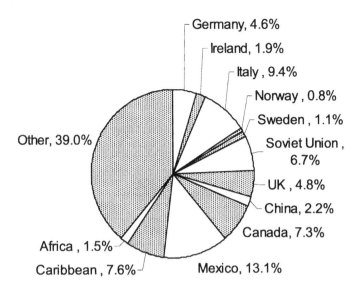

Figure 3-7: National Origin of Immigrants, 1900-2000

One hears a lot about divorce rates in the United States, with statements like "fifty percent of all marriages end in divorce." Although it has grown, the divorced population is actually a small fraction of the population in the United States.

Figure 3-8: Male Marital Status (Percentages)

Figure 3-9: Female Marital Status (Percent)

Marriage rates have fallen, but primarily because the "never married" category has grown. Some of the "never married" probably represent unmarried couples, since the proportion of children from unmarried women has risen fairly dramatically. Even so, marriage rates are greater than they were a century ago. However, a century ago there were more unrecorded and common-law marriages than probably there are today.

Figure 3-10: Percent of Births to Unwed Mothers

While we are on the subject, however, the much discussed crisis in teen-age pregnancy doesn't appear like such a crisis when viewed in terms of the proportion of all births that involve a teenage mother.

Figure 3-11: Percent of Births to Women Age 19 or less

3.1.2 Education

Why are the western nations rich, and many other nations poor? What creates the wealth of the developed nations? Modern economic analysis attributes much of the growth of the United States and other developed nations to its educated workforce, and not to natural resources. Japan, with a relative scarcity of natural resources but a highly educated workforce, is substantially richer than Brazil, with its abundance of natural resources.

Figure 3-12: Educational Attainment in Years (Percent of Population)

Just less than 85% of the US population completes 12 years of schooling, not counting kindergarten. Not all of these students graduate from high school, but they spent twelve years in school. The proportion that completes only five or fewer years of elementary school has dropped from about a quarter of the population to a steady 1.6%. At least four years of university now represents a bit more than a quarter of the population, which is a dramatic increase. Slightly fewer women (25% versus 28%) complete four years of university, although women are more likely to complete four years of high school.

Graduation rates are somewhat below the number of years completed, so that slightly less than three-quarters of the US population actually obtain their high school degree. Of those obtaining a high school degree, nearly half obtain a university or college degree.

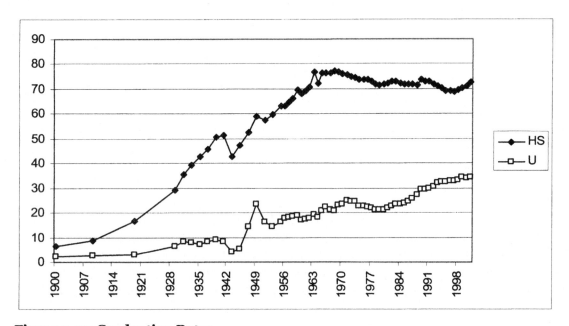

Figure 3-13: Graduation Rates

There are several interesting things to see in Figure 3-13. First, high school completion dropped significantly during World War II (1940-45) but rebounded after. Second, after World War II, college graduation spiked, as many US soldiers were sent to university by the government under a program called the "GI Bill."[16]

As the numbers of high school students rose, the portion of high school graduates going to university fell, meaning a larger segment of the population became high school educated. This increase represents the creation of the US middle class; previously, high school completion and university were in large part a sign of wealth. The creation of a large segment of the population who graduated from high school, but didn't attend university, led to a population with substantial skills and abilities, but no inherited wealth, who became the middle class.

High school completion has been declining for thirty years. This is surprising given the high rate of financial return to education in the United States. Much of the reduction in completion can be attributed to an increase in General Education Development, or GED, certification, which is a program that grants diplomas (often erroneously thought to be a

---

[16] The etymology of GI, as slang for US soldiers, is disputed, with candidates including "Government Issue," "General Infantry" and "Galvanized Iron," the latter a reference to trash cans that looked like German World War I artillery.

"General Equivalent Degree") after successfully passing examinations in five subject areas. Unfortunately, those people who obtain GED certification are not as successful as high school graduates, even marginal graduates, and indeed the GED certification does not seem to help students succeed, in comparison with high school graduation.[17]

3.1.3 Households and Consumption

There are approximately one hundred million households in the United States. The number of residents per household has consistently shrunk during this century, from over four to under three.

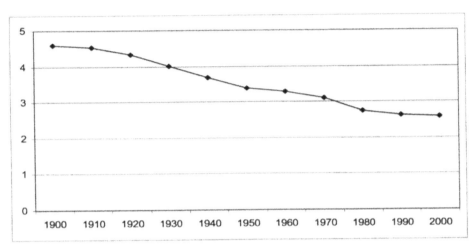

Figure 3-14: Household Occupancy

The shrinking size of households reflects a reduction not just in birthrates but also an increase in the number of people living alone. More women live alone than men, even though four times as many families with a single adult member are headed by women. This discrepancy – many more women both living on their own and living with children and no partner, even though there are about the same number of men and women born – is accounted for by the greater female longevity already noted above.

---

[17] In performing this kind of analysis, economists are very concerned with adjusting for the type of person. Smarter people are more likely to graduate from high school, but one doesn't automatically become smart by attending high school. Thus, care has been taken to hold constant innate abilities, measured by various measures like IQ scores and performance on tests, so that the comparison is between similar individuals, some of whom persevere to finish school, some of who don't. Indeed, some studies use identical twins.

Figure 3-15: Proportion of Households by Type

Where do we live? About 60% of households live in single family detached homes, meaning houses that stand alone. Another 5% or so live in single family attached houses, such as "row houses."   Slightly over 7½ % live in mobile homes or trailers, and the remainder live in multi-unit housing, including apartments and duplexes. Two-thirds of American families own their own homes, up from 43% in 1940. Slightly less than half a percent of the population is incarcerated in state and federal prisons. This represents a four-fold increase over 1925-1975.

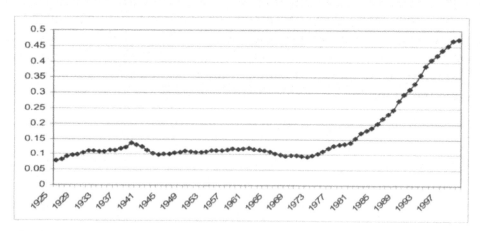

Figure 3-16: Percentage of Incarcerated Residents

Ten percent of households do not have an automobile, and 97.6% have a telephone. So-called "land line" telephones may start to fall as apartment dwellers, especially students, begin to rely exclusively on cell phones. Just under 99% of households have complete plumbing facilities (running water, bath or shower, flush toilet), up from 54.7% in 1940.

How much income do these households make? What is the distribution of income? One way of assessing the distribution is to use *quintiles* to measure dispersion. A quintile (or fifth) is a group of size 20%. Thus the top income quintile represents the top 20% of income earners, the next represents those ranking 60%-80%, and so on. Figure 3-17 shows the earnings of the top, middle and bottom quintiles.

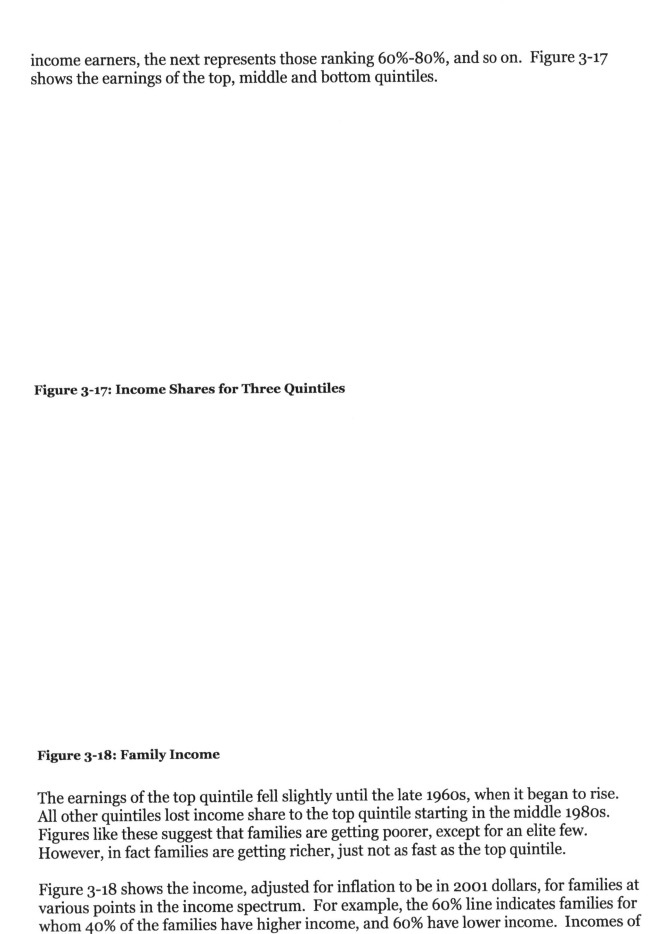

Figure 3-17: Income Shares for Three Quintiles

Figure 3-18: Family Income

The earnings of the top quintile fell slightly until the late 1960s, when it began to rise. All other quintiles lost income share to the top quintile starting in the middle 1980s. Figures like these suggest that families are getting poorer, except for an elite few. However, in fact families are getting richer, just not as fast as the top quintile.

Figure 3-18 shows the income, adjusted for inflation to be in 2001 dollars, for families at various points in the income spectrum. For example, the 60% line indicates families for whom 40% of the families have higher income, and 60% have lower income. Incomes of all groups has risen, although the richer families have seen their incomes rise faster than poorer families. That is readily seen when percentage changes are plotted in Figure 3-19.

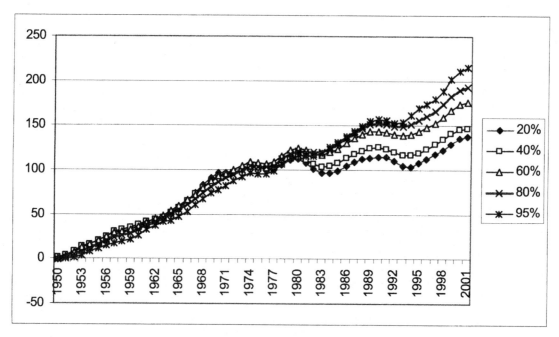

Figure 3-19: Family Income, Cumulative Percentage Change

Real income gains in percentage terms have been larger for richer groups, even though the poor have also seen substantially increased incomes.

If the poor have fared less well than the rich in percentage terms, how have African-Americans fared? After World War II, African-Americans families earned about 50% of white family income. This has risen gradually, noticeably in the 1960s after the 1964 Civil Rights Act that is credited with integrating workplaces throughout the southern United States. African-American family income lagged white income growth through the 1980s, but has been rising again.

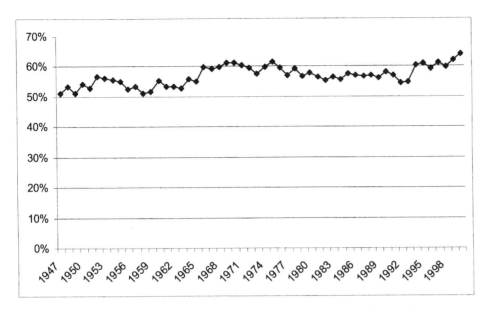

Figure 3-20: Black Family Income as a Percentage of White Income

These income measures attempt to actually measure purchasing power, and thus adjust for inflation. How much will $1 buy? This is a complicated question, because changes in prices aren't uniform – some goods get relatively cheaper, while others become more expensive, and the overall cost of living is a challenge to calculate. The price index typically used is the consumer price index (CPI), which adjusts for what it costs to buy a "standard" bundle of food, clothing, housing, electricity and other items. Figure 3-21 shows the CPI over most of past century, where 1982 is set as the reference year.

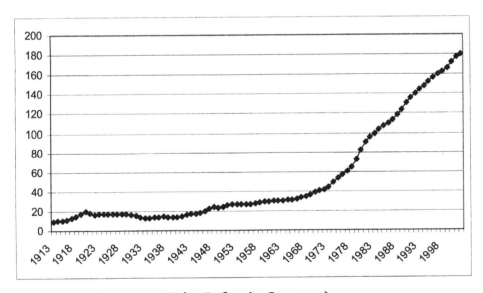

Figure 3-21: Consumer Price Index (1982 = 100)

3.1.3.1 (Exercise)   Have prices actually risen? Economists generally agree that the meaning of "prices have risen" is that you would prefer past prices to current prices. What makes this challenging is that the set of available products change over time. Cars have gone up significantly in price, but are also more reliable.

Would you be better off with your current income in 1913 than today? You would be very rich with current average income in 1913, but not have access to modern medicine, television, electronics, refrigeration, highways, and many other technologies. If you made $40,000 annually in 1913, how would you live and what would you buy? (Do some research.)

3.1.3.2 (Exercise)   Compare a $40,000 income in 1980 to the present. What differences are there in available products? In the quality of products? How rich does $40,000 make you in each time period? In which period would you choose to live, and why?

There have been three major inflations in the past century. Both World War I and World War II, with a large portion of the goods and services diverted to military use, saw significant inflations. In addition, there was a substantial inflation during the 1970s, after the Vietnam War in the 1960s. The price level fell during the Great Depression (1929-39). Falling price levels create investment problems, because inflation adjusted interest rates, which must adjust for a deflation, are forced to be high, since unadjusted interest rates cannot be negative.

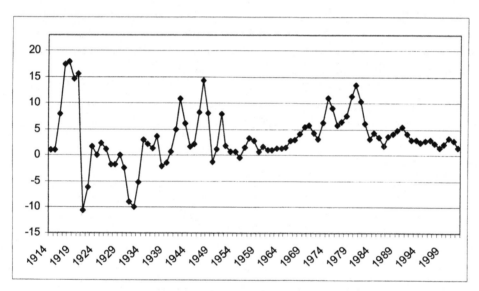

Figure 3-22: CPI Percent Changes

The cost of food has fallen quite dramatically over the past century. Figure 3-23 shows that the percentage of pre-tax household income spent on food has fallen from 25% to about 10%. This fall is a reflection of greater incomes, and of the fact that the real cost of food has fallen.

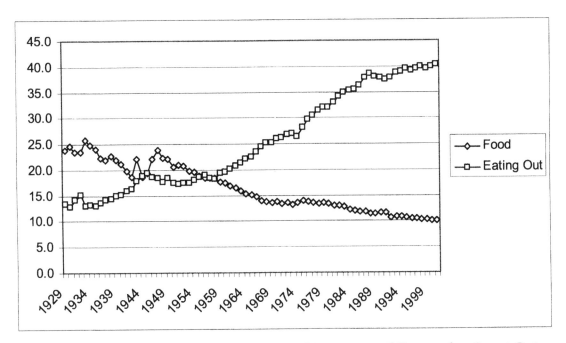

Figure 3-23: Food Expenditure as Percent of Income, and Proportion Spent Out

Moreover, a much greater fraction of expenditures on food are spent away from home, a fraction that has risen from under 15% to 40%.

How do we spend our income? The major categories are food, clothing, housing, medical, household operation, transportation, and recreation. The percentage of disposable income spent on these categories are shown, for the years 1929, 1965 and 2001, in Figure 3-24.

Figure 3-24: After Tax Income Shares

Food has shrunk substantially, but we enjoy more recreation, and spend a *lot* more staying healthy. (Food is larger than in Figure 3-23 because these figures use after tax disposable income, rather than pre-tax income.) This is in part a consequence of our aging population, but also of the increased technology available.

3.1.4 Production

We learned something about where we live and what we buy. Where do we get our income? Primarily we earn by providing goods and services. Nationally, we produce about eleven trillion dollars worth of goods and services. Broadly speaking, we spend that eleven trillion on personal consumption of goods and services, savings, and government. This, by the way, is often expressed as $Y = C + I + G$, which states that income (Y) is spent on consumption (C), investment (which comes from savings) and government. One can consume imports as well, so the short-term constraint looks like $Y + M = C + I + G + X$, where M is imports and X is exports.

How much does the United States produce? Economists measure output with the *gross domestic product* (GDP), which is the value of traded goods and services produced within the borders of the United States. GDP measures what is produced within the United States, and thus excludes output of Japanese factories owned by Americans, but includes the output of US factories owned by Japanese.

Importantly, GDP excludes non-traded goods and services. Thus, unpaid housework is not included. If you clean your own home, and your neighbor cleans his or her home, the cleaning does not contribute to GDP. On the other hand, if you and your neighbor pay each other to clean each other's homes, GDP goes up by the payments, even though the actual production of goods and services remains unchanged. Thus, GDP does not measure our total output as a nation, because it neglects unpaid services. Why does it neglect unpaid services? Primarily, because we can't readily measure them. Data on transactions is generated by tax information and reporting requirements imposed on businesses. For the same reason, GDP neglects illegal activities as well, such as illegal drug sales and pirated music sales. Thus, GDP is *not* a perfect measure of the production of our society. It is just the best measure we have.

Figure 3-25 shows the growth in GDP, and its components of personal consumption, government expenditures, and investment. The figures are expressed in constant 1996 dollars, that is, adjusted for inflation. The figure for government includes the government's purchases of goods and services – weapons, highways, rockets, pencils – but does not include transfer payments like social security and welfare programs. Transfer payments are excluded from this calculation because the actual dollars are spent by the recipient, not by the government. The cost of making the transfer payments (e.g. printing and mailing the checks), however, is included in the cost of government.

Figure 3-25: Output, Consumption, Investment and Government

It is often visually challenging to draw useful information from graphs like Figure 3-25, because economic activity is growing at a constant percentage. Consequently, economists often use a logarithmic scale, rather than a dollar scale. A logarithmic scale has the useful property that a straight line gives constant *percentage* growth. Consider a variable X that takes on values x_t at time t. Define $\%\Delta x$ to be the percentage change:

$$\%\Delta x = \frac{x_t - x_{t-1}}{x_{t-1}}.$$

Then

$$\log(x_t) = \log(x_{t-1}) + \log\left(\frac{x_t}{x_{t-1}}\right) = \log(x_{t-1}) + \log(1 + \%\Delta x)$$

Thus, if the percentage change is constant over time, $\log(x_t)$ will be a straight line over time. Moreover, for small percentage changes:

$$\log(1 + \%\Delta x) \approx \%\Delta x$$

so that the slope is approximately the growth rate.[18] Figure 3-26 shows these statistics with a logarithmic scale.

---

[18] The meaning of $\approx$ throughout this book is 'to the first order.' Here that means
$\lim\limits_{\%\Delta x \to 0} \dfrac{\log(1 + \%\Delta x) - \%\Delta x}{\%\Delta x} = 0$. Moreover, in this case the errors of the approximation are modest up to about 25% changes.

Figure 3-26: Major GDP Components in Log Scale

Immediately noticeable is the approximately constant growth rate from 1950 to the present, because a straight line with a log scale represents a constant growth rate. In addition, government has grown much more slowly (although recall that transfer payments, another aspect of government, aren't shown). A third feature is the volatility of investment – it shows much greater changes than output and consumption. Indeed, during the great depression (1929-39), income fell somewhat, consumption fell less, government was approximately flat, and investment plunged to 10% of its former level.

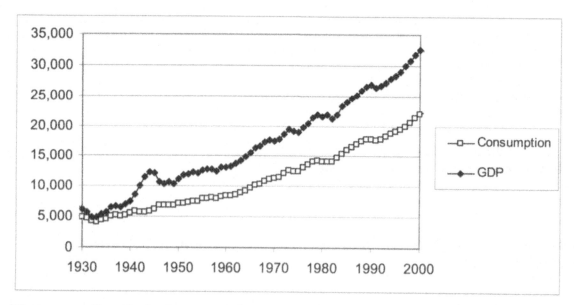

Figure 3-27: Per Capita Income and Consumption

Some of the growth in the American economy has arisen because there are more of us. Double the number of people, and consume twice as many goods, and individually we aren't better off. How much are we producing per capita, and how much are we consuming?

US output of goods and services, and consumption, have grown substantially over the past 75 years. In addition, consumption has been a steady percentage of income. This is more clearly visible when income shares are plotted in Figure 3-28.

Figure 3-28: Consumption, Investment and Government (% GDP)

Consumption was a very high portion of income during the Great Depression (1929-39), because income itself fell. Little investment took place. The wartime economy of World War II reduced consumption to below 50% of output, with government spending a similar fraction as home consumers. Otherwise, consumption has been a relatively stable 60-70% of income, rising modestly during the past twenty years, as the share of government shrank, and net imports grew. Net imports rose to 4% of GDP in 2001.

The most basic output of our economic system is food, and the US economy does a remarkable job producing food. The US has about 941 million acres under cultivation to produce food, which represents 41½ % of the surface area of the United States. Land use for agriculture peaked in 1952, at 1,206 million acres, and has been dwindling ever since, especially in the northeast where farms are being returned to forest through disuse. Figure 3-29 shows the output of agricultural products in the United States, adjusting to 1982 prices.

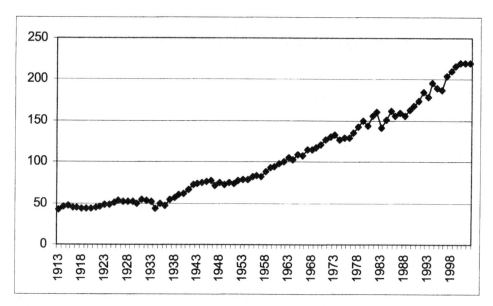

Figure 3-29: US Agricultural Output, 1982 constant dollars

The growth in output is more pronounced when viewed per worker involved in agriculture.

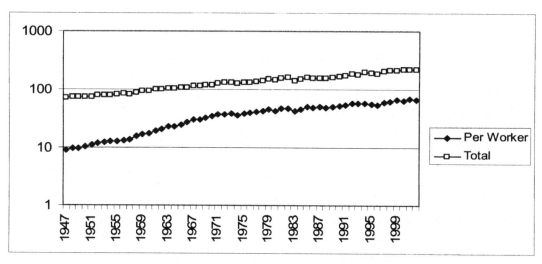

Figure 3-30: Agricultural Output, Total and Per Worker (1982 $, Log Scale)

Where do we work? Economists divide production into goods and services. Goods are historically divided into mining, construction and manufacturing. Mining includes production of raw materials of all kinds, including metals, oil, bauxite and gypsum. Construction involves production of housing and business space. Manufacturing involves the production of everything from computers to those little chef's hats that are placed on turkey legs. Figure 3-31 describes the major sectors of the US economy. Because the data come from firms, agriculture is excluded, although goods and services provided to farms would be included.

Figure 3-31: Major Non-Agricultural Sectors of US Economy, percent of GDP

Mining has diminished as a major factor in the US economy, a consequence of the growth of other sectors, and the reduction in the prices for raw materials. Contrary to many popular predictions, the prices of raw materials have fallen even as output and population have grown. We will see later in this book that the fall in prices of raw materials – ostensibly in fixed supply given the limited capacity of the earth – means that people expect a relative future abundance, either because of technological improvements in their use or because of large as yet undiscovered pools of the resources. An example of technological improvements is the substitution of fiber optic cable for copper wires. An enormous amount of copper has been recovered from telephone lines, and we can have more telephone lines and use less copper than was used in the past.

Manufacturing has become less important, for several reasons. Many manufactured goods cost less, pulling down the overall value. In addition, we import more manufactured goods than in the past. We produce more services. T& PU stands for transportation and public utilities, and includes electricity and telephone services and transportation including rail and air travel. This sector has shrunk as a portion of the entire economy, although the components have grown in absolute terms. We take more airplane trips than we have historically.

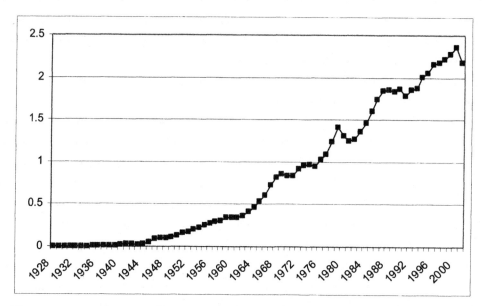

Figure 3-32: Air Travel Per Capita

Electricity production has risen dramatically.

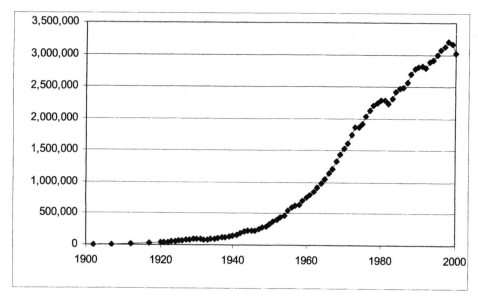

Figure 3-33: Electricity Production (M kwh)

However, energy use more generally has not grown as much, just doubling over the post-war period.

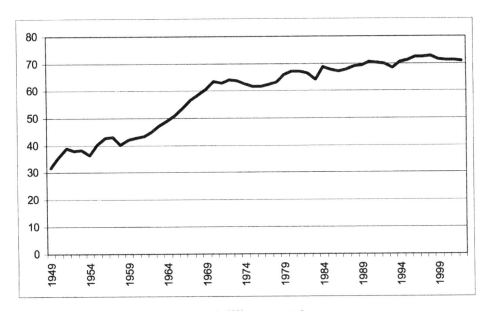

Figure 3-34: Energy Use (Quadrillion BTUs)

The number of automobiles per capita in the United States peaked in the early 1980s, which looks like a reduction in transportation since then. However, we still drive more than ever, suggesting the change is actually an increase in the reliability of automobiles.

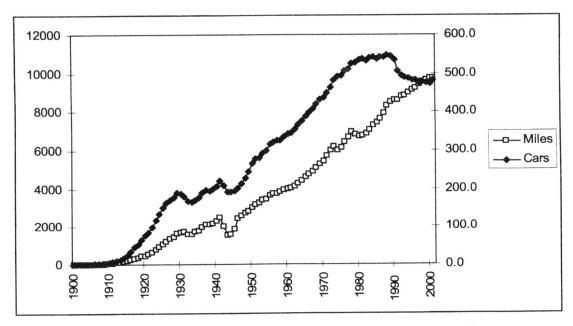

Figure 3-35: Cars Per Thousand Population and Miles Driven Per Capita

The cost of selling goods – wholesale and retail costs – remains relatively stable, as does "FIRE," which stands for finance, insurance, and real estate costs. Other services, ranging from restaurants to computer tutoring, have grown substantially. This is the so-called "service economy" that used to be in the news frequently, but is less so these days.

A bit more than 60% of the population works. The larger numbers in recent years are partially a reflection of the baby boom's entry into working years, reducing the proportion of elderly and children in American society. However, it is partially a reflection of an increased propensity for households to have two income earners.

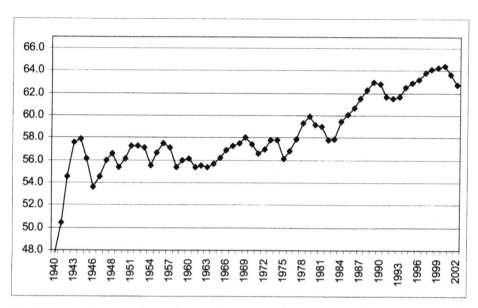

Figure 3-36: Percentage of Population Employed (Military & Prisoners Excluded)

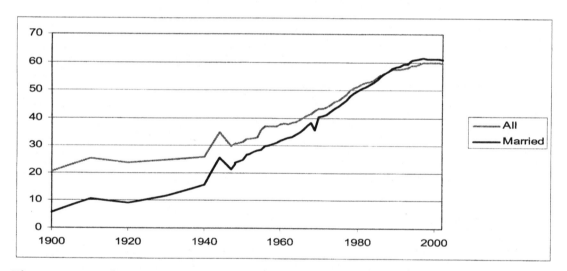

Figure 3-37: Labor Force Participation Rates, All Women and Married Women

Female participation in the labor force has risen quite dramatically in the United States. Figure 3-37 shows female labor force participation. The overall participation rate has roughly tripled during the century, and significantly exceed the rate prevailing during World War II, when many women went to work. In addition, participation of married women has now risen above the level for unmarried women. The participation rate for single women is even higher, currently at 68% it is higher than the overall average participation rate of all residents. The difference is primarily elderly women, who are disproportionately more likely to be widowed rather than married or single, and who are less likely to be working.

Another sector of the economy which has been much in the news is national defense. How much do we spend on the military? In this century, the large expenditure occurred during World War II, when about 50% of GDP was spent by the government, and 37% of GDP went to the armed forces. During the Korean War, we spent about 15% of GDP on military goods, and less than 10% of GDP during the Vietnam war. The military buildup during Ronald Reagan's presidency (1980-1988) increased our military expenditures from about 5½% to 6½% of GDP – a large percentage change in military expenditures, but a small diversion of GDP. The fall of the Soviet Union led the United States to reduce military expenditures, in what was called the "peace dividend," but again the effects were modest.

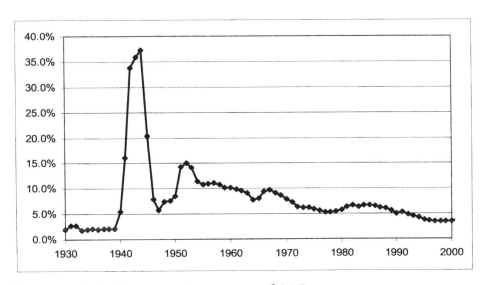

Figure 3-38: Defense as a Percentage of GDP

Historically, defense represents the largest expenditure by the federal government. However, as we see, defense has become a much smaller part of the economy overall. However, the federal government plays many other roles in the modern US economy.

3.1.5 Government

With a budget over two trillion dollars, the federal government represents just under 20% of the US economy. It is one of the largest organizations in the world; only nations are larger organizations, and only a handful of nations are larger.

The size of the federal government, as a percentage of GDP, is shown in Figure 3-39. Federal expenditures boomed during World War II (1940-45), but shrank back to nearly pre-war levels shortly afterward, with much of the difference attributable to veterans' benefits and continuing international involvement. Federal expenditures, as a percentage of GDP, continue to grow until Ronald Reagan's presidency in 1980, when they begin to shrink slightly after an initial growth. Figure 3-39 also shows federal revenues, and the deficit – the difference between expenditures and revenues, is apparent, especially for World War II and 1970-1998.

50.0															
45.0															
40.0															
35.0															
30.0															
25.0															
20.0															
15.0															
10.0															
5.0															
0.0															
	1930	1935	1940	1945	1950	1955	1960	1965	1970	1975	1980	1985	1990	1995	2000

Figure 3-39: Federal Expenditures and Revenues (Percent of GDP)

Much has been written about the federal government's "abdication" of various services, which are pushed onto state and local government. Usually this behavior is attributed to the Reagan presidency (1980-88). There is some evidence of this behavior in the post-war data, but the effect is very modest and long term. Most of the growth in state and local government occurred between 1947 and 1970, well before the Reagan presidency; state and local government has been stable since then. Moreover, the expenditure of the federal government, which shows ups and downs, has also been fairly stable. In any event, such effects are modest overall.

Figure 3-40: Federal, State & Local and Total Government Receipts (% GDP)

Figure 3-40 sets out the taxation at both the federal and state and local (merged to be regional) level. Figure 3-41 shows expenditures of the same entities. Both figures are stated as a percentage of GDP. State and local taxation and expenditures doubled over the postwar period. The two figures are very similar. The federal government's expenditures have varied more significantly than its revenues.

Figure 3-41: Federal, Regional and Total Expenditures as a Percent of GDP

A peculiarity of the US federal government is a penchant for "off-budget" expenditures. Originally, such off-budget items involved corporations like Intelsat (which commercialized satellite technology) and RCA (the Radio Corporation of America, which commercialized radio) and other semi-autonomous and self-sustaining operations. Over time, however, off-budget items became a way of hiding the growth of government, through a process that became known as "smoke and mirrors."

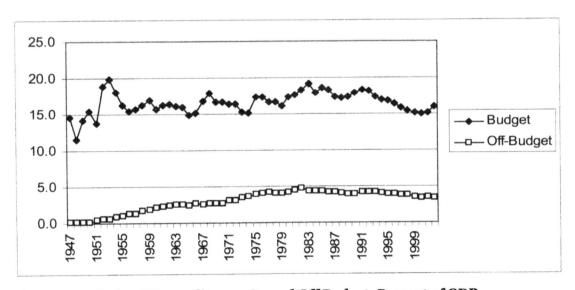

Figure 3-42: Federal Expenditures, On and Off Budget, Percent of GDP

During the 1980s, the public became aware of off-budget items. Political awareness made off-budget items cease to work as a device for evading balanced-budget requirements, and few new ones were created, although they continue to be debated. Sporadically there are attempts to push social security off-budget.

Figure 3-43: Federal and Regional Government Employment (000s)

Federal employees includes two major categories, uniformed military personnel and the executive branch. State and Local government is much larger and has tripled in size since 1962. The biggest growth areas involve public school teachers, police, corrections (prisons) and hospitals. About 850,000 of the federal employees work for the postal service.

Figure 3-44: Major Expenditures of the Federal Government

Figure 3-45: Major Transfer Payments (% of Federal Budget)

Transfers to individuals represent almost 50% of federal expenditures. These transfers are direct payments to individuals, in the form of a check. Such transfers include social security, Medicare, Medicaid, unemployment insurance, and veteran's benefits. Transfers to state and local governments are listed as regional. "Other grants" also involve sending checks, usually with strings attached. The growth in social security during the 1950s and 1960s is primarily a consequence of increasing benefit levels. The growth in Medicare and Medicaid payments over the period 1970-90, in contrast, is primarily a consequence of increased costs of existing programs rather than increases in benefit levels.

Figure 3-46: Social Security Revenue and Expenditure, $ millions

A question you may ask, quite reasonably, is whether the social security program can survive to the time when you retire. A common misunderstanding about social security is that it is an investment program – that the taxes individuals paid in are invested and returned at retirement. As Figure 3-46 makes clear, for most of its existence the social security program has paid out approximately what it took in.

The social security administration has been ostensibly investing money and has a current value of approximately 1.5 trillion dollars, which is a bit less than four times the current annual expenditure on social security. Unfortunately, this money is "invested" in the federal government, and thus is an obligation of the federal government, as opposed to an investment in the stock market. Consequently, from the perspective of someone hoping to retire in, say, 2050, this investment isn't much comfort, since the investment won't make it easier for the federal government to make the social security payments. The good news is that the government can print money. The bad news is that when it prints a lot of it, and the obligations of the social security administration are in the tens of trillions of dollars, it isn't worth very much.

Figure 3-47: Federal Debt, Total and Percent of GDP

The federal government runs deficits, spending more than it earned. In most of the past 75 years we see from Figure 3-39 that the government runs a deficit, bringing in less than it spends. Interest has been as high as 15% of the cost of the federal government (see Figure 3-44). How large is the debt, and how serious is it? Figure 3-47 gives the size of the federal debt, in absolute dollars and as a percent of GDP. The debt was increased dramatically during World War II (1940-45), but over the following 25 years, little was added to it, so that as a portion of growing GDP, the debt fell.

Starting in the late 1970s, the US began accumulating debt faster than we were growing, and the debt began to rise. That trend wasn't stabilized until the 1990s, and then only because the economy grew at an extraordinary rate by historical standards. The expenditures following the September 11, 2001 terrorist attacks, combined with a recession in the economy, have sent the debt rising again.

The national debt isn't out of control. At current 4% interest rates on federal borrowing, we spend about 2½ % of GDP on interest servicing the federal debt. The right evaluation of the debt is as a percentage of GDP; viewed as a percentage, the size of the debt is of moderate size – serious but not critical. The serious side of the debt is the coming retirement of the baby boom generation, which is likely to put additional pressure on the government.

An important distinction in many economic activities is the distinction between a *stock* and a *flow*. Your bank account represents a stock of money, the expenditures and income a flow. The national debt is a stock; the deficit is the addition to the debt and is a flow. If you think about a lake with incoming water and evaporation, the amount of water in the lake is the stock of water, the incoming stream minus evaporation the flow.

Table 3-1: Expenditures on Agencies as Percent of Non-Transfer Expenditures

Department or Agency	1977	1990	2002
Legislative	0.4	0.4	0.5
Judiciary	0.2	0.3	0.6
Agriculture	2.1	2.2	2.7
Commerce	3.2	0.7	0.7
Education	3.9	3.8	6.7
Energy	3.1	3.2	2.9
Health	3.7	4.6	8.3
Defense	43.8	59.2	46.9
Homeland Security	-	-	4.1
Housing & Urban Dev.	13.4	2.9	4.3
Interior	1.6	1.3	1.4
Justice	1.0	1.7	2.7
Labor	6.1	1.7	1.7
State	0.6	0.9	1.3
Transportation	2.2	2.6	2.1
Treasury	1.7	1.6	1.4
Veterans	2.3	2.6	3.3
Corps of Engineers	1.0	0.6	0.6
Environmental P.A.	1.1	1.1	1.1
Fed Emergency M.A.	0.2	0.4	0.0
GSA	0.2	0.5	0.0
Intl Assistance	2.8	2.7	1.9
NASA	1.6	2.5	2.0
NSF	0.3	0.4	0.7

Table 3-1 gives the expenditures on various agencies, as a percentage of the "discretionary" expenditures, where discretionary is a euphemism for expenditures that aren't transfers. Transfers, which are also known as entitlements, include social security, Medicare, aid to families with dependent children, unemployment insurance and veteran's benefits. In contrast, Table 3-1 gives the expenditures by the "Alphabet Soup" of federal agencies.

The National Science Foundation (NSF) provides funds for basic research. The general idea of government-funded research is that it is useful for ideas to be in the public domain, and moreover that some research isn't commercially viable, but is valuable nevertheless. Studying asteroids and meteors produces little if any revenue, but could, perhaps, save humanity one day in the event that we can deflect a large incoming asteroid. (Many scientists appear pessimistic about actually deflecting an asteroid.) Similarly, research into nuclear weapons might be commercially viable but as a society, we don't want firms selling nuclear weapons to the highest bidder. In addition to the NSF, the National Institutes of Health, also a government agency, fund a great deal of research. How much does the government spend on R&D? Figure 3-48 shows the history of R&D expenditures. The 1960s "space race" competition between the US and the Soviet Union led to the greatest federal expenditure on research and development, and it topped 2% of GDP. There was a modest increase during the Reagan presidency (1980-88) in defense R&D, which promptly returned to earlier levels.

Figure 3-48: Federal Spending on R&D, as a Percent of GDP

Where does the government get the money to buy all these things? As we see in Figure 3-49, the federal income tax currently produces just under 50% of federal revenue. Social Security and Medicare taxes produce the next largest portion, with around 30-35% of revenue. The rest comes from corporate profits taxes (about 10%), excise taxes like those imposed on cigarettes, liquor and cigarettes (under 5%) and other taxes like tariffs, fees, sales of property like radio spectrum and oil leases, and fines. The major change since World War II is the dramatic increase in social security, a consequence of the federal government's attempt to insure the future viability of the program, in the face of severely adverse demographics in the form of the retirement of the baby boom generation.

Figure 3-49: Sources of Federal Government Revenue

An important aspect of tax collection is that the income taxes, like the federal income tax as well as Social Security and Medicare taxes, are very inexpensive to collect, relative to sales taxes and excise taxes. Income taxes are straightforward to collect even relative to corporate income taxes. Quite reasonably, corporations can deduct expenses and the costs of doing business and are taxed on their profits, not on revenues. What is an allowable deduction, and what is not, make corporate profits complicated to administer. Moreover, from an economic perspective, corporate taxes are paid by consumers, in the form of higher prices for goods, at least when industries are competitive.

3.1.6 Trade

The United States is a major trading nation. Figure 3-50 presents total US imports and exports, including foreign investment and earnings (for example, earnings from US owned foreign assets). As is clear from this figure, the net trade surplus ended in the 1970s, and the US now runs substantial trade deficits, around 4% of GDP. In addition, trade is increasingly important in the economy.

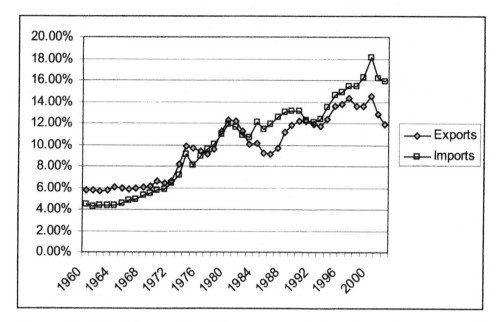

Figure 3-50: Total Imports and Exports as a Proportion of GDP

Figure 3-50 includes investment and earnings. When we think of trade, we tend to think of goods traded – American soybeans, movies and computers sold abroad, and automobiles, toys, shoes and wine purchased from foreign countries. Figure 3-51 shows the total trade in goods and services, as a percentage of US GDP. These figures are surprisingly similar, which shows that investment and earnings from investment are roughly balanced – the US invests abroad to a similar extent as foreigners invest in the US.

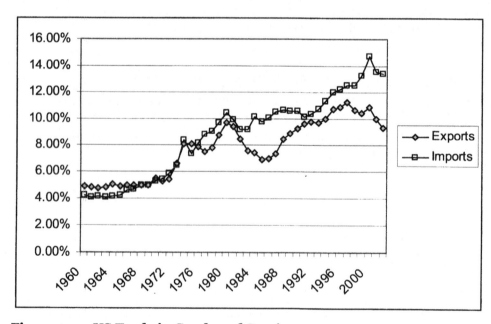

Figure 3-51: US Trade in Goods and Services

Figure 3-52 shows the earnings on US assets abroad, and the payments from US-based assets owned by foreigners. These accounts are roughly in balance, while the US used to earn about 1% of GDP from its ownership of foreign assets.

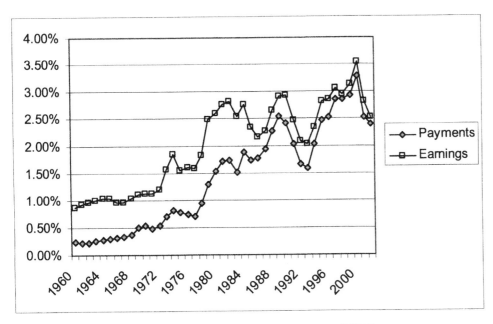

Figure 3-52: Income and Payments as a Percent of GDP

Who does the US trade with? Table 3-2 details the top fifteen trading partners., and the share of trade. The US and Canada remain the top trading countries of all pairs of countries. Trade with Mexico has grown substantially since the enactment of the 1994 North American Free Trade Act (NAFTA), which extended the earlier US – Canada agreement to include Mexico and Mexico is the US's second largest trading partner. Together, the top fifteen account for three-quarters of US foreign trade.

Table 3-2: Top US Trading Partners and Trade Volumes ($B)

Rank	Country	Exports Year-to-Date	Imports Year-to-Date	Total	Percent
	All Countries	533.6	946.6	1,480.2	100.0%
	Top 15 Countries	400.7	715.4	1,116.2	75.4%
1	Canada	123.1	167.8	290.9	19.7%
2	Mexico	71.8	101.3	173.1	11.7%
3	China	22.7	121.5	144.2	9.7%
4	Japan	36.0	85.1	121.0	8.2%
5	Germany	20.4	50.3	70.8	4.8%
6	United Kingdom	23.9	30.3	54.2	3.7%
7	Korea, South	17.5	29.6	47.1	3.2%
8	Taiwan	14.0	22.6	36.5	2.5%
9	France	13.4	20.0	33.4	2.3%
10	Italy	6.9	18.6	25.5	1.7%
11	Malaysia	7.2	18.0	25.2	1.7%
12	Ireland	5.2	19.3	24.5	1.7%
13	Singapore	13.6	10.1	23.7	1.6%
14	Netherlands	15.7	7.9	23.6	1.6%
15	Brazil	9.3	13.2	22.5	1.5%

3.1.7 Fluctuations

The US economy has recessions, a term which refers to a drop in gross domestic output. Recessions are officially called by the National Bureau of Economic Research, which keeps statistics on the economy and engages in various kinds of economic research. Generally a recession is called whenever output drops for half of a year.

Figure 3-53 shows the overall industrial production of the United States since World War II. Drops in output are clearly noticeable. The official recessions are also marked. There are three booms that lasted about a decade; these are the longest booms in US history and much longer than booms ordinarily lasted. Prior to World War II, a normal boom lasted 2½ years and the longest was four years. Recessions have historically lasted a 1½ to two years, a pattern that continues. Indeed, the average recession since World War II has been shorter than the average recession prior to that time.

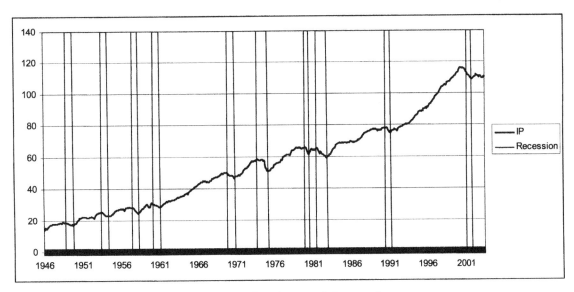

Figure 3-53: Postwar Industrial Production and Recessions

These fluctuations in output are known as the business cycle, which is not an exactly periodic cycle but instead a random cycle.

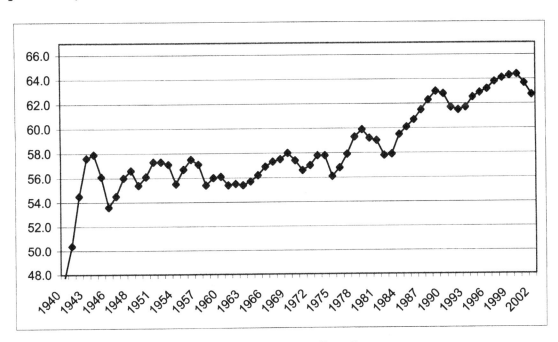

Figure 3-54: Percentage of the Population Employed

An important aspect of the business cycle is that many economic variables move together, or *covary*. Some economic variables vary less with the business cycle than others. Investment varies very strongly with the business cycle, while overall employment varies weakly. Interest rates, inflation, stock prices, unemployment and many other variables also vary systematically over the business cycle. Recessions are clearly visible in the percentage of the population employed, illustrated in Figure 3-54.

Some economic variables are much more variable than others. For example, investment, durable goods purchases, and utilization of production capacity vary more dramatically over the business cycle than consumption and employment. Figure 3-55 shows the percentage of industrial capacity utilized to produce manufactured goods. This series is more volatile than production itself, and responds more strongly to economic conditions.

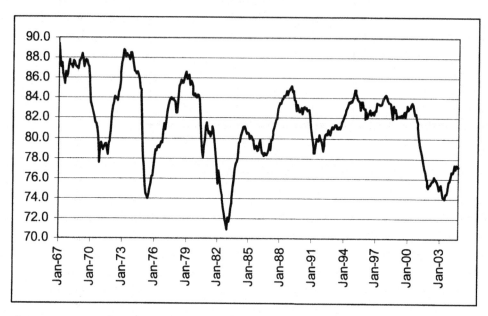

Figure 3-55: Industrial Factory Capacity Utilitzation (Source: FRED)

Most of the field of macroeconomics is devoted to understanding the determinants of growth and of fluctuations, but further consideration of this important topic is beyond the scope of a microeconomics text.

4 Producer Theory

The most basic theory of the *firm* views the firm as a means of transforming things into other, more valuable things, which is known as *production*. Thus, smelting of copper or gold removes impurities and makes the resulting product more valuable. Silicon valley transforms silicon, which is the primary ingredient of sand, along with a thousand other chemicals and metals, into computer chips used in everything from computers to toasters. Cooking transforms raw food, adding flavor and killing bacteria. Moving things to locations where they have higher value is a form of production. Moving stone to the location of a house where the stone can be installed in the exterior, or bringing the King Tut museum exhibit temporarily to Chicago, or a basketball team to the playoffs, are all examples of production. In this simplistic view, a firm is comprised of a technology or set of technologies for transforming things and then chooses the transformation to maximize the net profits. This "firm as a production function" view of the firm is adequate for some purposes, especially when products or services are relatively standardized and technologies widely available, but fares poorly when the internal organization of the firm matters a great deal. Nevertheless, the "firm as a production function" model is a natural starting point in the investigation of competition.

4.1 The Competitive Firm

4.1.1 Types of Firms

There are four major types of firms created in law, although these broad types have many subtypes. At the smallest end is the *proprietorship,* in which a firm is owned by a single individual (the proprietor) or perhaps a family, and operated by a relatively small number of people. The family farm, many restaurants, convenience stores, and laundromats are operated this way. Debts accrued by the proprietorship are the personal responsibility of the proprietor. Professionals like attorneys and accountants are often organized as *partnerships*. Partnerships share profits according to a formula (some equally by partner, some assigning shares or points to partners so that 'rainmakers' who generate more of the business obtain a larger share of the profits) and usually all are liable for losses incurred by the partnership. Thus, if a partner in a law firm steals a client's money and disappears, the other partners are generally responsible for the loss. In contrast, a *corporation* is, by a legal fiction, a person, which means a corporation itself can incur debt and the responsibility for repayment of that debt is with the corporation, not with the officers or owners of the corporation. When the energy trader company Enron collapsed, the shareholders in Enron lost their investment in the stock, but were not responsible for the remaining debts of the corporation. Moreover, executives of the company are also not financially responsible for debts of the corporation, provided the executives act legally and carry out their responsibilities appropriately. If a meteor strikes a manufacturing facility and bankrupts the corporation, the executives are not personally responsible for the debts the corporation fails to pay. On the other hand, breaking the law is not permitted, and executives at Archer Daniels Midland, the large agriculture firm, who colluded in the fixing of the price of lysine went to jail and were personally fined. The corporation was fined as well.

Corporations shield company executives and shareholders from liability, and are said to offer "limited liability." So why would anyone in their right mind organize a firm as a proprietorship or a partnership? Corporations cost money to organize, about $1,000 per year at the time of this writing, and are taxed, which is why many small businesses are organized as proprietorships: it is cheaper. Moreover, it may not be possible for a corporation owned by a family to borrow money to open a restaurant: potential lenders fear not being repaid in the event of bankruptcy, so insist on some personal liability on the part of the owners. So why are professional groups organized as partnerships and not corporations? The short answer is that a large variety of hybrid organizational forms exist. The distinctions have been blurred and organizations like "Chapter S Corporations" and "Limited Liability Partnerships" offer the advantages of partnerships (including avoidance of taxation) and corporations. The disadvantages to these forms is primarily larger legal fees, and limitations on the nature of ownership and rules specific to individual states.

It is usually the case that proprietorships are smaller than partnerships, and partnerships smaller than corporations, although there are some very large partnerships (e.g. the big four accounting firms) and some tiny corporations. The fourth kind can be of any size, for its distinction is not how it is organized internally but what it does with the revenue. The *non-profit* firm is prohibited from distributing a profit to its owners. Religious operations, academic associations, environmental groups, most zoos, industry associations, lobbying groups, many hospitals, credit unions (a type of bank), labor unions, private universities and charities are all organized as non-profit corporations. The major advantage of non-profit firms is that the government doesn't tax them. In exchange for avoiding taxes, non-profits must be engaged in government-approved activities, meaning generally that the non-profit operates for the benefit of some segment of society. So why can't you establish your own non-profit, that operates for the benefit of you, and avoid taxes? Generally you alone aren't enough of a socially worthy purpose to meet the requirements to form a non-profit.[19] Moreover, you can't establish a non-profit for a worthy goal and not serve that goal but just pay yourself all the money the corporation raises, because non-profits are prohibited from overpaying their managers, since overpaying the manager means not serving the worthy corporate goal as well as possible. Finally, commercial activities of non-profits are taxable. Thus, when the non-profit zoo sells stuffed animals in the gift-shop, generally the zoo collects sales tax and is potentially subject to corporate taxes.

The modern corporation is a surprisingly recent invention. Prior to World War I, companies were generally organized in a pyramid structure, with a president at the top, and vice-presidents who reported to him, etc. In a pyramid structure, there is a well-defined chain of command, and no one is ever below two distinct managers of the same level. The problem with a pyramid structure is that two retail stores that want to coordinate have to contact their managers, and possibly their managers' managers, and so on up the pyramid until a common manager is reached. There are circumstances where such rigid decision-making is unwieldy, and the larger the operation of a corporation, the more unwieldy it gets.

---

[19] Certainly some of the non-profit religious organizations created by televangelists suggest that the non-profit established for the benefit of a single individual isn't far-fetched.

Four companies – Sears, DuPont, General Motors and Standard Oil of New Jersey (Exxon) – found that the pyramid structure didn't work well for them. Sears found that its separate businesses of retail stores and mail order required a mix of shared inputs (purchased goods) but distinct marketing and warehousing of these goods. Consequently, retail stores and mail order needed to be separate business units, but purchasing had to answer to both of them. Similarly, DuPont's military business (e.g. explosives) and consumer chemicals were very different operations serving very different kinds of customers, yet often selling the same things, so again the inputs needed to be centrally produced and to coordinate with two separate corporate divisions. General Motors' many car divisions employ 'friendly rivalry,' in which technology and parts are shared across the divisions but the divisions compete in marketing their cars to consumers. Again, technology can't be under just one division, but instead is common to all. Finally, Standard Oil of New Jersey was attempting to create a company that managed oil products from oil exploration all the way through pumping gasoline into automobile gas tanks. With such varied operations all over the globe, Standard Oil of New Jersey required extensive coordination and found that the old business model needed to be replaced. These four companies independently invented the modern corporation, which is organized into separate business units. These business units run as semi-autonomous companies themselves, with one business unit purchasing, at a negotiated price, inputs from another unit, and selling outputs to a third. The study of the internal organization of firms and its ramifications for competitiveness is fascinating, but beyond the scope of this book.[20]

4.1.2 Production Functions

The firm transforms inputs into outputs. For example, a bakery takes inputs like flour, water, yeast, labor, and heat and makes loaves of bread. An earth-moving company takes capital equipment, ranging from shovels to bulldozers, and labor and digs holes. A computer manufacturer buys parts, generally "off-the-shelf" like disk-drives and memory, along with cases and keyboards and other parts that may be manufactured specially for the computer manufacturer, and uses labor to produce computers. Starbucks takes coffee beans, water, some capital equipment, and labor and produces brewed coffee.

Many if not all firms produce several outputs. However, we can view a firm producing multiple outputs as using several distinct production processes, and thus it is useful to start by looking at a firm that produces only one output. Generally, we can describe this firm as buying an amount x_1 of the first input, x_2 of the second input, and so on (we'll use x_n to denote the last input) and producing an amount y of the output, that is, the production function is

$$y = f(x_1, x_2, \ldots, x_n).$$

Mostly we will focus on two inputs in this section, but carrying out the analysis for more than two inputs is straightforward.

---

[20] If you want to know more about organization theory, I happily recommend *Competitive Solutions: The Strategist's Toolkit,* by R. Preston McAfee, Princeton: Princeton University Press, 2002.

Example: The *Cobb-Douglas* production function is the product of the *x*'s raised to powers, and comes in the form:

$$f(x_1, x_2, \ldots, x_n) = a_0 x_1^{a_1} x_2^{a_2} \ldots x_n^{a_n}$$

The constants a_1 through a_n are positive numbers, generally individually less than one. For example, with two goods, capital K and labor L, Cobb-Douglas can be expressed as $a_0 K^a L^b$. We will use this example frequently. It is illustrated, for $a_0 = 1$, $a = 1/3$ and $b = 2/3$, in Figure 4-1.

| 0.5 | 1 | 1.5 | 2 |

Figure 4-1: Cobb-Douglas Isoquants

Figure 4-1 shows three *isoquants* for the Cobb-Douglas production function. An isoquant, meaning "equal quantity," illustrates the input mixes that produce a given output level. In this case, given $a = 1/3$ and $b = 2/3$, we can solve $y = K^a L^b$ for K to obtain $K = y^3 L^{-2}$. Thus, $K = L^{-2}$ gives the combinations of inputs yielding an output of 1, and that is what the dark, solid line represents. The middle, grey dashed line represents an output of 2, and finally the dotted light-grey line represents an output of 3. Isoquants are familiar contour plots used, for example, to show the height of terrain or temperature on a map. Temperature isoquants are, not surprisingly, called isotherms.

Figure 4-2: The Production Function

Isoquants provide a natural way of looking at production functions and are a bit more useful to examine than 3-D plots like the one provided in Figure 4-2.

The *fixed-proportions production function* comes in the form

$$f(x_1, x_2, ..., x_n) = Min \{a_1 x_1, a_2 x_2, ..., a_n x_n\}$$

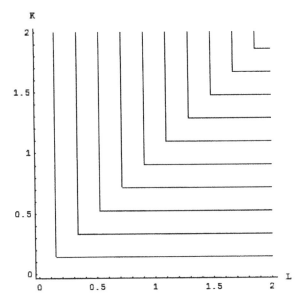

Figure 4-3: Fixed Proportions

The fixed proportions production function has the property that adding an input beyond a necessary level does no good. For example, the productive value of having more than one shovel per worker is pretty low, so that shovels and diggers are reasonably modeled as producing holes using a fixed proportions production function. Moreover, without a shovel or other digging implement like a backhoe, a bare-handed worker produces so little digging as to be nearly useless, so extra workers beyond the number of shovels have little effect. Ultimately, the size of the holes is pretty much determined by Min {number of shovels, number of diggers}. The Figure 4-3 illustrates the isoquants for fixed proportions. As we will see, fixed proportions makes the inputs "perfect complements."

Two inputs K and L are *perfect substitutes* in a production function f if they enter as a sum, that is, $f(K, L, x_3, ... , x_n) = g(K + cL, x_3, ... , x_n)$, for a constant c. With an appropriate scaling of the units of one of the variables, all that matters is the sum of the two variables, not the individual values. In this case, the isoquants are straight lines that are parallel to each other, as illustrated in the Figure 4-4.

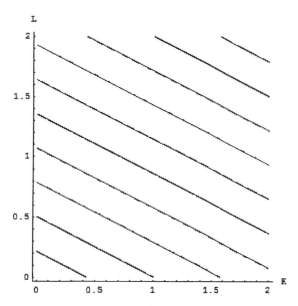

Figure 4-4: Perfect Substitutes

The *marginal product* of an input is just the derivative of the production function with respect to that input.[21] An important aspect of marginal products is that they are affected by the level of other inputs. For example, in the Cobb-Douglas case with two inputs[22] and for constant A:

$$f(K,L) = AK^{\alpha}L^{\beta},$$

the marginal product of capital is

$$\frac{\partial f}{\partial K}(K,L) = \alpha AK^{\alpha-1}L^{\beta}.$$

If α and β are between zero and one (the usual case), then the marginal product of capital increases in the amount of labor, and decreases in the amount of capital. For example, an extra computer is very productive in a situation with lots of workers and few computers, but not so productive in a situation where there are lots of computers and few people to operate them.

The *value of the marginal product* of an input is just the marginal product times the price of the output. If the value of the marginal product of an input exceeds the cost of that input, it is profitable to use more of the input.

Some inputs are more readily changed than others. It can take five years or more to order and obtain new passenger aircraft, four years to build an electricity generation

---

[21] This is a partial derivative, since it holds the other inputs fixed. Partial derivatives are denoted with the symbol ∂.

[22] The symbol α is the Greek letter "alpha." The symbol β is the Greek letter "beta." These are the first two letters of the Greek alphabet, and the word alphabet itself originates from these two letters.

facility or a pulp and paper mill. Very skilled labor – experienced engineers, animators, patent attorneys – is often hard to find and challenging to hire. It usually takes three to five years to hire even a small number of academic economists. On the other hand, it is possible to buy shovels, telephones, and computers and to hire a variety of temporary workers quite rapidly, in a matter of a day or so. Moreover, additional hours of work can be obtained by an existing labor force simply by hiring them "overtime," at least on a temporary basis. The amount of water or electricity a production facility uses can be varied second by second. If you run a restaurant, you can use more water tonight to wash dishes if you need it. If you start in the morning, you can probably get a few additional workers by that evening by paying overtime to those who aren't scheduled to work. It will probably take a few days or more to hire additional waiters and waitresses, and perhaps more than a few days to find a skilled chef. You can obtain more ingredients, generally the same day, and more plates and silverware pretty quickly. You can lease more space, but it will probably take more than a month to actually occupy a larger space, what with finding the space for rent, renting it, remodeling it and obtaining the necessary permits.

That some inputs or *factors* can be varied quickly, others only slowly, leads to the notions of the long-run and short-run. In the short-run, only some inputs can be adjusted, while in the long-run, all inputs can be adjusted. Traditionally, economists viewed labor as quickly adjustable, and capital equipment as more difficult to adjust. That is certainly right for airlines – obtaining new aircraft is a very slow process – and for large complex factories, and for relatively low-skilled and hence substitutable labor. On the other hand, obtaining workers with unusual skills is a slower process than obtaining warehouse or office space. Generally speaking, the long-run inputs are those that are expensive to adjust quickly, while the short-run factors can be adjusted in a relatively short time frame. What factors belong in which category is dependent on the context or application under consideration.

4.1.2.1 (Exercise)   For the Cobb-Douglas production function, suppose there are two inputs K and L, and the sum of the exponents is one. Show that if each input is paid the value of the marginal product per unit of the input, the entire output is just exhausted. That is, for this production function, show

$$K \frac{\partial f}{\partial K} + L \frac{\partial f}{\partial L} = f(K, L).$$

4.1.3 Profit Maximization

Consider an entrepreneur that would like to maximize profit, perhaps by running a delivery service. The entrepreneur uses two inputs, capital K (e.g. trucks) and labor L (e.g. drivers), and rents the capital at cost r per dollar of capital. The wage rate for drivers is w. The production function is $F(K, L)$, that is, given inputs K and L, the output is $F(K, L)$. Suppose p is the price of the output. This gives a profit of:[23]

---

[23] Economists often use the Greek letter π to stand for profit. There is little risk of confusion because economics doesn't use the ratio of the circumference to the diameter of a circle very often. On the other hand, the other two named constants, Euler's e and i, the square root of -1, appear fairly frequently in economic analysis.

$$\pi = pF(K,L) - rK - wL.$$

First, consider the case of a fixed level of K. The entrepreneur chooses L to maximize profit. The value L^* of L that maximizes the function π must satisfy:

$$0 = \frac{\partial \pi}{\partial L} = p\frac{\partial F}{\partial L}(K,L^*) - w.$$

This expression is known as a *first order condition*, because it says the first derivative of the function is zero.[24] The first order condition shows that we add workers to the production process until reaching a worker who just pays his salary, in that the value of the marginal product for that worker is equal to the cost of the worker.

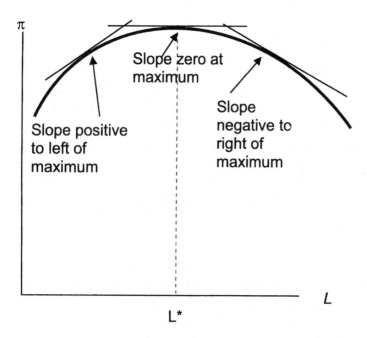

Figure 4-5: Profit-Maximizing Labor Input

In addition, a second characteristic of a maximum is that the second derivative is negative (or non-positive). This arises because, at a maximum, the slope goes from positive (since the function is increasing up to the maximum), to zero (at the maximum), to a negative number (because the function is falling as the variable rises past the maximum). This means that the derivative is falling, that is, the second derivative is negative. This logic is illustrated in the Figure 4-5.

---

[24] It is possible that $L=0$ is the best that entrepreneur can do. In this case, the derivative of profit with respect to L is not necessarily zero. The first order condition instead would be:

Either $0 = \frac{\partial \pi}{\partial L}$, or $L=0$ and $0 \geq \frac{\partial \pi}{\partial L}$. The latter pair of conditions reflects the logic that either the derivative is zero and we are at a maximum, or $L = 0$, in which case a small increase in L must not cause π to increase.

The second property is known as the *second order condition*, because it is a condition on the second derivative.[25] It is expressed as:

$$0 \geq \frac{\partial^2 \pi}{(\partial L)^2} = p \frac{\partial^2 F}{(\partial L)^2}(K, L^*).$$

This is enough of a mathematical treatment to establish comparative statics on the demand for labor. Here, we treat the choice L^* as a function of another parameter – the price p, the wage w, or the level of capital K. For example, to find the effect of the wage on the labor demanded by the entrepreneur, we can write:

$$0 = p \frac{\partial F}{\partial L}(K, L^*(w)) - w.$$

This expression recognizes that the choice L^* that the entrepreneur makes satisfies the first order condition, and results in a value that depends on w. But how does it depend on w? We can differentiate this expression to obtain:

$$0 = p \frac{\partial^2 F}{(\partial L)^2}(K, L^*(w)) L^{*\prime}(w) - 1,$$

or

$$L^{*\prime}(w) = \frac{1}{p \dfrac{\partial^2 F}{(\partial L)^2}(K, L^*(w))} \leq 0.$$

The second order condition lets the derivative be signed. This form of argument assumes that the choice L^* is differentiable, which is not necessarily true.

> Digression: In fact, there is a *revealed preference* form of argument that makes the point without calculus and makes it substantially more generally. Suppose $w_1 < w_2$ are two wage levels, and that the entrepreneur chooses L_1 when the wage is w_1 and L_2 when the wage is w_2. Then profit maximization requires that these choices are optimal. In particular, when the wage is w_1, the entrepreneur earns higher profit with L_1 than with L_2:
>
> $$pf(K, L_1) - rK - w_1 L_1 \geq pf(K, L_2) - rK - w_1 L_2.$$
>
> When the wage is w_2, the entrepreneur earns higher profit with L_2 than with L_1.

---

[25] The orders refer to considering small but positive terms Δ, which are sent to zero to reach derivatives. The value Δ^2, the "second order term" goes to zero faster than Δ, the first order term.

$$pf(K, L_2) - rK - w_2 L_2 \ge pf(K, L_1) - rK - w_2 L_1.$$

The sum of the left hand sides of these two expressions is at least as large as the sum of the right hand side of the two expressions:

$$pf(K, L_1) - rK - w_1 L_1 + pf(K, L_2) - rK - w_2 L_2 \ge$$
$$pf(K, L_1) - rK - w_2 L_1 + pf(K, L_2) - rK - w_1 L_2$$

A large number of terms cancel, to yield

$$-w_1 L_1 - w_2 L_2 \ge -w_2 L_1 - w_1 L_2.$$

This expression can be re-arranged to yield

$$(w_1 - w_2)(L_2 - L_1) \ge 0.$$

This shows that the higher labor choice must be associated with the lower wage. This kind of argument, sometimes known as a "revealed preference" kind of argument because choices by consumers were the first place the type of argument was applied, can be very powerful and general, because issues of differentiability are avoided. However, we will use the more standard differentiability type argument, because such arguments are usually more readily constructed.

The effect of an increase in the capital level K on the choice by the entrepreneur can be calculated by considering $L*$ as a function of the capital level K.

$$0 = p \frac{\partial F}{\partial L}(K, L*(K)) - w.$$

Differentiating this expression with respect to K, we obtain

$$0 = p \frac{\partial^2 F}{\partial K \partial L}(K, L*(K)) + p \frac{\partial^2 F}{(\partial L)^2}(K, L*(K)) L*'(K),$$

or,

$$L*'(K) = \frac{-\dfrac{\partial^2 F}{\partial K \partial L}(K, L*(K))}{\dfrac{\partial^2 F}{(\partial L)^2}(K, L*(K))}.$$

We know the denominator of this expression is not positive, thanks to the second order condition, so the unknown part is the numerator. We then obtain the conclusion that:

An increase in capital increases the labor demanded by the entrepreneur if

$\frac{\partial^2 F}{\partial K \partial L}(K, L^*(K)) > 0$, *and decreases the labor demanded if* $\frac{\partial^2 F}{\partial K \partial L}(K, L^*(K)) < 0$.

This conclusion looks like gobbledygook but is actually quite intuitive. Note that

$\frac{\partial^2 F}{\partial K \partial L}(K, L^*(K)) > 0$ means that an increase in capital increases the derivative of output with respect to labor, that is, an increase in capital increases the marginal product of labor. But this is the definition of a complement! That is, $\frac{\partial^2 F}{\partial K \partial L}(K, L^*(K)) > 0$ means that labor and capital are complements in production – an increase in capital increases the marginal productivity of labor. Thus an increase in capital will increase the demand for labor when labor and capital are complements, and will decrease the demand for labor when labor and capital are substitutes.

This is an important conclusion because different kinds of capital may be complements or substitutes for labor. Are computers complements or substitutes for labor? Some economists consider that computers are complements to highly skilled workers, increasing the marginal value of the most skilled, but substitute for lower skilled workers. In academia, the ratio of secretaries to professors has fallen dramatically since the 1970s as more and more professors use machines to perform secretarial functions. Computers are thought to have increased the marginal product of professors and reduced the marginal product of secretaries, so the number of professors rose and the number of secretaries fell.

The revealed preference version of the effect of an increase in capital is to posit two capital levels, K_1 and K_2, with associated profit-maximizing choices L_1 and L_2. The choices require, for profit maximization, that

$$pF(K_1, L_1) - rK_1 - wL_1 \geq pF(K_1, L_2) - rK_1 - wL_2$$

and

$$pF(K_2, L_2) - rK_2 - wL_2 \geq pF(K_2, L_1) - rK_2 - wL_1.$$

Again, adding the left-hand-sides together produces a result at least as large as the sum of the right hand sides:

$$pF(K_1, L_1) - rK_1 - wL_1 + pF(K_2, L_2) - rK_2 - wL_2 \geq \\ pF(K_2, L_1) - rK_2 - wL_1 + pF(K_1, L_2) - rK_1 - wL_2.$$

Eliminating redundant terms yields

$$pF(K_1, L_1) + pF(K_2, L_2) \geq pF(K_2, L_1) + pF(K_1, L_2),$$

or,

$$F(K_2,L_2)-F(K_1,L_2) \geq F(K_2,L_1)-,F(K_1,L_1)$$

or,

$$\int_{K_1}^{K_2} \frac{\partial F}{\partial K}(x,L_2)dx \geq \int_{K_1}^{K_2} \frac{\partial F}{\partial K}(x,L_1)dx,\ [26]$$

or

$$\int_{K_1}^{K_2} \frac{\partial F}{\partial K}(x,L_2)-\frac{\partial F}{\partial K}(x,L_1)dx \geq 0,$$

and finally,

$$\int_{K_1}^{K_2}\int_{L_1}^{L_2} \frac{\partial^2 F}{\partial K \partial L}(x,y)\,dy\,dx \geq 0,$$

Thus, if $K_2 > K_1$ and $\dfrac{\partial^2 F}{\partial K \partial L}(K,L) > 0$ for all K and L, then $L_2 \geq L_1$, that is, with complementary inputs, an increase in one input increases the optimal choice of the second input. In contrast, with substitutes, an increase in one input decreases the other input. While we still used differentiability of the production function to carry out the revealed preference argument, we did not need to establish that the choice $L*$ was differentiable to perform the analysis.

Example: Labor Demand with the Cobb-Douglas production function. The Cobb-Douglas production function has the form $F(K,L)=AK^{\alpha}L^{\beta}$, for constants A, α and β, all positive. It is necessary for $\beta<1$ for the solution to be finite and well-defined. The demand for labor satisfies

$$0 = p\frac{\partial F}{\partial L}(K,L*(K))-w = p\beta AK^{\alpha}L*^{\beta-1}-w,$$

or

---

[26] Here we use the standard convention that $\displaystyle\int_a^b ...\,dx = -\int_b^a ...\,dx.$

$$L^* = \left(\frac{p\beta AK^\alpha}{w} \right)^{1/1-\beta}.$$

When $\alpha+\beta=1$, L is linear in capital. Cobb-Douglas production is necessarily complementary, that is, an increase in capital increases labor demanded by the entrepreneur.

4.1.3.1 (Exercise)   For the fixed proportions production function Min $\{K, L\}$, find labor demand (capital fixed at K).

4.1.4 The Shadow Value

When capital K can't be adjusted in the short-run, it creates a constraint on the profit available on the entrepreneur – the desire to change K reduces the profit available to the entrepreneur. There is no direct value of capital, because capital is fixed. That doesn't mean we can't examine its value, however, and the value of capital is called a *shadow value* because it refers to the value associated with a constraint. Shadow value is well-established jargon.

What is the shadow-value of capital? Let's return to the constrained, short-run optimization problem. The profit of the entrepreneur is:

$$\pi = pF(K,L) - rK - wL.$$

The entrepreneur chooses the value L^* to maximize profit, but is stuck in the short-run with the level of capital inherited from a past decision. The shadow value of capital is the value of capital to profit, given the optimal decision L^*. Because

$$0 = \frac{\partial \pi}{\partial L} = p\frac{\partial F}{\partial L}(K,L^*) - w,$$

the shadow value of capital is

$$\frac{d\pi(K,L^*)}{dK} = \frac{\partial \pi(K,L^*)}{\partial K} = p\frac{\partial F}{\partial K}(K,L^*) - r.$$

Note that this could be negative; the entrepreneur might like to sell some capital but can't, perhaps because it is installed in the factory.

Any constraint has a shadow value. The term refers to the value of relaxing a constraint. The shadow value is zero when the constraint doesn't bind; for example, the shadow value of capital is zero when it is set at the profit-maximizing level. Technology binds the firm; the shadow value of a superior technology is the increase in profit associated with it. For example, parameterize the production technology by a parameter a, so that $aF(K, L)$ is produced. The shadow value of a given level of a is, in the short-run,

$$\frac{d\pi(K,L^*)}{da} = \frac{\partial\pi(K,L^*)}{\partial a} = pF(K,L^*).$$

A term is vanishing in the process of establishing the shadow value. The desired value L^* varies with the other parameters like K and a, but the effect of these parameters on L^* doesn't appear in the expression for the shadow value of the parameter because

$$0 = \frac{\partial\pi}{\partial L} \text{ at } L^*.$$

4.1.5 Input Demand

Over a long period of time, an entrepreneur can adjust both the capital and the labor used at the plant. This lets the entrepreneur maximize profit with respect to both variables K and L. We'll use a double star, **, to denote variables in their long-run solution. The approach to maximizing profit over two variables is to maximize it separately over each variable, thereby obtaining

$$0 = p\frac{\partial F}{\partial L}(K^{**},L^{**}) - w,$$

and

$$0 = p\frac{\partial F}{\partial K}(K^{**},L^{**}) - r.$$

We see for both capital and labor, the value of the marginal product is equal to purchase price of the input.

It is more of a challenge to carry out comparative statics exercises with two variables, and the general method won't be developed here.[27] However, we can illustrate one example as follows.

Example: The Cobb-Douglas production function implies choices of capital and labor satisfying two first order conditions, one each for labor and capital.[28]

$$0 = p\frac{\partial F}{\partial L}(K^{**},L^{**}) - w = p\beta A K^{**\alpha} L^{**\beta-1} - w,$$

$$0 = p\frac{\partial F}{\partial K}(K^{**},L^{**}) - w = p\alpha A K^{**\alpha-1} L^{**\beta} - r.$$

To solve this expression, first rewrite to obtain

---

[27] If you want to know more, the approach is to arrange the two equations as a vector with $\mathbf{x} = (K, L)$, $\mathbf{z} = (r/p, w/p)$, so that $\mathbf{0} = \mathbf{F}'(\mathbf{x}^{**}) - \mathbf{z}$, and then differentiate to obtain $\mathbf{dx}^{**} = (\mathbf{F}''(\mathbf{x}^{**}))^{-1}\mathbf{dz}$, which can then be solved for each comparative static.

[28] It is necessary for $\alpha+\beta<1$ for the solution to be finite and well-defined.

$w = p\beta AK^{**\alpha} L^{**\beta-1}$ and $r = p\alpha AK^{**\alpha-1} L^{**\beta}$, then divide the first by the second to yield

$\dfrac{w}{r} = \dfrac{\beta K^{**}}{\alpha L^{**}}$, or $K^{**} = \dfrac{\alpha w}{\beta r} L^{**}$. This can be substituted into either equation to obtain

$$L^{**} = \left(\frac{Ap\alpha^{\alpha}\beta^{1-\alpha}}{r^{\alpha}w^{1-\alpha}} \right)^{\frac{1}{1-\alpha-\beta}} \text{ and } K^{**} = \left(\frac{Ap\alpha^{1-\beta}\beta^{\beta}}{r^{1-\beta}w^{\beta}} \right)^{\frac{1}{1-\alpha-\beta}}.$$

While these expressions appear complicated, in fact the dependence on the output price p, and the input prices r and w are quite straightforward.

How do equilibrium values of capital and labor respond to a change in input prices or output price for the Cobb-Douglas production function? It is useful to cast these changes in percentage terms. It is straightforward to demonstrate that both capital and labor respond to a small percentage change in any of these variables with a constant percentage change.

4.1.5.1 (Exercise)   For the Cobb-Douglas production function $F(K,L) = AK^{\alpha}L^{\beta}$, show

$$\frac{r}{L^{**}}\frac{\partial L^{**}}{\partial r} = -\frac{\alpha}{1-\alpha-\beta}, \quad \frac{w}{L^{**}}\frac{\partial L^{**}}{\partial w} = -\frac{1-\alpha}{1-\alpha-\beta}, \quad \frac{p}{L^{**}}\frac{\partial L^{**}}{\partial p} = \frac{1}{1-\alpha-\beta},$$

$$\frac{r}{K^{**}}\frac{\partial K^{**}}{\partial r} = -\frac{1-\beta}{1-\alpha-\beta}, \quad \frac{w}{K^{**}}\frac{\partial K^{**}}{\partial w} = -\frac{\beta}{1-\alpha-\beta} \text{ and } \frac{p}{K^{**}}\frac{\partial K^{**}}{\partial p} = \frac{1}{1-\alpha-\beta}.$$

An important insight of profit maximization is that it implies minimization of costs of yielding the chosen output, that is, *profit-maximization entails efficient production*. The logic is straightforward. The profit of an entrepreneur is revenue minus costs, and the revenue is price times output. For the chosen output, then, the entrepreneur earns the revenue associated with the output, which is fixed since we are considering only the chosen output, minus the costs of producing that output. Thus, for the given output, maximizing profits is equivalent to maximizing a constant (revenue) minus costs. Since maximizing $-C$ is equivalent to minimizing C, the profit-maximizing entrepreneur minimizes costs. This is important because profit-maximization implies not being wasteful in this regard: a profit-maximizing entrepreneur produces at least cost.

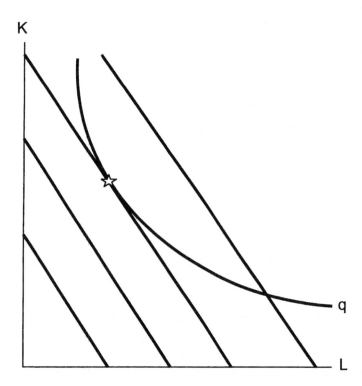

Figure 4-6: Tangency and Isoquants

There are circumstances where the cost-minimization feature of profit maximization can be used, and this is especially true when a graphical approach is taken. The graphical approach to profit-maximization is illustrated in Figure 4-6. The curve represents an isoquant, which holds constant the output. The straight lines represent "isocost" lines, which hold constant the expenditure on inputs. Isocost lines solve the problem

$rK + wL$ = constant

and thus have slope $\frac{dK}{dL} = -\frac{w}{r}$. Isocost lines are necessarily parallel – they have the same slope. Moreover, the cost associated with an isocost line rises the further northeast we go in the graph, or the further away from the origin.

What point on an isoquant minimizes total cost? The answer is the point associated with the lowest (most southwest) isocost that intersects the isoquant. This point will be tangent to the isoquant and is denoted by a star. At any lower cost, it isn't possible to produce the desired quantity. At any higher cost, it is possible to lower cost and still produce the quantity.

That cost minimization requires a tangency between the isoquant and the isocost has a useful interpretation. The slope of the isocost is minus the ratio of input prices. The slope of the isoquant measures the substitutability of the inputs in producing the output. Economists call this slope the *marginal rate of technical substitution*, which is the amount of one input needed to make up for a decrease in another input and hold output constant. Thus, one feature of cost minimization is that the input price ratio equals the marginal rate of technical substitution.

4.1.6 Myriad Costs

How much does it cost to produce a given quantity q? We already have a detailed answer to this question, but now need to focus less on the details and more on the "big picture." First, let's focus on the short-run, and suppose L is adjustable in the short-run, but K is not. Then the short-run total cost of producing q, given the capital level, is

$$SRTC(q|K) = \min_{L} \ rK + wL , \text{ over all } L \text{ satisfying } F(K,L) \geq q.$$

In words, this equation says the short-run total cost of the quantity q given the existing level K is the minimum cost, where L gets to vary (which is denoted by "min over L"), where the L considered is large enough to produce q. The vertical line | is used to indicate a condition or conditional requirement; here $|K$ indicates that K is fixed. The minimum lets L vary but not K. Finally, there is a constraint $F(K,L) \geq q$, which indicates that one has to be able to produce q with the mix of inputs because we are considering the short-run cost of q.

The short-run total cost of q given K has a simple form. First, since we are minimizing cost, the constraint $F(K,L) \geq q$ will be satisfied with equality, $F(K,L) = q$. This equation determines L, since K is fixed, that is, $F(K,L_S(q,K)) = q$ gives the short-run value of L, $L_S(q,K)$. Finally, the cost is then $rK + wL = rK + wL_S(q,K)$.

The *short-run marginal cost* given K is just the derivative of total cost with respect to q. To establish the short-run marginal cost, note that the equation $F(K,L) = q$ gives

$$\frac{\partial F}{\partial L}(K,L_S(q,K)) \, dL = dq,$$

or

$$\left.\frac{dL}{dq}\right|_{F=q} = \frac{1}{\dfrac{\partial F}{\partial L}(K,L_S(q,K))}.$$

The tall vertical line, subscripted with $F=q$, is used to denote the constraint $F(K,L) = q$ that is being differentiated. Thus, the short-run marginal cost is

$$SRMC(q|K) = SRTC'(q) = \frac{d}{dq}(rK + wL) = w\left.\frac{dL}{dq}\right|_{F=q} = \frac{w}{\dfrac{\partial F}{\partial L}(K,L_S(q,K))}.$$

There are two other short-run costs that will be needed to complete the analysis. First, there is the notion of the short-run average cost of production, which we obtain by dividing the total cost by the quantity:

$$SRAC(q \mid K) = \frac{SRTC(q \mid K)}{q}.$$

Finally, we need one more short-run cost: the short-run average variable cost. The variable cost eliminates the fixed costs of operation, which in this case are rK. That is,

$$SRAVC(q \mid K) = \frac{SRTC(q \mid K) - SRTC(0 \mid K)}{q} = \frac{wL_S(q \mid K)}{q}.$$

The short-run average variable cost is the average cost ignoring the investment in capital equipment.

The short-run average cost could also be called the short-run average total cost, since it is the average of the total cost per unit of output, but "average total" is a bit of an oxymoron.[29] Consequently, when total, fixed or variable is not specified, the convention is to mean total. Note that the marginal variable cost is the same as the marginal total costs, because the difference between variable cost and total cost is a constant – the cost of zero production, also known as the fixed cost of production.

At this point, we have identified four distinct costs, all relevant to the short-run. These are the total cost, the marginal cost, the average cost, and the average variable cost. In addition, all of these can be considered in the long-run as well. There are three differences in the long-run. First, the long-run lets all inputs vary, so the long-run total cost is

$$LRTC(q) = \min_{L,K} \ rK + wL \text{, over all } L \text{ and } K \text{ combinations satisfying } F(K,L) \geq q.$$

Second, since all inputs can vary, the long-run cost isn't conditioned on K. Finally, the long-run average variable cost is the same as the long-run average total cost. Because in the long-run a firm could use no inputs and thus incur no costs, the cost of producing zero is zero. Therefore, in the long-run, all costs are variable, and the long-run average variable cost is the long-run average total cost.

4.1.6.1 (Exercise)   For the Cobb-Douglas production function $F(K,L) = AK^{\alpha}L^{\beta}$, with $\alpha + \beta < 1$, with K fixed in the short-run but not in the long-run, and cost r of capital and w for labor, show

$$SRTC(q \mid K) = rK + w \left(\frac{q}{AK^{\alpha}} \right)^{\frac{1}{\beta}},$$

---

[29] An oxymoron is a word or phrase which is self-contradictory, like "jumbo shrimp," "stationary orbit," "virtual reality," "modern tradition," or "pretty ugly." Oxymoron comes from the Greek oxy, meaning sharp, and moros, meaning dull. Thus oxymoron is itself an oxymoron, so an oxymoron is self-descriptive. Another word which is self-descriptive is "pentasyllabic."

$$\text{SRAVC}(q|K) = w\frac{q^{\frac{1-\beta}{\beta}}}{\left(AK^{\alpha}\right)^{\frac{1}{\beta}}},$$

$$\text{SRMC}(q|K) = w\frac{q^{\frac{1-\beta}{\beta}}}{\beta\left(AK^{\alpha}\right)^{\frac{1}{\beta}}},$$

$$\text{LRTC}(q|K) = \left(\left(\frac{\alpha}{\beta}\right)^{\frac{\beta}{\alpha+\beta}} + \left(\frac{\beta}{\alpha}\right)^{\frac{\alpha}{\alpha+\beta}}\right) w^{\frac{\beta}{\alpha+\beta}} r^{\frac{\alpha}{\alpha+\beta}} \left(\frac{q}{A}\right)^{\frac{1}{\alpha+\beta}}.$$

Note that the easiest way to find the long-run total cost is to minimize the short-run total cost over K. Since this is a function of one variable, it is straightforward to identify the K that minimizes cost, and then plug that K into the expression for total cost.

One might want to distinguish the very short-run, from the short-run, from the medium run, from the long-run, from the very long-run. But a better approach is to view adjustment as a continuous process, with a gradual easing of the constraints. Faster adjustment costs more. Continuous adjustment is a more advanced topic, requiring an Euler equation approach.

4.1.7 Dynamic Firm Behavior

In this section, we consider a firm or entrepreneur that can't affect the price of output or the prices of inputs, that is, a competitive firm. How does such a competitive firm respond to price changes? When the price of the output rises, the firm earns profits

$$\pi = pq - c(q\,|\,K),$$

where $c(q|K)$ is the total cost of producing given that the firm currently has capital K. Assuming the firm produces at all, the firm maximizes profits by choosing the quantity q_s satisfying $0 = p - c'(q_s\,|\,K)$, that is, choosing the quantity where price equals marginal cost. However, this is a good strategy only if producing a positive quantity is desirable, that is, if $pq_s - c(q_s\,|\,K) \geq -c(0,K)$, which can be rewritten as $p \geq \dfrac{c(q_s\,|\,K) - c(0,K)}{q_s}$.

The right-hand-side of this inequality is the average variable cost of production, and thus the inequality implies that a firm will produce provided price exceeds the average variable cost. Thus, *the profit-maximizing firm produces the quantity q_s where price equals marginal cost, provided price is as large as minimum average variable cost. If price falls below minimum average variable cost, the firm shuts down.*

The behavior of the competitive firm is illustrated in Figure 4-7. The thick line represents the choice of the firm as a function of the price, which is on the vertical axis. Thus, if the price is below the minimum average variable cost (AVC), the firm shuts down. When price is above the minimum average variable cost, the marginal cost gives the quantity supplied by the firm. Thus, the choice of the firm is composed of two distinct segments – the marginal cost, where the firm produces the output where price equals marginal cost, and shutdown, where the firm makes a higher profit, or loses less money, by producing zero.

Figure 4-7 also illustrates the average total cost, which doesn't affect the short term behavior of the firm but does affect the long term behavior, because when price is below average total cost, the firm is not making a profit, but instead would prefer to exit over the long term. That is, when the price is between the minimum average variable cost and the minimum average total cost, it is better to produce than to shut down, but the return on capital was below the cost of capital. With a price in this intermediate area, a firm would produce, but would not replace the capital, and thus would shut down in the long-term if the price is expected to persist. As a consequence, minimum average total cost is the long-run "shut down" point for the competitive firm. (Shutdown may refer to reducing capital rather that literally setting capital to zero.) Similarly, in the long term, the firm produces the quantity where the price equals the long-run marginal cost.

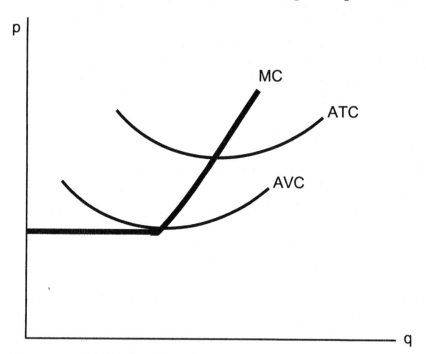

Figure 4-7: Short-Run Supply

Figure 4-7 illustrates one other fact: the minimum of average cost occurs at the point that marginal cost equals average cost. To see this, let $C(q)$ be total cost, so that average cost is $C(q)/q$. Then the minimum of average cost occurs at the point satisfying:

$$0 = \frac{d}{dq} \frac{C(q)}{q} = \frac{C'(q)}{q} - \frac{C(q)}{q^2}.$$

But this can be rearranged to imply $C'(q) = \frac{C(q)}{q}$, that is, marginal cost equals average cost at the minimum of average cost.

The long-run marginal cost has a complicated relationship to short-run marginal cost. The problem in characterizing the relationship between long-run and short-run marginal costs is that some costs are marginal in the long-run that are fixed in the short-run, tending to make long-run marginal costs larger than short-run marginal costs. However, in the long-run, the assets can be configured optimally, while some assets are fixed in the short-run, and this optimal configuration tends to make long-run costs lower.

Instead, it is more useful to compare the long-run average total costs and short-run average total costs. The advantage is that capital costs are included in short-run average total costs. The result is a picture like Figure 4-8.

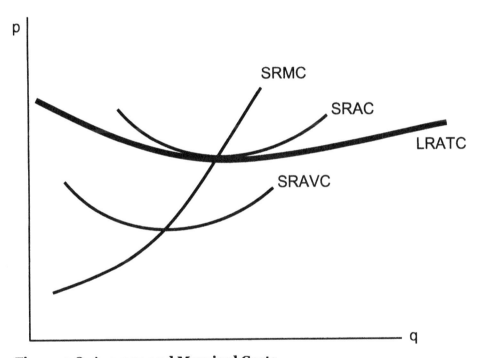

Figure 4-8: Average and Marginal Costs

In Figure 4-8, the short-run is unchanged – there is a short-run average cost, short-run average variable cost, and short-run marginal cost. The long-run average total cost has been added, in such a way that the minimum average total cost occurs at the same point as the minimum short-run average cost, which equals the short-run marginal cost. This is the lowest long-run average cost, and has the nice property that long-run average cost equals short-run average total cost equals short-run marginal cost. However, for a different output by the firm, there would necessarily be a different plant size, and the three-way equality is broken. Such a point is illustrated in Figure 4-9.

In Figure 4-9, the quantity produced is larger than the quantity that minimizes long-run average total cost. Consequently, as is visible in the picture, the quantity where short-run average cost equals long-run average cost does not minimize short-run average cost. What this means is that a factory designed to minimize the cost of producing a particular quantity won't necessarily minimize short-run average cost. Essentially, because the long-run average total cost is increasing, larger plant sizes are getting increasingly more expensive, and it is cheaper to use a somewhat "too small" plant and more labor than the plant size with the minimum short-run average total cost. However, this situation wouldn't likely persist indefinitely, because, as we shall see, competition tend to force price to the minimum long-run average total cost, and at that point, we have the three-way equality between long-run average total cost, short-run average total cost, and short-run marginal cost.

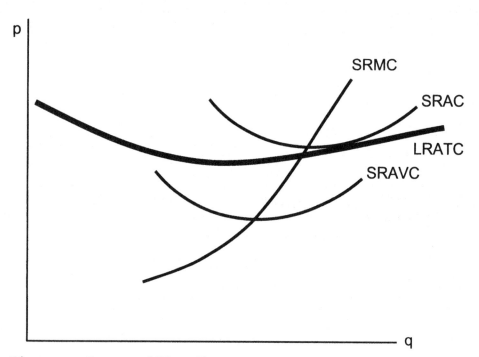

Figure 4-9: Increased Plant Size

4.1.7.1 (Exercise)   Suppose a company has total cost given by $rK + \dfrac{q^2}{2K}$, where capital K is fixed in the short-run. What is short-run average total cost and marginal cost? Plot these curves. For a given quantity q_0, what level of capital minimizes total cost? What is the minimum average total cost of q_0?

4.1.8 Economies of Scale and Scope

An economy of scale – that larger scale lowers cost – arises when an increase in output reduces average costs. We met economies of scale, and their opposite, diseconomies of scale, in the previous section, with an example where long-run average total cost initially fell, then rose, as quantity was increased.

What makes for an economy of scale? Larger volumes of productions permit the manufacture of more specialized equipment. If I am producing a million identical automotive tail lights, I can spend $50,000 on an automated plastic stamping machine and only affect my costs by five cents each. In contrast, if I am producing 50,000 units, the stamping machine increases my costs by a dollar each, and is much less economical.

Indeed, it is somewhat more of a puzzle as to what produces a diseconomy of scale. An important source of diseconomies are managerial in nature – organizing a large, complex enterprise is a challenge, and larger organizations tend to devote a larger percentage of their revenues to management of the operation. A bookstore can be run by a couple of individuals who rarely if ever engage in management activities, where a giant chain of bookstores needs finance, human resource, risk management and other "overhead" type expenses just in order to function. Informal operation of small enterprises is replaced by formal procedural rules in large organizations. This idea of managerial diseconomies of scale is reflected in the aphorism that "A platypus is a duck designed by a committee."

In his influential 1975 book *The Mythical Man-Month*, IBM software manager Fred Books describes a particularly severe diseconomy of scale. Adding software engineers to a project increases the number of conversations necessary between pairs of individuals. If there are n engineers, there are $\frac{1}{2} n (n - 1)$ pairs, so that communication costs rise at the square of the project size. This is pithily summarized in *Brooks' Law*: "Adding manpower to a late software project makes it later."

Another related source of diseconomies of scale involves system slack. In essence, it is easier to hide incompetence and laziness in a large organization than in a small one. There are a lot of familiar examples of this insight, starting with the Peter Principle, which states that people rise in organizations to the point of their own incompetence, which means eventually people cease to do the jobs that they do well.[30] That slack grows as an organization grows implies an diseconomy of scale.

Generally, for many types of products, economies of scale from production technology tend to reduce average cost, up to a point where the operation becomes difficult to manage, at which point diseconomies tend to prevent the firm from economically getting larger. Under this view, improvements in information technologies over the past twenty years have permitted firms to get larger and larger. While that seems logical, in fact firms aren't getting that much larger than they used to be, and the share of output produced by the top thousand firms has been relatively steady. That is, the growth in the largest firms just mirrors world output growth.

Related to an economy of scale is an *economy of scope*. An economy of scope is a reduction in cost associated with producing several distinct goods. For example, Boeing, which produces both commercial and military jets, can amortize some of its R&D costs over both types of aircraft, thereby reducing the average costs of each. Scope

---

[30] Laurence Johnston Peter (1919–1990).

economies work like scale economies, except they account for advantages of producing multiple products, where scale economies involve an advantage of multiple units of the same product.

Economies of scale can operate at the level of the individual firm but can also operate at an industry level. Suppose there is an economy of scale in the production of an input. For example, there is an economy of scale in the production of disc drives for personal computers. That means an increase in the production of PCs will tend to lower the price of disc drives, reducing the cost of PCs, which is a scale economy. In this case, it doesn't matter to the scale economy whether one firm or many firms are responsible for the increased production, and this is known as an *external economy of scale* or an *industry economy of scale,* because the scale economy operates at the level of the industry rather than in the individual firm. Thus, the long-run average cost of individual firms may be flat, while the long-run average cost of the industry slopes downward.

Even in the presence of an external economy of scale, there may be diseconomies of scale at the level of the firm. In such a situation, the size of any individual firm is limited by the diseconomy of scale, but nonetheless the average cost of production is decreasing in the total output of the industry, through the entry of additional firms. Generally there is an external diseconomy of scale if a larger industry drives up input prices, for example increasing land costs. Increasing the production of soybeans significantly requires using land that isn't so well suited for them, tending to increase the average cost of production. Such a diseconomy is an external diseconomy rather than operating at the individual farmer level. Second, there is an external economy if an increase in output permits the creation of more specialized techniques and a greater effort in R&D to lower costs. Thus, if an increase in output increases the development of specialized machine tools and other production inputs, an external economy will be present.

An economy of scale arises when total average cost falls as the number of units produced rises. How does this relate to production functions? We let $y=f(x_1,x_2,...,x_n)$ be the output when the n inputs $x_1, x_2,...,x_n$ are used. A rescaling of the inputs involves increasing the inputs by a fixed percentage, e.g. multiplying them all by the constant λ (the Greek letter lambda), where $\lambda>1$. What does this do to output? If output goes up by more than λ, we have an economy of scale (also known as *increasing returns to scale*): scaling up production increases output proportionately more. If output goes up by less than λ, we have a diseconomy of scale or *decreasing returns to scale*. And finally, if output rises by exactly λ, we have *constant returns to scale*. How does this relate to average cost? Formally, we have an economy of scale if

$$f(\lambda x_1,\lambda x_2,...,\lambda x_n) > \lambda f(x_1,x_2,...,x_n) \text{ if } \lambda>1.$$

This corresponds to decreasing average cost. Let w_1 be the price of input 1, w_2 the price of input 2, and so on. Then the average cost of producing $y=f(x_1,x_2,...,x_n)$ is

$$\text{AVC} = \frac{w_1 x_1 + w_2 x_2 + ... + w_n x_n}{f(x_1,x_2,...,x_n)}.$$

What happens to average cost as we scale up production by $\lambda > 1$? Call this $AVC(\lambda)$.

$$AVC(\lambda) = \frac{w_1\lambda x_1 + w_2\lambda x_2 + \dots + w_n\lambda x_n}{f(\lambda x_1, \lambda x_2, \dots, \lambda x_n)} = \lambda \frac{w_1 x_1 + w_2 x_2 + \dots + w_n x_n}{f(\lambda x_1, \lambda x_2, \dots, \lambda x_n)}$$

$$= \frac{\lambda f(x_1, x_2, \dots, x_n)}{f(\lambda x_1, \lambda x_2, \dots, \lambda x_n)} AVC(1)$$

Thus, average cost falls if there is an economy of scale and rises if there is a diseconomy of scale.

Another insight about the returns to scale concerns the value of the marginal product of inputs. Note that, if there are constant returns to scale:

$$x_1 \frac{\partial f}{\partial x_1} + x_2 \frac{\partial f}{\partial x_2} + \dots x_n \frac{\partial f}{\partial x_n} = \frac{d}{d\lambda} f(\lambda x_1, \lambda x_2, \dots, \lambda x_n)\Big|_{\lambda \to 1} =$$

$$= \lim_{\lambda \to 1} \frac{f(\lambda x_1, \lambda x_2, \dots, \lambda x_n) - f(x_1, x_2, \dots, x_n)}{\lambda - 1} = f(x_1, x_2, \dots, x_n)$$

The value $\frac{\partial f}{\partial x_1}$ is the marginal product of input x_1, and similarly $\frac{\partial f}{\partial x_2}$ is the marginal product of input 2, and so on. Consequently, if the production function exhibits constant returns to scale, it is possible to divide up output in such a way that each input receives the value of the marginal product. That is, we can give $x_1 \frac{\partial f}{\partial x_1}$ to the suppliers of input 1, $x_2 \frac{\partial f}{\partial x_2}$ to the suppliers of input 2, and so on, and this exactly uses up the all the output. This is known as "paying the marginal product," because each supplier is paid the marginal product associated with the input.

If there is a diseconomy of scale, then paying the marginal product is feasible, but there is generally something left over, too. If there are increasing returns to scale (an economy of scale), then it is not possible to pay all the inputs their marginal product, that is, $x_1 \frac{\partial f}{\partial x_1} + x_2 \frac{\partial f}{\partial x_2} + \dots x_n \frac{\partial f}{\partial x_n} > f(x_1, x_2, \dots, x_n)$.

4.1.8.1 (Exercise)   Given the Cobb-Douglas production function
$$f(x_1,x_2,...,x_n) = x_1^{a_1} x_2^{a_2} ... x_n^{a_n} ,$$ show there is constant returns to scale if
$a_1 + a_2 + ...a_n = 1$, increasing returns to scale if $a_1 + a_2 + ...a_n > 1$, and
decreasing returns to scale if $a_1 + a_2 + ...a_n < 1$.

4.1.8.2 (Exercise)   Suppose a company has total cost given by $rK + \dfrac{q^2}{2K}$ where capital
K can be adjusted in the long-run. Does this company have an economy of
scale, diseconomy of scale, or constant returns to scale in the long-run?

4.1.8.3 (Exercise)   A production function f is *homogeneous of degree r* if
$$f(\lambda x_1, \lambda x_2,...,\lambda x_n) = \lambda^r f(x_1,x_2,...,x_n).$$ Consider a firm with a production
function that is homogeneous of degree r. Suppose further that the firm pays
the value of marginal product for all its inputs. Show that the portion of
revenue left over is $1 - r$.

4.2 Perfect Competition Dynamics

The previous section developed a detailed analysis of how a competitive firm responds
to price and input cost changes. In this section, we consider how a competitive market
responds to demand or cost changes.

4.2.1 Long-run Equilibrium

The basic picture of a long-run equilibrium is presented in Figure 4-10. There are three
curves, all of which are already familiar. First, there is demand, considered in the first
chapter. Here demand is taken to be the "per period" demand. Second, there is the
short-run supply, which reflects two components – a shut down point at minimum
average variable cost, and quantity such that price equals short-run marginal cost above
that level. The short-run supply, however, is the market supply level, which means it
sums up the individual firm effects. Finally, there is the long-run average total cost at
the industry level, thus reflecting any external diseconomy or economy of scale. As
drawn in Figure 4-10, there is no long-run scale effect. The long-run average total cost
is also the long-run industry supply.[31]

As drawn, the industry is in equilibrium, with price equal to P_0, which is the long-run
average total cost, and also equating short-run supply and demand. That is, at the price
of P_0, and industry output of Q_0, no firm wishes to shut down, no firm can make positive
profits from entering, there is no excess output, and no consumer is rationed. Thus, no
market participant has an incentive to change their behavior, so the market is in both
long-run and short-run equilibrium.

---

[31] This may seem confusing, because supply is generally the *marginal* cost, not the average cost.
However, because a firm will quit producing in the long term if price falls below its minimum average
cost, the long-term supply is just the minimum average cost of the individual firms, because this is the
marginal cost of the industry.

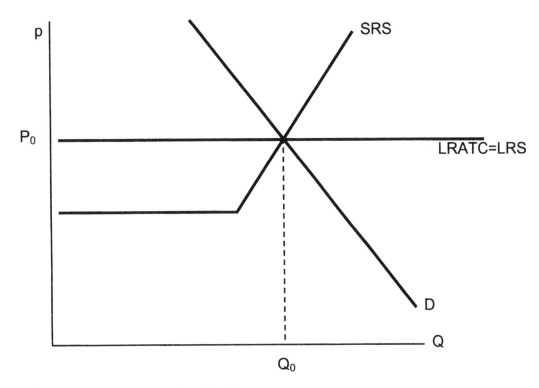

Figure 4-10: Long-Run Equilibrium

4.2.2 Dynamics with Constant Costs

Now consider an increase in demand. Demand might increase because of population growth, or because a new use for an existing product is developed, or because of income growth, or because the product becomes more useful. For example, the widespread adoption of the Atkins diet increased demand for high protein products like beef jerky and eggs. Suppose that the change is expected to be permanent. This is important because the decision of a firm to enter is based more on expectations of future demand than on present demand.

Figure 4-11 reproduces the equilibrium figure, but with the curves "grayed out" to indicate a starting position, and a darker new demand curve, labeled D_1.

The initial effect of the increased demand is that the price is bid up, because there is excess demand at the old price P_0. This is reflected by a change in both price and quantity to P_1 and Q_1, to the intersection of the short-run supply SRS and the new demand curve. This is a short-run equilibrium, and persists temporarily because, in the short-run, the cost of additional supply is higher.

At the new, short-run equilibrium, price exceeds the long-run supply cost. This higher price attracts new investment in the industry. It takes some time for this new investment to increase the quantity supplied, but over time the new investment leads to increased output, and a fall in the price, as illustrated in Figure 4-12.

Q_0 Q_1

Figure 4-11: A Shift in Demand

Q_0 Q_1 Q_2

Figure 4-12: Return to Long-Run Equilibrium

As new investment is attracted into the industry, the short-run supply shifts to the right, because with the new investment, more is produced at any given price level. This is illustrated with the darker short-run supply, SRS_2. The increase in price causes the price to fall back to its initial level, and the quantity to increase still further to Q_2.

It is tempting to think that the effect of a decrease in demand just retraces the steps of an increase in demand, but that isn't correct. In both cases, the first effect is the intersection of the new demand with the old short-run supply. Only then does the short-run supply adjust to equilibrate the demand with the long-run supply. That is, the initial effect is a short-run equilibrium, followed by adjustment of the short-run supply to bring the system into long-run equilibrium. Moreover, a small decrease in demand can have a qualitatively different effect in the short-run than a large decrease in demand, depending on whether the decrease is large enough to induce immediate exit of firms. This is illustrated in Figure 4-13.

Figure 4-13: A Decrease in Demand

In Figure 4-13, we start at the long-run equilibrium where LRS and D_0 and SRS_0 all intersect. If demand falls to D_1, the price falls to the intersection of the new demand and the old short-run supply, along SRS_0. At that point, exit of firms reduces the short-run supply and the price rises, following along the new demand D_1.

If, however, the decrease in demand is large enough to push the industry to minimum average variable cost, there is immediate exit. In Figure 4-14, the fall in demand from D_0 to D_1 is sufficient to push the price to minimum average variable cost, which is the shutdown point of suppliers. Enough suppliers have to shutdown to keep the price at this level, which induces a shift in of the short-run supply, to SRS_1. Then there is additional shutdown, shifting the short-run supply in still further, but driving up the price (along the demand curve) until the long-term equilibrium is reached.

P

Figure 4-14: A Big Decrease in Demand

Consider an increase in the price of an input into production. For example, an increase in the price of crude oil increases the cost of manufacturing gasoline. This tends to decrease (shift up) both the long-run supply and the short-run supply, by the amount of the cost increase. The effect is illustrated in Figure 4-15. The increased costs reduce both the short-run supply (prices have to be higher to in order to produce the same quantity) and the long-run supply. The short-run supply shifts upward to SRS_1, and the long-run supply to LRS_2. The short-run effect is to move to the intersection of the short-run supply and demand, which is at the price P_1 and the quantity Q_1. This price is below the long-run average cost, which is the long-run supply, so over time some firms don't replace their capital and there is *disinvestment* in the industry. This disinvestment causes the short-run supply to be reduced (move left) to SRS_2.

The case of a change in supply is more challenging because both the long-run supply and the short-run supply are shifted. But the logic – start at a long-run equilibrium, then look for the intersection of current demand and short-run supply, then look for the intersection of current demand and long-run supply – is the same whether demand or supply has shifted.

P

P
P
P

Q₂ Q₁ Q₀

Figure 4-15: A Decrease in Supply

4.2.3 General Long-run Dynamics

The previous section made two simplifying assumptions that won't hold in all applications of the theory. First, it assumed constant returns to scale, so that long-run supply is horizontal. A perfectly elastic long-run supply means that price always eventually returns to the same point. Second, the theory didn't distinguish long-run from short-run demand. But with many products, consumers will adjust more over the long-term than immediately. As energy prices rise, consumers buy more energy-efficient cars and appliances, reducing demand. But this effect takes time to be seen, as we don't immediately scrap our cars in response to a change in the price of gasoline. The short-run effect is to drive less in response to an increase in the price, while the long-run effect is to choose the appropriate car for the price of gasoline.

To illustrate the general analysis, we start with a long-run equilibrium. Figure 4-16 reflects a long-run economy of scale, because the long-run supply slopes downward, so that larger volumes imply lower cost. The system is in long-run equilibrium because the short-run supply and demand intersection occurs at the same price and quantity as the long-run supply and demand intersection. Both short-run supply and short-run demand are less elastic than their long-run counterparts, reflecting greater substitution possibilities in the long-run.

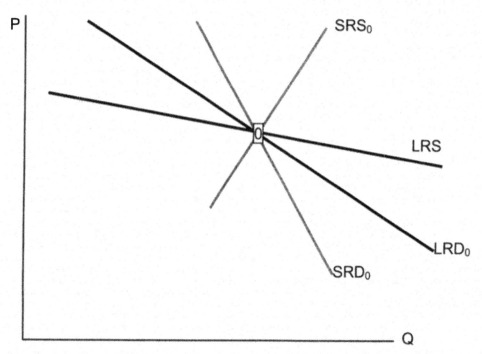

Figure 4-16: Equilibrium with External Scale Economy

Now consider a decrease in demand, decreasing both short-run and long-run demand. This is illustrated in Figure 4-17. To reduce the proliferation of curves, we color the old demand curves very faintly, and mark the initial long-run equilibrium with a zero inside a small rectangle.[32] The intersection of short-run supply and short-run demand is marked with the number 1. Both long-run supply and long-run demand are more elastic than their short-run counterparts, which has an interesting effect. The short-run demand tends to shift down over time, because the price associated with the short-run equilibrium is *above* the long-run demand price for the short-run equilibrium quantity. However, the price associated with the short-run equilibrium is below the long-run supply price at that quantity. The effect is that buyers see the price as too high, and are reducing their demand, while sellers see the price as too low, and so are reducing their supply. Both short-run supply and short-run demand fall, until a long-run equilibrium is achieved.

In this case, the long-run equilibrium involves higher prices, at the point labeled 2, because of the economy of scale in supply. This economy of scale means that the reduction in demand causes prices to rise over the long-run. The short-run supply and demand eventually adjust to bring the system into long-run equilibrium, as Figure 4-18 illustrates. The new long-run equilibrium has short-run demand and supply curves associated with it, and the system is in long-run equilibrium because the short-run demand and supply, which determine the current state of the system, intersect at the

---

[32] The short-run demand and long-run demand have been shifted down by the same amount, that is, both reflect an equal reduction in value. This kind of shift might arise if, for instance, a substitute had become cheaper, but the equal reduction is not essential to the theory. In addition, the fact of equal reductions often isn't apparent from the diagram, because of the different slopes – to most observers, it appears that short-run demand fell less than long-run demand. This isn't correct, however, and one can see this because the intersection of the new short-run demand and long-run demand occurs directly below the intersection of the old curves, implying both fell by equal amounts.

same point as the long-run demand and supply, which determine where the system is heading.

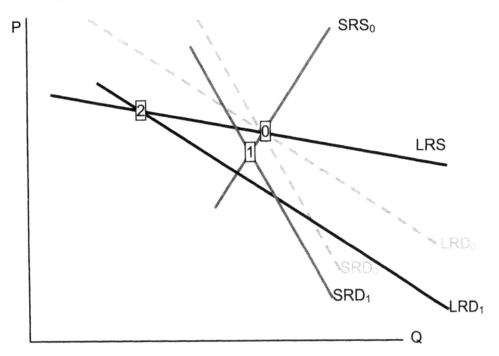

Figure 4-17: Decrease in Demand

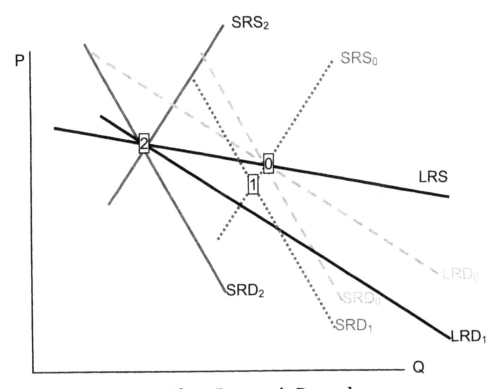

Figure 4-18: Long-run After a Decrease in Demand

There are four basic permutations of the dynamic analysis – demand increase or decrease, and a supply increase or decrease. Generally, it is possible for long-run supply to slope down – this is the case of an economy of scale – and for long-run demand to slope up.[33] This gives sixteen variations of the basic analysis. In all sixteen cases, the procedure is the same. Start with a long-run equilibrium, shift both the short-run and long-run levels of either demand or supply. The first stage is the intersection of the short-run curves. The system will then go to the intersection of the long-run curves.

An interesting example of competitive dynamics concepts is the computer memory market, which was discussed above. Most of the costs of manufacturing computer memory are fixed costs. The modern DRAM plant costs several billion dollars; the cost of other inputs – chemicals, energy, labor, silicon wafers – are modest in comparison. Consequently, the short-run supply is vertical until prices are very, very low; at any realistic price, it is optimal to run these plants 100% of the time.[34] The nature of the technology has let manufacturers cut the costs of memory by about 30% per year over the past forty years, demonstrating that there is a strong economy of scale in production. These two features – vertical short-run supply, strong economies of scale – are illustrated in the Figure 4-19. The system is started at the point labeled with the number 0, with a relatively high price, and technology which has made costs lower that this price. Responding to the profitability of DRAM, short-run supply shifts out (new plants are built and die-shrinks permits increasing output from existing plants). The increased output causes prices to fall, relatively dramatically because short-run demand is inelastic, and the system moves to the point labeled 1. The fall in profitability causes DRAM investment to slow, which lets demand catch up, boosting prices to the point labeled 2. (One should probably think of Figure 4-19 as being in a logarithmic scale.)

The point labeled with the number 2 looks qualitatively similar to the point labeled 1. The prices have followed a "saw-tooth" pattern, and the reason is due to the relatively slow adjustment of demand compared to supply, as well as the inelasticity of short-run demand, which creates great price swings as short-run supply shifts out. Supply can be increased quickly, and is increased "in lumps" because a die-shrink (making the chips smaller so that more fit on a given silicon wafer) tends to increase industry production by a large factor. This process can be repeated starting at the point labeled 2. The system is marching inexorably toward a long-run equilibrium in which electronic memory is very, very cheap even by 2004 standards and used in applications that haven't yet been considered, but the process of getting there is a wild ride, indeed. The saw-tooth pattern is illustrated in Figure 4-20, which shows DRAM industry revenues in billions of dollars from 1992 to 2003, and projections of 2004 and 2005.[35]

---

[33] The demand situation analogous to an economy of scale in supply is a *network externality*, in which the addition of more users of a product increases the value of the product. Telephones are a clear example – suppose you were the only person with a phone – but other products like computer operating systems and almost anything involving adoption of a standard represent examples of network externalities. When the slope of long-run demand is greater than the slope of long-run supply, the system will tend to be inefficient, because an increase in production produces higher average value and lower average cost. This usually means there is another equilibrium at a greater level of production.

[34] The plants are expensive in part because they are so clean, because a single speck of dust falling on a chip ruins the chip. The Infineon DRAM plant in Virginia stopped operations only when a snow-storm prevented workers and materials from reaching the plant.

[35] Two distinct data sources were used, which is why there are two entries for each of 1998 and 1999.

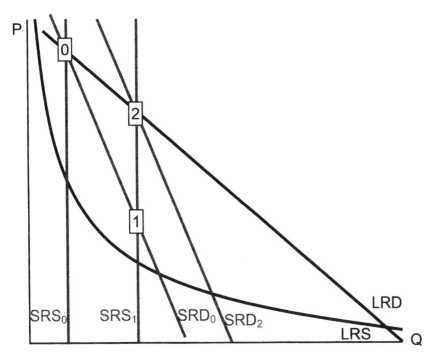

Figure 4-19: DRAM Market

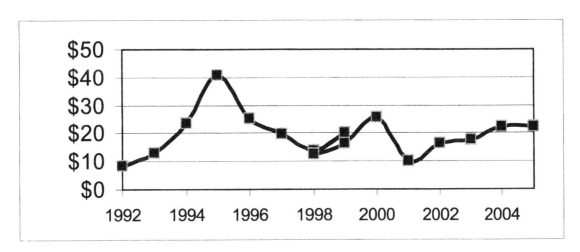

Figure 4-20: DRAM Revenue Cycle

4.2.3.1 (Exercise)   Land close to the center of a city is in fixed supply, but it can be used more intensively by using taller buildings. When the population of a city increases, illustrate the long- and short-run effects on the housing markets using a graph.

4.2.3.2 (Exercise)   Emus can be raised on a wide variety of ranch land, so that there are constant returns to scale in the production of emus in the long-run. In the short-run, however, the population of emus is limited by the number of breeding pairs of emus and the supply is essentially vertical. Illustrate the long- and short-run effects of an increase in demand for emus. (In the late 1980s, there was a speculative bubble in emus, with prices reaching $80,000 per breeding pair, in contrast to $2,000 or so today.)

4.2.3.3 (Exercise)   There are long-run economies of scale in the manufacture of computers and their components. There was a shift in demand away from desktop computers and toward notebook computers around the year 2001. What are the short- and long-run effects? Illustrate your answer with two diagrams, one for the notebook market and one for the desktop market. Account for the fact that the two products are substitutes, so that if the price of notebook computers rises, some consumers shift to desktops. (To answer this question, start with a time 0 and a market in long-run equilibrium. Shift demand for notebooks out and demand for desktops in. What happens in the short-run? What happens in the long-run to the prices of each? What does that price effect do to demand for each?)

4.3 Investment

The distinction between the short-run supply and the long-run supply is governed by the time that investment takes. Some of the difference between the short-run demand and the long-run demand arises because we don't scrap capital goods – cars, fridges, and air conditioners – in response to price changes. In both cases, investment is an important component of the responsiveness of supply and demand. In this section, we take a first look at investment. We will take a second look at investment from a somewhat different perspective later when we consider basic finance tools near the end of the book. Investment goods require expenditures today to produce future value, so we begin the analysis by examining the value of future payments.

4.3.1 Present value

The promise of $1 in the future is not worth $1 today. There are a variety of reasons why a promise of future payments is not worth the face value today, some of which involve risk that the money may not be paid. Let's set aside such risk for the moment; we'll consider risk separately later. Even when the future payment is perceived to occur with negligible risk, nevertheless most people prefer $1 today to $1 payable a year hence. One way of expressing this is that the *present value* – the value today – of a future payment of a dollar is less than a dollar. From a present value perspective, future payments are *discounted*.

From the individual perspective, one reason that you should value a future payment less than a current payment is due to *arbitrage*.[36] Suppose you are going to need $10,000 one year from now, to put a down-payment on a house. One way of producing $10,000 is to buy a government bond that pays $10,000 a year from now. What will that bond cost you? At current interest rates, a secure bond[37] will cost around $9700. This means

---

[36] Arbitrage is the process of buying and selling in such a way to make a profit. For example, if wheat is selling for $3 per bushel in New York, but $2.50 per bushel in Chicago, one can buy in Chicago and sell in New York and profit by $0.50 per bushel, minus any transaction and transportation cost. Such arbitrage tends to force prices to differ by no more than transaction costs. When these transaction costs are small, as with gold, prices will be about the same worldwide.

[37] Economists tend to consider US federal government securities secure, because the probability of such a default is very, very low.

that no one should willing to pay $10,000 for a future payment of $10,000, because instead one can have the future $10,000, by buying the bond, and have $300 left over to spend on cappuccinos or economics textbooks. In other words, if you will pay $10,000 for a secure promise to repay the $10,000 a year hence, then I can make a successful business selling you the secure promise for $10,000, and pocketing $300.

This arbitrage consideration also suggests how to value future payments: discount them by the relevant interest rate.

Example (Auto loan): You are buying a $20,000 car, and you are offered the choice to pay it all today in cash, or to pay $21,000 in one year. Should you pay cash (assuming you have that much in cash) or take the loan? The loan is at a 5% annual interest rate, because the repayment is 5% higher than the loan amount. This is a good deal for you if your alternative is to borrow money at a higher interest rate, e.g. on (most) credit cards. It is also a good deal if you have savings that pay more than 5% -- if buying the car with cash entails cashing in a certificate of deposit that pays more than 5%, then you would be losing the difference. If, on the other hand, you are currently saving money that pays less than 5% interest, paying off the car is a better deal.

The formula for present value is to discount by the amount of interest. Let's denote the interest rate for the next year as r_1, the second year's rate as r_2, and so on. In this notation, a $1 invested would pay $1+r_1$ next year, or $(1+r_1)\times(1+r_2)$ after 2 years, or $(1+r_1)\times(1+r_2)\times(1+r_3)$ after 3 years. That is, r_i is the interest rate that determines the value, at the end of year i, of $1 invested at the start of year i. Then, if we obtain a stream of payments A_0 immediately, A_1 at the end of year 1, A_2 at the end of year 2, and so on, the present value of that stream is

$$PV = A_0 + \frac{A_1}{1+r_1} + \frac{A_2}{(1+r_1)(1+r_2)} + \frac{A_2}{(1+r_1)(1+r_2)(1+r_3)} + \dots$$

Example (Consolidated annuities or *Consols*): What is the value of $1 paid at the end of each year forever, with a fixed interest rate r? Suppose the value is v. Then[38]

$$v = \frac{1}{1+r} + \frac{1}{(1+r)^2} + \frac{1}{(1+r)^3} + \dots = \frac{1}{1-\frac{1}{1+r}} - 1 = \frac{1}{r}.$$

At a 5% interest rate, $1 million per year paid forever is worth $20 million today. Bonds that pay a fixed amount every year forever are known as consols; no current government issues consols.

Example (Mortgages): Again, fix an interest rate r, but this time let r be the monthly interest rate. A mortgage implies a fixed payment per month for a large number of

---

[38] This development uses the formula, for $-1<a<1$, that $\frac{1}{1-a} = 1+a+a^2+\dots$ which is readily verified.

Note that this formula involves an infinite series.

months (e.g. 360 for a 30 year mortgage). What is the present value of these payments over n months? A simple way to compute this is to use the consol value, because

$$M = \frac{1}{1+r} + \frac{1}{(1+r)^2} + \frac{1}{(1+r)^3} + \ldots + \frac{1}{(1+r)^n} = \frac{1}{r} - \frac{1}{(1+r)^{n+1}} - \frac{1}{(1+r)^{n+2}} - \frac{1}{(1+r)^{n+3}} \ldots$$

$$= \frac{1}{r} - \frac{1}{(1+r)^n} \left(\frac{1}{(1+r)} + \frac{1}{(1+r)^2} + \frac{1}{(1+r)^3} \ldots \right)$$

$$= \frac{1}{r} - \frac{1}{(1+r)^n} \frac{1}{r} = \frac{1}{r} \left(1 - \frac{1}{(1+r)^n} \right).$$

Thus, at a monthly interest rate of ½%, paying $1 per month for 360 months produces a present value M of $\frac{1}{.005} \left(1 - \frac{1}{(1.005)^{360}} \right) = 166.79$ Thus, to borrow $100,000, one would have to pay $\frac{\$100,000}{166.79} = \$599.55$ per month. It is important to remember that a different loan amount just changes the scale; borrowing $150,000 requires a payment of $\frac{\$150,000}{166.79} = \$899.33$ per month, because $1 per month generates $166.79 in present value.

Example (Simple and Compound Interest): In the days before calculators, it was a challenge to actually solve interest rate formulas, so certain simplifications were made. One of these was "simple" interest, which means that daily or monthly rates are translated into annual rates by incorrect formulas. For example, with an annual rate of 5%, the simple interest daily rate is $\frac{5\%}{365} = .07692\%$. That this is incorrect can be seen from the calculation that $\left(1 + \frac{.05}{365} \right)^{365} = 1.051267\%$ Simple interest increases the annual rate, so it benefits lenders and harms borrowers. (Consequently, banks advertise the accurate annual rate on savings accounts – when consumers like the number to be larger – and not on mortgages, although banks are required by law to disclose – but not to advertise widely – actual annual interest on mortgages.)

Obligatory Lottery Example: You win the lottery, and the paper reports you've won $20 million. You're going to be paid $20 million, but is it worth $20 million? In fact, you get $1 million per year for 20 years. However, in contrast to our formula, you get the first million right off the bat, so the value is

$$PV = 1 + \frac{1}{1+r} + \frac{1}{(1+r)^2} + \frac{1}{(1+r)^3} + \ldots + \frac{1}{(1+r)^{19}} = 1 + \frac{1}{r} \left(1 - \frac{1}{(1+r)^{19}} \right).$$

Table 3.1 computes the present value of our $20 million dollar lottery, listing the results in thousands of dollars, at various interest rates. At ten percent interest, the value of the lottery is less than half the "number of dollars" paid, and even at 5%, the value of the stream of payments is 65% of the face value.

r	3%	4%	5%	6%	7%	10%
PV (000s)	$15,324	$14,134	$13,085	$12,158	$11,336	$9,365

The lottery example shows that interest rates have a dramatic impact on the value of payments made in the distant future. Present value analysis is the number one tool used in MBA programs, where it is known as Net Present Value or NPV analysis. It is accurate to say that the majority of corporate investment decisions are guided by an NPV analysis.

Example (Bond prices): A standard *treasury bill* has a fixed future value. For example it may pay $10,000 in one year. It is sold at a discount off the face value, so that a one-year $10,000 bond might sell for $9,615.39, producing a 4% interest rate. To compute the effective interest rate r, the formula relating the future value FV, the number of years n, and the price is

$$(1+r)^n = \frac{FV}{Price}, \text{ or } r = \left(\frac{FV}{Price}\right)^{1/n} - 1.$$

We can see from either formula that treasury bill prices move inversely to interest rates – an increase in interest rates reduces treasury prices. Bonds are a bit more complicated. Bonds pay a fixed interest rate set at the time of issue during the life of the bond, generally collected semi-annually, and the face value is paid at the end of the term. These bonds were often sold on long terms, as much as 30 years. Thus, a three-year $10,000 bond at 5% with semi-annual payments would pay $250 at the end of each half year for three years, and pay $10,000 at the end of the three years. The net present value, with an annual interest rate r, is

$$NPV = \frac{\$250}{(1+r)^{1/2}} + \frac{\$250}{(1+r)^1} + \frac{\$250}{(1+r)^{3/2}} + \frac{\$250}{(1+r)^2} + \frac{\$250}{(1+r)^{5/2}} + \frac{\$250}{(1+r)^3} + \frac{\$10000}{(1+r)^3}.$$

The net present value will be the price of the bond. Initially, the price of the bond should be the face value, since the interest rate is set as a market rate. The U.S. Treasury quit issuing such bonds in 2001, replacing them with bonds in which the face value is paid and then interest paid semi-annually.

4.3.1.1 (Exercise)   At a 7% annual interest rate, what is the present value of $100 paid at the end of one year, and $200 paid at the end of the second year?

4.3.1.2 (Exercise)   Compute the NPV of the 3 year, $10,000 bond, with $250 payments semi-annually, that was described above, at an interest rate of 4%.

4.3.1.3 (Exercise)   You can finance your $20,000 car with a straight 5% loan paid monthly over 5 years, or get one year interest free, but then pay 7% over the following four years. Which is a better deal? (Hint: In both cases, figure out the fixed monthly payments that produce a net present value equal to $20,000.)

4.3.1.4 (Exercise)   You win the lottery. At what interest rate should you accept $7 million today over twenty annual payments of $500,000?

4.3.2 Investment

A simple investment project involves spending an investment, I, and then reaping a return over time. If you dig a mine, drill an oil well, build an apartment building or a factory, or buy a share of stock, you spend money now, in the hopes of earning money subsequently. We will set aside the very important risk issue until the next subsection, and ask how to make the decision to invest.

The *NPV* approach involves assigning a rate of return r that is reasonable for, and specific to, the project and then computing the present value of the expected stream of payments. Since the investment is initially expended, it is counted as negative revenue. This gives an expression that looks like:

$$ NPV = -I + \frac{R_1}{1+r} + \frac{R_2}{(1+r)^2} + \frac{R_3}{(1+r)^3} + \dots. $$

where R_1 represents first year revenues, R_2 represents second year revenues, etc.[39] The investment is then made when *NPV* is positive – since this would add to the net value of the firm.

Carrying out an NPV analysis essentially requires two things. First, investment and revenues must be estimated. This is a challenge, especially for new products where there is no direct way of estimating demand, or with uncertain outcomes like oil wells or technological research.[40] Second, an appropriate rate of return must be identified. The rate of return is a problem, mostly because of risk associated with the payoffs to the investment, but also because of the incentives of project managers to inflate the payoffs and minimize the costs to make the project look more attractive to upper management. In addition, most investment undertaken by corporations is financed not with borrowing but with retained earnings, that is, with profits from previous activities. Thus a company that undertakes one investment can't carry out some other investment, and the interest rate has to account for the internal corporate value of funds. As a result of these factors, interest rates of 15%-20% are common for evaluating the NPV of projects of major corporations.

---

[39] The most common approach is to treat revenues within a year as if they are received at the midpoint, and then discount appropriately for that mid-year point. The present discussion oversimplifies in this regard.

[40] The building of the famed Sydney Opera House, which looks like billowing sails over Sydney harbor, was estimated to cost $7 million and actually cost $105 million. A portion of the cost overrun was due to the fact that the original design neglected to install air conditioning. When this oversight was discovered, it was too late to install a standard unit, which would interfere with the excellent acoustics, so instead an ice hockey floor was installed as a means of cooling the building.

Example (Silver Mine): A company is considering whether to develop a silver mine in Mexico. The company estimates that developing the mine (building roads and opening a large hole in the ground) would require $4 million per year for four years and no revenues would accrue during this time. Starting in year 5 the expenses fall to $2 million per year, and $6 million in net revenue is earned off the mined silver for each of the subsequent 40 years. If the company values funds at 18%, should it develop the mine?

The earnings from the mine are calculated in the following table. First, the NPV of the investment phase during years 0, 1, 2, and 3 is

$$NPV = -4 + \frac{-4}{1.18} + \frac{-4}{(1.18)^2} + \frac{-4}{(1.18)^3} = -12.697.$$

A dollar earned in each of years 4 through 43 have a present value of

$$\frac{1}{(1+r)^4} + \frac{1}{(1+r)^5} + \frac{1}{(1+r)^6} + ... + \frac{1}{(1+r)^{43}} = \frac{1}{(1+r)^3} \times \frac{1}{r}\left(1 - \frac{1}{(1+r)^{40}}\right) = 13.377$$

The mine is just profitable at 18%, in spite of the fact that its $4 million payments are made in four years, after which point $4 million dollar revenues are earned for forty years. The problem in the economics of mining is that 18% makes those future revenues have quite modest present values.

Year	Earnings ($M) / yr	PV ($M)
0-3	-4	-12.697
4-43	4	13.377
Net		0.810

There are other approaches to deciding whether to take an investment. In particular, the *Internal Rate of Return* approach solves the equation NPV=0 for the interest rate, and then the project is undertaken if the rate of return is sufficiently high. This approach is flawed because the equation may have more than one solution, or no solutions and it is not transparent what the right thing to do should be in these events. Indeed, the IRR approach gets the profit-maximizing answer only if it agrees with NPV. A second approach is the payback period, which asks how many years a project must be run before profitability is reached. The problem with the payback period is deciding between projects – if I can only do one of two projects, the one with the higher NPV makes the most money for the company. The one with the faster payback may make a quite small amount of money very quickly; it isn't apparent that this is a good choice. When a company is in risk of bankruptcy, a short payback period might be valuable, although this would ordinarily be handled by employing a higher interest rate in an NPV analysis. NPV does a good job when the question is whether to undertake a project or not, and it does better than other approaches to investment decisions. For this reason, NPV has become the most common approach to investment decisions. Indeed, NPV analysis is more common than all other approaches combined. NPV does a poor job, however, when the question is whether to undertake a project, or delay the project. That is, NPV answers "yes or no" to investment, but when the choice is "yes or wait," NPV requires amendment.

4.3.2.1 (Exercise)   Suppose that, without a university education, you'll earn $25,000 per year. A university education costs $20,000 per year, and you forgo the $25,000/year you would have earned for four years. However, you earn $50,000 per year for the following forty years. At 7%, what is the NPV of the university education?

4.3.2.2 (Exercise)   Now that you've decided to go to university based on the previous answer, suppose that you can attend East State U, paying $3,000 per year for four years and earning $40,000 when you graduate, or North Private U, paying $22,000 per year for the four years and earning $50,000 when you graduate. Which is the better deal at 7%?

4.3.3 Investment Under Uncertainty

Risk has a cost, and people, and corporations, buy insurance against financial risk.[41] The standard approach to investment under uncertainty is to compute an NPV, with the revenues composed of expected values, and the interest rate used adjusted to compensate for the risk.

For example, consider a project like oil exploration. The risks are enormous. Half of all underwater tracts in the Gulf Coast near Louisiana and Texas that are leased are never drilled, because later information makes them a bad bet. Half of all the tracts that are drilled are dry. So right off the bat, three-quarters of the tracts that are sold produce zero or negative revenue, and positive costs. To see how the economics of such a risky investment might be developed, suppose that the relevant rate of return for such investments is 18%. Suppose further the tract can be leased for $500,000 and the initial exploration costs $1 million. If the tract has oil (with a 25% probability), it produces $1 million per year for twenty years, and then runs dry. This gives an expected revenue of $250,000 per year. To compute the expected net present value, we first compute the returns:

Table 4-1: Oil Tract Return

	Expected revenue	EPV
0	-$1.5M	-$1.5M
1-20	$0.25M	$1.338M
Net		-$0.162

At 18%, the investment is a loss – the risk is too great given the average returns.

A very important consideration for investment under uncertainty is the choice of interest rate. The most important thing to understand is that the interest rate is specific

---

[41] For example, NBC spent $6 million in buying an insurance policy against US nonparticipation in the 1980 Moscow summer Olympic games, and the US didn't participate (because of the Soviet invasion of Afghanistan), and NBC was paid $94 million from the policy.

to the project, and not to the investor. This is perhaps the most important insight of corporate finance generally: the interest rate should adjust for the risk associated with the project and not the investor. For example, suppose hamburger retailer McDonald's is considering investing in a cattle ranch in Peru. McDonald's is overall a very low-risk firm, but this particular project is quite risky, because of local conditions. McDonald's still needs to adjust for the market value of the risk it is undertaking, and that value is a function of the project risk, not the risk of McDonald's other investments.

This basic insight of corporate finance – the appropriate interest rate is determined by the project, not the investor – is counter-intuitive to most of us because it doesn't apply to our personal circumstances. For individuals, the cost of borrowing money is mostly a function of their own personal circumstances, and thus the decision of whether to pay cash for a car or borrow the money is not so much a function of the car being purchased but of the wealth of the borrower. Even so, personal investors borrow money at distinct interest rates. Mortgage rates on houses are lower than interest rates on automobiles, and interest rates on automobiles lower than on credit cards. This is because the "project" of buying a house has less risk associated for it: the percentage loss to the lender in event of borrower default is lower on a house than on a car. Credit cards carry the highest interest rates because they are unsecured by any asset.

One way of understanding why the interest rate is project-specific but not investor-specific is to think about undertaking the project by creating a separate firm to make the investment. The creation of subsidiary units is a common strategy, in fact. This subsidiary firm created to operate a project has a value equal to the NPV of the project using the interest rate specific to the subsidiary, which is the interest rate for the project, independent of the parent. For the parent company, owning such a firm is a good thing if the firm has positive value, and not otherwise.[42]

Investments in oil are subject to another kind of uncertainty: price risk. Prices of oil fluctuate and aren't constant. Moreover, oil pumped and sold today is not available for the future. Should you develop and pump the oil you have today, or should you hold out and sell in the future? This question, known as the *option value of investment*, is generally somewhat challenging and arcane, but a simple example provides a useful insight.

To develop this example, let's set aside some extraneous issues first. Consider a very simple investment, in which either C is invested or not.[43] If C is invested, a value V is generated. The cost C is a constant; it could correspond to drilling or exploration costs, or in the case of a stock option, the *strike price* of the option, which is the amount one pays to obtain the share of stock. The value V, in contrast, varies from time to time in a random fashion. To simplify the analysis, we assume that V is uniformly distributed on the interval $[0,1]$, so that the probability of V falling in an interval $[a, b]$ is $b-a$ if $0 \leq a \leq b \leq 1$. The option only has value if $C<1$, which we assume for the rest of this section.

---

[42] It may seem that synergies between parent and subsidiary are being neglected here, but synergies should be accounted for at the time they produce value, i.e. as part of the stream of revenues of the subsidiary.

[43] This theory is developed in striking generality by Avinash Dixit and Robert Pindyck, *Investment Under Uncertainty*, Princeton University Press, 1994.

The first thing to note is that the optimal rule to make the investment is *cutoff value*, that is, to set a level V_0 and exercise the option if, and only if, $V \geq V_0$. This is because, if you are willing to exercise the option and generate value V, you should be willing to exercise the option and obtain even more value. The NPV rule simply says $V_0 = C$, that is, invest whenever it is profitable. The purpose of the example developed below is to provide some insight into how far wrong the NPV rule will be when option values are potentially significant.

Now consider the value of option to invest, given that the investment rule $V \geq V_0$ is followed. Call this option value $J(V_0)$. If the realized value V exceeds V_0, one obtains V-C. Otherwise, one delays the investment, producing a discounted level of the same value. This logic says

$$J(V_0) = (1 - V_0)\left(\frac{1 + V_0}{2} - C\right) + V_0\left(\frac{1}{1+r} J(V_0)\right).$$

This expression for $J(V_0)$ arises as follows. First, the hypothesized distribution of V is uniform on $[0,1]$. Consequently, the value of V will exceed V_0 with probability 1- V_0. In this event, the expected value of V is the midpoint of the interval $[V_0, 1]$, which is ½(V_0+1). The value ½(V_0+1) - C is the average payoff from the strategy of investing whenever $V \geq V_0$, which is obtained with probability 1- V_0. Second, with probability V_0, the value falls below the cutoff level V_0. in this case, no investment is made, and instead, we wait until the next period. The expected profits of the next period are $J(V_0)$ and these profits are discounted in the standard way.

The expression for J is straightforward to solve:

$$J(V_0) = \frac{(1 - V_0)\left(\frac{1 + V_0}{2} - C\right)}{1 - \frac{V_0}{1+r}}.$$

Rudimentary calculus shows

$$J'(V_0) = \frac{1 + 2rC + V_0^2 - 2(1+r)\,V_0}{2(1+r)\left(1 - \frac{V_0}{1+r}\right)^2}.$$

First, note that $J'(C) > 0$ and $J'(1) < 0$, which together imply the existence of a maximum at a value V_0 between C and 1, satisfying $J'(V_0) = 0$. Second, the solution occurs at

$$V_0 = (1+r) - \sqrt{(1+r)^2 - (1 + 2rC)} = (1+r) - \sqrt{r^2 + 2r(1 - C)}.$$

The positive root of the quadratic has $V_0 > 1$, which entails never investing, and hence is not a maximum. The profit-maximizing investment strategy is to invest whenever the value exceeds V_0 given by the negative root in the formula. There are a couple of notable features about this solution. First, at $r=0$, $V_0 = 1$. This is because $r=0$ corresponds to no discounting, so there is no loss in holding out for the highest possible value. Second, as $r \to \infty$, $V_0 \to C$. As $r \to \infty$, the future is valueless, so it is worth investing if the return is anything over costs. These are not surprising findings, quite the opposite – they should hold in any reasonable formulation of such an investment strategy. Moreover, they show that the NPV rule, which requires $V_0 = C$, is correct only if the future is valueless.

How does this solution behave? The solution is plotted as a function of r, for $C=0$, 0.25 and 0.5, in Figure 4-21.

The horizontal axis represents interest rates, so this picture shows *very* high interest rates by current standards, up to 200%. Even so, V_0 remains substantially above C. That is, even when the future has very little value because two-thirds of the value is destroyed by discounting each period, the optimal strategy deviates significantly from the NPV strategy. Figure 4-22 shows a close-up of that picture for a more reasonable range of interest rates, for interest rates of zero to ten percent

Figure 4-21: Investment Strike Price Given Interest Rate r in Percent

Figure 4-22 shows the cutoff values of investment for three values of C, the cost of the investment. These three values are 0 (lowest curve), 0.25 (the middle dashed curve), and 0.5, the highest, dotted line. Consider the lowest curve, with $C=0$. The NPV of this project is *always* positive – there are no costs and revenues are positive. Nevertheless, because the investment can only be made once, it pays to hold out for a higher level of payoff, indeed, for 65% or more of the maximum payoff. The economics at an interest rate of 10% is as follows. By waiting, there is a 65% chance that ten percent of the potential value of the investment is lost. However, there is a 35% of an even higher value. The optimum value of V_0 trades these considerations off against each other.

For $C = 0.25$, at 10% the cutoff value for taking an investment is 0.7, nearly three times the actual cost of the investment. Indeed, the cutoff value incorporates two separate costs: the actual expenditure on the investment C, and the lost opportunity to invest in the future. The latter cost is much larger than the expenditure on the investment in many circumstances, and in this example, can be quantitatively much larger than the actual expenditure on the investment.

Some investments can be replicated. There are over 13,000 McDonald's restaurants in the United States, and building another doesn't foreclose building even more. For such investments, NPV analysis gets the right answer, provided that appropriate interest rates and expectations are used. Other investments are difficult to replicate or logically impossible to replicate – having pumped and sold the oil from a tract, that tract is now dry. For such investments, NPV is consistently wrong because it neglects the value of the option to delay the investment. A correct analysis adds a lost value for the option to delay the cost of the investment, a value which can be quantitatively large, as we have seen.

Figure 4-22 Investment Strike Price Given Interest Rate *r* in Percent

Example: When should you refinance a mortgage? Suppose you are paying 10% on a $100,000 mortgage, and it costs $5,000 to refinance, but refinancing permits you to lock in a lower interest rate, and hence pay less. When is it a good idea? To answer this question, we assume that the $5,000 cost of refinancing is built into the loan, so that in essence you borrow $105,000 at a lower interest rate when you refinance. This is actually the most common method of refinancing a mortgage.

To simplify the calculations, we will consider a mortgage that is never paid off, that is, one pays the same amount per year forever. If the mortgage isn't refinanced, one pays ten percent of the $100,000 face value of the mortgage each year, or $10,000 per year. If one refinances at interest rate r, one pays $r \times \$105,000$ per year, so the NPV of refinancing is

NPV = $10,000 - r × $105,000.

Thus NPV is positive whenever $r < \dfrac{10}{105} = 9.52\%$.

Should you refinance when the interest rate drops to this level? No. At that level, you would exactly break even, but would also be carrying a $105,000 mortgage rather than a $100,000 mortgage, making it harder to benefit from any further interest rate decreases. The only circumstance in which refinancing at 9.52% is sensible is if interest rates can't possibly fall further.

When should you refinance? That depends on the nature and magnitude of the randomness governing interest rates, preferences over money today versus money in the future, and attitudes to risk. The model developed in this section is not a good guide to answering this question, primarily because the interest rates are strongly correlated over time. However, an approximate guide to implementing the option theory of investment is to seek an NPV of twice the investment, which would translate into a refinance point of around 8.5%.

4.3.3.1 (Exercise) You are searching for a job. The net value of jobs that arise is uniformly distributed on the interval [0,1]. When you accept a job, you must stop looking at subsequent jobs. If you can interview with one employer per week, what jobs should you accept? Use a 7% annual interest rate.

Hint: Relate the job search problem to the investment problem, where accepting a job is equivalent to making the investment. What is c in the job search problem? What is the appropriate interest rate?

4.3.4 Resource Extraction

For the past sixty years, the world has been "running out of oil." There are news stories about the end of the reserves being only ten, fifteen or twenty years away. The tone of these stories is that, at that time, we will run out of oil completely and prices will be extraordinarily high. Industry studies counter that more oil continues to be found and that the world is in no danger of running out of oil.

If you believe that the world will run out of oil, what should you do? You should *buy and hold*. That is, if the price of oil in twenty years is going to be $1,000 per barrel, then you can buy oil at $40 and hold it for twenty years, and sell it at $1,000. The rate of return from this behavior is the solution to

$$(1+r)^{20} = \frac{1000}{40}.$$

This equation solves for $r = 17.46\%$, which represents a healthy rate of return on investment. This substitution is part of a general conclusion known as the *Ramsey*[44]

---

[44] The solution to this problem is known as *Ramsey pricing*, after the discoverer Frank Ramsey (1903-1930).

rule: for resources in fixed supply, prices rise at the interest rate. With a resource in fixed supply, owners of the resource will sell at the point maximizing the present value of the resource. Even if they do not, others can buy the resource at the low present value of price point and resell at the high present value, and make money.

The Ramsey rule implies that prices of resources in fixed supply rise at the interest rate. An example of the Ramsey rule in action concerns commodities that are temporarily fixed in supply, such as grains, after the harvest. During the period between harvests, these products rise in price on average at the interest rate, where the interest rate includes storage and insurance costs, as well as the cost of funds.

Example: Let time run $t = 0, 1, \ldots$ and suppose the demand for a resource in fixed supply has constant elasticity: $p(Q) = aQ^{-1/\varepsilon}$. Suppose there is a total stock R of the resource, and the interest rate is fixed at r. What is the price and consumption of the resource at each time?

Solution: Let Q_t represent the quantity consumed at time t. Then the arbitrage condition requires:

$$aQ_0^{-1/\varepsilon}(1+r)^t = p(Q_0)(1+r)^t = p(Q_t) = aQ_t^{-1/\varepsilon}.$$

Thus, $Q_t = Q_0(1+r)^{-t\varepsilon}$.

Finally, the resource constraint implies

$$R = (Q_0 + Q_1 + Q_2 + \ldots) = Q_0\left(1 + (1+r)^{-\varepsilon} + (1+r)^{-2\varepsilon} + \ldots\right) = \frac{Q_0}{1 - (1+r)^{-\varepsilon}}.$$

This solves for the initial consumption Q_0. Consumption in future periods declines geometrically, thanks to the constant elasticity assumption.

Market arbitrage insures the availability of the resource in the future, and drives the price up to ration the good. The world runs out slowly, and the price of a resource in fixed supply rises on average at the interest rate.

Resources like oil and minerals are ostensibly in fixed supply – there is only so much oil, or gold, or bauxite, or palladium in the earth. Markets, however, behave as if there is an unlimited supply, and with good reason. People are inventive, and find substitutes. England's wood shortage of 1651 didn't result in England being cold permanently, nor was England limited to the wood it could grow as a source of heat. Instead, coal was discovered. The shortage of whale oil in the mid-nineteenth century led to the development of oil resources as a replacement. If markets expect that price increases will lead to substitutes, then we rationally should use more today, trusting that technological developments will provide substitutes.[45] Thus, while some believe we are running out of oil, most investors are betting that we are not, and that energy will not be very expensive in the future, either because of continued discovery of oil, or because of the creation of alternative energy sources. If you disagree, why not invest and take the bet? If you bet on future price increases, that will tend to increase the price today, encouraging conservation today, and increase the supply in the future.

4.3.4.1 (Exercise)   With an elasticity of demand of 2, compute the percentage of the resource that is used each year if the interest rate is 10%. If the interest rate falls, what happens to the proportion quantity used?

4.3.5 A Time to Harvest

A tree grows slowly, but is renewable, so the analysis of Section 4.3.4 doesn't help us understand when it is most profitable to cut the tree down. Consider harvesting for pulp and paper use. In this use, the amount of wood chips is what matters to the profitability of cutting down the tree, and the biomass of the tree provides a direct indication of this. Suppose the biomass sells for a net price p, which has the costs of harvesting and replanting deducted from it , and the biomass of the tree is $b(t)$ when the tree is t years old. It simplifies the analysis slightly to use continuous time discounting

$$e^{-\rho t} = \left(\frac{1}{1+r}\right)^t,$$

where $\rho = \log(1+r)$.

Consider the policy of cutting down trees when they are T years old. This induces a cutting cycle of length T. A brand new tree will produce a present value of profits of:

$$e^{-\rho T} pb(T) + e^{-2\rho T} pb(T) + e^{-3\rho T} pb(T) + \ldots = \frac{e^{-\rho T} pb(T)}{1 - e^{-\rho T}} = \frac{pb(T)}{e^{\rho T} - 1}.$$

This profit arises because the first cut occurs at time T, with discounting $e^{-\rho T}$, and produces a net gain of $pb(T)$. The process then starts over, with a second tree cut down at time $2T$, and so on.

Profit maximization gives a first order condition on the optimal cycle length T of

$$0 = \frac{d}{dT} \frac{pb(T)}{e^{\rho T} - 1} = \frac{pb'(T)}{e^{\rho T} - 1} - \frac{pb(T)\rho e^{\rho T}}{\left(e^{\rho T} - 1\right)^2}.$$

This can be rearranged to yield:

_____

[45] Unlike oil and trees, whales were overfished and there was no mechanism for arbitraging them into the future, that is, no mechanism for capturing and saving whales for later use. This problem, known as the tragedy of the commons, results in too much use and is taken up in Section 6.3.6. Trees have also been over-cut, most notably on Easter Island.

$$\frac{b'(T)}{b(T)} = \frac{\rho}{1 - e^{-\rho T}}.$$

The left hand side of this equation is the growth rate of the tree. The right hand side is approximately the continuous-time discount factor, at least when T is large, as it tends to be for trees, which are usually on a 20 to 80 year cycle, depending on the species. This is the basis for a conclusion: cut down the tree slightly before it is growing at the interest rate. The higher are interest rates, the shorter the cycle on which the trees should be cut down.

The pulp and paper use of trees is special, because the tree is going to be ground up into wood chips. What happens when the object is to get boards from the tree, and larger boards sell for more? In particular, it is more profitable to get a 4 × 4 than two 2 × 4s. Doubling the diameter of the tree, which approximately raises the biomass by a factor of six to eight, more than increases the value of the timber by the increase in the biomass.

It turns out our theory is already capable of handling this case. The only adaptation is a change in the interpretation of the function b. Now, rather than representing the biomass, $b(t)$ must represent the value in boards of a tree that is t years old. (The parameter p may be set to one.) The only amendment to the rule for cutting down trees is that the most profitable point in time to cut down the tree occurs slightly before the time when the value (in boards) of the tree is growing at the interest rate.

For example, lobsters become more valuable as they grow; the profit-maximizing time to harvest lobsters is governed by the same equation, where $b(T)$ is the value of a lobster of age T. Prohibiting the harvest of lobsters under age T is a means of insuring the profit-maximizing capture of lobsters, and preventing over-fishing, a topic considered in section 6.3.6.

The implementation of the formula is illustrated in Figure 4-23. The dashed line represents the growth rate $\frac{b'(T)}{b(T)}$, while the solid line represents the discount rate, which was set at 5%. Note that the best time to cut down the trees is when they are approximately 28.7 years old, and at that time, they are growing at 6 ½ %. Figure 4-23 also illustrates another feature of the optimization – there may be multiple solutions to the optimization problem, and the profit-maximizing solution involves $\frac{b'(T)}{b(T)}$ cutting $\frac{\rho}{1 - e^{-\rho T}}$ from above.

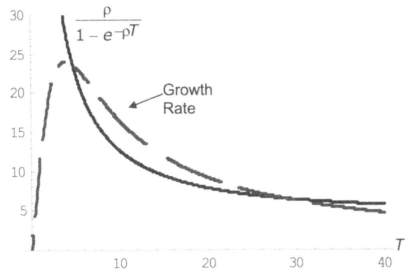

Figure 4-23: Optimal Solution for T

The U.S. Department of the Interior is in charge of selling timber rights on federal lands. The Department uses the policy of *maximum sustainable yield* to determine the time that the tree is cut down. Maximum sustainable yield maximizes the long-run average value of the trees cut down, that is, it maximizes

$$\frac{b(T)}{T}.$$

4.3.5.1 (Exercise)   Show maximum sustainable yield results in cutting down the tree when it is T years old, where T satisfies

$$\frac{b'(T)}{b(T)} = \frac{1}{T}.$$

Maximum sustainable yield is actually a special case of the policies considered here, and arises for a discount factor of 0. It turns out (thanks to a formula known variously as L'Hôpital's or L'Hospital's rule) that

$$\lim_{\rho \to 0} \frac{\rho}{1 - e^{-\rho T}} = \frac{1}{T}.$$

Thus, the rule $\dfrac{b'(T)}{b(T)} = \dfrac{\rho}{1 - e^{-\rho T}} \to \dfrac{1}{T}$ as $\rho \to 0$, and this is precisely the same rule that arises under maximum sustainable yield.

Thus, the Department of the Interior acts as if the interest rate is zero, when it is not. The justification given is that the Department is valuing future generations at the same level as current generations, that is, increasing the supply for future generations, while slightly harming the current generation of buyers. The major consequence of the

Department's policy of maximum sustainable yield is to force cutting of timber even when prices are low during recessions.

4.3.5.2 (Exercise)   Suppose the growth rate of trees satisfies $\frac{b'(T)}{b(T)} = te^{-t}$. Numerically approximate the efficient time to cut the tree if $\rho = 0.1$. How does this compare to the solution of maximum sustainable yield?

4.3.6 Collectibles

Many people purchase durable goods as investments, including Porsche Speedsters, Tiffany lamps, antique telephones, postage stamps and coins, baseball cards, original Barbie dolls, antique credenzas, autographs, original rayon Hawaiian shirts, old postcards, political campaign buttons, old clocks and even Pez dispensers. How is the value of, say, a 1961 Porsche Speedster or a $500 bill from the confederacy, which currently sells for over $500, determined?

Figure 4-24: The Porsche Speedster

The theory of resource prices can be adapted to cover these items, which are in fixed supply. There are four major differences that are relevant. First, using the item doesn't consume it; the goods are durable. I can own an "I Like Ike" campaign button for years, then sell the same button. Second, these items may depreciate. Cars wear out even when they aren't driven, and the brilliant color of Pez dispensers fades. Every time a standard 27 ½ pound gold bar, like the kind in the Fort Knox depository, is moved, approximately $5 in gold wears off the bar. Third, the goods may cost something to store. Fourth, the population grows, and some of the potential buyers are not yet born.

To understand the determinants of the prices of collectibles, it turns out to create a major simplification to perform the analysis in continuous time. Let t, ranging from zero to infinity, be the continuous time variable. If the good depreciates at rate δ, and q_0 is the amount available at time 0, the quantity available at time t is

$$q(t) = q_0 e^{-\delta t}.$$

For simplicity, assume that there is constant elasticity of demand ε. If g is the population growth rate, the quantity demanded, for any price p, is given by

$$x_d(p,t) = ae^{gt}p^{-\varepsilon},$$

for a constant a which represents the demand at time 0. This represents demand for the good for direct use, but neglects the investment value of the good – that the good can be resold for a higher price later. In other words, x_d captures the demand for looking at Pez dispensers or driving Porsche Speedsters, but does not incorporate the value of being able to resell these items.

The demand equation can be used to generate the lowest use value to a person owning the good at time t. That marginal use value v arises from the equality of supply and demand:

$$q_0 e^{-\delta t} = q(t) = x_d(v,t) = ae^{gt}v^{-\varepsilon}$$

or

$$v^{\varepsilon} = \frac{a}{q_0}e^{(\delta+g)t}.$$

Thus, the use value to the marginal owner of the good at time t satisfies

$$v = \left(\frac{a}{q_0}\right)^{1/\varepsilon} e^{\frac{\delta+g}{\varepsilon}t}.$$

An important aspect of this development is that the value to the owner is found without reference to the price of the good. The reason this calculation is possible is that the individuals with high values will own the good, and the number of goods and the values of people are assumptions of the theory. Essentially, we already know that the price will ration the good to the individuals with high values, so computing the lowest value individual who holds a good at time t is a straightforward "supply equals demand" calculation. Two factors increase the marginal value to the owner – there are fewer units available because of depreciation, and there are more high-value people demanding them, because of population growth. Together, these factors make the marginal use value grow at the rate $\frac{\delta+g}{\varepsilon}$.

Assume that s is the cost of storage per unit of time and per unit of the good, so that storing x units for a period of length Δ costs $sx\Delta$. This is about the simplest possible storage cost technology.

The final assumption that we make is that all potential buyers use a common discount rate r, so that the discount of money or value received Δ units of time in the future is $e^{-r\Delta}$. It is worth a brief digression why it is sensible to assume a common discount rate, when it is evident that many people have different discount rates. Different discount rates induce gains from trade in borrowing and lending, and create an incentive to have banks. While banking is an interesting thing to study, this section is concerned with collectibles, not banks. If we have different discount factors, then we must also introduce banks, which would complicate the model substantially. Otherwise, we would intermingle the theory of banking and the theory of collectibles. It is probably a good idea to develop a joint theory of banking and collectibles given the investment potential of collectibles, but it is better to start with the pure theory of either one before developing the joint theory.

Consider a person who values the collectible at v. Is it a good thing for this person to own a unit of the good at time t? Let p be the function that gives the price across time, so that $p(t)$ is the price at time t. Buying the good at time t and then selling what remains (recall that the good depreciates at rate δ) at time $t+\Delta$ gives a net value of

$$\int_0^\Delta e^{-ru}(v-s)du - p(t) + e^{-r\Delta}e^{-\delta\Delta}p(t+\Delta).$$

For the marginal person, that is, the person who is just indifferent to buying or not buying at time t, this must be zero at every moment in time, for $\Delta=0$. If v represents the value to a marginal buyer (indifferent to holding or selling) holding the good at time t, then this expression should come out to be zero. Thus, dividing by Δ,

$$0 = \lim_{\Delta\to 0} \frac{1}{\Delta}\int_0^\Delta e^{-ru}(v-s)du - \frac{p(t)}{\Delta} + \frac{e^{-(r+\delta)\Delta}p(t+\Delta)}{\Delta}$$

$$= \lim_{\Delta\to 0} v - s + \frac{p(t+\Delta)-p(t)}{\Delta} - \frac{1-e^{-(r+\delta)\Delta}}{\Delta}p(t+\Delta) = v - s + p'(t) - (r+\delta)p(t).$$

Recall that the marginal value is $v = \left(\dfrac{a}{q_0}\right)^{1/\varepsilon} e^{\frac{\delta+g}{\varepsilon}t}$, which gives

$$p'(t) = (r+\delta)p(t) + s - v = (r+\delta)p(t) + s - \left(\frac{a}{q_0}\right)^{1/\varepsilon} e^{\frac{\delta+g}{\varepsilon}t}.$$

The general solution to this differential equation is

$$p(t) = e^{(r+\delta)t}\left(p(0) + \frac{1-e^{-(r+\delta)t}}{(r+\delta)}s - \left(\frac{a}{q_0}\right)^{1/\varepsilon}\frac{1-e^{-\left(r+\delta-\frac{\delta+g}{\varepsilon}\right)t}}{r+\delta-\frac{\delta+g}{\varepsilon}} \right).$$

It turns out that this equation only makes sense if $r + \delta - \frac{\delta + g}{\varepsilon} > 0$, for otherwise the present value of the marginal value goes to infinity, so there is no possible finite initial price. Provided demand is elastic and discounting is larger than growth rates (which is an implication of equilibrium in the credit market), this condition will be met.

What is the initial price? It must be the case that the present value of the price is finite, for otherwise the good would always be a good investment for everyone at time 0, using the "buy and hold for resale" strategy. That is,

$$\lim_{t \to \infty} e^{-rt} p(t) < \infty.$$

This condition implies

$$\lim_{t \to \infty} e^{\delta t} \left(p(0) + \frac{1 - e^{-(r+\delta)t}}{(r+\delta)} s - \left(\frac{a}{q_0} \right)^{1/\varepsilon} \frac{1 - e^{-\left(r + \delta - \frac{\delta + g}{\varepsilon}\right)t}}{r + \delta - \frac{\delta + g}{\varepsilon}} \right) < \infty$$

and thus

$$p(0) + \frac{1}{(r+\delta)} s - \left(\frac{a}{q_0} \right)^{1/\varepsilon} \frac{1}{r + \delta - \frac{\delta + g}{\varepsilon}} = 0.$$

This equation may take on two different forms. First, it may be solvable for a non-negative price, which happens if

$$p(0) = \left(\frac{a}{q_0} \right)^{1/\varepsilon} \frac{1}{r + \delta - \frac{\delta + g}{\varepsilon}} - \frac{1}{(r+\delta)} s \geq 0.$$

Second, it may require destruction of some of the endowment of the good. Destruction must happen if the quantity of the good q_0 at time 0 satisfies

$$\left(\frac{a}{q_0} \right)^{1/\varepsilon} \frac{1}{r + \delta - \frac{\delta + g}{\varepsilon}} - \frac{1}{(r+\delta)} s < 0.$$

In this case, there is too much of the good, and an amount must be destroyed to make the initial price zero. Since the initial price is zero, the good is valueless at time zero, and destruction of the good makes sense – at the current quantity, the good is too costly to store for future profits. Enough is destroyed to insure indifference between holding the good as a collectible and destroying it. Consider, for example, the $500 confederate bill pictured in Figure 4-25. Many of these bills were destroyed at the end of the US Civil War, when the currency became valueless, burned as a source of heat. Now, an uncirculated version retails for $900.

The amount of the good that must be destroyed is such that the initial price is zero. As q_0 is the initial (pre-destruction) quantity, the amount at time zero after the destruction is the quantity $q(0)$ satisfying

$$0 = p(0) = \left(\frac{a}{q(0)}\right)^{1/\varepsilon} \frac{1}{r + \delta - \frac{\delta + g}{\varepsilon}} - \frac{1}{(r+\delta)} s \ .$$

Figure 4-25: $500 Confederate States Bill

Given this construction, we have that

$$p(0) + \frac{1}{(r+\delta)} s - \left(\frac{a}{q(0)}\right)^{1/\varepsilon} \frac{1}{r + \delta - \frac{\delta + g}{\varepsilon}} = 0,$$

where either $q(0)=q_0$ and $p(0) \geq 0$, or $q(0) < q_0$ and $p(0)=0$.

Destruction of a portion of the stock of a collectible, followed by price increases, is actually a quite common phenomenon. In particular, consider the "Model 500" telephone by Western Electric illustrated in Figure 4-26. This ubiquitous classic phone was retired as the US switched to tone dialing and push-button phones in the 1970s, and millions of phones – perhaps over 100 million – wound up in landfills. Now, the phone is a collectible and rotary phone enthusiasts work to keep them operational.

Figure 4-26: Western Electric Model 500 Telephone

The solution for $p(0)$ dramatically simplifies the expression for $p(t)$:

$$p(t) = e^{(r+\delta)t}\left(p(0) + \frac{1-e^{-(r+\delta)t}}{(r+\delta)}s - \left(\frac{a}{q(0)}\right)^{1/\varepsilon}\frac{1-e^{-\left(r+\delta-\frac{\delta+g}{\varepsilon}\right)t}}{r+\delta-\frac{\delta+g}{\varepsilon}}\right)$$

$$= e^{(r+\delta)t}\left(\frac{-e^{-(r+\delta)t}}{(r+\delta)}s + \left(\frac{a}{q(0)}\right)^{1/\varepsilon}\frac{e^{-\left(r+\delta-\frac{\delta+g}{\varepsilon}\right)t}}{r+\delta-\frac{\delta+g}{\varepsilon}}\right)$$

$$= \left(\frac{a}{q(0)}\right)^{1/\varepsilon}\frac{e^{\frac{\delta+g}{\varepsilon}t}}{r+\delta-\frac{\delta+g}{\varepsilon}} - \frac{s}{r+\delta}$$

This formula lets us compare different collectibles. The first insight is that storage costs enter linearly into prices, so that growth rates are approximately unaffected by storage costs. That gold is easy to store, while stamps and art require control of humidity and temperature to preserve value and are hence more expensive to store, affects the level of prices but not the growth rate. However, depreciation and the growth of population affect the growth rate, and they do so in combination with the demand elasticity. With more elastic demand, prices grow more slowly and start at a lower level.

4.3.7 Summer Wheat

Typically, wheat harvested in the fall has to last until the following harvest. How should prices evolve over the season? If I know that I need wheat in January, should I buy it at harvest time and store it myself, or wait and buy it in January? We can use a theory analogous to the theory of collectibles developed in Section 4.3.6 to determine the evolution of prices for commodities like wheat, corn, orange juice, and canola oil.

Unlike collectibles, buyers need not hold for their personal use, since there is no value in admiring the wheat in your home. Let $p(t)$ be the price at time t and suppose that the year has length T. Generally there is a substantial amount of uncertainty regarding the size of wheat harvests and most countries maintain an excess inventory as a precaution. However, if the harvest were not uncertain, there would be no need for a precautionary holding, and instead we would consume the entire harvest over the course of a year, at which point the new harvest comes in. It is such a model that is investigated in this section.

Let δ represent the depreciation rate (which for wheat includes the quantity eaten by rodents) and s be the storage cost. Buying at time t and reselling at $t+\Delta$ should be a break-even proposition. If one purchases at time t, it costs $p(t)$ to buy the good. Reselling at $t+\Delta$, the storage cost is about $s\Delta$. (This is not the precisely relevant cost, but rather it is the present value of the storage cost, and hence the restriction to small values of Δ.) The good depreciates to only have $e^{-\delta\Delta}$ left to sell, and discounting reduces the value of that amount by the factor $e^{-r\Delta}$. For this to be a breakeven proposition, for small Δ,

$$0 = e^{-r\Delta}e^{-\delta\Delta}p(t+\Delta) - s\Delta - p(t),$$

or

$$\frac{p(t+\Delta)-p(t)}{\Delta} = \frac{1-e^{-(r+\delta)\Delta}}{\Delta}p(t+\Delta) - s.$$

Taking the limit as $\Delta \to 0$,

$$p'(t) = (r+\delta)p(t) - s.$$

This arbitrage condition insures that it is a break-even proposition to invest in the good; the profits from the price appreciation are exactly balanced by depreciation, interest and storage costs. We can solve the differential equation to obtain:

$$p(t) = e^{(r+\delta)t}\left(p(0) + \frac{1-e^{-(r+\delta)t}}{r+\delta}s \right) = e^{(r+\delta)t}p(0) + \frac{e^{(r+\delta)t}-1}{r+\delta}s.$$

The unknown is $p(0)$. The constraint on $p(0)$, however, is like the resource extraction problem – $p(0)$ is determined by the need to use up the harvest over the course of the year.

Suppose demand has constant elasticity ε. Then the quantity used comes in the form $x(t) = ap(t)^{-\varepsilon}$. Let $z(t)$ represent the stock at time t. Then the equation for the evolution of the stock is $z'(t) = -x(t) - \delta z(t)$. This equation is obtained by noting that the flow out of stock is composed of two elements: depreciation δz and consumption x. The stock evolution equation solves for

$$z(t) = e^{-\delta t}\left(q(0) - \int_0^t e^{\delta u} x(u)\, du \right).$$

Thus, the quantity of wheat is consumed exactly if

$$\int_0^T e^{\delta u} x(u)\, du = q(0).$$

But this equation determines the initial price through

$$q(0) = \int_0^T e^{\delta u} x(u)\, du = \int_0^T e^{\delta u} a p(u)^{-\varepsilon}\, du = \int_0^T e^{\delta u} a \left(e^{(r+\delta)u} p(0) + \frac{e^{(r+\delta)u}-1}{r+\delta} s \right)^{-\varepsilon} du$$

This equation doesn't lead to a closed form for $p(0)$ but is readily estimated, which provides a practical means of computing expected prices for commodities in temporarily fixed supply.

Generally, the price equation produces a "saw-tooth" pattern, which is illustrated in Figure 4-27. The increasing portion is actually an exponential, but of such a small degree that it looks linear. When the new harvest comes in, prices drop abruptly as the inventory grows dramatically, and the same pattern is repeated.

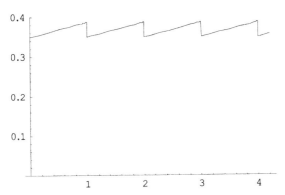

Figure 4-27: Prices over a Cycle for Seasonal Commodities

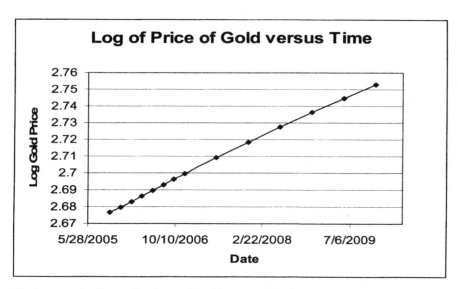

Figure 4-28: Log of Price of Gold over Time

How well does the theory work? Figure 4-28 shows the log of the future price of gold over time. The relevant data comes from a futures market which establishes, at one moment in time, the price of gold for future delivery, and thus represents today's estimate of the future price of gold. These data, then, represent the expected future price at a particular moment in time (the afternoon of October 11, 2005), and thus correspond to the prices in the theory, since perceived risks are fixed. (Usually in the real world, risk plays a salient role.) We can observe that prices are approximately an exponential, because the log of prices is approximately linear. However, the estimate of $r+\delta$ is surprisingly low, at an annual level of less than 0.03, or 3% for both discounting and depreciation. Depreciation of gold is low, but this still represents a very low interest rate.

5 Consumer Theory

Consumer theory is to demand as producer theory is to supply. The major difference is that producer theory assumes that sellers are motivated by profit, and profit is something that one can usually directly measure. Moreover, the costs that enter into profit arise from physical properties of the production process – how many coffee cups come from the coffee cup manufacturing plant? In contrast, consumer theory is based on what people like, so it begins with something that we can't directly measure, but must infer. That is, consumer theory is based on the premise that we can infer what people like from the choices they make.

Now, inferring what people like from choices they make does not rule out mistakes. But our starting point is to consider the implications of a theory in which consumers don't make mistakes, but make choices that give them the most satisfaction.

Economists think of this approach as analogous to studying gravitation in a vacuum before thinking about the effects of air friction. There is a practical consideration that dictates ignoring mistakes. There are many kinds of mistakes, e.g. "I meant to buy toothpaste but forgot and bought a toothbrush," a memory problem, "I thought this toothpaste was better but it is actually worse," a learning issue, and "I meant to buy toothpaste but I bought crack instead," a self-control issue. All of these kinds of mistakes lead to distinct theories. Moreover, we understand these alternative theories by understanding the basic theory first, and then seeing what changes these theories lead to.

5.1 *Utility Maximization*

Economists use the term *utility* in a peculiar and idiosyncratic way. Utility refers not to usefulness but to the flow of pleasure or happiness that a person enjoys – some measure of the satisfaction a person experiences. Usefulness might contribute to utility, but so does style, fashion, or even whimsy.

The term *utility* is unfortunate not just because it suggests usefulness, but because it makes the economic approach to behavior appear more limited than it actually is. We will make very few assumptions about the form of utility that a consumer might have. That is, we will attempt to avoid making value judgments about the preferences a consumer holds – whether they like smoking cigarettes or eating only carrots, watching Arnold Schwarzenegger movies or spending time with a hula hoop. Consumers like whatever it is that they like; the economic assumption is that they attempt to obtain the goods that they like. It is the consequences of the pursuit of happiness that comprise the core of consumer theory.

In this chapter, we will focus on two goods. In many cases, the generalization to an arbitrary number of goods is straightforward. Moreover, in most applications it won't matter because we can view one of the goods as a "composite good" reflecting consumption of a bunch of other goods.[46]

---

[46] Thus, for example, savings for future consumption, or to provide for descendents, or to give to your alma mater, are all examples of consumption. Our consumer will, in the end, always spend all of her

As a starting point, suppose the two goods are X and Y. To distinguish the quantity of the good from the good itself, we'll use capital letters to indicate the good and a lower case letter to indicate the quantity consumed. If X is rutabagas, a consumer who ate three of them would have $x=3$. How can we represent preferences for this consumer? To fix ideas, suppose the consumer is both hungry and thirsty and the goods are beer and pizza. The consumer would like more of both, reflected in greater pleasure for greater consumption. Items one might consume are generally known as "bundles," as in bundles of goods and services, and less frequently as "tuples," a short-form for the "n-tuple," meaning a list of n quantities. Since we will focus on two goods, both of these terms are strained in the application; a bundle because a bundle of two things isn't much of a bundle, and a tuple because what we have here is a "two-tuple," also known as a pair. But part of the job of studying economics is to learn the language of economics, and bundles it is.

One might naturally consider measuring utility on some kind of physical basis – production of dopamine in the brain, for example – but it turns out that the actual quantities of utility don't matter for the theory we develop. What matters is whether a bundle produces more than another, or less, or the same. Let $u(x, y)$ represent the utility a consumer gets from consuming x units of beer and y units of pizza. The function u guides the consumer's choice, in the sense that, if the consumer can choose either (x_1, y_1) or (x_2, y_2), we expect him to choose (x_1, y_1) if $u(x_1, y_1) > u(x_2, y_2)$.

But notice that a doubling of u would lead to the same choices, because

$u(x_1, y_1) > u(x_2, y_2)$ if and only if $2u(x_1, y_1) > 2u(x_2, y_2)$.

Thus, doubling the utility doesn't change the preferences of the consumer. But the situation is more extreme than this. Even exponentiating the utility doesn't change the consumer's preferences, because

$u(x_1, y_1) > u(x_2, y_2)$ if and only if $e^{u(x_1, y_1)} > e^{u(x_2, y_2)}$.

Another way to put this is that there are no natural units for utility, at least until such time as we are able to measure pleasure in the brain.

It is possible to develop the theory of consumer choice without supposing that a utility function exists at all. However, it is expedient to begin with utility, to simplify the analysis for introductory purposes.

5.1.1 Budget or Feasible Set

Suppose a consumer has a fixed amount of money to spend, M. There are two goods X and Y, with associated prices p_X and p_Y. The feasible choices the consumer can make satisfy $p_X x + p_Y y \leq M$. In addition, we will focus on consumption and rule out

---

income, although this happens because we adopt a very broad notion of spending. In particular, savings are "future spending."

negative consumption, so $x \geq 0$ and $y \geq 0$. This gives a *budget set* or *feasible set* illustrated in Figure 5-1.

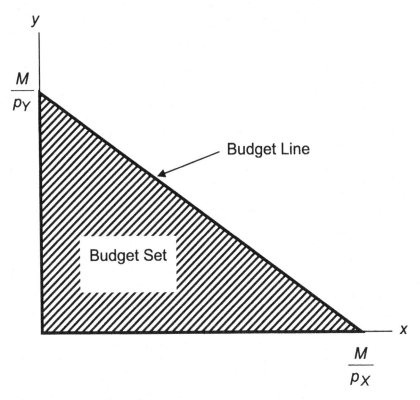

Figure 5-1: Budget Set

In this diagram, the feasible set of purchases that satisfy the budget constraint are illustrated with shading. If the consumer spends all her money on X, she can consume the quantity $x = \dfrac{M}{p_X}$. Similarly, if she spends all of her money on Y, she consumes $\dfrac{M}{p_Y}$ units of Y. The straight line between them, known as the budget line, represents the most of the goods she can consume. The slope of the budget line is $-\dfrac{p_X}{p_Y}$.

An increase in the price of one good pivots or rotates the budget line. Thus, if the price of X increases, the endpoint $\dfrac{M}{p_Y}$ remains the same, but $\dfrac{M}{p_X}$ falls. This is illustrated in Figure 5-2.

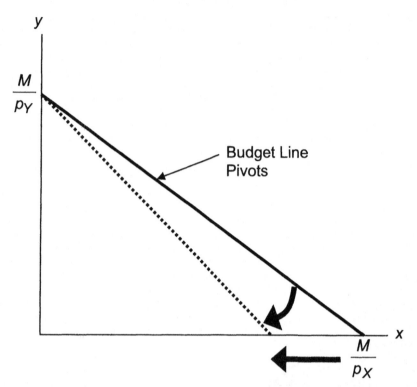

Figure 5-2: Effect of an Increase in Price on the Budget

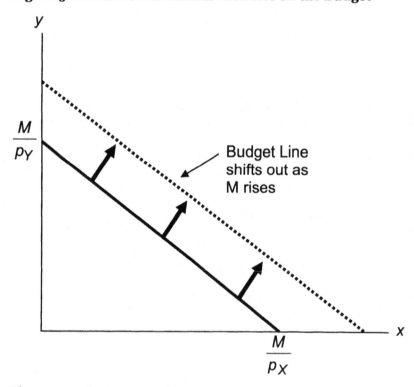

Figure 5-3: An Increase in Income

The effect of increasing the available money M is to increase both $\dfrac{M}{p_X}$ and $\dfrac{M}{p_Y}$ proportionately. This means an increase in M shifts the budget line out (away from the origin) in a parallel fashion, as in Figure 5-3.

An increase in both prices by the same proportional factor has an effect identical to a decrease in income. Thus, one of the three financial values – the two prices and income – is redundant. That is, we can trace out all the possible budget lines with any two of the three parameters. This can prove useful; we can arbitrarily set p_X to be the number one without affecting the generality of the analysis. When setting a price to one, that related good is called the *numeraire*, and essentially all prices are denominated with respect to that one good. A real world example of a numeraire occurred when the currency used was based on gold so that the prices of other goods are denominated in terms of the value of gold.

Money is not necessarily the only constraint on the consumption of goods that a consumer faces. Time can be equally important. One can own all the compact discs in the world, but they are useless if one doesn't actually have time to listen to them. Indeed, when we consider the supply of labor, time will be a major issue – supplying labor (working) uses up time that could be used to consume goods. In this case there will be two kinds of budget constraints – a financial one and a temporal one. At a fixed wage, time and money translate directly into one another and the existence of the time constraint won't present significant challenges to the theory. The conventional way to handle the time constraint is to use as a baseline working "full out," and then view leisure as a good which is purchased at a price equal to the wage. Thus, if you earn $20/hour, we would set your budget at $480/day, reflecting 24 hours of work, but then permit you to buy leisure time, during which eating, sleeping, brushing teeth and every other non-work activity is accomplished at a price equal to $20 per hour.

5.1.1.1 (Exercise)   Graph the budget line for apples and oranges, with prices of $2 and $3 respectively and $60 to spend. Now increase the price of apples from $2 to $4 and draw the budget line.

5.1.1.2 (Exercise)   Suppose that apples cost $1 each. Water can be purchased for 0.5 cents per gallon up to 20,000 gallons, and 0.1 cent per gallon for each gallon beyond 20,000 gallons. Draw the budget constraint for a consumer who spends $200 per month on apples and water.

5.1.1.3 (Exercise)   Graph the budget line for apples and oranges, with prices of $2 and $3 respectively and $60 to spend. Now increase expenditure to $90 and draw the budget line.

5.1.2 Isoquants

With two goods, we can graphically represent utility by considering the contour map of utility. Utility contours are known as *isoquants*, meaning "equal quantity," and are also known as *indifference curves*, since the consumer is indifferent between points on the line. We have met this idea already in the description of production functions, where the curves represented input mixes that produced a given output. The *only* difference here is that the output being produced is consumer "utility" instead of a single good or service.

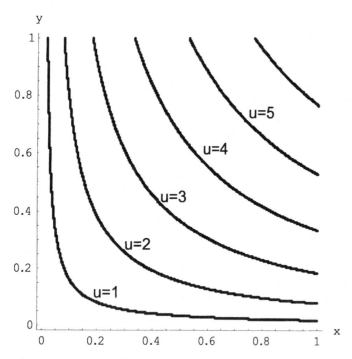

Figure 5-4: Utility Isoquants

Figure 5-4 provides an illustration of isoquants or indifference curves. Each curve represents one level of utility. Higher utilities occur to the northeast, further away from the origin. As with production isoquants, the slope of the indifference curves has the interpretation of the tradeoff between the two goods. The amount of Y that the consumer is willing to give up to obtain an extra bit of X is the slope of the indifference curve. Formally, the equation

$$u(x, y) = u_0$$

defines an indifference curve for the reference utility u_0. Differentiating in such a way as to preserve the equality, we obtain the slope of the indifference curve:

$$\frac{\partial u}{\partial x}dx + \frac{\partial u}{\partial y}dy = 0 \ \text{ or } \ \left.\frac{dy}{dx}\right|_{u=u_0} = -\frac{\partial u/\partial x}{\partial u/\partial y}.$$

This slope is known as the marginal rate of substitution and reflects the tradeoff, from the consumer's perspective, between the goods. That is to say, the marginal rate of substitution (of Y for X) is the amount of Y the consumer is willing to lose to obtain an extra unit of X.

An important assumption concerning isoquants is reflected in the diagram: "midpoints are preferred to extreme points." Suppose the consumer is indifferent between (x_1, y_1)

and (x_2, y_2), that is, $u(x_1, y_1) = u(x_2, y_2)$. Then we say *preferences are convex* if any point on the line segment connecting (x_1, y_1) and (x_2, y_2) is at least as good as the extremes. Formally, a point on the line segment connecting (x_1, y_1) and (x_2, y_2) comes in the form

$$(\alpha x_1 + (1 - \alpha) x_2, \alpha y_1 + (1 - \alpha) y_2),$$

for α between zero and one. This is also known as a "convex combination" between the two points. When α is zero, the segment starts at (x_2, y_2) and proceeds in a linear fashion to (x_1, y_1) at α equal to one. Preferences are convex if, for any α between 0 and 1,

$$u(x_1, y_1) = u(x_2, y_2) \text{ implies } u(\alpha x_1 + (1 - \alpha) x_2, \alpha y_1 + (1 - \alpha) y_2) \geq u(x_1, y_1).$$

This property is illustrated in Figure 5-5. The line segment that connects two points on the indifference curve lies to the northeast of the indifference curve, which means the line segment involves strictly more consumption of both goods than some points on the indifference curve, which means that it is preferred to the indifference curve. Convex preferences mean that a consumer prefers a mix to any two equally valuable extremes. Thus, if the consumer likes black coffee and also likes drinking milk, the consumer prefers some of each (not necessarily mixed) to only drinking coffee or only drinking milk. This sounds more reasonable if you think of the consumer's choices on a monthly basis; if you like drinking 60 cups of coffee, and no milk, per month the same as 30 glasses of milk and no coffee, convex preferences entails preferring 30 cups of coffee and 15 glasses of milk to either extreme.

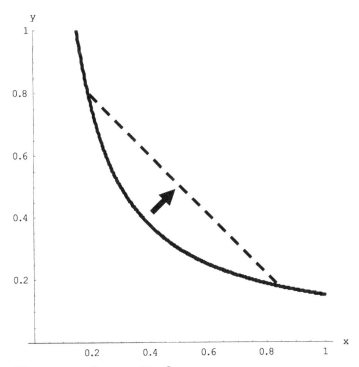

Figure 5-5: Convex Preferences

How does a consumer choose which bundle to select? The consumer is faced with the problem of maximizing $u(x, y)$ subject to $p_X x + p_Y y \leq M$.

We can derive the solution to the consumer's problem as follows. First, "solve" the budget constraint $p_X x + p_Y y \leq M$ for y, to obtain $y \leq \dfrac{M - p_X x}{p_Y}$. If Y is a good, this constraint will be satisfied with equality and all the money will be spent. Thus, we can write the consumer's utility as

$$u\left(x, \frac{M - p_X x}{p_Y}\right).$$

The first order condition for this problem, maximizing it over x, has

$$0 = \frac{d}{dx} u\left(x, \frac{M - p_X x}{p_Y}\right) = \frac{\partial u}{\partial x} - \frac{p_X}{p_Y}\frac{\partial u}{\partial y}.$$

This can be re-arranged to obtain the marginal rate of substitution (MRS).

$$\frac{p_X}{p_Y} = \frac{\partial u / \partial x}{\partial u / \partial y} = -\frac{dy}{dx}\bigg|_{u = u_0} = MRS.$$

The first order condition requires that the slope of the indifference curve equals the slope of the budget line, that is, there is a tangency between the indifference curve and the budget line. This is illustrated in Figure 5-6. Three indifference curves are drawn, two of which intersect the budget line, but are not tangent. At these intersections, it is possible to increase utility by moving "toward the center," until the highest of the three indifference curves is reached. At this point, further increases in utility are not feasible, because there is no intersection between the set of bundles that produce a strictly higher utility and the budget set. Thus, the large black dot is the bundle that produces the highest utility for the consumer.

It will later prove useful to also state the second order condition, although we won't use this condition now:

$$0 \geq \frac{d^2}{(dx)^2} u\left(x, \frac{M - p_X x}{p_Y}\right) = \frac{\partial^2 u}{(\partial x)^2} - \frac{p_X}{p_Y}\frac{\partial^2 u}{\partial x \partial y} + \left(\frac{p_X}{p_Y}\right)^2 \frac{\partial^2 u}{(\partial y)^2}.$$

Note that the vector $(u_1, u_2) = \left(\dfrac{\partial u}{\partial x}, \dfrac{\partial u}{\partial y}\right)$ is the gradient of u, and the gradient points in the direction of steepest ascent of the function u. Second, the equation which characterizes the optimum,

$$0 = p_X \frac{\partial u}{\partial y} - p_Y \frac{\partial u}{\partial x} = \left(\frac{\partial u}{\partial x}, \frac{\partial u}{\partial y} \right) \bullet (-p_Y, p_X),$$

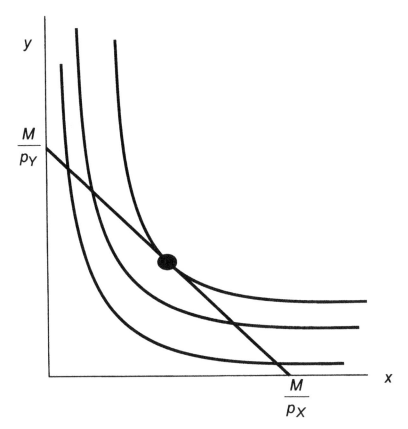

Figure 5-6: Graphical Utility Maximization

where • is the "dot product" which multiplies the components of vectors and then adds them, says that the vectors (u_1, u_2) and (-p_Y, p_X) are perpendicular, and hence that *the rate of steepest ascent of the utility function is perpendicular to the budget line.*

When does this tangency approach fail to solve the consumer's problem? There are three ways it can fail. First, the utility might not be differentiable. We will set aside this kind of failure with the remark that fixing points of non-differentiability is mathematically challenging but doesn't lead to significant alterations in the theory. The second failure is that a tangency didn't maximize utility. Figure 5-7 illustrates this case. Here, there is a tangency, but it doesn't maximize utility. In Figure 5-7, the dotted indifference curve maximizes utility given the budget constraint (straight line). This is exactly the kind of failure that is ruled out by convex preferences. In Figure 5-7, preferences are not convex, because if we connect two points on the indifference curves and look at a convex combination, we get something less preferred, with lower utility, not more preferred as convex preferences would require.

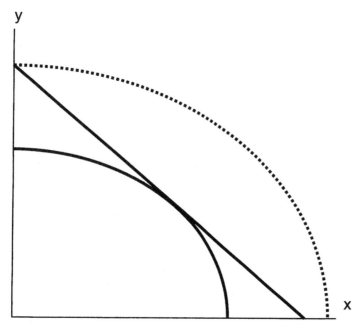

Figure 5-7: "Concave" Preferences, Prefer Boundaries

The third failure is more fundamental: the derivative might fail to be zero because we've hit the boundary of $x=0$ or $y=0$. This is a fundamental problem because in fact there are many goods that we do buy zero of, so zeros for some goods are not uncommon solutions to the problem of maximizing utility. We will take this problem up in a separate section, but we already have a major tool to deal with it: convex preferences. As we shall see, convex preferences insure that the consumer's maximization problem is "well-behaved."

5.1.3 Examples

The Cobb-Douglas utility function comes in the form $u(x,y) = x^\alpha y^{1-\alpha}$. Since utility is zero if either of the goods is zero, we see that a consumer with Cobb-Douglas preferences will always buy some of each good. The marginal rate of substitution for Cobb-Douglas utility is

$$-\frac{dy}{dx}\bigg|_{u=u_0} = \frac{\partial u/\partial x}{\partial u/\partial y} = \frac{\alpha y}{(1-\alpha)x}.$$

Thus, the consumer's utility maximization problem yields

$$\frac{p_X}{p_Y} = -\frac{dy}{dx}\bigg|_{u=u_0} = \frac{\partial u/\partial x}{\partial u/\partial y} = \frac{\alpha y}{(1-\alpha)x}.$$

Thus, using the budget constraint, $(1-\alpha)xp_X = \alpha y p_Y = \alpha(M - xp_X)$.

This yields $x = \dfrac{\alpha M}{p_X}$, $y = \dfrac{(1-\alpha)M}{p_Y}$.

Cobb-Douglas utility results in *constant expenditure shares*. No matter what the price of X or Y, the expenditure xp_X on X is αM. Similarly, the expenditure on Y is $(1-\alpha)M$. This makes the Cobb-Douglas utility very useful for computing examples and homework exercises.

5.1.3.1 (Exercise)   Consider a consumer with utility $u(x,y) = \sqrt{xy}$. If the consumer has \$100 to spend, and the price of X is \$5 and the price of Y is \$2, graph the budget line, and then find the point that maximizes the consumer's utility given the budget. Draw the utility isoquant through this point. What are the expenditure shares?

5.1.3.2 (Exercise)   Consider a consumer with utility $u(x,y) = \sqrt{xy}$. Calculate the slope of the isoquant directly, by solving $u(x,y) = u_0$ for y as a function of x and the utility level u_0. What is the slope $-\left.\dfrac{dy}{dx}\right|_{u=u_0}$? Verify that it satisfies the formula given above.

5.1.3.3 (Exercise)   Consider a consumer with utility $u(x,y) = (xy)^2$. Calculate the slope of the isoquant directly, by solving $u(x,y) = u_0$ for y as a function of x and the utility level u_0. What is the slope $-\left.\dfrac{dy}{dx}\right|_{u=u_0}$? Verify that the result is the same as in the previous exercise. Why is it the same?

When two goods are perfect complements, they are consumed proportionately. The utility that gives rise to perfect complements is in the form $u(x, y) = \min \{x, \beta y\}$ for some constant β (the Greek letter beta). First observe that with perfect complements, consumers will buy in such a way that $x = \beta y$. The reason is that, if $x > \beta y$, some expenditure on x is a waste since it brings in no additional utility, and the consumer gets higher utility by decreasing x and increasing y. This lets us define a "composite good" which involves buying some amount y of Y and also buying βy of X. The price of this composite commodity is $\beta p_X + p_Y$, and it produces utility $u = \dfrac{M}{\beta p_X + p_Y}$. In this way, perfect complements boil down to a single good problem.

5.1.3.4 (Exercise)   The case of perfect substitutes arises when all that matters to the consumer is the sum of the products – e.g. red shirts and green shirts for a color-blind consumer. In this case, $u(x, y) = x + y$. Graph the isoquants for perfect substitutes. Show that the consumer maximizes utility by spending their entire income on whichever product is cheaper.

If the only two goods available in the world were pizza and beer, it is likely that *satiation* would set in at some point. How many pizzas can you eat per month? How much beer can you drink? [Don't answer that.]

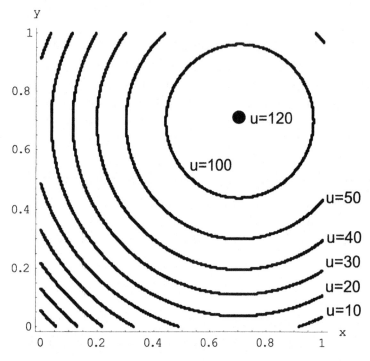

Figure 5-8: Isoquants for a Bliss Point

What does satiation mean for isoquants? It means there is a point that maximizes utility, which economists call a *bliss point*. An example is illustrated in Figure 5-8. Near the origin, the isoquants behave as before. However, as one gets full of pizza and beer, a point of maximum value is reached, illustrated by a large black dot. What does satiation mean for the theory? First, if the bliss point isn't within reach, the theory behaves as before. With a bliss point within reach, consumption will stop at the bliss point. A feasible bliss point entails having a zero value of money. There may be people with a zero value of money, but even very wealthy people, who reach satiation in goods that they personally consume, often like to do other things with the wealth and appear not to have reached satiation overall.

5.1.3.5 (Exercise)   Suppose $u(x,y) = x^{\alpha} + y^{\alpha}$ for $\alpha < 1$. Show

$$x = \frac{M}{p_X\left(1 + \left(\dfrac{p_Y}{p_X}\right)^{\alpha}\right)}, \text{ and } y = \frac{M}{p_Y\left(1 + \left(\dfrac{p_X}{p_Y}\right)^{\alpha}\right)}.$$

5.1.3.6 (Exercise)   Suppose one consumer has the utility function u (which is always a positive number), and a second consumer has utility w. Suppose, in addition, that for any x, y, $w(x, y) = (u(x, y))^2$, that is, the second person's utility is the square of the first. Show that these consumers make the same choices – that is, $u(x_a, y_a) \geq u(x_b, y_b)$ if and only $w(x_a, y_a) \geq w(x_b, y_b)$.

5.1.4 Substitution Effects

It would be a simpler world if an increase in the price of a good always entailed buying less of it. Alas, it isn't so, as the following diagram illustrates. In this diagram, an increase in the price of Y causes the budget line to pivot around the intersection on the X axis, since the amount of X that can be purchased hasn't changed. In this case, the quantity y of Y demanded rises.

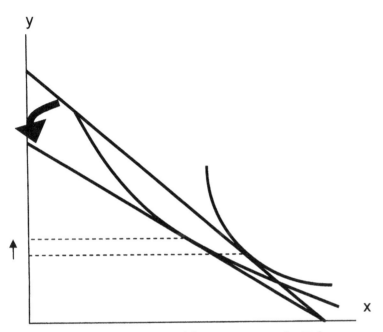

Figure 5-9: Substitution with an Increase in Price

At first glance, this increase in the consumption of a good in response to a price increase sounds implausible, but there are examples where it makes sense. The primary example is leisure. As wages rise, the cost of leisure (forgone wages) rises. But as people feel wealthier, they choose to work fewer hours. The other examples given, which are hotly debated in the "tempest in a teapot" kind of way, involve people subsisting on a good like potatoes but occasionally buying meat. When the price of potatoes rises, they can no longer afford meat and buy even more potatoes than before.

Thus, the logical starting point on substitution – what happens to the demand for a good when the price of that good increases? – does not lead to a useful theory. As a result, economists have devised an alternative approach, based on the following logic. An increase in the price of a good is really a composition of two effects: an increase in the relative price of the good, and a decrease in the purchasing power of money. As a result, it is useful to examine these two effects separately. The substitution effect considers the change in the relative price, with a sufficient change in income to keep the consumer on the same utility isoquant.[47] The income effect changes only income.

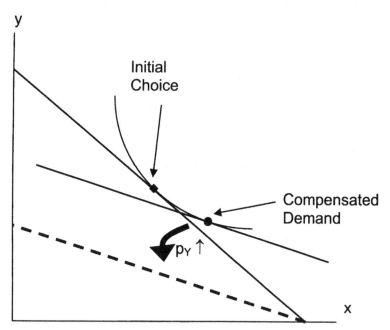

Figure 5-10: Substitution Effect

To graphically illustrate the substitution effect, consider Figure 5-10. The starting point is the tangency between the isoquant and the budget line, denoted with a diamond shape and labeled "Initial Choice." The price of Y rises, pivoting the budget line inward. The new budget line is illustrated with a heavy, dashed line. To find the substitution effect, increase income from the dashed line until the original isoquant is reached. Increases in income shift the budget line out in a fashion parallel to the original. We reach the original isoquant at a point labeled with a small circle, a point sometimes called the *compensated* demand, because we have compensated the consumer for the price increase by increasing income just enough to leave her unharmed, on the same isoquant. The substitution effect is just the difference between these points – the substitution in response to the price change, holding constant the utility of the consumer.

We can readily see that the substitution effect of a price increase in Y is to decrease the consumption of Y and increase the consumption of X.[48] The income effect is the change in consumption resulting from the change in income. The effect of any change in price can be decomposed into the substitution effect, which holds utility constant and changes the relative prices, and the income effect, which adjusts for the loss of purchasing power arising from the price increase.

---

[47] Some authors instead change the income enough to make the old bundle affordable. This approach has the virtue of being readily computed, but the disadvantage that the substitution effect winds up increasing the utility of the consumer. Overall the present approach is more economical for most purposes.
[48] To construct a formal proof, first show that if p_Y rises and y rises, holding utility constant, the initial choice prior to the price increase is feasible after the price increase. Use this to conclude that after the price increase it is possible to have strictly more of both goods, contradicting the hypothesis that utility was held constant.

Example (Cobb-Douglas): Recall that the Cobb-Douglas utility comes in the form $u(x,y) = x^\alpha y^{1-\alpha}$. Solving for x, y we obtain

$$x = \frac{\alpha M}{p_X}, \quad y = \frac{(1-\alpha)M}{p_Y}, \text{ and } u(x,y) = \alpha^\alpha (1-\alpha)^{1-\alpha} \frac{M}{p_X^\alpha p_Y^{1-\alpha}}.$$

Thus, consider a multiplicative increase Δ in p_Y, that is, multiplying p_Y by $\Delta > 1$. In order to leave utility constant, M must rise by $\Delta^{1-\alpha}$. Thus, x rises by the factor $\Delta^{1-\alpha}$ and y falls, by the factor $\Delta^{-\alpha} < 1$. This is the substitution effect.

What is the substitution effect of a small change in the price p_Y for any given utility function, not necessarily Cobb-Douglas? To address this question, it is helpful to introduce some notation. We will subscript the utility to indicate partial derivative, that is,

$$u_1 = \frac{\partial u}{\partial x}, \quad u_2 = \frac{\partial u}{\partial y}.$$

Note that, by the definition of the substitution effect, we are holding utility constant, so $u(x, y)$ is being held constant. This means, locally, that

$$0 = du = u_1 \, dx + u_2 \, dy .^{49}$$

In addition, we have $M = p_X x + p_Y y$, so

$$dM = p_X dx + p_Y dy + y dp_Y$$

Finally, we have the optimality condition

$$\frac{p_X}{p_Y} = \frac{\partial u / \partial x}{\partial u / \partial y}$$

which is convenient to write as $p_X u_2 = p_Y u_1$. Differentiating this equation, and letting

$$u_{11} = \frac{\partial^2 u}{(\partial x)^2}, \quad u_{12} = \frac{\partial^2 u}{\partial x \partial y} \text{ and } u_{22} = \frac{\partial^2 u}{(\partial y)^2}, \text{ we have}$$

$$p_X(u_{12}dx + u_{22}dy) = u_1 \, dp_Y + p_Y(u_{11}dx + u_{12}dy).$$

---

[49] Writing dx for an unknown infinitesimal change in x can be put on a formal basis. The easiest way to do so is to think of dx as representing the derivative of x with respect to a parameter, which will be p_Y.

For a given dp_Y, we now have three equations in three unknowns dx, dy, and dM. However, dM only appears in one of the three. Thus, the effect of a price change on x and y can be solved by solving two equations:

$$0 = u_1\,dx + u_2\,dy \text{ and}$$

$$p_X(u_{12}dx + u_{22}dy) = u_1\,dp_Y + p_Y(u_{11}dx + u_{12}dy)$$

for the two unknowns dx and dy. This is straightforward and yields:

$$\frac{dx}{dp_Y} = -\frac{p_Y u_1}{p_X^2 u_{11} + 2p_X p_Y u_{12} + p_Y^2 u_{22}} \text{ and}$$

$$\frac{dy}{dp_Y} = \frac{p_Y u_2}{p_X^2 u_{11} + 2p_X p_Y u_{12} + p_Y^2 u_{22}}.$$

These equations imply that x rises and y falls.[50] We immediately see

$$\frac{\dfrac{dy}{dp_Y}}{\dfrac{dx}{dp_Y}} = -\frac{u_1}{u_2} = -\frac{p_X}{p_Y}.$$

Thus, the change in (x,y) follows the budget line locally. (This is purely a consequence of holding utility constant.)

To complete the thought while we are embroiled in these derivatives, note that $p_X u_2 = p_Y u_1$ implies that $p_X dx + p_Y dy = 0$.

Thus, the amount of money necessary to compensate the consumer for the price increase, keeping utility constant, can be calculated from our third equation:

$$dM = p_X dx + p_Y dy + y\,dp_Y = y\,dp_Y.$$

The amount of income necessary to insure the consumer makes no losses from a price increase in Y is the amount that lets them buy the bundle they originally purchased, that is, the increase in the amount of money is precisely the amount needed to cover the increased price of y. This shows that locally there is no difference from a substitution effect that keeps utility constant (which is what we explored) and one that provides sufficient income to permit purchasing the previously purchased consumption bundle, at least when small changes in prices are contemplated.

---

[50] This is a consequence of the fact that $p_X^2 u_{11} + 2p_X p_Y u_{12} + p_Y^2 u_{22} < 0$, which follows from the already stated second order condition for a maximum of utility.

5.1.5 Income Effects

Wealthy people buy more caviar than poor people. Wealthier people buy more land, medical services, cars, telephones, and computers than poorer people, because they have more money to spend on goods and services, and overall, buy more of them. But wealthier people also buy fewer of some goods, too. Rich people buy fewer cigarettes and processed cheese food. You don't see billionaires waiting in line at McDonald's, and that probably isn't because they have an assistant to wait for them. For most goods, at a sufficiently high income, the purchase tends to trail off as income rises.

When an increase in income causes a consumer to buy more of a good that good is called a *normal good* for that consumer. When the consumer buys less, the good is called an *inferior* good, which is an example of sensible jargon that is rare in any discipline. That is, an inferior good is any good whose quantity demanded falls as incomes rise. At a sufficiently low income, almost all goods are normal goods, while at a sufficiently high income, most goods become inferior. Even a Ferrari is an inferior good against some alternatives, such as Lear jets.

The curve that shows the path of consumption as incomes rise is known as an Engel curve.[51] An Engel curve graphs $(x(M), y(M))$ as M varies, where $x(M)$ is the amount of X chosen with income M, and similarly $y(M)$ is the amount of is the amount of Y. An example of an Engel curve is illustrated in Figure 5-11.

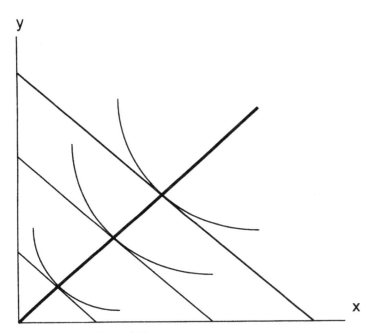

Figure 5-11: Engel Curve

---

[51] The Engel curve is named for Ernst Engel (1821-1896), a statistician, not for Friedrich Engels, who wrote with Karl Marx.

Example (Cobb-Douglas): Since the equations $x = \dfrac{\alpha M}{p_X}$, $y = \dfrac{(1-\alpha)M}{p_Y}$ define the optimal consumption, the Engel curve is a straight line through the origin with slope $\dfrac{(1-\alpha)p_X}{\alpha p_Y}$.

5.1.5.1 (Exercise)   Show that, in the case of perfect complements, the Engel curve does not depend on prices.

An inferior good has the quantity fall as incomes rise. Note that, with two goods, at least one is normal good – they can't both be inferior goods, for otherwise when income rose, less of both would be purchased. An example of an inferior good is illustrated in Figure 5-12. Here, as incomes rise, the consumption of x rises, reaches a maximum, then begins to decline. In the declining portion, X is an inferior good.

The definition of the substitution effect now permits us to decompose the effect of a price change into a substitution effect and an income effect. This is illustrated in Figure 5-13.

What is the mathematical form of the income effect? This is actually more straightforward to compute than the substitution effect computed above. As with the substitution effect, we differentiate the conditions $M = p_x x + p_y y$ and $p_x u_2 = p_y u_1$, holding p_X and p_Y constant, to obtain:

$$dM = p_X dx + p_Y dy \text{ and } p_X(u_{12}dx + u_{22}dy) = p_Y(u_{11}dx + u_{12}dy).$$

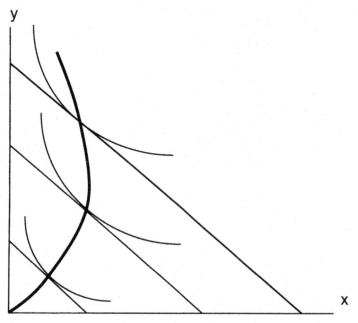

Figure 5-12: Backward Bending – Inferior Good

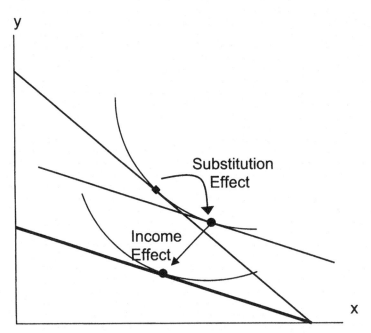

y

Substitution
Effect

Income
Effect

x

Figure 5-13: Income and Substitution Effects

The second condition can also be written as

$$\frac{dy}{dx} = \frac{p_Y u_{11} - p_X u_{12}}{p_X u_{22} - p_Y u_{12}}.$$

This equation alone defines the slope of the Engel curve, without determining how large a change arises from a given change in M. The two conditions together can be solved for the effects of M on X and Y. The Engel curve is given by

$$\frac{dx}{dM} = \frac{p_Y^2 u_{11} - 2 p_X u_{12} + p_X^2 u_{22}}{p_X u_{22} - p_Y u_{12}} \text{ and } \frac{dy}{dM} = \frac{p_Y^2 u_{11} - 2 p_X u_{12} + p_X^2 u_{22}}{p_Y u_{11} - p_X u_{12}}.$$

Note (from the second order condition) that good Y is inferior if $p_Y u_{11} - p_X u_{12} > 0$, or if $\frac{u_{11}}{u_1} - \frac{u_{12}}{u_2} > 0$, or $\frac{u_1}{u_2}$ is increasing in x. Since $\frac{u_1}{u_2}$ is locally constant when M increases, equaling the price ratio, and an increase in y increases $\frac{u_1}{u_2}$ (thanks to the second order condition), the only way to keep $\frac{u_1}{u_2}$ equal to the price ratio is for x to fall. This property characterizes an inferior good – an increase in the quantity of the good increases the marginal rate of substitution of that good for another good.

5.1.5.2 (Exercise)   Compute the substitution effect and income effect associated with a multiplicative price increase Δ in p_Y, that is, multiplying p_Y by $\Delta > 1$, for the case of Cobb-Douglas utility $u(x,y) = x^\alpha y^{1-\alpha}$.

5.2 Additional Considerations

Let us revisit the maximization problem considered in this chapter. The consumer can spend M on either or both of two goods. This yields a payoff of $h(x) = u\left(x, \dfrac{M - p_X x}{p_Y}\right)$.

When is this problem well behaved? First, if h is a *concave* function of x, which implies $h''(x) \le 0$,[52] then any solution to the first order condition is in fact a maximum. To see this, note that $h''(x) \le 0$ entails $h'(x)$ decreasing. Moreover, if the point x^* satisfies $h'(x^*) = 0$, then for $x \le x^*$, $h'(x) \ge 0$, and for $x \ge x^*$, $h'(x) \le 0$, because $h'(x)$ gets smaller as x gets larger, and $h'(x^*) = 0$. Now consider $x \le x^*$. Since $h'(x) \ge 0$, h is increasing as x gets larger. Similarly, for $x \ge x^*$, $h'(x) \le 0$, which means h gets smaller as x gets larger. Thus, h concave and $h'(x^*) = 0$ means that h is maximized at x^*.

Thus, a *sufficient* condition for the first order condition to characterize the maximum of utility is that $h''(x) \le 0$, for all x, p_X, p_Y, and M. Letting $z = \dfrac{p_X}{p_Y}$, this is equivalent to

$$u_{11} - 2z u_{12} + z^2 u_{22} \le 0 \text{ for all } z > 0.$$

In turn, we can see that this requires (i) $u_{11} \le 0$ ($z=0$) and (ii) $u_{22} \le 0$ ($z \to \infty$), and (iii)

$$\sqrt{u_{11} u_{22}} - u_{12} \ge 0 \ \left(z = \sqrt{u_{11}/u_{22}} \right). \text{ In addition, since}$$

$$-\left(u_{11} + 2z u_{12} + z^2 u_{22}\right) = \left(\sqrt{-u_{11}} - z\sqrt{-u_{22}}\right)^2 + 2z\left(\sqrt{u_{11}u_{22}} - u_{12}\right),$$

(i), (ii) and (iii) are sufficient for $u_{11} + 2z u_{12} + z^2 u_{22} \le 0$.

Therefore, if (i) $u_{11} \le 0$ and (ii) $u_{22} \le 0$, and (iii) $\sqrt{u_{11} u_{22}} - u_{12} \ge 0$, a solution to the first order conditions characterizes utility maximization for the consumer. We will assume that these conditions are met for the remainder of this chapter.

5.2.1 Corner Solutions

When will a consumer specialize and consume zero of a good? A necessary condition for the choice of x to be zero is that the consumer doesn't benefit from consuming a very small x, that is, $h'(0) \le 0$. This means

---

[52] The definition of concavity is that h is concave if $0 < a < 1$ and for all x, y, $h(ax+(1-a)y) \ge ah(x) + (1-a)h(y)$. It is reasonably straightforward to show this implies the second derivative of h is negative, and if h is twice differentiable, the converse is true as well.

$$h'(0) = u_1\left(0, M\big/p_Y\right) - u_2\left(0, M\big/p_Y\right) p_X\big/p_Y \le 0,$$

or

$$\frac{u_1\left(0, M\big/p_Y\right)}{u_2\left(0, M\big/p_Y\right)} \le p_X\big/p_Y.$$

Moreover, if the concavity of h is met, as assumed above, then this condition is sufficient to guarantee that the solution is zero. To see that, note that concavity of h implies h' is decreasing. Combined with $h'(0) \le 0$, that entails h maximized at 0. An important class of examples of this behavior are *quasilinear* utility. Quasilinear utility comes in the form $u(x, y) = y + v(x)$, where v is a concave function ($v''(x) \le 0$ for all x).

5.2.1.1 (Exercise)   Demonstrate that the quasilinear consumer will consume zero X if and only if $v'(0) \le \dfrac{p_x}{p_y}$, and that the consumer instead consumes zero Y if

$v'\left(M\big/p_X\right) \ge \dfrac{p_x}{p_y}$. The quasilinear utility isoquants, for $v(x) = (x + 0.03)^{0.3}$, are illustrated in Figure 5-14. Note that even though the isoquants curve, they are nonetheless parallel to each other

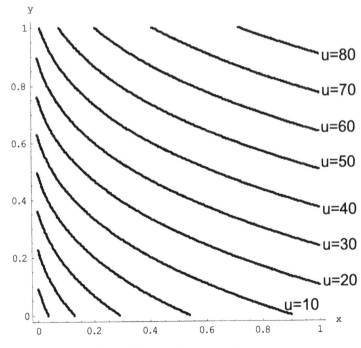

Figure 5-14: Quasilinear Isoquants

The procedure for dealing with corners is generally this. First, check concavity of the h function. If h is concave, we have a procedure to solve the problem; when h is not concave, an alternative strategy must be devised. There are known strategies for some cases that are beyond the scope of this text. Given h concave, the next step is to check the endpoints, and verify that $h'(0) > 0$ (for otherwise $x=0$ maximizes the consumer's utility) and that $h'\left(M / p_X\right) < 0$ (for otherwise $y=0$ maximizes the consumer's utility).

Finally, at this point we seek the interior solution $h'(x) = 0$. With this procedure we can insure we find the actual maximum for the consumer, rather than a solution to the first order conditions that doesn't maximize the consumer's utility.

5.2.2 Labor Supply

Consider a taxi driver who owns a car or convenience store owner, or anyone else who can set his own hours. Working has two effects on this consumer – more goods consumption, but less leisure consumption. To model this, we let x be the goods consumption, L the amount of non-work time or *leisure*, and working time $T - L$, where T is the amount of time available for activities of all kinds. The variable L includes a lot of activities that aren't necessarily fun, like trips to the dentist and haircuts and sleeping, but for which the consumer isn't paid, and which represent choices. One could argue that sleeping isn't really a choice, in the sense that one can't choose zero sleep, but this can be handled by adjusting T to represent "time available for chosen behavior" so that $T - L$ is work time and L the chosen non-work activities. We set L to be leisure rather than labor supply because it is leisure that is the good thing, whereas most of us view working as something we are willing to do provided we're paid for it.

Labor supply is different from other consumption because the wage enters the budget constraint twice – first as the price of leisure and second as income from working. One way of expressing this is to write the consumer's budget constraint as

$$px + wL = M + wT.$$

Here, M represents non-work income, such as gifts, government transfers, and interest income. We drop the subscript on the price of X, and use w as the wage. Finally, we use a capital L for leisure because a small el looks like the number one. The somewhat Dickensian idea is that the consumer's maximal budget entails working the total available hours T, and any non-worked hours are purchased at the wage rate w. Alternatively, one could express the budget constraint so as to reflect that expenditures on goods px equals the total money, which is the sum of non-work income M and work income $w(T - L)$, or

$$px = M + w(T - L).$$

These two formulations of the budget constraint are mathematically equivalent.

The strategy for solving the problem is also equivalent to the standard formulation, although there is some expositional clarity used by employing the budget constraint to eliminate x. That is, we write the utility $u(x,L)$

$$h(L) = u\left(\frac{M + w(T - L)}{p}, L\right).$$

As before, we obtain the first order condition

$$0 = h'(L^*) = -u_1\left(\frac{w}{p}\right) + u_2$$

where the partial derivatives u_1 and u_2 are evaluated at $\left(\dfrac{M + w(T - L^*)}{p}, L^*\right)$. Note that the first order condition is the same as the standard two-good theory developed already. This is because the effect so far is merely to require two components to income: M and wT, both of which are constant. It is only when we evaluate the effect of a wage increase that we see a difference.

To evaluate the effect of a wage increase, differentiate the first order condition to obtain

$$0 = \left(u_{11}\left(\frac{w}{p}\right)^2 - 2u_{12}\left(\frac{w}{p}\right) + u_{22}\right)\frac{dL}{dw} - \frac{u_1}{p} - \left(\frac{w}{p}\right)u_{11}\frac{T-L}{p} + u_{12}\frac{T-L}{p}$$

Since $u_{11}\left(\dfrac{w}{p}\right)^2 - 2u_{12}\left(\dfrac{w}{p}\right) + u_{22} < 0$ by the standard second order condition,

$\dfrac{dL}{dw} > 0$ if, and only if, $\dfrac{u_1}{p} + \left(\dfrac{w}{p}\right)u_{11}\dfrac{T-L}{p} - u_{12}\dfrac{T-L}{p} < 0$, that is, these expressions are equivalent to one another. Simplifying the latter, we obtain

$$\frac{-\left(\dfrac{w}{p}\right)u_{11}\dfrac{T-L}{p} + u_{12}\dfrac{T-L}{p}}{\dfrac{u_1}{p}} > 1, \text{ or,}$$

$$(T-L)\frac{-\left(\dfrac{w}{p}\right)u_{11} + u_{12}}{u_1} > 1, \text{ or,}$$

$$\frac{\partial}{\partial L}Log(u_1) > \frac{1}{T-L} = -\frac{\partial}{\partial L}Log(T-L), \text{ or,}$$

$$\frac{\partial}{\partial L}Log(u_1) + \frac{\partial}{\partial L}Log(T-L) > 0, \text{ or,}$$

$$\frac{\partial}{\partial L} Log(u_1(T-L)) > 0.$$

Since the logarithm is increasing, this is equivalent to $u_1(T-L)$ being an increasing function of L. That is, L rises with an increase in wages, and hours worked falls, if the marginal utility of goods times the hours worked is an increasing function of L, holding constant everything else, but evaluated at the optimal values. The value u_1 is the marginal value of an additional good, while the value T-L is the hours worked. Thus, in particular, if goods and leisure are substitutes, so that an increase in L decreases the marginal value of goods, then an increase in the wage must decrease leisure, and labor supply increases in the wage. The case where the goods are complements holds a hope for a decreasing labor supply, so we consider first the extreme case of complements.

Example (perfect complements): $u(x, L)$= Min $\{x, L\}$

In this case, the consumer will make consumption and leisure equal to maximize the utility, so

$$\frac{M + w(T - L^*)}{p} = L*$$

or

$$L* = \frac{\dfrac{M + wT}{p}}{1 + \dfrac{w}{p}} = \frac{M + wT}{p + w}.$$

Thus, L is increasing in the wage if pT>M, that is, if M is sufficiently small that one can't buy all one's needs and not work at all. (This is the only reasonable case for this utility function.) With strong complements between goods and leisure, an increase in the wage induces fewer hours worked.

Example (Cobb-Douglas): $h(L) = \left(\dfrac{M + w(T - L)}{p}\right)^{\alpha} L^{1-\alpha}.$

The first order condition gives

$$0 = h'(L) = -\alpha\left(\frac{M + w(T - L)}{p}\right)^{\alpha-1} L^{1-\alpha}\frac{w}{p} + (1-\alpha)\left(\frac{M + w(T - L)}{p}\right)^{\alpha} L^{-\alpha}$$

or

$$\alpha L \frac{w}{p} = (1-\alpha)\frac{M + w(T-L)}{p}$$

$$\frac{w}{p} L = (1-\alpha)\frac{M + wT}{p}$$

$$\text{or } L = (1-\alpha)\left(\frac{M}{w} + T\right)$$

If M is high enough, the consumer doesn't work but takes $L=T$; otherwise, the equation gives the leisure, and labor supply is given by

$$T - L = Max\left\{0, \alpha T - (1-\alpha)\left(M/w\right)\right\}$$

Labor supply increases with the wage, no matter how high the wage goes.

5.2.2.1 (Exercise)   Show that an increase in the wage increases the consumption of goods, that is, x increases when the wage increases.

The wage affects not just the price of leisure, but also the income level; this makes it possible that the income effect of a wage increase dominates the substitution effect. Moreover, we saw that this is more likely when the consumption of goods takes time, that is, the goods and leisure are complements.

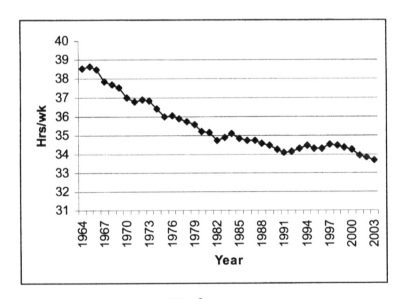

Figure 5-15: Hours per Week

As a practical matter, for most developed nations, increases in wages are associated with fewer hours worked. The average workweek prior to 1950 was 55 hours, which fell to 40 hours by the mid-1950s. The workweek has gradually declined since then, as Figure 5-15 illustrates.

Thought Question: Does a bequest motive – the desire to give money to others – change the likelihood that goods and leisure are complements?

5.2.3 Compensating Differentials

A number of physicists have changed careers, to become researchers in finance or financial economics. Research in finance pays substantially better than research in physics, and yet requires many of the same mathematical skills like stochastic calculus. Physicists who see their former colleagues driving Porsches and buying summer houses are understandably annoyed that finance research – which is intellectually no more difficult or challenging than physics – pays so much better. Indeed, some physicists say that other fields – finance, economics, and law – "shouldn't" pay more than physics.

The difference in income between physics researchers and finance researchers is an example of a *compensating differential*. A compensating differential is income or costs that equalize different choices. There are individuals who could become either physicists or finance researchers. At equal income, too many choose physics and too few choose finance, in the sense that there is a surplus of physicists, and a shortage of finance researchers. Finance salaries must exceed physics salaries in order to induce some of the researchers capable of doing either one to switch to finance, which compensates those individuals for doing the less desirable task.

Jobs that are dangerous or unpleasant must pay more than jobs requiring similar skills but without the bad attributes. Thus, oil field workers in Alaska's North Slope, well above the Arctic Circle, earn a premium over workers in similar jobs in Houston, Texas. The premium – or differential pay – must be such that the marginal worker is indifferent between the two choices – the extra pay compensates the worker for the adverse working conditions. This is why it is known in economics jargon by the phrase of a *compensating* differential.

The high salaries earned by professional basketball players are not compensating differentials. These salaries are not created by a need to induce tall people to choose basketball over alternative jobs like painting ceilings, but instead are payments that reflect the rarity of the skills and abilities involved. Compensating differentials are determined by alternatives, not by direct scarcity. Professional basketball players are well-paid for the same reason that Picasso's paintings are expensive: there aren't very many of them relative to demand.

A compensating differential is a feature of other choices as well as career choices. For example, many people would like to live in California, for its weather and scenic beauty. Given the desirability of California over, say, Lincoln, Nebraska or Rochester, New York, there must be a compensating differential for living in Rochester, and two significant ones are air quality and housing prices. Air quality worsens as populations rise, thus tending to create a compensating differential. In addition, the increase in housing prices also tends to compensate – housing is inexpensive in Rochester, at least compared to California.[53]

---

[53] There are other compensations besides housing to living in Rochester – cross-country skiing, proximity to mountains and lakes. Generally employment is only a temporary factor that might compensate,

Housing prices also compensate for location within a city. For most people, it is more convenient – both in commuting time and for services – to be located near the central business district than in the outlying suburbs. The main compensating differentials are school quality, crime rates, and housing prices. We can illustrate the ideas with a simple model of a city.

5.2.4 Urban Real Estate Prices

An important point to understand is that the good in limited supply in cities is not physical structures like houses, but the land on which the houses sit. The cost of building a house in Los Angeles is quite similar to the cost of building a house in Rochester, New York. The big difference is the price of land. A $1 million house in Los Angeles might be a $400,000 house sitting on a $600,000 parcel of land. The same house in Rochester might be $500,000 – a $400,000 house on a $100,000 parcel of land.

Usually, land is what fluctuates in value, rather than the price of the house that sits on the land. When the newspaper reports that house prices rose, in fact what rose was land prices, for the price of housing has changed only at a slow pace, reflecting increased wages of house builders and changes in the price of lumber and other inputs. These do change, but historically the changes have been small compared to the price of land.

We can construct a simple model of a city to illustrate the determination of land prices. Suppose the city is constructed in a flat plane. People work at the origin (0,0). This simplifying assumption is intended to capture the fact that a relatively small, central portion of most cities involves business, with a large area given over to housing. The assumption is extreme, but not unreasonable as a description of some cities.

Suppose commuting times are proportional to distance from the origin. Let $c(t)$ be the cost to the person of a commute of time t, and let the time taken be $t = \lambda r$, where r is the distance. The function c should reflect both the transportation costs and the value of time lost. The parameter λ accounts for the inverse of the speed in commuting, with a higher λ indicating slower commuting. In addition, we assume that people occupy a constant amount of land. This assumption is clearly wrong empirically, and we will consider making house size a choice variable later.

A person choosing a house priced at $p(r)$ at distance r thus pays $c(\lambda r) + p(r)$ for the combination of housing and transportation. People will choose the lowest cost alternative. If people have identical preferences about housing and commuting, then house prices p will depend on distance, and will be determined by $c(\lambda r) + p(r)$ equal to a constant, so that people are indifferent to the distance from the city center – decreased commute time is exactly compensated by increased house prices.

---

because employment tends to be mobile, too, and move to the location the workers prefer, when that is possible. It is not possible on Alaska's North Slope.

The remaining piece of the model is to figure out the constant. To do this, we need to figure out the area of the city. If the total population is N, and people occupy an area of one per person, the city size r_{max} satisfies $N = \pi r_{max}^2$, and thus

$$r_{max} = \sqrt{\frac{N}{\pi}}$$

At the edge of the city, the value of land is given by some other use, like agriculture. From the perspective of the determinant of the city's prices, this value is approximately constant. As the city takes more land, the change in agricultural land is a very small portion of the total land used for agriculture. Let the value of agricultural land be v per housing unit size. Then the price of housing $p(r_{max}) = v$, because that is the value of land at the edge of the city. This lets us compute the price of all housing in the city:

$$c(\lambda r) + p(r) = c(\lambda r_{max}) + p(r_{max}) = c(\lambda r_{max}) + v = c\left(\lambda \sqrt{\frac{N}{\pi}}\right) + v$$

or

$$p(r) = c\left(\lambda \sqrt{\frac{N}{\pi}}\right) + v - c(\lambda r) \ .$$

This equation produces housing prices like those illustrated in Figure 5-16, where the peak is the city center. The height of the figure indicates the price of housing.

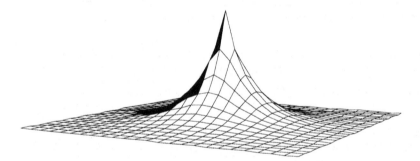

Figure 5-16: House Price Gradient

It is straightforward to verify that house prices increase in the population N and the commuting time parameter λ, as one would expect. To quantify the predictions, we consider a city with a population of 1,000,000, a population density of 10,000 per square mile, and an agricultural use value of $6 million per square mile. To translate these assumptions into the model's structure, first note that a population density of 10,000 per square mile creates a fictitious "unit of measure" of about 52.8 feet, which we'll call a purlong, so that there is one person per square purlong (2788 square feet). Then the agricultural value of a property is $v = \$600$ per square purlong. Note that this density requires a city of radius r_{max} equal to 564 purlongs, which is 5.64 miles.

The only remaining structure to identify in the model is the commuting cost c. To simplify the calculations, let c be linear. Suppose that the daily cost of commuting is $2 per mile (roundtrip), so that the present value of daily commuting costs in perpetuity is about $10,000 per mile.[54] This translates into a cost of commuting of $100.00 per purlong. Thus, we obtain

$$p(r) = c\left(\lambda\sqrt{\frac{N}{\pi}}\right) + \upsilon - c(\lambda r) = \$100\left(\sqrt{\frac{N}{\pi}} - r\right) + \$600 = \$57,000 - \$100r .$$

Thus, the same 2788 square foot property at the city edge sells for $600, versus $57,000 less than six miles away at the city center. With reasonable parameters, this model readily creates dramatic differences in land prices, based purely on commuting time.

As constructed, a quadrupling of population approximately doubles the price of land in the central city. This probably understates the change, since a doubling of the population would likely increase road congestion, increasing λ and further increasing the price of central city real estate.

As presented, the model contains three major unrealistic assumptions. First, everyone lives in an identically-sized piece of land. In fact, however, the amount of land used tends to fall as prices rise. At $53 per square foot, most of us buy a lot less land than at twenty cents per square foot. As a practical matter, the reduction of land per capita is accomplished both through smaller housing units and through taller buildings, which produce more housing floor space per acre of land. Second, people have distinct preferences, and the disutility of commuting, as well as the value of increased space, vary with the individual. Third, congestion levels are generally endogenous – the more people that live between two points, the greater the traffic density and consequently the lower the level of λ. The first two problems arise because of the simplistic nature of consumer preferences embedded in the model, while the third is an equilibrium issue requiring consideration of transportation choices.

This model can readily be extended to incorporate different types of people, different housing sizes, and endogenous congestion. To illustrate such generalizations, consider making the housing size endogenous. Suppose preferences are represented by the utility function:

$$u = H^\alpha - \lambda r - p(r)H ,$$

where H is the house size that the person chooses, and r is the distance they choose. This adaptation of the model reflects two issues. First, the transport cost has been set to be linear in distance, for simplicity. Second, the marginal value of housing decreases in the house size, but the value of housing doesn't depend on distance from the center. For

---

[54] Figure 250 working days per year, for an annual cost of about $500 per mile, yielding a present value at 5% interest of $10,000. See Section 4.3.1. With a time value of $25 per hour, and an average speed of 40 mph (1.5 minutes per mile), the time cost is 62.5 cents per minute. Automobile costs (gas, car depreciation, insurance) are about 35-40 cents per mile. Thus the total is around $1 per mile, which doubles with roundtrips.

these preferences to make sense, $\alpha<1$ (otherwise either zero or an infinite house size emerges). A person with these preferences optimally would choose a house size of

$$H = \left(\frac{\alpha}{p(r)}\right)^{\frac{1}{1-\alpha}}$$

resulting in utility

$$u^* = \left(\alpha^{\frac{\alpha}{1-\alpha}} - \alpha^{\frac{1}{1-\alpha}}\right) p(r)^{\frac{-\alpha}{1-\alpha}} - \lambda r$$

Utility at every location is constant, so $\left(\dfrac{\alpha^{\frac{\alpha}{1-\alpha}} - \alpha^{\frac{1}{1-\alpha}}}{u^* + \lambda r}\right)^{\frac{1-\alpha}{\alpha}} = p(r)$.

A valuable attribute of the form of the equation for p is that the general form depends on the equilibrium values only through the single number u^*. This functional form produces the same qualitative shapes as in Figure 5-16. Using the form, we can solve for the housing size H.

$$H(r) = \left(\frac{\alpha}{p(r)}\right)^{\frac{1}{1-\alpha}} = \alpha^{\frac{1}{1-\alpha}} \left(\frac{u^* + \lambda r}{\alpha^{\frac{\alpha}{1-\alpha}} - \alpha^{\frac{1}{1-\alpha}}}\right)^{\frac{1}{\alpha}} = \left(\frac{u^* + \lambda r}{\alpha^{-1} - 1}\right)^{\frac{1}{\alpha}} = \left(\frac{\alpha}{1-\alpha}(u^* + \lambda r)\right)^{\frac{1}{\alpha}}.$$

The space in the interval $[r, r+\Delta]$ is $\pi(2r\Delta+\Delta^2)$. In this interval, there are approximately

$$\frac{\pi(2r\Delta + \Delta^2)}{H(r)} = \pi(2r\Delta + \Delta^2)\left(\frac{1-\alpha}{\alpha(u^* + \lambda r)}\right)^{\frac{1}{\alpha}}$$ people. Thus, the number of people within r_{max}

of the city center is

$$\int_0^{r_{max}} 2\pi r \left(\frac{1-\alpha}{\alpha(u^* + \lambda r)}\right)^{\frac{1}{\alpha}} dr = N$$

This equation, when combined with the value of land on the periphery:

$$v = p(r_{max}) = \left(\frac{\alpha^{\frac{\alpha}{1-\alpha}} - \alpha^{\frac{1}{1-\alpha}}}{u^* + \lambda r_{max}} \right)^{\frac{1-\alpha}{\alpha}}$$

jointly determine r_{max} and u^*.

5.2.4.1 (Exercise)   For the case of $\alpha = \frac{1}{2}$, solve for the equilibrium values of u^* and r_{max}.

When different people have different preferences, the people with the highest disutility of commuting will tend to live closer to the city center. These tend to be people with the highest wages, since one of the costs of commuting is time that could have been spent working.

5.2.5 Dynamic Choice

The consumption of goods doesn't take place in a single instance, but over time. How does time enter into choice? We're going to simplify the problem a bit, and focus only on consumption and set aside working for the time being. Let x_1 be consumption in the first period, x_2 in the second period. Suppose the value of consumption is the same in each period, so that

$$u(x_1, x_2) = v(x_1) + \delta v(x_2),$$

where δ is called the rate of "pure" time preference. The consumer is expected to have income M_1 in the first period and M_2 in the second. There is a market for loaning and borrowing, which we assume has a common interest rate r.

The consumer's budget constraint, then, can be written

$$(1+r)(M_1 - x_1) = x_2 - M_2.$$

This equation says that the net savings in period 1, plus the interest on the net savings in period 1 equals the net expenditure in period 2. This is because whatever is saved in period 1 earns interest and can then be spent in period 2; alternatively, whatever is borrowed in period 1 must be paid back with interest in period 2. Rewriting the constraint:

$$(1+r)x_1 + x_2 = (1+r)M_1 + M_2.$$

This equation is known as the *intertemporal budget constraint*. It has two immediate consequences. First, $1+r$ is the price of period 2 consumption in terms of period 1 consumption. Thus, the interest rate gives the relative prices. Second, the relevant income is "permanent income" rather than "current income." That is, a change in incomes that leaves the present value of income the same should have no effect on the choice of consumption.

Once again, as with the labor supply, a change in the interest rate affects not just the price of consumption, but also the budget for consumption. Put another way, an increase in the interest rate represents an increase in budget for net savers, but a decrease in budget for net borrowers.

As always, we rewrite the optimization problem to eliminate one of the variables, to obtain

$$u = v(x_1) + \delta v\big((1+r)(M_1 - x_1) + M_2\big)$$

Thus the first order conditions yield

$$0 = v'(x_1) - (1+r)\delta v'(x_2)$$

This condition says that the marginal value of consumption in period 1, $v'(x_1)$, equals the marginal value of consumption in period 2, $\delta v'(x_2)$, times the interest factor. That is, the marginal present values are equated. Note that the consumer's private time preference, δ, need not be related to the interest rate. If the consumer values period 1 consumption more than does the market, so $\delta(1+r) < 1$, then $v'(x_1) < v'(x_2)$, that is, the consumer consumes more in period 1 than in period 2.[55] Similarly, if the consumer's discount of future consumption is exactly equal to the market discount, $\delta(1+r) = 1$, the consumer will consume the same amount in both periods. Finally, if the consumer values period 1 consumption less than the market, $\delta(1+r) > 1$, the consumer will consume more in period 2. In this case, the consumer is more patient than the market.

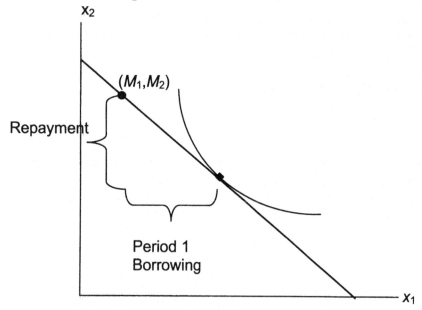

Figure 5-17: Borrowing and Lending

---

[55] As usual, we are assuming that utility is concave, which in this instance means the second derivative of v is negative, which means the derivative of v is decreasing. In addition, to insure an interior solution, it is useful to require the *Inada* conditions: $v'(0) = \infty,\ v'(\infty) = 0$.

Whether the consumer is a net lender or borrower depends not just on the preference for earlier versus later consumption, but also on incomes. This is illustrated in Figure 5-17. In this figure, the consumer's income mostly comes in the second period. As a consequence, the consumer borrows in the first period, and repays in the second period.

The effect of an interest rate increase is to pivot the budget constraint around the point (M_1, M_2). Note that this point is *always* feasible – that is, it is feasible to consume one's own endowment. The effect of an increase in the interest rate is going to depend on whether the consumer is a borrower or a lender. As Figure 5-18 illustrates, the net borrower borrows less in the first period – the price of first period consumption has risen and the borrower's wealth has fallen. It is not clear whether the borrower consumes less in the second period because the price of second period consumption has fallen even though wealth has fallen, too, two conflicting effects.

An increase in interest rates is a benefit to a net lender. The lender has more income, and the price of period 2 consumption has fallen. Thus the lender must consume more in the second period, but only consumes more in the first period (lends less) if the income effect outweighs the substitution effect. This is illustrated in Figure 5-19.

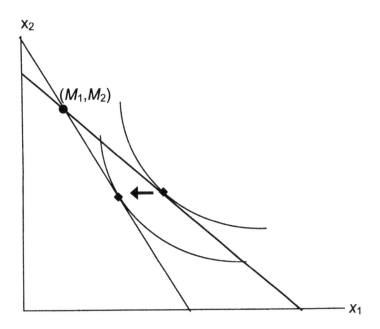

Figure 5-18: Interest Rate Change

The government from time to time will rebate a portion of taxes to "stimulate" the economy. An important aspect of the effects of such a tax rebate is the effect to which consumers will spend the rebate, versus savings the rebate, because the stimulative effects of spending are thought to be larger than the stimulative effects of savings.[56] The

---

[56] This belief shouldn't be accepted as necessarily true; it was based on a model that has since been widely rejected by the majority of economists. The general idea is that spending creates demand for goods, thus

theory suggests how people will react to a "one-time" or transitory tax rebate, compared to a permanent lowering of taxes. In particular, the budget constraint for the consumer spreads lifetime income over the lifetime. Thus, for an average consumer that might spend a present value of $750,000 over a lifetime, a $1,000 rebate is small potatoes. On the other hand, a $1,000/year reduction is worth $20,000 or so over the lifetime, which should have twenty times the effect of the transitory change on the current expenditure.

Tax rebates are not the only way we receive one-time payments. Money can be found, or lost, and we can have unexpected costs or windfall gifts. From an intertemporal budget constraint perspective, these transitory effects have little significance, and thus the theory suggests people shouldn't spend much of a windfall gain in the current year, nor cut back significantly when they have a moderately-sized unexpected cost.

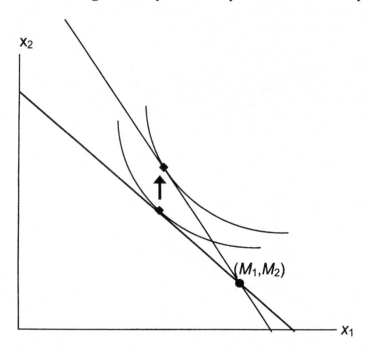

Figure 5-19: Interest Rate Increase on Lenders

As a practical matter, most individuals can't borrow at the same rate at which they lend. Many students borrow on credit cards at very high interest rates, and obtain a fraction of that in interest on savings. That is to say, borrowers and lenders face different interest rates. This situation is readily explored with a diagram like Figure 5-20. The cost of a first period loan is a relatively high loss of x_2, and similarly the value of first period savings is a much more modest increase in second period consumption. Such effects tend to favor "neither a borrower nor a lender be," as Shakespeare recommends, although it is still possible for the consumer to optimally borrow in the first period (e.g. if $M_1=0$) or in the second period (if M_2 is small relative to M_1).

---

encouraging business investment in production. However, savings encourage investment by producing loanable funds, so it isn't at all obvious whether spending or savings have a larger effect.

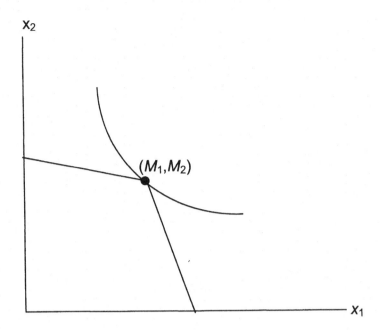

Figure 5-20: Different Rates for Borrowing and Lending

Differences in interest rates causes transitory changes in income to have much larger effects than the intertemporal budget constraint would suggest, and may go a long way to explaining why people don't save much of a windfall gain, and suffer a lot temporarily, rather than a little for a long time, when they have unexpected expenses. This is illustrated in Figure 5-21.

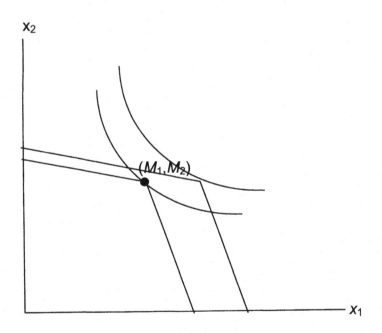

Figure 5-21: The Effect of a Transitory Income Increase

5.2.6 Risk

There are many risks in life, even if one doesn't add to these risks by intentionally buying lottery tickets. Gasoline prices go up and down, the demand for people trained in your major fluctuates, house prices change. How do people value gambles? The starting point for the investigation is the *von Neumann-Morgenstern* utility function. The idea of a von Neumann-Morgenstern utility function for a given person is that for each possible outcome x, there is a value $v(x)$ assigned by the person, and the average value of v is the value the person assigns to the risky outcome. This is a "state of the world" approach, in the sense that each of the outcomes is associated with a state of the world, and the person maximizes the expected value of the various possible states of the world. Value here doesn't mean a money value, but a psychic value or utility.

To illustrate the assumption, consider equal probabilities of winning $100 and winning $200. The expected outcome of this gamble is $150 – the average of $100 and $200. However, the expected value of the outcome could be anything between the value of $100 and the value of $200. The von Neumann-Morgenstern utility is $\frac{1}{2}v(\$100) + \frac{1}{2}v(\$200)$.

The von Neumann-Morgenstern formulation has certain advantages, including the logic that what matters is the average value of the outcome. On the other hand, in many tests, people behave in ways not consistent with the theory.[57] Nevertheless, the von Neumann approach is the prevailing model of behavior under risk.

To introduce the theory, we will consider only money outcomes, and mostly the case of two money outcomes. The person has a Neumann-Morgenstern utility function v of these outcomes. If the possible outcomes are $x_1, x_2, \ldots, x_n$ and these occur with probability $\pi_1, \pi_2, \ldots, \pi_n$ respectively, the consumer's utility is

$$u = \pi_1 v(x_1) + \pi_2 v(x_2) + \ldots + \pi_n v(x_n) = \sum_{i=1}^{n} \pi_i v(x_i)$$

This is the meaning of "having a von Neumann-Morgenstern utility function" – that utility can be written in this weighted sum form.

The first insight that flows from this definition is that a individual dislikes risk if v is concave. To see this, note that the definition of concavity posits that v is concave if, for all π in [0,1], and all values x_1 and x_2,

$$v(\pi x_1 + (1-\pi)x_2) \geq \pi v(x_1) + (1-\pi)v(x_2)$$

For smoothly differentiable functions, concavity is equivalent to a second derivative that is not positive. Using induction, the definition of concavity can be generalized to show:

---

[57] For example, people tend to react more strongly to very unlikely events than is consistent with the theory.

$$v(\pi_1 x_1 + \pi_2 x_2 + \ldots + \pi_n x_n) \geq \pi_1 v(x_1) + \pi_2 v(x_2) + \ldots + \pi_n v(x_n)$$

That is, a consumer with concave value function prefers the average outcome to the random outcome. This is illustrated in Figure 5-22. There are two possible outcomes, x_1 and x_2. The value x_1 occurs with probability π and x_2 with probability $1-\pi$. This means the average or expected outcome is $\pi x_1 + (1-\pi)x_2$. The value $v(\pi x_1 + (1-\pi)x_2)$ is the value at the expected outcome $\pi x_1 + (1-\pi)x_2$, while $\pi v(x_1) + (1-\pi)v(x_2)$ is the average of the value of the outcome. As is plainly visible in the picture, concavity makes the average outcome preferable to the random outcome. People with concave von Neumann-Morganstern utility functions are known as *risk averse* people.

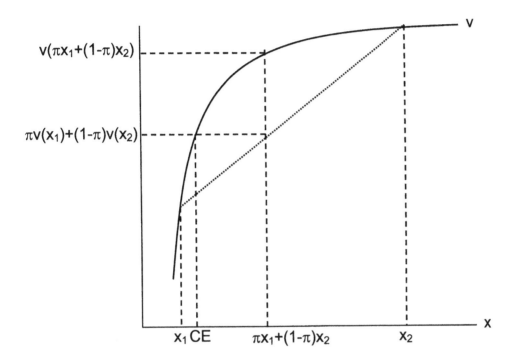

Figure 5-22: Expected Utility and Certainty Equivalents

A useful concept is the *certainty equivalent* of a gamble. The certainty equivalent is an amount of money that provides equal utility to the random payoff of the gamble. The certainty equivalent is labeled *CE* in the diagram. Note that CE is less than the expected outcome, if the person is risk averse. This is because risk averse individuals prefer the expected outcome to the risky outcome.

The *risk premium* is defined to be the difference between the expected payoff (in the graph, this is expressed as $\pi x_1 + (1 - \pi)x_2$) and the certainty equivalent. This is the cost of risk – it is the amount of money an individual would be willing to pay to avoid risk. This means as well that the risk premium is the value of insurance. How does the risk premium of a given gamble change when the base wealth is increased? It can be shown that the risk premium falls as wealth increases for any gamble if, and only if,[58]

---

[58] R. Preston McAfee and Daniel Vincent, The Price Decline Anomaly, *Journal of Economic Theory 60*, June, 1993, 191-212.

$-\dfrac{v''(x)}{v'(x)}$ is decreasing.

The measure $\rho(x) = -\dfrac{v''(x)}{v'(x)}$ is known as the Arrow-Pratt[59] measure of risk aversion, and also as the measure of absolute risk aversion. To get an idea why this measure matters, consider a quadratic approximation to v. Let μ be the expected value and σ^2 be the expected value of $(x - \mu)^2$. Then we can approximate $v(CE)$ two different ways.

$$v(\mu) + v'(\mu)(CE - \mu) \approx v(CE) = E\{v(x)\} \approx E\{v(\mu) + v'(\mu)(x - \mu) + \tfrac{1}{2}v''(\mu)(x - \mu)^2\},$$

thus

$$v(\mu) + v'(\mu)(CE - \mu) \approx E\{v(\mu) + v'(\mu)(x - \mu) + \tfrac{1}{2}v''(\mu)(x - \mu)^2\}.$$

Canceling $v(\mu)$ from both sides and noting that the average value of x is μ, so $E(x-\mu)=0$, we have

$$v'(\mu)(CE - \mu) \approx \tfrac{1}{2}v''(\mu)\sigma^2 .$$

Then, dividing by $v'(x)$,

$$\mu - CE \approx -\tfrac{1}{2}\frac{v''(\mu)}{v'(\mu)}\sigma^2 = \tfrac{1}{2}\rho(\mu)\sigma^2 .$$

That is, the risk premium, the difference between the average outcome and the certainty equivalent, is approximately equal to the Arrow-Pratt measure, times half the variance, at least when the variance is small.

5.2.6.1 (Exercise)   Use a quadratic approximation on both sides to sharpen the estimate of the risk premium. First, note

$$v(\mu) + v'(\mu)(CE - \mu) + \tfrac{1}{2}v''(\mu)(CE - \mu)^2 \approx v(CE)$$
$$= E\{v(x)\} \approx E\{v(\mu) + v'(\mu)(x - \mu) + \tfrac{1}{2}v''(\mu)(x - \mu)^2\}.$$

Conclude that $\mu - CE \approx \dfrac{1}{\rho}\left(\sqrt{1+\rho^2\sigma^2} - 1\right)$. This approximation is exact to the second order.

The translation of risk into dollars, by way of a risk premium, can be assessed even for large gambles if we are willing to make some technical assumptions. Suppose the utility

---

[59] The measure was named after its discoverers Nobel laureate Kenneth Arrow and John Pratt.

has constant absolute risk aversion or CARA, that is $\rho = -\dfrac{v''(x)}{v'(x)}$ is a constant. This turns out to imply, after setting the utility of zero to zero, that

$$v(x) = \frac{1}{\rho}(1 - e^{-\rho x}).$$

(This formulation is derived by setting $v(0)=0$ handling the case of $\rho=0$ with appropriate limits.) Now also assume that the gamble x is normally distributed with mean μ and variance σ^2. Then the expected value of $v(x)$ is

$$Ev(x) = \frac{1}{\rho}\left(1 - e^{-\rho\left(\mu - \frac{\rho}{2}\sigma^2\right)}\right).$$

It is an immediate result from this formula that the certainty equivalent, with CARA preferences and normal risks, is $\mu - \dfrac{\rho}{2}\sigma^2$. Hence the risk premium of a normal distribution for a CARA individual is $\dfrac{\rho}{2}\sigma^2$. This formulation will appear when we consider agency theory and the challenges of motivating a risk averse employee when outcomes have a substantial random component.

An important aspect of CARA with normally distributed risks is that the preferences of the consumer are linear in the mean of the gamble and the variance. In fact, given a choice of gambles, the consumer selects the one with the highest value of $\mu - \dfrac{\rho}{2}\sigma^2$. Such preferences are often called "mean variance preferences," and they comprise the foundation of modern finance theory.

5.2.6.2 (Exercise)   Suppose $u(x) = x^{0.95}$ for a consumer with a wealth level of \$50,000. Consider a gamble with equal probability of winning \$100 and losing \$100 and compute the risk premium associated with the gamble.

5.2.6.3 (Exercise)   Suppose $u(x) = x^{0.99}$ for a consumer with a wealth level of \$100,000. A lottery ticket costs \$1 and pays \$5,000,000 with the probability $\dfrac{1}{10,000,000}$. Compute the certainty equivalent of the lottery ticket.

5.2.6.4 (Exercise)   The return on U.S. government treasury investments is approximately 3%. Thus, a \$1 investment returns \$1.03 after one year. Treat this return as risk-free. The stock market (S&P 500) returns 7% on average and has a variance that is around 16% (the variance of return on a \$1 investment is \$0.16). Compute the value of ρ for a CARA individual. What is the risk premium associated equal probabilities of a $100 gain or loss given the value of ρ?

5.2.7 Search

In most communities, every Wednesday grocery stores advertise sale prices in a newspaper insert, and these prices vary from week to week. Prices can vary a lot from week to week and from store to store. The price of gasoline varies as much as fifteen cents per gallon in a one mile radius. Decide you want a specific Sony television, and you may see distinct prices at Best Buy, Circuit City, and other electronics retailers. For many goods and services, there is substantial variation in prices, which implies that there are gains for buyers to search for the best price.

The theory of consumer search behavior is just a little bit arcane, but the basic insight will be intuitive enough. The general idea is that, from the perspective of a buyer, the price that is offered is random, and has a probability density function $f(p)$. If a consumer faces a cost of search (e.g. if you have to visit a store, in person, telephonically or virtually, the cost includes your time and any other costs necessary to obtain a price quote), the consumer will set a *reservation price*, which is a maximum price they will pay without visiting another store. That is, if a store offers a price below p^*, the consumer will buy, and otherwise they will visit another store, hoping for a better price.

Call the reservation price p^* and suppose that the cost of search is c. Let $J(p^*)$ represent the expected total cost of purchase (including search costs). Then J must equal

$$J(p^*) = c + \int_0^{p^*} pf(p)dp + \int_{p^*}^{\infty} J(p^*)f(p)dp \, .$$

This equation arises because the current draw (which costs c) could either result in a price less than p^*, in which case observed price, with density f, will determine the price paid p, or the price will be too high, in which case the consumer is going to take another draw, at cost c, and on average get the average price $J(p^*)$. It is useful to introduce the cumulative distribution function F, with $F(x) = \int_0^x f(p)dp$. Note that something has to happen, so $F(\infty)=1$.

We can solve the equality for $J(p^*)$,

$$J(p^*) = \frac{\int_0^{p^*} pf(p)dp + c}{F(p^*)} \, .$$

This expression has a simple interpretation. The expected price $J(p^*)$ is composed of two terms. The first is the expected price, which is $\int_0^{p^*} p\frac{f(p)}{F(p^*)}dp$. This has the interpretation of the average price conditional on that price being less than p^*. This is because $\dfrac{f(p)}{F(p^*)}$ is in fact the density of the random variable which is the price given that

the price is less than p^*. The second term is $\dfrac{c}{F(p^*)}$. This is the expected search costs,

and it arises because $\dfrac{1}{F(p^*)}$ is the expected number of searches. This arises because the odds of getting a price low enough to be acceptable is $F(p^*)$. There is a general statistical property underlying the number of searches. Consider a basketball player who successfully shoots a free throw with probability y. How many throws on average must he throw to sink one basket? The answer is $1/y$. To see this, note that the probability that exactly n throws are required is $(1-y)^{n-1}y$. This is because n are required means $n-1$ must fail (probability $(1-y)^{n-1}$) and then the remaining one go in, with probability y. Thus, the expected number of throws is

$$y + 2(1-y)y + 3(1-y)^2 y + 4(1-y)^3 y + \ldots$$

$$= y(1 + 2(1-y) + 3(1-y)^2 + 4(1-y)^3 + \ldots)$$

$$= y\big((1+(1-y)+(1-y)^2+(1-y)^3+\ldots) + (1-y)(1+(1-y)+(1-y)^2+(1-y)^3+\ldots)$$

$$+ (1-y)^2(1+(1-y)+(1-y)^2+(1-y)^3+\ldots) + (1-y)^3(1+(1-y)+(1-y)^2+\ldots) + \ldots$$

$$= y\left(\frac{1}{y} + (1-y)\frac{1}{y} + (1-y)^2\frac{1}{y} + (1-y)^3\frac{1}{y} + \ldots\right) = \frac{1}{y}.$$

Our problem has the same logic, where a successful basketball throw corresponds to finding a price less than p^*.

The expected total cost of purchase, given a reservation price p^* is given by

$$J(p^*) = \frac{\displaystyle\int_0^{p^*} pf(p)dp + c}{F(p^*)}.$$

But what value of p^* minimizes cost? Let's start by differentiating:

$$J'(p^*) = p^*\frac{f(p^*)}{F(p^*)} - \frac{f(p^*)\displaystyle\int_0^{p^*} pf(p)dp + c}{F(p^*)^2}$$

$$= \frac{f(p^*)}{F(p^*)}\left(p^* - \frac{\int_0^{p^*} pf(p)dp + c}{F(p^*)} \right) = \frac{f(p^*)}{F(p^*)}(p^* - J(p^*)).$$

Thus, if $p^* < J(p^*)$, J is decreasing, and it lowers cost to increase p^*. Similarly, if $p^* > J(p^*)$, J is increasing in p^*, and it reduces cost to decrease p^*. Thus, minimization occurs at a point where $p^* = J(p^*)$.

Moreover, there is only one such solution to the equation $p^* = J(p^*)$ in the range where f is positive. To see this, note that at any solution to the equation $p^* = J(p^*)$, $J'(p^*) = 0$ and

$$J''(p^*) = \frac{d}{dp^*}\left(\frac{f(p^*)}{F(p^*)}(p^* - J(p^*)) \right)$$

$$= \left(\frac{d}{dp^*} \frac{f(p^*)}{F(p^*)} \right)(p^* - J(p^*)) + \frac{f(p^*)}{F(p^*)}(1 - J'(p^*)) = \frac{f(p^*)}{F(p^*)} > 0.$$

This means that J takes a minimum at this value, since its first derivative is zero and its second derivative is positive, and that is true about any solution to $p^* = J(p^*)$. Were there to be two such solutions, J' would have to be both positive and negative on the interval between them, since J is increasing to the right of the first (lower) one, and decreasing to the left of the second (higher) one. Consequently, the equation $p^* = J(p^*)$ has a unique solution that minimizes the cost of purchase.

Consumer search to minimize cost dictates setting a reservation price equal to the expected total cost of purchasing the good, and purchasing whenever the price offered is lower than that level. That is, it is not sensible to "hold out" for a price lower than what you expect to pay on average, although this might be well useful in a bargaining context rather than in a store searching context.

Example (Uniform): Suppose prices are uniformly distributed on the interval $[a,b]$. For p^* in this interval,

$$J(p^*) = \frac{\int_0^{p^*} pf(p)dp + c}{F(p^*)} = \frac{\int_a^{p^*} p\frac{dp}{b-a} + c}{\frac{p^* - a}{b-a}}$$

$$= \frac{\frac{1}{2}(p^{*2} - a^2) + c(b-a)}{p^* - a} = \frac{1}{2}(p^* + a) + \frac{c(b-a)}{p^* - a}.$$

Thus, the first order condition for minimizing cost is

$$0 = J'(p^*) = \frac{1}{2} - \frac{c(b-a)}{(p^*-a)^2}, \text{ implying } p^* = a + \sqrt{2c(b-a)}.$$

There are a couple of interesting observations about this solution. First, not surprisingly, as $c \to 0$, $p^* \to a$, that is, as the search costs go to zero, one holds out for the lowest possible price. This is sensible in the context of the model, but in the real search situations delay may also have a cost that isn't modeled here. Second, $p^* < b$, the maximum price, if $2c < (b-a)$. Put another way, if the *most* you can save by a search is twice the search cost, don't search, because the expected gains from search will be half the maximum gains (thanks to the uniform distribution) and the search unprofitable.

The third observation, which is much more general than the specific uniform example, is that the expected price is a concave function of the cost of search (second derivative negative). That is in fact true for any distribution. To see this, define a function

$$H(c) = \min_{p^*} J(p^*) = \min_{p^*} \frac{\int_0^{p^*} pf(p)dp + c}{F(p^*)}.$$

Since $J'(p^*) = 0$,

$$H'(c) = \frac{\partial}{\partial c} J(p^*) = \frac{1}{F(p^*)}.$$

It then needs only a modest effort to show p^* is increasing in c, from which it follows that H is concave. This means that the effects of an increase in c are passed on at a decreasing rate. Moreover, it means that a consumer should rationally be risk averse about the cost of search.

5.2.7.1 (Exercise)   Suppose that there are two possible prices, 1 and 2, and that the probability of the lower price 1 is x. Compute the consumer's reservation price, which is the expected cost of searching, as a function of x and the cost of search c. For what values of x and c should the consumer accept 2 on the first search, or continue searching until the lower price 1 is found?

5.2.8 Edgeworth Box

The Edgeworth[60] box considers a two person, two good "exchange economy." That is, two people have utility functions of two goods and endowments (initial allocations) of the two goods. The Edgeworth box is a graphical representation of the exchange problem facing these people, and also permits a straightforward solution to their exchange problem.

---

[60] Francis Edgeworth, 1845-1926, introduced a variety of mathematical tools including calculus for considering economics and political issues, and was certainly among the first to use advanced mathematics for studying ethical problems.

The Edgeworth box is represented in Figure 5-23. Person 1 is "located" in the lower left (southwest) corner, and person 2 in the upper right (northeast). The X good is given on the horizontal axis, the Y good on the vertical. The distance between them is the total amount of the good they have between them. A point in the box gives the allocation of the good – the distance to the lower left to person 1, remainder to person 2. Thus, for the point illustrated, person 1 obtains (x_1, y_1), and person 2 obtains (x_2, y_2). The total amount of each good available to the two people will be fixed.

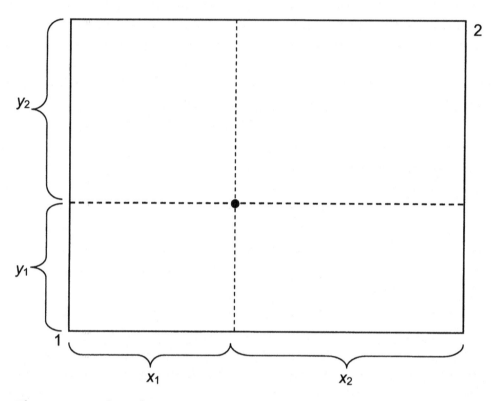

Figure 5-23: The Edgeworth Box

What points are efficient? The economic notion of efficiency is that an allocation is efficient if it is impossible to make one person better off without harming the other, that is, the only way to improve 1's utility is to harm 2, and vice versa. Otherwise, if the consumption is inefficient, there is a re-arrangement that makes both parties better off, and the parties should prefer such a point. Now, there is no sense of fairness embedded in the notion, and there is an efficient point in which one person gets everything and the other nothing. That might be very unfair, but it could still be the case that improving 2 must necessarily harm 1. The allocation is efficient if there is no waste or slack in the system, even if it is wildly unfair. To distinguish this economic notion, it is sometimes called *Pareto Efficiency*.[61]

We can find the Pareto-efficient points by fixing person 1's utility and then asking what point, on the indifference isoquant of person 1, maximizes person 2's utility? At that

---

[61] Vilfredo Pareto, 1848-1923, was a pioneer in replacing concepts of utility with abstract preferences, which was later adopted by the economics profession and remains the modern approach.

point, any increase in person 2's utility must come at the expense of person 1, and vice versa, that is, the point is Pareto-efficient. An example is illustrated in Figure 5-24.

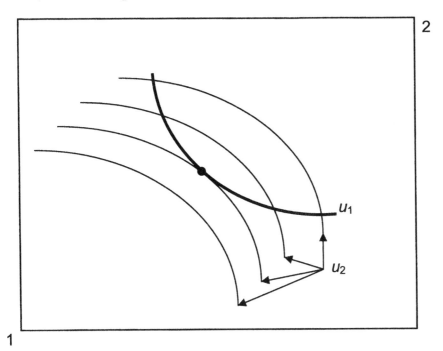

Figure 5-24: An Efficient Point

In Figure 5-24, the isoquant of person 1 is drawn with a dark thick line. This utility level is fixed. It acts like the "budget constraint" for person 2. Note that person 2's isoquants face the opposite way because a movement southwest is good for 2, since it gives him more of both goods. Four isoquants are graphed for person 2, and the highest feasible isoquant, which leaves person 1 getting the fixed utility, has the Pareto-efficient point illustrated with a large dot. Such points occur at tangencies of the isoquants.

This process, of identifying the points that are Pareto-efficient, can be carried out for every possible utility level for person 1. What results is the set of Pareto-efficient points, and this set is also known as the *contract curve*. This is illustrated with the thick line in Figure 5-25. Every point on this curve maximizes one person's utility given the other, and they are characterized by the tangencies in the isoquants.

The contract curve need not have a simple shape, as Figure 5-25 illustrates. The main properties are that it is increasing and goes from person 1 consuming zero of both goods to person 2 consuming zero of both goods.

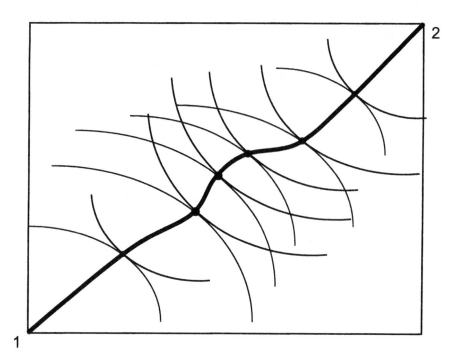

Figure 5-25: The Contract Curve

Example: Suppose both people have Cobb-Douglas utility. Let the total endowment of each good be 1, so that $x_2 = 1 - x_1$. Then person 1's utility can be written as $u_1 = x^\alpha y^{1-\alpha}$, and 2's utility is $u_2 = (1-x)^\beta (1-y)^{1-\beta}$. Then a point is Pareto-efficient if

$$\frac{\alpha y}{(1-\alpha)x} = \frac{\partial u_1 / \partial x}{\partial u_1 / \partial y} = \frac{\partial u_2 / \partial x}{\partial u_2 / \partial y} = \frac{\beta(1-y)}{(1-\beta)(1-x)}.$$

Thus, solving for y, a point is on the contract curve if

$$y = \frac{(1-\alpha)\beta x}{(1-\beta)\alpha + (\beta-\alpha)x} = \frac{x}{\dfrac{(1-\beta)\alpha}{(1-\alpha)\beta} + \dfrac{\beta-\alpha}{(1-\alpha)\beta}x} = \frac{x}{x + \left(\dfrac{(1-\beta)\alpha}{(1-\alpha)\beta}\right)(1-x)}.$$

Thus, the contract curve for the Cobb-Douglas case depends on a single parameter $\dfrac{(1-\beta)\alpha}{(1-\alpha)\beta}$. It is graphed for a variety of examples (α and β) in Figure 5-26.

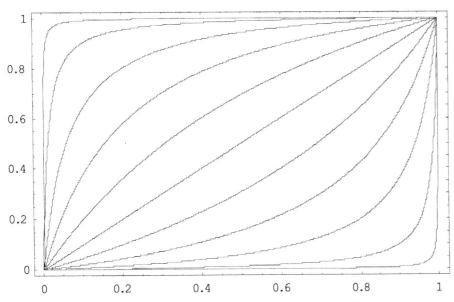

Figure 5-26: Contract Curves with Cobb-Douglas Utility

5.2.8.1 (Exercise)   If two individuals have the same utility function concerning goods, is the contract curve the diagonal? Why or why not?

5.2.8.2 (Exercise)   For two individuals with Cobb-Douglas preferences, when is the contract curve the diagonal?

The contract curve provides the set of efficient points. What point will actually be chosen? Let's start with an endowment of the goods. An endowment is just a point in the Edgeworth box, which gives the initial ownership of both goods for both people. The endowment is marked with a triangle in Figure 5-27. Note that this point gives the endowment of both person 1 and 2, because it shows the shares of each.

Figure 5-27 also shows isoquants for persons 1 and 2 going through the endowment. Note that the isoquant for 1 is concave toward the point labeled 1, and the isoquant for 2 is concave toward the point labeled 2. These utility isoquants define a reservation utility level for each person – the utility they could get alone, without exchange. This "no exchange" state is known as *autarky*. There are a variety of efficient points that give these people at least as much as they get under autarky, and those points are along the contract curve but have a darker line.

In Figure 5-27, starting at the endowment, the utility of both players is increased by moving in the general direction of the southeast, that is, down and to the right, until the contract curve is reached. This involves person 1 getting more X (movement to the right) in exchange for giving up some Y (movement down). Thus, we can view the increase in utility as a trade – 1 trades some of his Y for some of 2's X.

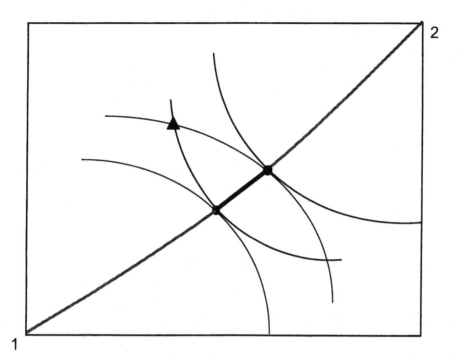

Figure 5-27: Individually Rational Efficient Points

In principle, any of the darker points on the contract curve, which give both people at least as much as they achieve under autarky, might result from trade. The two people get together and agree on exchange that puts them at any point along this segment of the curve, depending on the bargaining skills of the players. But there is a particular point, or possibly a set of points, that result from exchange using a *price system*. A price system involves a specific price for trading Y for X, and vice versa, that is available to both parties. In this diagram, prices define a straight line, whose slope is the negative of the Y for X price (the X for Y price is the reciprocal).

Figure 5-28 illustrates trade with a price system. The O in the center is the point on the contract curve connected to the endowment (triangle) by a straight line (the price line), in such a way that the straight line is tangent to both 1 and 2's isoquants at the contract curve. This construction means that, if each person took the price line as a budget constraint, they would maximize their utility function by choosing the point labeled O.

That a price line that (i) goes through the endowment and (ii) goes through the contract curve at a point tangent to both people's utility exists is relatively easy to show. Consider lines that satisfy property (ii) and let's see if we can find one that goes through the endowment. Start on the contract curve at the point that maximizes 1's utility given 2's reservation utility, and you can easily see that the price line through that point passes above and to the right of the endowment. The similar price line maximizing 2's utility given 1's reservation utility passes below and to the left of the endowment. These price lines are illustrated with dotted lines. Thus, by continuity, somewhere in between is a price line that passes through the endowment.

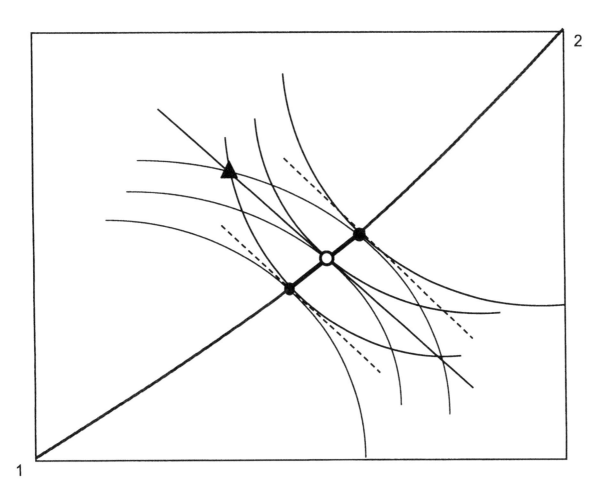

Figure 5-28: Equilibrium with a Price System

The point marked with the O represents an *equilibrium* of the price system, in the sense that supply and demand are equated for both goods. Note that, given the endowment and given the price through the endowment, both parties maximize utility by going to the O. To see this, it may help to consider a version of the picture that only shows person 2's isoquants and the price line.

Figure 5-29 removes player 1's isoquants, leaving only player 2's isoquants and the price line through the endowment. The price line through the endowment is the budget facing each player at that price. Note that, given this budget line, player 2, who gets more the less player 1 gets, maximizes utility at the middle isoquant, given the budget. That is, taking the price as given, player 2 would choose the O given player 2's endowment. The logic for player 1 is analogous. This shows that, if both players believe that they can buy or sell as much as they like at the tradeoff of the price through the O, both will trade to reach the O. This means that, if the players accept the price, a balance of supply and demand emerges. In this sense, we have found an equilibrium price.

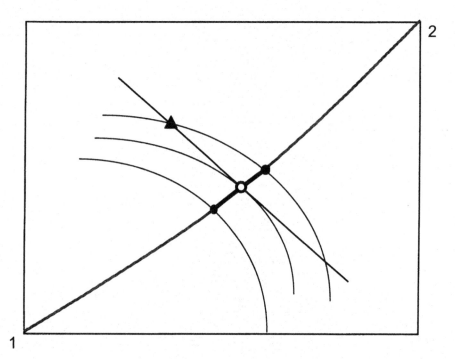

Figure 5-29: Illustration of Price System Equilibrium

In the Edgeworth box, we see that, given an endowment, it is possible to reach some Pareto-efficient point using a price system. Moreover, any point on the contract curve arises from as an equilibrium of the price system for some endowment. The proof of this proposition is startlingly easy. To show that a particular point on the contract curve is an equilibrium for some endowment, just start with an endowment equal to the point on the contract curve. No trade can occur because the starting point is Pareto-efficient – any gain by one party entails a loss by the other.

Furthermore, if a point in the Edgeworth box represents an equilibrium using a price system (that is, if the quantity supplied equals the quantity demanded for both goods), it must be Pareto-efficient. At an equilibrium to the price system, each player's isoquant is tangent to the price line, and hence tangent to each other. This implies the equilibrium is Pareto-efficient.

Two of these three propositions – any equilibrium of the price system is Pareto-efficient, any Pareto-efficient point is an equilibrium of the price system for some endowment, are known as the first and second *welfare theorems* of *general equilibrium*. They have been demonstrated by Nobel laureates Kenneth Arrow and Gerard Debreu, for an arbitrary number of people and goods. They also demonstrated the third proposition, that for any endowment, there exists an equilibrium of the price system, with the same high level of generality.

5.2.9 General Equilibrium

We will illustrate general equilibrium, for the case when all consumers have Cobb-Douglas utility in an exchange economy. An exchange economy is an economy where the supply of each good is just the total endowment of that good and there is no production. Suppose there are N people, indexed by $n = 1, 2, ..., N$. There are G goods, indexed by $g = 1, 2, ..., G$. Person n has Cobb-Douglas utility, which we can represent using exponents $\alpha(n,g)$, so that the utility of person n can be represented as

$\prod_{g=1}^{G} x(n,g)^{\alpha(n,g)}$, where $x(n,g)$ is person n's consumption of good g. Assume that

$\alpha(n,g) \geq 0$ for all n and g, which amounts to assuming that the products are in fact goods. Without any loss of generality, we can require

$$\sum_{g=1}^{G} \alpha(n,g) = 1,$$

for each n. (To see this, note that maximizing the function U is equivalent to maximizing the function U^{β} for any positive β.)

Let $y(n,g)$ be person n's endowment of good g. The goal of general equilibrium is to find prices $p_1, p_2, ..., p_G$ for the goods, in such a way that demand for each good exactly equals supply of the good. The supply of good g is just the sum of the endowments of that good. The prices yield a wealth for person n equal to

$$W_n = \sum_{g=1}^{G} p_g y(n,g).$$

We will assume that $\sum_{n=1}^{N} \alpha(n,g)y(n,i) > 0$ for every pair of goods g and i. This assumption states that for any pair of goods, there is at least one agent that values good g and has an endowment of good i. The assumption insures that there is always someone willing and able to trade if the price is sufficiently attractive. The assumption is much stronger than necessary but useful for exposition. The assumption also insures the endowment of each good is positive.

Cobb-Douglas utility simplifies the analysis because of a feature that we already met in the case of two goods, but which holds in general: the share of wealth for a consumer n on good g equals the exponent $\alpha(n,g)$. Thus, the total demand for good g is

$$X_g = \sum_{n=1}^{N} \frac{\alpha(n,g)W_n}{p_g}.$$

The equilibrium conditions, then, can be expressed as saying supply (sum of the endowments) equals demand, or, for each good g,

$$\sum_{n=1}^{N} y(n,g) = X_g = \sum_{n=1}^{N} \frac{\alpha(n,g)W_n}{p_g}.$$

We can rewrite this expression, provided $p_g > 0$ (and it must be for otherwise demand is infinite), to be

$$p_g - \sum_{i=1}^{G} p_i \frac{\sum_{n=1}^{N} y(n,i)\alpha(n,g)}{\sum_{n=1}^{N} y(n,g)} = 0.$$

Let $\mathbf{B}$ be the $G \times G$ matrix whose (g, i) term is

$$b_{gi} = \frac{\sum_{n=1}^{N} y(n,i)\alpha(n,g)}{\sum_{n=1}^{N} y(n,g)}.$$

Let $\mathbf{p}$ be the vector of prices. Then we can write the equilibrium conditions as

$$(\mathbf{I}-\mathbf{B})\mathbf{p}=\mathbf{o},$$

where $\mathbf{o}$ is the zero vector. Thus, for an equilibrium (other than $\mathbf{p}=\mathbf{o}$) to exist, $\mathbf{B}$ must have an eigenvalue equal to 1, and a corresponding eigenvector $\mathbf{p}$ that is positive in each component. Moreover, if such an eigenvector, eigenvalue pair exists, it is an equilibrium, because demand is equal to supply for each good.

The actual price vector is not completely identified, because if $\mathbf{p}$ is an equilibrium price vector, so is any positive scalar times $\mathbf{p}$. Scaling prices doesn't change the equilibrium because both prices and wealth (which is based on endowments) rise by the scalar factor. Usually economists assign one good to be a numeraire, which means all other goods are indexed in terms of that good, and the numeraire's price is artificially set to be 1. We will treat any scaling of a price vector as the same vector.

The relevant theorem is the Perron-Frobenius theorem.[62] It states that if $\mathbf{B}$ is a positive matrix (each component positive), then there is an eigenvalue $\lambda > 0$ and an associated positive eigenvector $\mathbf{p}$, and moreover λ is the largest (in absolute value) eigenvector of $\mathbf{B}$.[63] This conclusion does most of the work of demonstrating the existence of an

---

[62] Oskar Perron, 1880 - 1975 and Georg Frobenius, 1849 – 1917.

[63] The Perron-Frobenius theorem, as usually stated, only assumes that $\mathbf{B}$ is non-negative and that $\mathbf{B}$ is irreducible. It turns out that a strictly positive matrix is irreducible, so this condition is sufficient to invoke the theorem. In addition, we can still apply the theorem even when $\mathbf{B}$ has some zeros in it, provided that it is irreducible. Irreducibility means that the economy can't be divided into two economies, where the people in one economy can't buy from the people in the second because they aren't endowed with anything the people in the first value. If $\mathbf{B}$ is not irreducible, then some people may wind up consuming zero of things they value.

equilibrium. The only remaining condition to check is that the eigenvalue is in fact 1, so that $(\mathbf{I}-\mathbf{B})\mathbf{p}=\mathbf{0}$.

Suppose the eigenvalue is λ. Then $\lambda\mathbf{p} = \mathbf{Bp}$. Thus for each g,

$$\lambda p_g = \sum_{i=1}^{G} \frac{\displaystyle\sum_{n=1}^{N} \alpha(n,g)y(n,i)}{\displaystyle\sum_{m=1}^{N} y(m,g)} p_i \, ,$$

or

$$\lambda p_g \sum_{m=1}^{N} y(m,g) = \sum_{i=1}^{G}\sum_{n=1}^{N} \alpha(n,g)y(n,i)p_i \, .$$

Summing both sides over g,

$$\lambda \sum_{g=1}^{G} p_g \sum_{m=1}^{N} y(m,g) = \sum_{g=1}^{G}\sum_{i=1}^{G}\sum_{n=1}^{N} \alpha(n,g)y(n,i)p_i$$

$$= \sum_{i=1}^{G}\sum_{n=1}^{N}\sum_{g=1}^{G} \alpha(n,g)y(n,i)p_i = \sum_{i=1}^{G}\sum_{n=1}^{N} y(n,i)p_i \, .$$

Thus $\lambda=1$ as desired.

The Perron-Frobenius theorem actually provides two more useful conclusions. First, the equilibrium is unique. This is a feature of the Cobb-Douglas utility and does not necessarily occur for other utility functions. Moreover, the equilibrium is readily approximated. Denote by $\mathbf{B}^t$ the product of $\mathbf{B}$ with itself t times. Then for any positive vector $\mathbf{v}$, $\lim_{t\to\infty} \mathbf{B}^t \mathbf{v} = \mathbf{p}$. While approximations are very useful for large systems (large numbers of goods), the system can readily be computed exactly with small numbers of goods, even with a large number of individuals. Moreover, the approximation can be interpreted in a potentially useful manner. Let $\mathbf{v}$ be a candidate for an equilibrium price vector. Use $\mathbf{v}$ to permit people to calculate their wealth, which for person n is $W_n = \sum_{i=1}^{G} v_i y(n,i)$. Given the wealth levels, what prices clear the market? Demand for good g is

$$x_g(v) = \sum_{n=1}^{N} \alpha(n,g)W_n = \sum_{i=1}^{G} v_i \sum_{n=1}^{N} \alpha(n,g)y(n,i)$$

and the market clears, given the wealth levels, if $p_g = \dfrac{\sum\limits_{i=1}^{G} v_i \sum\limits_{n=1}^{N} \alpha(n,g) y(n,i)}{\sum\limits_{n=1}^{N} y(n,g)}$, which is

equivalent to $\mathbf{p} = \mathbf{B}\mathbf{v}$. This defines an iterative process. Start with an arbitrary price vector, compute wealth levels, then compute the price vector that clears the market for the given wealth levels. Use this price to recalculate the wealth levels, and then compute a new market-clearing price vector for the new wealth levels. This process can be iterated, and in fact converges to the equilibrium price vector from any starting point.

We finish this section by considering three special cases. If there are two goods, we can let $a_n = \alpha(n, 1)$, and then conclude $\alpha(n, 2) = 1 - a_n$. Then let

$$Y_g = \sum_{n=1}^{N} y(n,g)$$

be the endowment of good g. Then the matrix $\mathbf{B}$ is

$$\mathbf{B} = \begin{pmatrix} \dfrac{1}{Y_1} \sum\limits_{n=1}^{N} y(n,1) a_n & \dfrac{1}{Y_1} \sum\limits_{n=1}^{N} y(n,2) a_n \\[2em] \dfrac{1}{Y_2} \sum\limits_{n=1}^{N} y(n,1)(1-a_n) & \dfrac{1}{Y_2} \sum\limits_{n=1}^{N} y(n,2)(1-a_n) \end{pmatrix}$$

$$= \begin{pmatrix} \dfrac{1}{Y_1} \sum\limits_{n=1}^{N} y(n,1) a_n & \dfrac{1}{Y_1} \sum\limits_{n=1}^{N} y(n,2) a_n \\[2em] \dfrac{1}{Y_2}\left(Y_1 - \sum\limits_{n=1}^{N} y(n,1) a_n \right) & 1 - \dfrac{1}{Y_2} \sum\limits_{n=1}^{N} y(n,2) a_n \end{pmatrix}$$

The relevant eigenvector of $\mathbf{B}$ is

$$\mathbf{p} = \begin{pmatrix} \sum\limits_{n=1}^{N} y(n,2) a_n \\[2em] \sum\limits_{n=1}^{N} y(n,1)(1-a_n) \end{pmatrix}.$$

The overall level of prices is not pinned down – any scalar multiple of $\mathbf{p}$ is also an equilibrium price – so the relevant term is the price ratio, which is the price of good 1 in terms of good 2, or

$$\frac{p_1}{p_2} = \frac{\sum\limits_{n=1}^{N} y(n,2)a_n}{\sum\limits_{n=1}^{N} y(n,1)(1-a_n)}.$$

We can readily see that an increase in the supply of good 1, or a decrease in the supply of good 2, decreases the price ratio. An increase in the preference for good 1 increases the price of good 1. When people who value good 1 relatively highly are endowed with a lot of good 2, the correlation between preference for good 1 a_n and endowment of good 2 is higher. The higher the correlation, the higher is the price ratio. Intuitively, if the people who have a lot of good 2 want a lot of good 1, the price of good 1 is going to be higher. Similarly, if the people who have a lot of good 1 want a lot of good 2, the price of good 1 is going to be lower. Thus, the correlation between endowments and preferences also matters to the price ratio.

In our second special case, we consider people with the same preferences, but who start with different endowments. Hypothesizing identical preferences sets aside the correlation between endowments and preferences found in the two good case. Since people are the same, $\alpha(n, g) = A_g$ for all n. In this case,

$$b_{gi} = \frac{\sum\limits_{n=1}^{N} y(n,i)\alpha(n,g)}{\sum\limits_{n=1}^{N} y(n,g)} = A_g \frac{Y_i}{Y_g},$$

where as before $Y_g = \sum\limits_{n=1}^{N} y(n,g)$ is the total endowment of good g. The matrix **B** has a special structure, and in this case, $p_g = \frac{A_g}{Y_g}$ is the equilibrium price vector. Prices are proportional to the preference for the good divided by the total endowment for that good.

Now consider a third special case, where no common structure is imposed on preferences, but endowments are proportional to each other, that is, the endowment of person n is a fraction w_n of the total endowment. This implies that we can write $y(n, g) = w_n Y_g$, an equation assumed to hold for all people n and goods g. Note that by construction, $\sum\limits_{n=1}^{N} w_n = 1$, since the value w_n represents n's share of the total endowment.
In this case, we have

$$b_{gi} = \frac{\sum\limits_{n=1}^{N} y(n,i)\alpha(n,g)}{\sum\limits_{n=1}^{N} y(n,g)} = \frac{Y_i}{Y_g} \sum_{n=1}^{N} w_n \alpha(n,g).$$

These matrices also have a special structure, and it is readily verified that the equilibrium price vector satisfies

$$p_g = \frac{1}{Y_g} \sum_{n=1}^{N} w_n \alpha(n,g).$$

This formula receives a similar interpretation – the price of good g is the strength of preference for good g, where strength of preference is a wealth-weighted average of the individual preference, divided by the endowment of the good. Such an interpretation is guaranteed by the assumption of Cobb-Douglas preferences, since these imply that individuals spend a constant proportion of their wealth on each good. It also generalizes the conclusion found in the two good case to more goods, but with the restriction that the correlation is now between wealth and preferences. The special case has the virtue that individual wealth, which is endogenous because it depends on prices, can be readily determined.

5.2.9.1 (Exercise)   Consider a consumer with Cobb-Douglas utility,

$$U = \prod_{i=1}^{G} x_i^{a_i} ,$$

where $\sum\limits_{i=1}^{G} a_i = 1$, and facing the budget constraint $W = \sum\limits_{i=1}^{G} p_i x_i$. Show that the consumer maximizes utility by choosing $x_i = \dfrac{a_i W}{p_i}$ for each good i. Hint: Express the budget constraint as $x_G = \dfrac{1}{p_G}\left(W - \sum\limits_{i=1}^{G-1} p_i x_i \right)$, and thus utility as

$$U = \left(\prod_{i=1}^{G-1} x_i^{a_i} \right) \left(\frac{1}{p_G}\left(W - \sum_{i=1}^{G-1} p_i x_i \right) \right)^{a_G}.$$ This function can now be maximized in an unconstrained fashion. Verify that the result of the maximization can be expressed as $p_i x_i = \dfrac{a_i}{a_G} p_G x_G$, and thus $W = \sum\limits_{i=1}^{G} p_i x_i = \sum\limits_{i=1}^{G} \dfrac{a_i}{a_G} p_G x_G = \dfrac{p_G x_G}{a_G}$, which yields $p_i x_i = a_i W$.

6 Market Imperfections

We have so far focused on unimpeded markets, and seen that markets may perform efficiently.[64] In this chapter, we examine impediments to the efficiency of markets. Some of these impediments are imposed on otherwise efficiently functioning markets, as occurs with taxes. Others, such as monopoly or pollution, are problems that may arise in some circumstances, and may require correction by the government.

6.1 Taxes

There are a variety of types of taxes, such as income taxes, property taxes, ad valorem (percentage of value) taxes, and excise taxes (taxes on a specific good like cigarettes or gasoline). Here, we are primarily concerned with *sales taxes*, which are taxes on goods and services sold at retail. Our insights into sales taxes translate naturally into some other taxes.

6.1.1 Effects of Taxes

Consider first a fixed tax such as a twenty cent tax on gasoline. The tax could either be imposed on the buyer or the supplier. It is imposed on the buyer if the buyer pays a price for the good, and then also pays the tax on top of that. Similarly, if the tax is imposed on the seller, the price charged to the buyer includes the tax. In the United States, sales taxes are generally imposed on the buyer – the stated price does not include the tax – while in Canada, the sales tax is generally imposed on the seller.

An important insight of supply and demand theory is that it doesn't matter – to anyone – whether the tax is imposed on the supplier or the buyer. The reason is that ultimately the buyer cares only about the total price paid, which is the amount the supplier gets plus the tax, and the supplier cares only about the net to the supplier, which is the total amount the buyer pays minus the tax. Thus, with a twenty cent tax, a price of $2.00 to the buyer is a price of $1.80 to the seller. Whether the buyer pays $1.80 to a seller and additional twenty cents in tax, or pays $2.00, produces the same outcome to both the buyer and seller. Similarly, from the seller's perspective, whether the sellers charge $2.00 and then pay twenty cents to the government, or charges $1.80 and pay no tax, leads to the same profit.[65]

---

[64] The standard term for an unimpeded market is a *free market*, which is free in the sense of "free of external rules and constraints." In this terminology, eBay is free market, even though it charges for the use of the market.

[65] There are two minor issues here that won't be considered further. First, the party who collects the tax has a legal responsibility and it could be that businesses have an easier time complying with taxes than individual consumers. The transaction costs associated with collecting taxes could create a difference arising from who pays the tax. Such differences will be ignored in this book. Second, if the tax is percentage tax, it won't matter to the outcome but the calculations are more complicated, because a ten percent tax on the seller at a seller's price of $1.80 is different from a ten percent tax on a buyer's price of $2.00. Then the equivalence between taxes imposed on the seller and taxes imposed on the buyer requires different percentages that produce the same effective tax level. In addition, there is a political issue: imposing the tax on buyers makes the presence and size of taxes more transparent to voters.

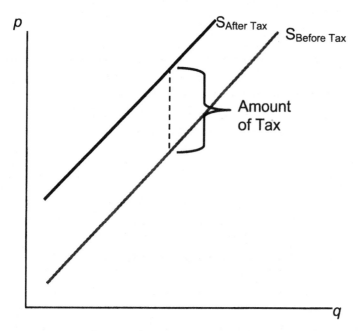

Figure 6-1: Effect of a Tax on Supply

First, consider a tax imposed on the seller. At a given price p, and tax t, each seller obtains $p-t$, and thus supplies the amount associated with this net price. Taking the before tax supply to be $S_{\text{Before Tax}}$, the after tax supply is shifted up by the amount of the tax. This is the amount that covers the marginal value of the last unit, plus providing for the tax. Another way of saying this is that at any lower price, the sellers would reduce the number of units offered. The change in supply is illustrated in Figure 6-1.

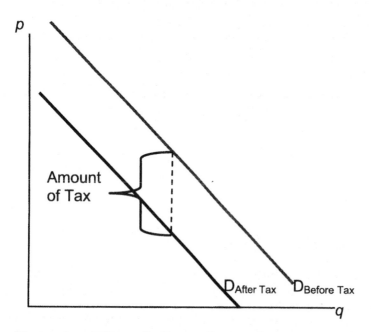

Figure 6-2: Effect of a Tax on Demand

Now consider the imposition of a tax on the buyer, illustrated in Figure 6-2. In this case, the buyer pays the price of the good, p, plus the tax, t. This reduces the willingness to pay for any given unit by the amount of the tax, thus shifting down the demand curve by the amount of the tax.

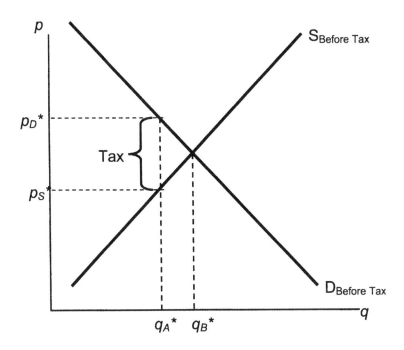

Figure 6-3: Effect of a Tax on Equilibrium

In both cases, the effect of the tax on the supply-demand equilibrium is to shift the quantity toward a point where the before tax demand minus the before tax supply is the amount of the tax. This is illustrated in Figure 6-3. The quantity traded before a tax was imposed was q_B^*. When the tax is imposed, the price that the buyer pays must exceed the price the sellers receive, by the amount equal to the tax. This pins down a unique quantity, denoted q_A^*. The price the buyer pays is denoted by p_D^* and the sellers receive that amount minus the tax, which is noted as p_S^*. The relevant quantities and prices are illustrated in Figure 6-3.

Another thing notable from this picture is that the price that buyers pay rises, but generally by less than the tax. Similarly, the price the sellers obtain falls, but by less than the tax. These changes are known as the *incidence* of the tax – is a tax mostly borne by buyers, in the form of higher prices, or by sellers, in the form of lower prices net of taxation?

There are two main effects of a tax: a fall in the quantity traded, and a diversion of revenue to the government. These are illustrated in Figure 6-4. First, the revenue is just the amount of the tax times the quantity traded, which is the area of the shaded rectangle. The tax raised of course uses the after tax quantity q_A^* because this is the quantity traded once the tax is imposed.

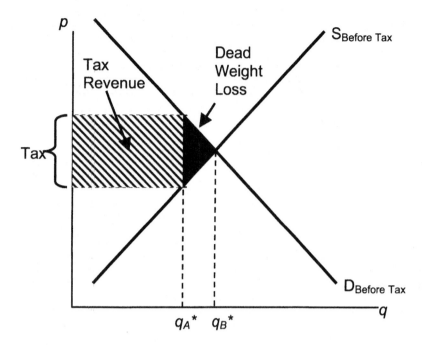

Figure 6-4: Revenue and Dead weight Loss

In addition, a tax reduces the quantity traded, thereby reducing some of the gains from trade. Consumer surplus falls because the price to the buyer rises, and producer surplus (profit) falls because the price to the seller falls. Some of those losses are captured in the form of the tax, but there is a loss captured by no party – the value of the units that would have been exchanged were there no tax. The value of those units is given by the demand, and the marginal cost of the units is given by the supply. The difference, shaded in black in the diagram, is the lost gains from trade of units that aren't traded because of the tax. These lost gains from trade are known as a *dead weight loss*. That is, the dead weight loss is the buyers' values minus the sellers' costs of units that are not economic to trade *only* because of a tax or other interference in the market. The net lost gains from trade, measured in dollars, of these lost units is illustrated by the black triangular region in the diagram.

The dead weight loss is important because it represents a loss to society much the same as if resources were simply thrown away or lost. The dead weight loss is value that people don't enjoy, and in this sense can be viewed as an opportunity cost of taxation. That is, to collect taxes, we have to take money away from people, but obtaining a dollar in tax revenue actually costs society more than a dollar. The costs of raising tax revenues include the money raised (which the taxpayers lose), the direct costs of collection like tax collectors and government agencies to administer tax collection, and the dead weight loss – the lost value created by the incentive effects of taxes, which reduce the gains for trade. The dead weight loss is part of the overhead of collecting taxes. An interesting issue, to be considered in the subsequent section, is the selection of activities and goods to tax in order to minimize the dead weight loss of taxation.

Without more quantification, only a little more can be said about the effect of taxation. First, a small tax raises revenue approximately equal to the tax level times the quantity, or tq. Second, the drop in quantity is also approximately proportional to the size of the tax. Third, this means the size of the dead weight loss is approximately proportional to the tax squared. Thus, small taxes have an almost zero dead weight loss per dollar of revenue raised, and the overhead of taxation, as a percentage of the taxes raised, grows when the tax level is increased. Consequently, the cost of taxation tends to rise in the tax level.

6.1.1.1 (Exercise) Suppose demand is given by $q_d(p) = 1 - p$ and supply $q_s(p) = p$, with prices in dollars. If sellers pay a 10 cent tax, what is the after tax supply? Compute the before tax equilibrium price and quantity, and the after tax equilibrium quantity, and buyer's price and seller's price.

6.1.1.2 (Exercise) Suppose demand is given by $q_d(p) = 1 - p$ and supply $q_s(p) = p$, with prices in dollars. If buyers pay a 10 cent tax, what is the after tax demand? Do the same computations as the previous exercise and show that the outcomes are the same.

6.1.1.3 (Exercise) Suppose demand is given by $q_d(p) = 1 - p$ and supply $q_s(p) = p$, with prices in dollars. Suppose a tax of t cents is imposed, $t \leq 1$. What is the equilibrium quantity traded, as a function of t? What is the revenue raised by the government, and for what level of taxation is it highest?

6.1.2 Incidence of Taxes

How much does the quantity fall when a tax is imposed? How much does the buyer's price rise and the price to the seller fall? The elasticities of supply and demand can be used to answer this question. To do so, we consider a percentage tax t and employ the methodology introduced in Chapter 2 and assume constant elasticity of both demand and supply. Let the equilibrium price to the seller be p_s and the equilibrium price to the buyer be p_b. As before, we will denote the demand function by $q_d(p) = ap^{-\varepsilon}$ and supply function by $q_s(p) = bp^{\eta}$. These prices are distinct because of the tax, and the tax determines the difference:

$$p_b = (1+t) p_s.$$

Equilibrium requires

$$ap_d^{-\varepsilon} = q_d(p_b) = q_s(p_s) = bp_s^{\eta}.$$

Thus,

$$a\big((1+t)p_s\big)^{-\varepsilon} = ap_d^{-\varepsilon} = q_d(p_b) = q_s(p_s) = bp_s^{\eta}.$$

This solves for

$$p_s = \left(\frac{a}{b}\right)^{1/\eta+\varepsilon}(1+t)^{-\varepsilon/\eta+\varepsilon},$$

and

$$q^* = q_s(p_s) = bp_s^{\eta} = b\left(\frac{a}{b}\right)^{\eta/\eta+\varepsilon}(1+t)^{-\varepsilon\eta/\eta+\varepsilon} = a^{\eta/\eta+\varepsilon}b^{\varepsilon/\eta+\varepsilon}(1+t)^{-\varepsilon\eta/\eta+\varepsilon}.$$

Finally, $p_d = (1+t)p_s = \left(\frac{a}{b}\right)^{1/\eta+\varepsilon}(1+t)^{\eta/\eta+\varepsilon}.$

Recall the approximation $(1+t)^r \approx 1 + rt$.

Thus, a small proportional tax increases the price to the buyer by approximately $\dfrac{\eta t}{\varepsilon + \eta}$,

and decreases the price to the seller by $\dfrac{\varepsilon t}{\varepsilon + \eta}$. The quantity falls by approximately $\dfrac{\eta \varepsilon t}{\varepsilon + \eta}$.

Thus, the price effect is mostly on the "relatively inelastic party." If demand is inelastic, ε is small, then the price decrease to the seller will be small and the price increase to the buyer close to the entire tax. Similarly, if demand is very elastic, ε is very large, and the price increase to the buyer will be small and the price decrease to the seller close to the entire tax.

We can rewrite the quantity change as $\dfrac{\eta \varepsilon t}{\varepsilon + \eta} = \dfrac{t}{\dfrac{1}{\varepsilon} + \dfrac{1}{\eta}}$. Thus the effect of a tax on quantity

is small if either the demand or the supply is inelastic. To minimize the distortion in quantity, it is useful to impose taxes on goods that either have inelastic demand, or inelastic supply.

For example, cigarettes are a product with very inelastic demand and moderately elastic supply. Thus a tax increase will generally increase the price almost the entire amount of the tax. In contrast, travel tends to have relatively elastic demand, so taxes on travel – airport, hotel and rental car taxes – tend not to increase the final prices so much, but have large quantity distortions.

6.1.2.1 (Exercise)   For the case of constant elasticity (of both supply and demand), what tax rate maximizes the government's revenue? How does the revenue-maximizing tax rate change when demand becomes more inelastic?

6.1.3 Excess Burden of Taxation

The presence of the dead-weight loss implies that raising $1 in taxes costs society more than $1. But how much more? This idea – that the cost of taxation exceeds the taxes raised – is known as the *excess burden of taxation,* or just the excess burden. We can quantify the excess burden with a remarkably sharp formula.

To start, we will denote the marginal cost of the quantity q by $c(q)$ and the marginal value by $v(q)$. The elasticities of demand and supply are given by the standard formulae:

$$\varepsilon = -\frac{dq\big/q}{dv\big/v} = -\frac{v(q)}{qv'(q)} \quad \text{and} \quad \eta = \frac{dq\big/q}{dc\big/c} = \frac{c(q)}{qc'(q)}.$$

Consider an *ad valorem* tax that will be denoted by t. If sellers are charging $c(q)$, the *ad valorem* (at value) tax is $tc(q)$, and the quantity q^* will satisfy

$$v(q^*) = (1 + t)c(q^*).$$

From this equation, we immediately deduce

$$\frac{dq^*}{dt} = \frac{c(q^*)}{v'(q^*)-(1+t)c'(q^*)} = \frac{c(q^*)}{-\dfrac{v(q^*)}{\varepsilon q^*}-(1+t)\dfrac{c(q^*)}{\eta q^*}} = -\frac{q^*}{(1+t)\left(\dfrac{1}{\varepsilon}+\dfrac{1}{\eta}\right)} = -\frac{q^*\varepsilon\eta}{(1+t)(\varepsilon+\eta)}.$$

Tax revenue is given by

$$Tax = tc(q^*)q^*.$$

The effect on taxes collected, *Tax*, of an increase in the tax rate t is

$$\frac{dTax}{dt} = c(q^*)q^* + t(c(q^*)+q^*c'(q^*))\frac{dq^*}{dt} = c(q^*)\left(q^* - t\left(1+\frac{1}{\eta}\right)\frac{q^*\varepsilon\eta}{(1+t)(\varepsilon+\eta)}\right)$$

$$= \frac{c(q^*)q^*}{(1+t)(\varepsilon+\eta)}\big((1+t)(\varepsilon+\eta)-t(1+\eta)\varepsilon\big) = \frac{c(q^*)q^*}{(1+t)(\varepsilon+\eta)}\big(\varepsilon+\eta-t\eta(\varepsilon-1)\big).$$

Thus, tax revenue is maximized when the tax rate is t_{max}, given by

$$t_{max} = \frac{\varepsilon+\eta}{\eta(\varepsilon-1)} = \frac{\varepsilon}{\varepsilon-1}\left(\frac{1}{\eta}+\frac{1}{\varepsilon}\right).$$

The value $\dfrac{\varepsilon}{\varepsilon-1}$ is the monopoly markup rate, which we will meet in Section 6.5. Here, it is applied to the sum of the inverse elasticities.

The gains from trade (including the tax) is the difference between value and cost for the traded units, and thus is

$$GFT = \int_0^{q*} v(q) - c(q) \; dq.$$

Thus, the change in the gains from trade as taxes increase is given by

$$\frac{dGFT}{dTax} = \frac{\partial GFT\big/\partial t}{\partial Tax\big/\partial t} = \frac{(v(q^*)-c(q^*))\dfrac{dq^*}{dt}}{\dfrac{c(q^*)q^*}{(1+t)(\varepsilon+\eta)}(\varepsilon+\eta-t\eta(\varepsilon-1))} = -\frac{(v(q^*)-c(q^*))\dfrac{q^*\varepsilon\eta}{(1+t)(\varepsilon+\eta)}}{\dfrac{c(q^*)q^*}{(1+t)(\varepsilon+\eta)}(\varepsilon+\eta-t\eta(\varepsilon-1))}$$

$$= -\frac{(tc(q^*))\varepsilon\eta}{c(q^*)(\varepsilon+\eta-t\eta(\varepsilon-1))} = -\frac{\varepsilon\eta t}{\varepsilon+\eta-t\eta(\varepsilon-1)} = -\frac{\varepsilon}{\varepsilon-1}\frac{t}{t_{max}-t}.$$

The value t_{max} is the value of the tax rate t that maximizes the total tax take. This remarkable formula permits the quantification of the cost of taxation. The minus sign indicates it is a loss – the dead weight loss of monopoly, as taxes are raised, and it is composed of two components. First, there is the term $\dfrac{\varepsilon}{\varepsilon-1}$, which arises from the change in revenue as quantity is changed, thus measuring the responsiveness of revenue to a quantity change. The second term provides for the change in the size of the welfare loss triangle. The formula can readily be applied in practice to assess the social cost of taxation, knowing only the tax rate and the elasticities of supply and demand.

The formula for the excess burden is a local formula – it calculates the increase in the dead weight loss associated with raising an extra dollar of tax revenue. All elasticities, including those in t_{max}, are evaluated locally around the quantity associated with the current level of taxation. The calculated value of t_{max} is value given the local elasticities; if elasticities are not constant, this value will not necessarily be the actual value that maximizes the tax revenue. One can think of t_{max} as the projected value. It is sometimes more useful to express the formula directly in terms of elasticities rather than in terms of the projected value of t_{max}, in order to avoid the potential confusion between the projected (at current elasticities) and actual (at the elasticities relevant to t_{max}) value of t_{max}. This level can be read directly from the derivation above:

$$\frac{dGFT}{dTax} = -\frac{\varepsilon\eta t}{\varepsilon+\eta-\eta(\varepsilon-1)t}.$$

6.2 Price Floors and Ceilings

A *price floor* is a minimum price at which a product or service is permitted to sell. Many agricultural goods have price floors imposed by the government. For example, tobacco sold in the United States has historically been subject to a quota and a price floor set by the Secretary of Agriculture. Unions may impose price floors as well. For example, the Screen Actors Guild imposes minimum rates for guild members, generally pushing up the price paid for actors above that which would prevail in an unconstrained market.

(The wages of big name stars aren't generally affected by SAG, because these are individually negotiated.) The most important example of a price floor is the *minimum wage*, which imposes a minimum amount that a worker can be paid per hour.

A *price ceiling* is a maximum price that can be charged for a product or service. Rent control imposes a maximum price on apartments (usually set at the historical price plus an adjustment for inflation) in many U.S. cities. Taxi fares in New York, Washington, D.C. and other cities are subject to maximum legal fares. During World War II, and again in the 1970s, the United States imposed price controls to limit inflation, imposing a maximum price for legal sale of many goods and services. For a long time, most U.S. states limited the legal interest rate that could be charged (these are called *usury laws*) and this is the reason so many credit card companies are located in South Dakota. South Dakota was the first state to eliminate such laws. In addition, ticket prices for concerts and sporting events are often set below the equilibrium price. Laws prohibiting scalping then impose a price ceiling. Laws preventing scalping are usually remarkably ineffective in practice, of course.

6.2.1 Basic Theory

The theory of price floors and ceilings is readily articulated with simple supply and demand analysis. Consider a price floor – a minimum legal price. If the price floor is low enough – below the equilibrium price – there are no effects, because the same forces that tend to induce a price equal to the equilibrium price continue to operate. If the price floor is higher than the equilibrium price, there will be a *surplus*, because at the price floor, more units are supplied than are demanded. This surplus is illustrated in Figure 6-5.

In Figure 6-5, the price floor is illustrated with a horizontal line and is above the equilibrium price. Consequently, at the price floor, a larger quantity is supplied than is demanded, leading to a surplus. There are units that are socially efficient to trade but aren't traded – because their value is less than the price floor. The gains from trade associated with these units, which is lost due to the price floor, represent the dead weight loss.

The price increase created by a price floor will increase the total amount paid by buyers when the demand is inelastic, and otherwise will reduce the amount paid. Thus, if the price floor is imposed in order to be a benefit to sellers, we would not expect to see the price increased to the point where demand becomes elastic, for otherwise the sellers receive less revenue. Thus, for example, if the minimum wage is imposed in order to increase the average wages to low-skilled workers, then we would expect to see the total income of low-skilled workers rise. If, on the other hand, the motivation for the minimum wage is primarily to make low-skilled workers a less effective substitute for union workers, and hence allow union workers to increase their wage demands, then we might observe a minimum wage which is in some sense "too high" to be of benefit to low-skilled workers.

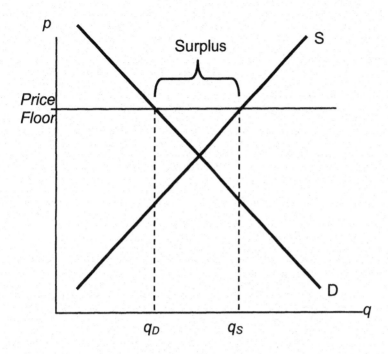

Figure 6-5: A Price Floor

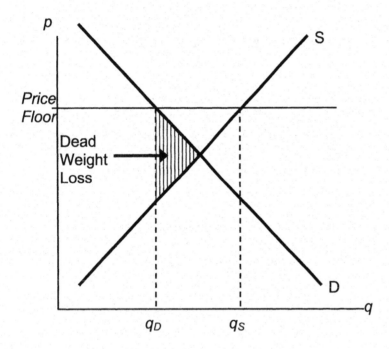

Figure 6-6: Dead weight Loss of a Price Floor

The dead weight loss illustrated in Figure 6-6 is the difference between the value of the units not traded, and value is given by the demand curve, and the cost of producing these units. The triangular shaped region representing the difference between value and cost is illustrated in the above diagram, in the shaded region.

However, this is the *minimum* loss to society associated with a price floor. Generally there will be other losses. In particular, the loss given above assumes that suppliers who don't sell don't produce. As a practical matter, some suppliers who won't in the end sell may still produce because they hope to sell. In this case additional costs are incurred and the dead weight loss will be larger to reflect these costs.

Example: Suppose both supply and demand are linear, with the quantity supplied equal to the price, and the quantity demanded equal to one minus the price. In this case, the equilibrium price, and the equilibrium quantity, are both ½. A price floor of $p > ½$ induces a quantity demanded of $1-p$. How many units will suppliers offer, if a supplier's chance of trading is random? Suppose $q \geq 1-p$ units are offered. A supplier's chance of selling is $\frac{1-p}{q}$. Thus, the marginal supplier (who has a marginal cost of q by assumption) has a probability $\frac{1-p}{q}$ of earning p, and a certainty of paying q. Exactly q units will be supplied when this is a break-even proposition for the marginal supplier, that is,

$$\frac{1-p}{q}p - q = 0, \text{ or } q = \sqrt{p(1-p)}.$$

The dead weight loss then includes not just the triangle illustrated in the previous picture, but also the cost of the $\sqrt{p(1-p)} - (1-p)$ unsold units.

6.2.1.1 (Exercise)   In this example, show that the quantity produced is less than the equilibrium quantity, which is ½. Compute the gains from trade, given the overproduction of suppliers. What is the dead weight loss of the price floor?

6.2.1.2 (Exercise)   Suppose that units aren't produced until after a buyer has agreed to purchase, as typically occurs with services. What is the dead weight loss in this case? (Hint: what potential sellers will offer their services? What is the average cost of supply of this set of potential sellers?)

The Screen Actors Guild, a union of actors, has some ability to impose minimum prices (a price floor) for work on regular Hollywood movies. If the Screen Actors Guild would like to maximize the total earnings of actors, what price should they set in the linear demand and supply example?

The effects of a price floor include lost gains from trade, because too few units are traded (inefficient exchange), units produced that are never consumed (wasted production), and more costly units produced than necessary (inefficient production)

A price ceiling is a maximum price. Analogous to a low price floor, a price ceiling that is larger than the equilibrium price has no effect. Tell me that I can't charge more than a billion dollars for this book (which is being given away free) and it won't affect the price charged or the quantity traded. Thus, the important case of a price ceiling is a price ceiling less than the equilibrium price.

In this case, which should now look familiar, the price is forced below the equilibrium price, and too few units are supplied, while a larger number are demanded, leading to a shortage. The dead weight loss is illustrated in Figure 6-7, and again represents the loss associated with units that are valued more than they cost but aren't produced.

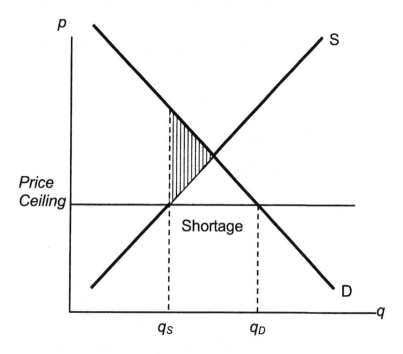

Figure 6-7: A Price Ceiling

Analogous to the case of a price floor, there can be additional losses associated with a price ceiling. In particular, some lower value buyers may succeed in purchasing, denying the higher value buyers the ability to purchase. This effect results in buyers with high values failing to consume, and hence their value is lost.

6.2.1.3 (Exercise)   Adapt the price floor example above to the case of a price ceiling, with $p < \frac{1}{2}$, and compute the lost gains from trade if buyers willing to purchase are all able to purchase with probability q_S/q_D. (Hint: Compute the value of q_D units; the value realized by buyers collectively will be that amount times the probability of trade.)

In addition to the misallocation of resources (too few units, and units not allocated to those who value them the most), price ceilings tend to encourage illegal trade as people attempt to exploit the prohibited gains from trade. For example, it became common practice in New York to attempt to bribe landlords to offer rent-controlled apartments, and such bribes could exceed $50,000. In addition, potential tenants expended a great deal of time searching for apartments, and a common strategy was to read the obituaries late at night, when the *New York Times* had just come out, hoping to find an apartment that would be vacant and available for rent.

An important and undesirable by-product of price ceilings is discrimination. In a free or unconstrained market, discrimination against a particular group, based on race, religion, or other factors, requires transacting not based on price but on another factor. Thus, in a free market, discrimination is costly – discrimination entails, for instance, not renting an apartment to the highest bidder, but the highest bidder of the favored group. In contrast, with a price ceiling, there is a shortage, and sellers can discriminate at lower cost, or even at no cost. That is, if there are twice as many people seeking apartments as there are apartments at the price ceiling, landlords can "pick and choose" among prospective tenants and still get the maximum legal rent. Thus a price ceiling has the undesirable by-product of reducing the cost of discrimination.

6.2.2 Long- and Short-run Effects

Both demand and supply tend to be more elastic in the long-run. This means that the quantity effects of price floors and ceilings tend to be larger over time. An extreme example of this is rent control, a maximum price imposed on apartments.

Rent control is usually imposed in the following way: as a prohibition or limitation on price increases. For example, New York City's rent control, imposed during World War II, prevented landlords from increasing rent, even when their own costs increased, such as when property taxes increased. This law was softened in 1969 to be gradually replaced by a rent stabilization law that permitted modest rent increases for existing tenants.

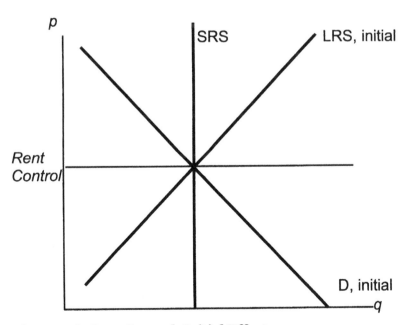

Figure 6-8: Rent Control, Initial Effect

Thus the nature of rent control is that it begins with at most minor effects because it doesn't bind until the equilibrium rent increases. Moreover, the short-run supply of apartments tends to be extremely inelastic, because one doesn't tear down an apartment or convert it to a condominium (there were limitations on this) or abandon it without a pretty significant change in price. Demand also tends to be relatively inelastic, because one has to live somewhere and the alternatives to renting in the city are to live a long distance away or buy (which is relatively expensive), neither of which is a very good substitute for many consumers. Long-run demand and short-run demand are not very different and are treated as being identical. Finally, the long-run supply is much more elastic than the short-run supply, because in the long-run a price increase permits the creation of apartments from warehouses (lofts), rooms rented in houses, etc. Thus, the apartment market in New York is characterized by inelastic short-run supply, much more elastic long-run supply, and inelastic demand. This is illustrated in Figure 6-8.

We start with a rent control law that has little or no immediate effect because it is set at current rents. Thus, in the near term, tenants' fears of price increases are eased and there is little change in the apartment rental market. This is not to say there is zero effect – some companies considering building an apartment on the basis of an expectation of higher future rents may be deterred, and a few marginal apartments may be converted to other uses because the upside potential for the owner has been removed, but such effects are modest at best.

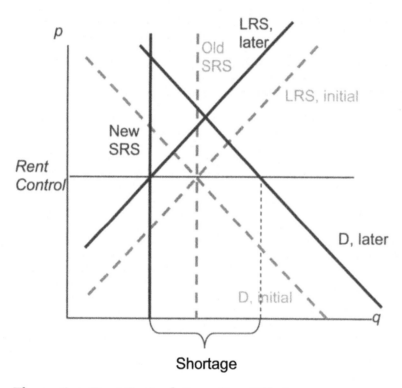

Figure 6-9: Rent Control, Long-Run Effect

Over time, however, the demand for apartments grows as the city population and incomes grow. Moreover, as the costs of operating an apartment rise due to property tax increases, wage increases and cost of maintenance increases, the supply is reduced. This has little effect on the short-run supply but a significant effect on the long-run supply. The supply reduction and demand increases cause a shortage, but results in few apartments being lost because the short-run supply is very inelastic. Over time, however, apartments are withdrawn from the market and the actual quantity falls, even as the demand rises, and the shortage gets worse and worse. These changes are illustrated in Figure 6-9. The old values of demand, short-run supply and long-run supply are illustrated in dashed grey lines. The new values, reflecting an increase in demand, a fall in long-run supply, and a reduction in the number available set of apartments (where the rent control covers the long-run cost) are given in dark black lines.

The shortage is created by two separate factors – demand is increasing as incomes and population rise, and supply is decreasing as costs rise. This reduces the quantity of available housing units supplied and increases the demand for those units.

How serious is the threat that units will be withdrawn from the market? In New York City, over 200,000 apartment units were abandoned by their owners, usually because the legal rent didn't cover the property taxes and legally mandated maintenance. In some cases, tenants continued to inhabit the buildings even after the electricity and water were shut off. It is fair to say that rent control devastated large areas of New York City, such as the Bronx. So why would New York, and so many other communities, impose rent control on itself?

6.2.3 Political Motivations

The politics of rent control are straightforward. First, rent control involves a money transfer from landlords to tenants, because tenants pay less than they would absent the law, and landlords obtain less revenue. In the short-run, due to the inelastic short-run supply, the effect on the quantity of apartments is small, so rent control is primarily just a transfer from landlords to tenants.

In a city like New York, the majority of people rent. A tiny fraction of New Yorkers are landlords. Thus, it is easy to attract voters to support candidates who favor rent control – most renters will benefit, while landlords don't. The numbers of course don't tell the whole story, because while landlords are small in numbers, they are wealthier on average, and thus likely have political influence beyond the number of votes they cast. However, even with their larger economic influence, the political balance favors renters. In the 100*ab* zip codes of Manhattan (first three digits are 100), 80% of families were renters in the year 2000. Thus, a candidate who runs on a rent control platform appeals to large portion of the voters.

Part of the attraction of rent control is that there is little economic harm in the short-run, and most of that harm falls on new residents to New York. As new residents generally haven't yet voted in New York, potential harm to them has only a small effect on most existing New Yorkers, and thus isn't a major impediment to getting voter support for rent control. The slow rate of harm to the city is important politically because the election cycle encourages a short time horizon – if successful at lower office, a politician hopes to move on to higher office, and is unlikely to be blamed for the long-run damage to New York by rent control.

Rent control is an example of a political situation sometimes called the *tyranny of the majority,* where a majority of people have an incentive to confiscate the wealth of a minority. But there is another kind of political situation that is in some sense the reverse, where a small number of people care a great deal about something, and the majority are only slightly harmed on an individual basis. No political situation appears more extreme in this regard than that of refined sugar. There are few U.S. cane sugar producers (nine in 1997), yet the U.S. imposes quotas that raise domestic prices much higher than world prices, in some years tripling the price Americans pay for refined sugar. The domestic sugar producers benefit, while consumers are harmed. But consumers are harmed by only a small amount each, perhaps twelve to fifteen cents per pound – which is not enough to build a consensus to defeat politicians who accept donations from sugar producers. This is a case where *concentrated benefits and diffused costs* determine the political outcome. Because there aren't many sugar producers, it is straightforward for them to act as a single force. In contrast, it is pretty hard for consumers to become passionate about twelve cents per pound increase in the domestic sugar price when they consume about 60 pounds per year of sugar.

6.2.4 Price Supports

A price support is a combination of two programs – a minimum price or price floor, and government purchase of any surplus. Thus, a price support is different from a price floor, because with a price floor, any excess production by sellers was a burden on the sellers. In contrast, with a price support, any excess production is a burden on the government.

The U.S. Department of Agriculture operates a price support for cheese, and has possessed warehouses full of cheese in the past. There are also price supports for milk and other agricultural products.

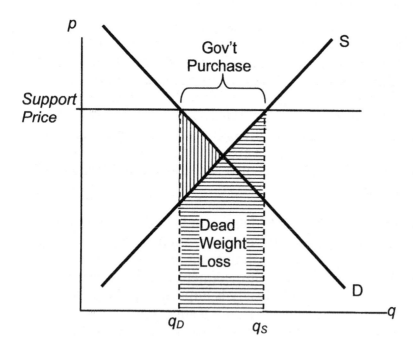

Figure 6-10: Price Supports

Figure 6-10 illustrates the effect of a support program. The government posts a price, called the *support price*, and purchases any excess production offered on the market.

The government purchases, which are the difference between the quantity supplied and quantity demanded, are illustrated on the diagram. The cost of the program to the government is the support price times this quantity purchased, which is the area of the rectangle directly underneath the words "Gov't Purchases."

There are two kinds of dead weight loss in a price support program. First, consumers who would like to buy at the equilibrium price are deterred by the higher prices, resulting in the usual dead weight loss, illustrated with the vertical shading. In addition, however, there are goods produced that are then either destroyed or put in warehouses and not consumed, which means the costs of production of those goods is also lost, resulting in a second dead weight loss. That loss is the cost of production, which is given by the supply curve, and thus is the area under the supply curve, for the government purchases. It is shaded in a horizontal fashion. The total dead weight loss of the price support is the sum of these two individual losses. Unlike the case of a price floor or ceiling, a price support creates no ambiguity about what units are produced, or which consumers are willing and able to buy, and thus the rationing aspect of a price floor or ceiling is not present for a price support, nor is the incentive to create a black market other than that created by selling the warehouse full of product.

6.2.5 Quantity Restrictions and Quotas

The final common way that governments intervene in market transactions is to impose a quota. A quota is a maximal production quantity, usually set based on historical production. In tobacco, peanuts, hops, California oranges, and other products, producers have production quotas based on their historical production. Tobacco quotas were established in the 1930s and today a tobacco farmer's quota is a percentage of the 1930s level of production. The percentage is set annually by the Secretary of Agriculture. Agricultural products are not the only products with quotas. The right to drive a tax in New York requires a medallion issued by the city, and there are a limited number of medallions. This is a quota. Is it a restrictive quota? The current price of a New York taxi medallion – the right to drive a taxi legally in New York City – is $300,000 (2004 number). This adds approximately $30,000-$40,000 annually to the cost of operating a taxi in New York, using a risk adjusted interest rate.

What are the effects of a quota? A quota restricts the quantity below that which would otherwise prevail, forcing the price up, which is illustrated in Figure 6-11. It works like a combination of a price floor and a prohibition on entry.

Generally, the immediate effects of a quota involve a transfer of money from buyers to sellers. The inefficient production and surplus of the price floor are avoided because a production limitation created the price increase. This transfer has an undesirable and somewhat insidious attribute. Because the right to produce is a capital good, it maintains a value, which must be captured by the producer. For example, an individual who buys a taxi medallion today, and pays $300,000, makes no economic profits – he captures the foregone interest on the medallion through higher prices but no more than that. The individuals who received the windfall gain were those who were driving taxis and were grandfathered in to the system, and issued free medallions. Those people – who were driving taxis 70 years ago and thus are mostly dead at this point – received a windfall gain from the establishment of the system. Future generations pay for the program, which provides no net benefits to the current generation; all the benefits were captured by people long since retired.

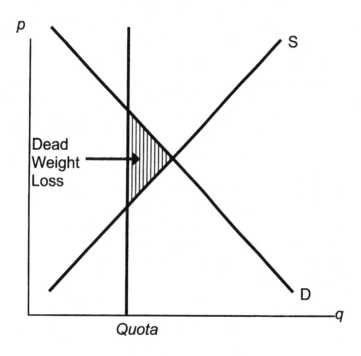

Figure 6-11: A Quota

Does this mean it is harmless to eliminate the medallion requirement? Unfortunately not. The current medallion owners, who if they bought recently paid a lot of money for their medallions, would see the value of these investments destroyed. Thus, elimination of the program would harm current medallion owners.

If the right to produce is freely tradable, the producers will remain the efficient producers, and the taxi medallions are an example of this. Taxi medallions can be bought and sold. Moreover, a medallion confers the right to operate a taxi, but doesn't require that the owner of the medallion actually drive the taxi. Thus, a "medallion owning company" can lease the right to drive a taxi to an efficient driver, thereby eliminating any inefficiency associated with who drives a taxi.

In contrast, because tobacco farming rights aren't legally tradable across county lines, tobacco is very inefficiently grown. The average size of a burley tobacco farm is less than five acres, so some are much smaller. There are tobacco farms in Florida and Missouri, which only exist because of the value of the quota – if they could trade their quota to a farm in North Carolina or Kentucky, which are much better suited to producing cigarette tobacco, it would pay to do so. In this case, the quota, which locked in production rights, also locked in production which gets progressively more inefficient as the years pass.

Quotas based on historical production have the problem that they don't evolve as production methods and technology evolve, thus tending to become progressively more inefficient. Tradable quotas eliminate this particular problem, but continue to have the problem that future generations are harmed with no benefits.

6.2.5.1 (Exercise)   Suppose demand for a product is $q_d = 1 - p$, and the marginal cost of production is c. A quota at level $Q \leq 1 - c$ is imposed. What is the value of the quota, per unit of production? Use this to derive the demand for the quota as a function of the level of quota released to the market. If the government wishes to sell the quota, how much should they sell to maximize the revenue on the product?

6.3 *Externalities*

When the person sitting next to you lights up a cigarette, he gets nicotine, and the cigarette company gets some of his money. You just suffer, with no compensation. If your neighbor's house catches fire because he fell asleep with that cigarette burning in his hand, your house may burn to the ground. The neighbor on the other side who plays very loud music late into the night before your big economics test enjoys the music, and the record company and stereo component companies get his money. You flunk out of college and wind up borrowing $300,000 to buy a taxi medallion. Drunk drivers, cell phones ringing in movies, loud automobiles, polluted air, and rivers polluted to the point that they catch fire like Cleveland's Cuyahoga did, are all examples where a transaction between two parties harmed other people. These are "external effects."

But external effects are not necessarily negative. The neighbor who plants beautiful flowers in her yard brightens your day. Another's purchase of an electric car reduces the smog you breathe. Your neighbor's investment in making his home safe from fire conveys a safety advantage to you. Indeed, even your neighbor's investment in her own education may provide an advantage to you – you may learn useful things from your neighbor. Inventions and creations, whether products or poetry, produce value for others. The creator of a poem, or a mathematical theorem, provides a benefit to others.

These effects are called *external effects*, or *externalities*. An externality is any effect on people not involved in a particular transaction. Pollution is the classic example. When another person buys and smokes cigarettes, there is a transaction between the cigarette company and the smoker. But if you are sitting near the smoker, you are an affected party not directly compensated from the transaction, at least before taxes were imposed on cigarettes. Similarly, you pay nothing for the benefits you get from viewing your neighbor's flowers, nor is there a direct mechanism to reward your neighbor for her efforts.

Externalities will generally cause competitive markets to behave inefficiently from a social perspective, absent a mechanism to involve all the affected parties. Without such a mechanism, the flower-planter will plant too few beautiful flowers, for she has no reason to take account of your preferences in her choices. The odious smoker will smoke too much, and too near others, and the loud neighbor will play music much too late into the night. Externalities create a *market failure*, that is, a competitive market does not yield the socially efficient outcome.

Education is viewed as creating an important positive externality. Education generates many externalities, including more and better employment, less crime, and fewer negative externalities of other kinds. It is widely believed that educated voters elect better politicians.[66] Educated individuals tend to make a society wealthy, an advantage to all of society's members. As a consequence, most societies subsidize education, in order to promote it.

A major source of externalities arises in communicable diseases. Your vaccination not only reduces the likelihood that you contract a disease, but also makes it less likely that you infect others with the disease.

6.3.1 Private and Social Value, Cost

Let's consider pollution as a typical example. A paper mill produces paper, and a bad smell is an unfortunate by-product of the process. Each ton of paper produced increases the amount of bad smells produced. The paper mill incurs a marginal cost, associated with inputs like wood and chemicals and water. For the purposes of studying externalities, we will refer to the paper mill's costs as a *private cost*, the cost to the paper mill itself. In addition, there are *external costs*, which are the costs borne by others, which arise in this case from the smell. Adding the private costs and the external costs yields the social costs. These costs, in their marginal form, are illustrated in Figure 6-12.

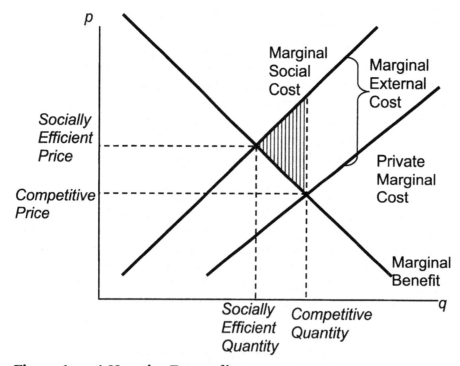

Figure 6-12: A Negative Externality

In Figure 6-12, the demand has been labeled "marginal benefit," for reasons that will become apparent, but it is at this point just the standard demand, the marginal value of

---

[66] This is a logical proposition, but there is scant evidence in favor of it. There is evidence that educated voters are more likely to vote, but little evidence that they vote for better candidates.

the product. The paper mill's costs have been labeled marginal private cost to reflect the fact that these costs are only the mill's costs and don't include the cost of the bad smell imposed on others. The marginal social cost is obtained by adding the marginal external cost to the marginal private cost. The marginal external cost isn't graphed on the diagram, but the size of it is illustrated at one quantity, and it is generally the difference between marginal social cost and marginal private cost.

Left to its own devices, the paper market would equate the marginal private cost and the marginal benefit, to produce the competitive quantity sold at the competitive price. Some of these units – all of those beyond the quantity labeled "Socially Efficient Quantity," are bad from a social perspective – they cost more to society than they provide in benefits. This is because the social cost of these units includes pollution, but paper buyers have no reason to worry about pollution or even to know it is being created in the process of manufacturing paper.

The dead weight loss of these units is a shaded triangle. The loss arises because the marginal social cost of the units exceeds the benefit, and the difference between the social cost and the benefits yields the loss to society. This is a case where too much is produced because the market has no reason to account for all the costs; some of the costs are borne by others.

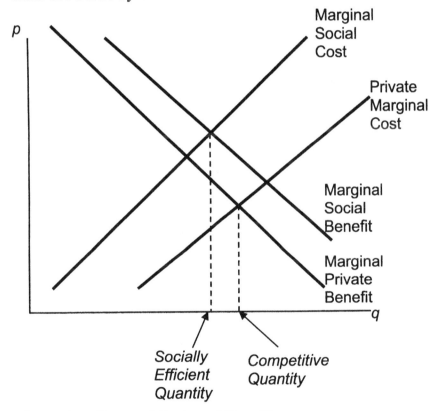

Figure 6-13: External Costs and Benefits

Generally, a negative externality like pollution creates a marginal social cost higher than the marginal private cost. Similarly, a positive externality like beautification creates a higher marginal social benefit than the marginal private benefit (demand). These are to some extent conventions – one could have incorporated a positive externality by a reduction in cost – but the convention remains. An example of a product that produces both positive and negative externalities is illustrated in Figure 6-13. Street lights are an example of a product that produces both externalities – most of us like lit streets, but they are terrible for astronomers. Similarly, large highways produce benefits for commuters and harm to nearby residents.

The marginal private benefit and the marginal private cost give the demand and supply of a competitive market, and hence the competitive quantity results from the intersection of these two. The marginal social benefit and the marginal social cost gives the value and cost from a social perspective; equating these two generates the socially efficient outcome. This can be either greater or less than the competitive outcome depending on which externality is larger.

Example (Tragedy of the Commons): Consider a town on a scenic bay filled with lobsters. The town members collect and eat lobsters, and over time the size of the lobsters collected falls, until they are hardly worth searching for. This situation persists indefinitely; few large lobsters are caught and it is barely worth one's time attempting to catch them.

The tragedy of the commons is a problem with a *common resource*, in this case the lobster bay. Catching lobsters creates an externality, by lowering the productivity of other lobster catchers. The externality leads to over-fishing, since individuals don't take into account the negative effect they have on each other, ultimately leading to a nearly useless resource and potentially driving the lobsters into extinction. As a consequence, the lobster catch is usually regulated.

6.3.1.1 (Exercise)   A child who is vaccinated against polio is more likely to contract polio (from the vaccine) than an unvaccinated child. Does this fact imply that programs forcing vaccination on schoolchildren are ill-advised? Include with your answer with a diagram illustrating the negative marginal benefit of vaccination, and a horizontal axis representing the proportion of the population vaccinated.

6.3.1.2 (Exercise)   The total production from an oil field generally depends on the rate at which the oil is pumped, with faster rates leading to lower total production but earlier production. Suppose two different producers can pump from the field. Illustrate, using an externality diagram where the horizontal axis is the rate of production for one of the producers, the difference between the socially efficient outcome and the equilibrium outcome. Like many other states, Texas' law requires that when multiple people own land over a single oil field, the output is shared among the owners, with each owner obtaining a share equal to proportion of the field under their land. This process is called *unitization*. Does it solve the problem of externalities in pumping and yield an efficient outcome? Why or why not?

6.3.2 Pigouvian Taxes

Arthur Cecil Pigou, 1877-1959, proposed a solution to the problem of externalities that has become a standard approach. This simple idea is to impose a per-unit tax on a good generating negative externalities equal to the marginal externality at the socially efficient quantity. Thus, if at the socially efficient quantity, the marginal external cost is a dollar, then a one dollar per unit tax would lead to the right outcome. This is illustrated in Figure 6-14.

The tax that is added is the difference, at the socially efficient quantity, between the marginal social cost and the marginal private cost, which equals the marginal external cost. The tax level need not equal the marginal external cost at other quantities, and the diagram reflects a marginal external cost that is growing as the quantity grows. Nevertheless, the new supply curve created by the addition of the tax intersects demand (the marginal benefit) at the socially efficient quantity. As a result, the new competitive equilibrium, taking account of the tax, is efficient.

6.3.2.1 (Exercise)   Identify the tax revenue produced by a Pigouvian tax in Figure 6-14. What is the relationship between the tax revenue and the damage produced by the negative externality? Is the tax revenue sufficient to pay those damaged by the external effect an amount equal to their damage? Hint: Is the marginal external effect increasing or decreasing.

The case of a positive externality is similar. In this case, a subsidy is needed to induce the efficient quantity. It is left as an exercise.

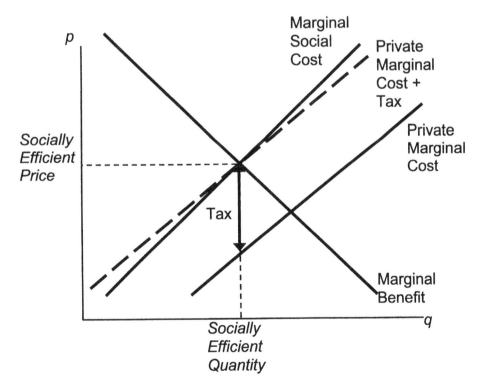

Figure 6-14: The Pigouvian Tax

6.3.2.2 (Exercise)   Identify on a diagram the Pigouvian subsidy needed to induce the efficient quantity in the case of a positive externality. When is the subsidy expended smaller than the total external benefit?

6.3.2.3 (Exercise)   Use the formulae for estimating the effect of a tax on quantity to deduce the size of the tax needed to adjust for an externality when the marginal social cost is twice the marginal private cost.

Taxes and subsidies are fairly common instruments to control externalities. We subsidize higher education with state universities, and the federal government provides funds for research and limited funds for the arts. Taxes on cigarettes and alcoholic beverages are used to discourage these activities, perhaps because smoking and drinking alcoholic beverages create negative externalities. (Cigarettes and alcohol also have inelastic demands, which make them good candidates for taxation since there is only a small distortion of the quantity.) However, while important in some arenas, taxes and subsidies are not the most common approach to regulation of externalities.

6.3.3 Quotas

The Pigouvian tax and subsidy approach to dealing with externalities has several problems. First, it requires knowing the marginal value or cost of the external effect, and this may be a challenge to estimate. Second, it requires the imposition of taxes and permits the payment of subsidies, which encourages what might be politely termed as "misappropriation of funds." That is, once a government agency is permitted to tax some activities and subsidize others, there will be a tendency to tax things people in the agency don't like, and subsidize "pet" projects, using the potential for externalities as an excuse rather than a real reason. U.S. politicians have been especially quick to see positive externalities in oil, cattle and the family farm, externalities that haven't been successfully articulated. (The Canadian government, in contrast, sees externalities in film-making and railroads.)

An alternative to the Pigouvian tax or subsidy solution is to set a quota, which is a limit on the activity. Quotas can be maxima or minima, depending on whether the activity generates negative or positive externalities. We set maximum levels of many pollutants rather than tax them, and ban some activities, like lead in gasoline or paint, or chlorofluorocarbons (CFCs) outright (a quota equal to zero). We set maximum amounts of impurities, like rat feces, in foodstuffs. We impose minimum educational attainment (eighth grade or age 16, whichever comes first), minimum age to drive, minimum amount of rest time for truck drivers and airline pilots. A large set of regulations govern electricity and plumbing, designed to promote safety, and these tend to be "minimum standards." Quotas are a much more common regulatory strategy for dealing with externalities than taxes and subsidies.

The idea behind a quota is to limit the quantity to the efficient level. If a negative externality in pollution means our society pollutes too much, then impose a limit or quantity restriction on pollution. If the positive externality of education means individuals in our society receive too little education from the social perspective, force them to go to school.

As noted, quotas have the advantage that they address the problem without letting the government spend more money, limiting the government's ability to misuse funds. On the other hand, quotas have the problem of identifying who should get the quota; quotas will often misallocate the resource. Indeed, a small number of power plants account for almost half of the man-made sulfur dioxide pollution emitted into the atmosphere, primarily because these plants historically emitted a lot of pollution and their pollution level was set by their historical levels. Quotas tend to harm new entrants compared to existing firms, and discourage the adoption of new technology. Indeed, the biggest polluters must stay with old technology in order to maintain their right to pollute.

6.3.3.1 (Exercise)   If a quota is set to the socially efficient level, how does the value of a quota right compare to the Pigouvian tax?

6.3.3.2 (Exercise)   Speeding (driving fast) creates externalities by increasing the likelihood and severity of automobile accidents, and most countries put a limit on speed, but one could instead require fast drivers to buy a permit to speed. Discuss the advantages and disadvantages of "speeding permits."

6.3.4 Tradable Permits and Auctions

A solution to inefficiencies in the allocation of quota rights is to permit trading them. Tradable permits for pollution create a market in the right to pollute, and thereby create a tax on polluting: the emission of pollution requires the purchase of permits to pollute, and the price of these permits represents a tax on pollution. Thus, tradable permits represent a hybrid of a quota system and a Pigouvian taxation system – a quota determines the overall quantity of pollution as in a quota system, determining the supply of pollution rights, but the purchase of pollution rights acts like a tax on pollution, a tax whose level is determined by the quota supply and demand.

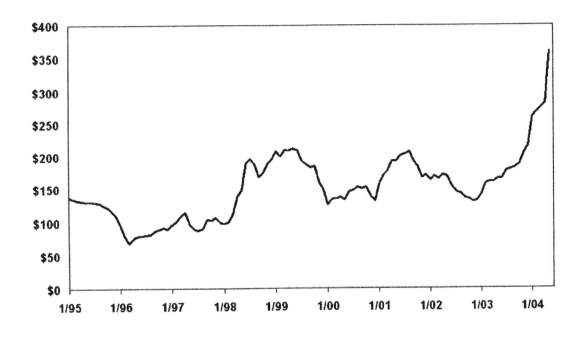

Figure 6-15: SO₂ Permit Prices

The United States has permitted the trading of permits for some pollutants, like sulfur dioxide. Figure 6-15 shows the price of sulfur dioxide permits over the past decade.[67] Each permit conveys the right to emit one ton of sulfur dioxide into the air. The overall pollution level is being reduced over time, which accounts for some of the increase in prices. These prices represent significant taxes on large polluters, as a coal-fired power plant, using coal with high sulfur content, can annually produce as much as 200,000 tons of sulfur dioxide.

The major advantage of a tradable permits system is that it creates the opportunity for efficient exchange – one potential polluter can buy permits from another, leaving the total amount of pollution constant. Such exchange is efficient because it uses the pollution in the manner creating the highest value, eliminating a bias toward "old" sources. Indeed, a low value polluter might sell its permits and just shut down, if the price of pollution were high enough.

A somewhat unexpected advantage of tradable permits was the purchase of permits by environmental groups like the Sierra Club. Environmental groups can buy permits and then not exercise them, as a way of cleaning the air. In this case, the purchase of the permits creates a major positive externality on the rest of society, since the environmental group expends its own resources to reduce pollution of others.

Tradable permits offer the advantages of a taxation scheme – efficient use of pollution – without needing to estimate the social cost of pollution directly. This is especially valuable when the strategy is to set a quantity equal to the current quantity, and then gradually reduce the quantity to reduce the effects of the pollution. The price of permits can be a very useful instrument is assessing the appropriate time to reduce the quantity, since high permit prices, relative to likely marginal external costs, suggests that the quantity of the quota is too low, while low prices suggest that the quantity is too large and should be reduced.

6.3.5 Coasian Bargaining

The negative externality of a neighbor playing loud music late at night is not ordinarily solved with a tax or with a quota, but instead though an agreement. When there aren't many individuals involved, the individuals may be able to solve the problem of externalities without involving a government, but through negotiation. This insight was developed by Nobel laureate Ronald Coase (1910 –).

Coase offered the example of a cattle ranch next to a farm. There is a negative externality, in that the cattle tend to wander over to the farm and eat the crops, rather than staying on the ranch. What happens next depends on *property rights*, which are the rights that come with ownership.

One of three things might be efficient from a social perspective. It might be efficient to erect a fence to keep the cows away from the crops. It might be efficient to close down

---

[67] Source: Environmental Protection Agency, July 22, 2004,
http://www.epa.gov/airmarkets/trading/so2market/alprices.html

the farm. Finally, it might be efficient to close down the ranch, if the farm is valuable enough, and the fence costs more than the value of the ranch.

If the farmer has a right not to have his crops eaten, and can confiscate the cows if they wander onto the farm, then the rancher will have an incentive to erect a fence to keep the cows away, if that is the efficient solution. If the efficient solution is to close down the ranch, then the rancher will do that, since the farmer can confiscate the cows if they go to the farm and it isn't worth building the fence by hypothesis. Finally, if the efficient solution to the externality is to close down the farm, the rancher will have an incentive to buy the farm in order to purchase the farm's rights, so that he can keep the ranch in operation. Since it is efficient to close down the farm only if the farm is worth less than the ranch, there is enough value in operating the ranch to purchase the farm at its value and still have money left over – that is there are gains from trade from selling the farm to the rancher. In all three cases, if the farmer has the property rights, the efficient outcome is reached.

Now suppose instead that the rancher has the rights, and that the farmer has no recourse if the cows eat his crops. If shutting down the farm is efficient, the farmer has no recourse but to shut down. Similarly, if building the fence is efficient, the farmer will build the fence to protect his crops. Finally, if shutting down the ranch is efficient, the farmer will buy the ranch from the rancher, in order to be able to continue to operate the more valuable farm. In all cases, the efficient solution is reached through negotiation.

Coase argued that bargaining can generally solve problems of externalities, and that the real problem is ill-defined property rights. If the rancher and the farmer can't transfer their property rights, then the efficient outcome may not arise. In the Coasian view of externalities, if an individual owned the air, air pollution would not be a problem, because the owner would charge for the use and wouldn't permit an inefficient level of pollution. The case of air pollution demonstrates some of the limitations of the Coasian approach, because ownership of the air, or even the more limited right to pollute into the air, would create an additional set of problems, a case where the cure is likely worse than the disease.

Bargaining to solve the problem of externalities is often feasible when a small number of people are involved. When a large number of people are potentially involved, as with air pollution, bargaining is unlikely to be successful in addressing the problem of externalities, and a different approach required.

6.3.6 Fishing and Extinction

Consider an unregulated fishing market like the lobster market considered above, and let S be the stock of fish. The purpose of this example is illustrative of the logic, rather than an exact accounting of the biology of fish populations, but is not unreasonable. Let S be the stock of a particular species of fish. Our starting point is an environment without fishing: how does the fish population change over time? Denote the change over time in the fish population by $\dot{S}$ ($\dot{S}$ is notation for the derivative with respect to time, notation that dates back to Sir Isaac Newton.) We assume that population growth follows the logistic equation $\dot{S} = rS(1-S)$. This equation reflects two underlying assumptions. First, mating and reproduction is proportional to the stock of fish S. Second, survival is proportional to the amount of available resources 1-S, where 1 is set to be the maximum sustainable population. (Set the units of the number of fish so that 1 is the full population.)

The dynamics of the number of fish is illustrated in Figure 6-16. On the horizontal axis is the number of fish, and on the vertical axis is the change in S. When $\dot{S} > 0$, S is increasing over time, and the arrows on the horizontal axis reflect this. Similarly, if $\dot{S} < 0$, S is decreasing.

Absent fishing, the value 1 is a *stable steady state* of the fish population. It is a steady state because, if $S=1$, $\dot{S} = 0$, that is, there is no change in the fish population. It is stable because the effect of a small perturbation – S near but not exactly equal to 1 – is to return to 1. (In fact, the fish population is very nearly globally stable – start with any population other than zero and the population returns to 1.)[68]

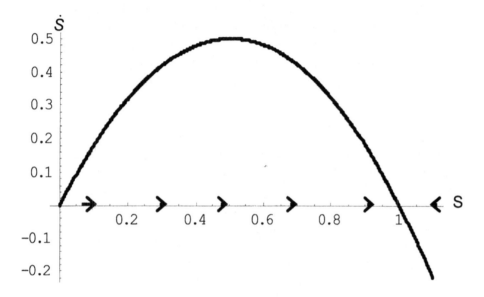

Figure 6-16: Fish Population Dynamics

Now we introduce a human population and turn to the economics of fishing. Suppose that a boat costs b to launch and operate, and that it captures a fixed fraction a of the total stock of fish S, that is, each boat catches aS. Fish sell for a price $p = Q^{-1/\varepsilon}$, where the price arises from the demand curve, which in this case has constant elasticity ε, and Q is the quantity of fish offered for sale. Suppose there be n boats launched; then the quantity of fish caught is $Q=naS$. Fishers enter the market as long as profits are positive, which leads to zero profits for fishers, that is, $b = \left(\frac{Q}{n}\right)p(Q)$. This equation

---

[68] It turns out that there is a closed form solution for the fish population: $S(t) = \dfrac{S(0)}{S(0) + (1 - S(0))e^{-rt}}$.

makes a company just indifferent to launching an additional boat, because the costs and revenues are balanced. These two equations yield two equations in the two unknowns n and Q:

$$n = \frac{Qp(Q)}{b} = \frac{1}{b}Q^{\frac{\varepsilon-1}{\varepsilon}} \text{, and}$$

$Q=naS$. These two equations solve for the number of fish caught:

$$Q = \left(\frac{aS}{b}\right)^{\varepsilon}$$

and the number of boats $n = \dfrac{a^{\varepsilon-1}}{b^{\varepsilon}}S^{\varepsilon-1}$.

Subtracting the capture by humans from the growth in the fish population yields:

$$\dot{S} = rS(1-S) - \left(\frac{aS}{b}\right)^{\varepsilon}.$$

Thus, a steady state satisfies $0 = \dot{S} = rS(1-S) - \left(\dfrac{aS}{b}\right)^{\varepsilon}.$

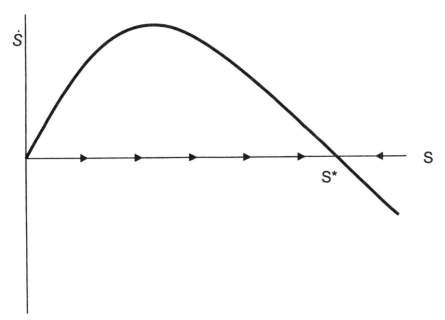

Figure 6-17: Fish Population Dynamics with Fishing

Will human fishing drive the fish to extinction? Extinction must occur when the only stable solution to the stock of fish is zero. Consider first the case when demand is elastic ($\varepsilon > 1$). In this case, for S near zero but positive, $\dot{S} \approx rS > 0$, because the other terms are small relative to the linear term. Thus, with elastic demand, there is always a steady state without extinction. (Extinction is also an equilibrium, too, but over-fishing won't get the system there.) This equilibrium is illustrated in Figure 6-17.

The dark curve represents $\dot{S}$, and thus for S between 0 and the point labeled S^*, $\dot{S}$ is positive and thus S is increasing over time. Similarly, to the right of S^*, S is decreasing. Thus, S^* is stable under small perturbations in the stock of fish and is an equilibrium.

We see that if demand for fish is elastic, fishing will not drive the fish to extinction. Even so, fishing will reduce the stock of fish below the efficient level, because individual fishers don't take account of the externality they impose – their fishing reduces the stock for future generations. The level of fish in the sea converges to S^* satisfying

$$0 = rS^*(1-S^*) - \left(\frac{aS^*}{b}\right)^\varepsilon.$$

In contrast, if demand is inelastic, fishing may drive the fish to extinction. For example, if $r=2$ and $a=b=1$, and $\varepsilon=0.7$, extinction is necessary, as is illustrated in Figure 6-18.

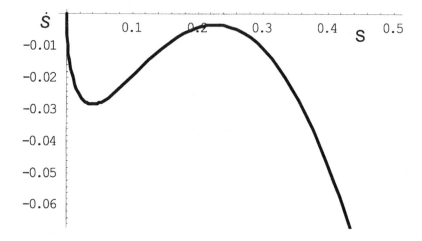

Figure 6-18: Fish Population Dynamics: Extinction

Figure 6-18 shows that, for the given parameters, the net growth of the fish population is negative for every value of the stock S. Thus the population of fish consistently dwindles. This is a case when the fishing externality (overfishing today reduces the stock of fish tomorrow) has particularly dire consequences. The reason why the elasticity of demand matters is that, with inelastic demand, the fall in the stock of fish increases the price by a large amount (enough so that total revenue rises). This, in turn, increases the number of fishing boats, in spite of the fall in the catch. In contrast, with elastic demand, the number of fishing boats falls as the stock falls, reducing the proportion of fish caught, and thus preventing extinction. We see this for the equation for the number of fishing boats

$$n = \frac{a^{\varepsilon-1}}{b^{\varepsilon}} S^{\varepsilon-1}$$

which reflects the fact that *fishing effort rises as the stock falls if and only if demand is inelastic.*

It is possible, even with inelastic demand, for there to be a stable fish population: not all parameter values lead to extinction. Using the same parameters as before, but with ε=0.9, we obtain a stable outcome illustrated in Figure 6-19.

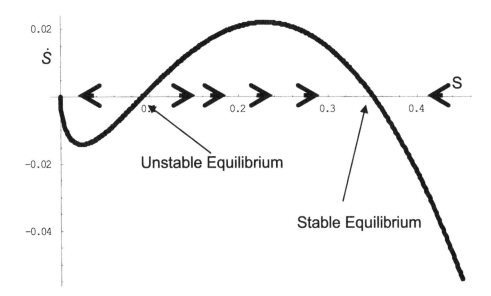

Figure 6-19: Possibility of Multiple Equilibria

In addition to the stable equilibrium outcome, there is an unstable steady state, which might either converge upward or downward. It is a feature of fishing with inelastic demand that there is a region where extinction is inevitable, for when the stock is near zero, the high demand price induced by inelasticity forces sufficient fishing to insure extinction.

As a consequence of the fishing externality, nations attempt to regulate fishing, both by extending their own reach 200 miles into the sea, and by treaties limiting fishing in the open sea. These regulatory attempts have met with only modest success at preventing over-fishing.

What is the efficient stock of fish? This is a challenging mathematical problem, but some insight can be gleaned via a steady state analysis. A steady state arise when $\dot{S} = 0$. If a constant amount Q is removed, a steady state in the stock must occur at $0 = \dot{S} = rS(1-S) - Q$. This maximum catch then occurs at $S = \frac{1}{2}$, and $Q = \frac{1}{4} r$. This is not the efficient level, for it neglects the cost of boats, and the efficient stock will actually be larger. More generally, it is never efficient to send the population below the maximum point on the survival curve plotted in Figure 6-16.

Conceptually, fishing is an example of the tragedy of the commons externality already discussed. However, the threat of a permanent extinction and alluring possibility of solving dynamic models make it a particularly dramatic example.

6.3.6.1 (Exercise)   Suppose $\varepsilon = 1$. For what parameter values are fish necessarily driven to extinction? Can you interpret this condition to say that the demand for caught fish exceeds the production via reproduction?

6.4 Public Goods

A public good has two attributes: *nonexcludability*, which means the producer can't prevent the use of the good by others, and *nonrivalry*, which means that many people can use the good simultaneously.

6.4.1 Examples

Consider a company offering a fireworks display. Pretty much anyone nearby can watch the fireworks, and people with houses in the right place have a great view of them. The company that creates the fireworks can't compel those with nearby homes to pay for the fireworks, and so a lot of people get to watch them without paying. This will make it difficult or impossible for the fireworks company to make a profit. In addition, fireworks offer nonrivalry, in that one person's viewing of the display doesn't impinge significantly on another's viewing. Nonrivalry has the implication that the efficient price is zero, since the marginal cost of another viewer is zero.

The classic example of a public good is national defense. National defense is clearly non-excludable, for if we spend the resources necessary to defend our national borders, it isn't going to be possible to defend everything except one apartment on the second floor of a three story apartment on East Maple Street. Once we have kept our enemies out of our borders, we've protected everyone within the borders. Similarly, the defense of the national borders exhibits a fair degree of nonrivalry, especially insofar as the strategy of defense is to deter an attack in the first place. That is, the same expenditure of resources protects all.

It is theoretically possible to exclude some from the use of a poem, or a mathematical theorem, but exclusion is generally quite difficult. Both poems and theorems are nonrivalrous. Similarly, technological and software inventions are non-rivalrous, even though a patent grants the right to exclude the use by others. Another good that permits exclusion at a cost is a highway. A toll highway shows that exclusion is possible on the highways. Exclusion is quite expensive, partly because the tollbooths require staffing, but mainly because of the delays imposed on drivers associated with paying the tolls – the time costs of toll roads are high. Highways are an intermediate case where exclusion is possible only at a significant cost, and thus should be avoided if possible. Highways are also rivalrous at high congestion levels, but nonrivalrous at low congestion levels. That is, the marginal cost of an additional user is essentially zero for a sizeable number of users, but then marginal cost grows rapidly in the number of users. With fewer than 700 cars per lane per hour on a four lane highway, generally the flow of traffic is unimpeded.[69] As congestion grows beyond this level, traffic slows down and congestion sets in. Thus, west Texas interstate highways are usually nonrivalrous, while Los Angeles freeways are usually very rivalrous.

Like highways, recreational parks are nonrivalrous at low use levels, becoming rivalrous as they become sufficiently crowded. Also like highways, it is possible but expensive to exclude potential users, since exclusion requires fences and a means for admitting some but not others. (Some exclusive parks provide keys to legitimate users, while others use gatekeepers to charge admission.)

6.4.2 Free-Riders

Consider a neighborhood association which is considering buying land and building a park in the neighborhood. The value of the park is going to depend on the size of the park, and we suppose for simplicity that the value in dollars of the park to each household in the neighborhood is $S^b n^{-a}$, where n is the number of park users, S is the size of the park and a and b a are parameters satisfying $0 < a \leq b < 1$. This functional form builds in the property that larger parks provide more value at a diminishing rate, but there is an effect from congestion. The functional form gives a reason for parks to be public – it is more efficient for a group of people to share a large park than for each individual to possess a small park, at least if $b > a$, because the gains from a large park exceed the congestion effects. That is, there is a scale advantage – doubling the number of people and the size of the park increases each individual's enjoyment.

How much will selfish individuals voluntarily contribute to the building of the park? That of course depends on what they think others will contribute. Consider a single household, and suppose that household thinks the others will contribute S_{-1} to the building of the park. Should the household contribute, and if so, how much? If the household contributes s, the park will have size $S = S_{-1} + s$, which the household values at $(S_{-1} + s)^b n^{-a}$. Thus, the net gain to a household that contributes s when the others contribute S_{-1} is $(S_{-1} + s)^b n^{-a} - s$.

6.4.2.1 (Exercise) Verify that individual residents gain from contributing to the park if $S < (bn^{-a})^{\frac{1}{1-b}}$ and gain from reducing their contributions if $S > (bn^{-a})^{\frac{1}{1-b}}$.

The previous exercise shows that individual residents gain from their marginal contribution if and only if the park is smaller than $S_0 = (bn^{-a})^{\frac{1}{1-b}}$. Consequently, under voluntary contributions, the only equilibrium park size is S_0. That is, for any park size smaller than S_0, citizens will voluntarily contribute to make the park larger. For any larger size, no one is willing to contribute.

---

[69] The effect of doubling the number of lanes from 2 to 4 is dramatic. A two lane highway generally flows at 60 mph or more provided there are fewer than 200 cars per lane per hour, while a four lane highway can accommodate 700 cars per lane per hour at the same speed.

Under voluntary contributions, as the neighborhood grows in number, the size of the park shrinks. This makes sense – the benefits of individual contributions to the park mostly accrue to others, which reduces the payoff to any one contributor.

How large *should* the park be? The total value of the park of size S to the residents together is n times the individual value, which gives a collective value of $S^b n^{1-a}$, and the park costs S, so from a social perspective the park should be sized to

maximize $S^b n^{1-a} - S$, which yields an optimal park of size $S^* = (bn^{1-a})^{\frac{1}{1-b}}$. Thus, as the neighborhood grows, the park should grow, but as we saw the park would shrink if the neighborhood has to rely on voluntary contributions. This is because people contribute individually as if they were building the park for themselves, and don't account for the value they provide to their neighbors when they contribute. Under individual contributions, the hope that others contribute leads individuals not to contribute. Moreover, use of the park by others reduces the value of the park to each individual, so that the size of the park shrinks as the population grows under individual contributions. In contrast, the park ought to grow *faster* than the number of residents grows, as the per capita park size is $S^*/n = b^{\frac{1}{1-b}} n^{\frac{b-a}{1-b}}$, which is an increasing function of n.[70]

The lack of incentive for individuals to contribute to a social good is known as a *free-rider problem*. The term refers to the individuals who don't contribute, who are said to *free-ride* on the contributions of others. There are two aspects of the free-rider problem apparent in this simple mathematical model. First, the individual incentive to contribute to a public good is reduced by the contributions of others, and thus individual contributions tend to be smaller when the group is larger. Put another way, the size of the free-rider problem grows as the community grows larger. Second, as the community grows larger, the optimal size of the public good grows. The market failure under voluntary contributions is greater the larger is the community. In the theory presented, the optimal size of the public good is $S^* = (bn^{1-a})^{\frac{1}{1-b}}$, and the actual size under voluntary contributions is $S_0 = (bn^{-a})^{\frac{1}{1-b}}$, a gap that gets very large as the number of people grows.

The upshot is that people will voluntarily contribute too little from a social perspective, by free-riding on the contributions of others. A good example of the provision of public goods is a co-authored term paper. This is a public good because the grade given to the paper is the same for each author, and the quality of the paper depends on the sum of the efforts of the individual authors. Generally, with two authors, both work pretty hard on the manuscript in order to get a good grade. Add a third author and it is a virtual

---

[70] Reminder: In making statements like should and ought, there is no conflict in this model because every household agrees about the optimal size of the park, so that a change to a park size of S*, paid with equal contributions, maximizes every household's utility.

certainty that two of the authors think the third didn't work as hard and was a free-rider on the project.

The term paper example also points to the limitations of the theory. Many people are not as selfish as the theory assumed and will contribute more than would be privately optimal. Moreover, with small numbers, bargaining between the contributors and the division of labor (each works on a section) may help reduce the free-rider problem. Nevertheless, even with these limitations, the free-rider problem is very real and it gets worse the more people are involved. The theory shows that if some individuals contribute more than their share in an altruistic way, the more selfish individuals contribute even less, undoing some of the good done by the altruists.

6.4.2.2 (Exercise)   For the model presented in this section, compute the elasticity of the optimal park size with respect to the number of residents, that is, the percent change in S^* for a small percentage change in n. [Hint: use the linear approximation trick $(1+\Delta)^r \approx r\Delta$ for Δ near zero.]

6.4.2.3 (Exercise)   For the model of this section, show that an individual's utility when the park is optimally sized and the expenses are shared equally among the n individuals is $u = \left(b^{\frac{b}{1-b}} - b^{\frac{1}{1-b}} \right) n^{\frac{b-a}{1-b}}$. Does this model predict an increase in utility from larger communities?

6.4.2.4 (Exercise)   Suppose two people, person 1 and person 2, want to produce a playground to share between them. The value of the playground of size S to each person is $\sqrt{S}$, where S is the number of dollars spent building it. Show that under voluntary contributions, the size of the playground is ¼ and that the efficient size is 1.

6.4.2.5 (Exercise)   For the previous exercise, now suppose person 1 offers "matching funds," that is, offers to contribute an equal amount to the contributions of the person 2. How large a playground will person 2 choose?

6.4.3 Provision with Taxation

Faced with the fact that voluntary contributions produce an inadequate park, the neighborhood turns to taxes. Many neighborhood associations or condominium associations have taxing authority, and can compel individuals to contribute. Clearly in the example from the previous section, and indeed a solution is to require each resident to contribute the amount 1, resulting in a park that is optimally sized at n. Generally it is possible in principle to provide the correct size of the public good using taxes to fund it. However, it will be a challenge in practice, which can be illustrated with a slight modification of the example.

Let individuals have different strengths of preferences, so that individual i values the public good of size S at $v_i S^b n^{-a}$ in dollars. (It is useful to assume that no two people have the same v values to simplify arguments.) The optimal size of the park for the neighborhood is $n^{\frac{-a}{1-b}}\left(b\sum_{i=1}^{n}v_i\right)^{\frac{1}{1-b}} = (b\bar{v})^{\frac{1}{1-b}}n^{\frac{1-a}{1-b}}$, where $\bar{v} = \frac{1}{n}\sum_{i=1}^{n}v_i$ is the average value. Again, taxes can be assessed to pay for an optimally-sized park, but some people (those with small v values) will view that as a bad deal, while others (with large v) view it as a good deal. What will the neighborhood choose?

If there are an odd number of voters in the neighborhood, the prediction is that the park will serve the *median voter* the best.[71] With equal taxes, an individual obtains $v_i S^b n^{-a} - S/n$. If there are an odd number of people, n can be written as $2k+1$. The median voter is the person for whom k have values v_i larger than hers, and k have values smaller. Consider increasing S. If the median voter likes it, then so do all the people with higher v's, and the proposition to increase S passes. Similarly, a proposal to decrease S will get a majority if the median voter likes it. If the median voter likes reducing S, all the individuals with smaller v_i will vote for it as well. Thus, we can see that voting maximizes the preferences of the median voter, and simple calculus shows that entails $S = (bv_k)^{\frac{1}{1-b}}n^{\frac{1-a}{1-b}}$.

Unfortunately, voting does not result in an efficient outcome generally, and only does so when the average value equals the median value. On the other hand, voting generally performs much better than voluntary contributions. The park size can either be larger or smaller under median voting than is efficient.[72]

6.4.3.1 (Exercise)   For the model of this section, show that, under voluntary contributions, only one person contributes, and that person is the person with the largest v_i. How much do they contribute? [Hint: which individual i is willing to contribute at the largest park size? Given the park this individual desires, can anyone else benefit from contributing at all?]

6.4.3.2 (Exercise)   Show that if all individuals value the public good equally, voting on the size of the good results in the efficient provision of the public good.

6.4.4 Local Public Goods

The example in the previous section showed that there are challenges to a neighborhood's provision of public goods created by differences in the preferences of the public good. Voting does not generally lead to the efficient provision of the public good, and does so only in special circumstances, like agreement of preferences.

---

[71] The voting model used is that there is a status quo, which is a planned size of S. Anyone can propose to change the size of S, and the neighborhood votes yes or no. If an S exists such that no replacement gets a majority vote, that S is an equilibrium under majority voting.

[72] The general principle here is that the median voting will do better when the distribution of values is such that the average of n values exceeds the median, which in turn exceeds the maximum divided by n. This is true for most empirically relevant distributions.

A different solution was proposed by Tiebout[73] in 1956. This solution works only when the public goods are local in nature – people living nearby may or may not be excludable, but people living further away can be excluded, and such goods are called "local public goods." Schools are local – more distant people can readily be excluded. Parks are harder to exclude from, but are still local in nature; few people will drive 30 miles to use a park.

Suppose that there are a variety of neighborhoods, some with high taxes, better schools, big parks, beautifully maintained trees on the streets, frequent garbage pickup, a first-rate fire department, extensive police protection and spectacular fireworks displays, and others with lower taxes and more modest provision of public goods. People will tend to move to the neighborhood that fits their preferences. The result is neighborhoods that are relatively homogeneous with respect to the desire for public goods. That homogeneity, in turn, makes voting work better. That is, the ability of people to choose their neighborhoods to suit their preferences over taxes and public goods will make the neighborhood provision of public goods more efficient. The "Tiebout theory" shows that local public goods will tend to be efficiently provided. In addition, even private goods like garbage collection and schools can be efficiently provided publicly if they are local goods, and there are enough distinct localities to offer a broad range of services.

6.4.4.1 (Exercise)   Consider a baby-sitting cooperative, where parents rotate supervision of the children of several families. Suppose that, if the sitting service is available with frequency Y, the value placed by person i is $v_i Y$ and the costs of contribution y is $\frac{1}{2} ny^2$, where Y is the sum of the individual contributions and n is the number of families. Rank $v_1 \geq v_2 \geq ... \geq v_n$. (i) What is the size of the service under voluntary contributions? (Hint: Let y_i be the contribution of family i. Identify the payoff of family j as

$$v_j\left(y_j + \sum_{i \neq j} y_i\right) - \frac{1}{2}n\left(y_j\right)^2$$

What value of y_j maximizes this expression?)

(ii) What contributions maximize the total social value

$$\left(\sum_{j=1}^{n} v_j\right)\left(\sum_{j=1}^{n} y_j\right) - \frac{1}{2}n\sum_{i=1}^{n}\left(y_j\right)^2 ?$$ [Hint: Are the values of y_i different for different i?]

(iii) Let $\mu = \frac{1}{n}\sum_{j=1}^{n} v_j$ and $\sigma^2 = \frac{1}{n}\sum_{j=1}^{n}(v_j - \mu)^2$. Conclude that, under voluntary contributions, the total value generated by the cooperative is $\frac{n}{2}\left(\mu^2 - \sigma^2\right)$ (Hint:

[73] Charles Tiebout, 1919-1962. His surname is pronounced "tee-boo."

It helps to know that

$$\sigma^2 = \frac{1}{n}\sum_{j=1}^{n}(v_j - \mu)^2 = \frac{1}{n}\sum_{j=1}^{n}v_j^2 - \frac{2}{n}\sum_{j=1}^{n}\mu v_j + \frac{1}{n}\sum_{j=1}^{n}\mu^2 = \frac{1}{n}\sum_{j=1}^{n}v_j^2 - \mu^2 .)$$

6.5 Monopoly

We have spent a great deal of time on the competitive model, and we now turn to the polar opposite case, that of monopoly. A monopoly is a firm that faces a downward sloping demand, and has a choice about what price to charge – an increase in price doesn't send most or all of the customers away to rivals.

There are very few pure monopolies. The U.S. post office has a monopoly in first-class mail, but faces competition by FedEx and other express mail companies, as well as by faxes and email, in the broader "send documents to others" market. Microsoft has a great deal of market power, but a small percentage of personal computer users choose Apple or Linux operating systems. There is only one U.S. manufacturer of aircraft carriers.

However, there are many firms that have *market power* or *monopoly power*, which means that they can increase their price above marginal cost and sustain sales for a long period of time.[74] The theory of monopoly is applicable to such firms, although they may face an additional and important constraint: a price increase may affect the behavior of rivals. The behavior of rivals is the subject of the next chapter.

A large market share is not a proof of monopoly, nor is a small market share proof that a firm lacks monopoly power. U.S. Air dominated air traffic to Philadelphia and Pittsburgh, but still lost money. Porsche has a small share of the automobile market, or even the high-end automobile market, but still has monopoly power in that market.

6.5.1 Sources of Monopoly

There are three basic sources of monopoly. The most common source is to be granted a monopoly by the government, either through patents, in which case the monopoly is temporary, or through a government franchise. Intelsat was a government franchise that was granted a monopoly on satellite communications, a monopoly that ultimately proved lucrative indeed. Many cities and towns license a single cable TV company or taxi company, although usually basic rates and fares are set by the terms of the license agreement. New drugs are granted patents that provide a monopoly for a period of time. (Patents generally last twenty years, but pharmaceutical drugs have their own patent laws.) Copyright also confers a monopoly for a supposedly limited period of time. Thus, the Disney Corporation owns copyrights on Mickey Mouse, copyrights which by law should have expired, but have been granted an extension by Congress each time they were due to expire. Copyrights create monopoly power over music as well as cartoon characters, and Time-Warner owns the rights to the song "Happy Birthday to

---

[74] These terms are used somewhat differently by different authors. Both require downward sloping demand, and usually some notion of sustainability of sales. Some distinguish the terms by whether they are "large" or not, others by how long the price increase can be sustained. We won't need such distinctions here.

You," and receives royalties every time it is played on the radio or other commercial venue.[75] Many of the Beatles songs which McCartney co-authored were purchased by Michael Jackson. This book is copyrighted under terms that expressly prohibit commercial use but permit most other uses.

A second source of monopoly is a large economy of scale. The scale economy needs to be large relative to the size of demand. If the average cost when a single firm serves the entire market is lower than when two or more firms serve the market, a monopoly can be the result. For example, long distance telephone lines were expensive to install, and the first company to do so, A.T. & T., wound up being the only provider of long distance service in the United States. Similarly, scale economies in electricity generation meant that most communities had a single electricity provider prior to the 1980s, when new technology made relatively smaller scale generation more efficient.

The demand-side equivalent of an economy of scale is a *network externality*. A network externality arises when others' use of a product makes it more valuable to each consumer. Standards are a common source of network externality. That AA batteries are standardized makes them more readily accessible, helps drive down their price through competition and economies of scale, and thus makes the AA battery more valuable. AA batteries are available everywhere, unlike proprietary batteries. Fax machines are valuable only if others have similar machines. In addition to standards, a source of network externality is third-party products. Choosing Microsoft Windows as a computer operating system means that there is more software available than for Macintosh or Linux, as the widespread adoption of Windows has led a large variety of software to be written for it. The JVC Video Home System of VCRs came to dominate the Sony Beta system, primarily because there were more movies to rent in the VHS format than in the Beta format at the video rental store. In contrast, recordable DVD has been hobbled by incompatible standards of DVD+R and DVD-R, a conflict not resolved even as the next generation – 50GB discs such as Sony's Blu-ray – start to reach the market. DVDs themselves were slow to be adopted by consumers, because few discs were available for rent at video rental stores, which is a consequence of few adoptions of DVD players. As DVD players became more prevalent, and the number of discs for rent increased, the market *tipped* and DVDs came to dominate VHS.

The third source of monopoly is control of an essential, or a sufficiently valuable, input to the production process. Such an input could be technology that confers a cost advantage. For example, software is run by a computer operating system, and needs to be designed to work well with the operating system. There have been a series of allegations that Microsoft kept secret some of the "application program interfaces" used by Word as a means of hobbling rivals. If so, access to the design of the operating system itself is an important input.

6.5.2 Basic Analysis

Even a monopoly is constrained by demand. A monopoly would like to sell lots of units at very high prices, but higher prices necessarily lead to a loss in sales. So how does a monopoly choose its price and quantity?

---

[75] Fair use provisions protect individuals with non-commercial uses of copyrighted materials.

A monopoly can choose price, or a monopoly can choose quantity and let the demand dictate the price. It is slightly more convenient to formulate the theory in terms of quantity rather than price, because costs are a function of quantity. Thus, we let $p(q)$ be the demand price associated with quantity q, and $c(q)$ be the cost of producing q. The monopoly's profits are

$$\pi = p(q)q - c(q).$$

The monopoly earns the revenue pq and pays the cost c. This leads to the first order condition, for the profit-maximizing quantity q_m:

$$0 = \frac{\partial \pi}{\partial q} = p(q_m) + q_m p'(q_m) - c'(q_m).$$

The term $p(q) + qp'(q)$ is known as *marginal revenue*. It is the derivative of revenue pq with respect to quantity. Thus, a monopoly chooses a quantity q_m where marginal revenue equals marginal cost, and charges the maximum price $p(q_m)$ the market will bear at that quantity. Marginal revenue is below demand $p(q)$ because demand is downward sloping. That is, $p(q) + qp'(q) < p(q)$.

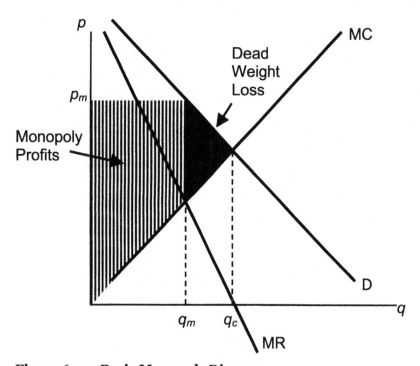

Figure 6-20: Basic Monopoly Diagram

6.5.2.1 (Exercise)   If demand is linear, $p(q) = a - bq$, what is marginal revenue? Plot demand and marginal revenue, and total revenue $qp(q)$ as a function of q.

6.5.2.2 (Exercise) For the case of constant elasticity of demand, what is marginal revenue?

6.5.2.3 (Exercise) If both demand and supply have constant elasticity, compute the monopoly quantity and price.

The choice of monopoly quantity is illustrated in Figure 6-20. The key points of this diagram are, first, that marginal revenue lies below the demand curve. This occurs because marginal revenue is the demand $p(q)$ plus a negative number. Second, the monopoly quantity equates marginal revenue and marginal cost, but the monopoly price is higher than the marginal cost. Third, there is a dead weight loss, for the same reason that taxes create a dead weight loss: the higher price of the monopoly prevents some units from being traded that are valued more highly than they cost. Fourth, the monopoly profits from the increase in price, and the monopoly profit is shaded. Fifth, since under competitive conditions supply equals marginal cost, the intersection of marginal cost and demand corresponds to the competitive outcome. We see that the monopoly restricts output and charges a higher price than would prevail under competition.

We can rearrange the monopoly pricing formula to produce an additional insight.

$$p(q_m) - c'(q_m) = -q_m p'(q_m)$$

or

$$\frac{p(q_m) - c'(q_m)}{p(q_m)} = \frac{-q_m p'(q_m)}{p(q_m)} = \frac{1}{\varepsilon}.$$

The left hand side of this equation is known as the *price-cost margin* or *Lerner Index*.[76] The right hand side is one over the elasticity of demand. This formula relates the markup over marginal cost to the elasticity of demand. It is important because perfect competition forces price to equal marginal cost, so this formula provides a measure of the deviation from competition, and in particular says that the deviation from competition is small when the elasticity of demand is large, and vice versa.

Marginal cost will always be at least zero or larger. If marginal cost is less than zero, the least expensive way to produce a given quantity is to produce more and throw some away. Thus, the price-cost margin is no greater than one, and as a result, *a monopolist produces in the elastic portion of demand.* One implication of this observation is that if demand is everywhere inelastic (e.g. $p(q) = q^{-a}$ for $a>1$), the optimal monopoly quantity is essentially zero, and in any event would be no more than one molecule of the product.

---

[76] Abba Lerner, 1903-1982. Note that $\dfrac{1}{\dfrac{-q_m p'(q_m)}{p(q_m)}} = -\dfrac{\dfrac{1}{q_m}}{\dfrac{p'(q_m)}{p(q_m)}} = -\dfrac{\dfrac{dq}{q}}{\dfrac{dp}{p}} = \varepsilon,$ which is used in the

derivation.

In addition, the effects of monopoly are related to the elasticity of demand. If demand is very elastic, the effect of monopoly on prices is quite limited. In contrast, if the demand is relatively inelastic, monopolies will increase prices by a large margin.

We can rewrite the formula to obtain

$$p(q_m) = \frac{\varepsilon}{\varepsilon - 1} c'(q_m).$$

Thus, a monopolist marks up marginal cost by the factor $\frac{\varepsilon}{\varepsilon - 1}$, at least when $\varepsilon > 1$. This formula is sometimes used to justify a "fixed markup policy," which means a company adds a constant percentage markup to its products. This is an ill-advised policy not justified by the formula, because the formula suggests a markup which depends on the demand for the product in question and thus not a fixed markup for all products a company produces.

6.5.3 Effect of Taxes

A tax imposed on a seller with monopoly power performs differently than a tax imposed on a competitive industry. Ultimately a perfectly competitive industry must pass on all of a tax to consumers, because in the long-run the competitive industry earns zero profits. In contrast, a monopolist might absorb some portion of a tax even in the long-run.

To model the effect of taxes on a monopoly, consider a monopolist who faces a tax rate t per unit of sales. This monopolist earns

$$\pi = p(q)q - c(q) - tq .$$

The first order condition for profit maximization yields

$$0 = \frac{\partial \pi}{\partial q} = p(q_m) + q_m p'(q_m) - c'(q_m) - t .$$

Viewing the monopoly quantity as a function of t, we obtain:

$$\frac{dq_m}{dt} = \frac{1}{2p'(q_m) + q_m p''(q_m) - c''(q_m)} < 0 ,$$

with the sign following from the second order condition for profit maximization. In addition, the change in price satisfies

$$p'(q_m) \frac{dq_m}{dt} = \frac{p'(q_m)}{2p'(q_m) + q_m p''(q_m) - c''(q_m)} > 0.$$

Thus, a tax causes a monopoly to increase its price. In addition, the monopoly price rises by less than the tax if $p'(q_m)\dfrac{dq_m}{dt} < 1$, or

$$p'(q_m) + q_m p''(q_m) - c''(q_m) < 0.$$

This condition need not be true, but is a standard regularity condition imposed by assumption. It is true for linear demand and increasing marginal cost. It is false for constant elasticity of demand, $\varepsilon > 1$ (which is the relevant case, for otherwise the second order conditions fail) and constant marginal cost. In the latter case (constant elasticity and marginal cost), a tax on a monopoly increases price by more than the amount of the tax.

6.5.3.1 (Exercise)   Use a revealed preference argument to show that a per unit tax imposed on a monopoly causes the quantity to fall. That is, hypothesize quantities q_b before the tax, and q_a after the tax, and show that two facts – the before tax monopoly preferred q_b to q_a and the taxed monopoly made higher profits from q_b together imply the $q_b \leq q_a$.

6.5.3.2 (Exercise)   When both demand and supply have constant elasticity, use the results of 6.5.2.3 (Exercise) to compute the effect of a proportional tax (i.e. a portion of the price paid to the government).

6.5.4 Price Discrimination

Pharmaceutical drugs for sale in Mexico are generally priced substantially below their U.S. counterparts. Pharmaceutical drugs in Europe are also cheaper than in the U.S., although not as inexpensive as in Mexico, with Canadian prices usually between the U.S. and European prices. (The comparison is between identical drugs produced by the same manufacturer.)

Pharmaceutical drugs differ in price across countries primarily because demand conditions vary. The formula

$$p(q_m) = \frac{\varepsilon}{\varepsilon - 1} c'(q_m).$$

shows that a monopoly seller would like to charge a higher markup over marginal cost to customers with less elastic demand than to customers with more elastic demand, because $\dfrac{\varepsilon}{\varepsilon - 1}$ is a decreasing function of ε, for $\varepsilon > 1$. Charging different prices for the same product to different customers is known as *price discrimination*. In business settings, it is sometimes known as *value-based pricing*, which is a more palatable term to tell to customers.

Computer software vendors often sell a "student" version of their software, usually at substantially reduced prices, and requiring proof of being a student to qualify for the lower price. Such student discounts are examples of price discrimination, and students have more elastic demand than business users. Similarly, the student and senior citizen discounts at movies and other venues sell the same thing – a ticket to the show – for different prices, and thus qualify as price discrimination.

In order for a seller to price-discriminate, the seller must be able to
- identify (approximately) the demand of groups of customers
- prevent arbitrage

Arbitrage is also known as "buying low and selling high," and represents the act of being an intermediary. Since price discrimination requires charging one group a higher price than another, there is potentially an opportunity for arbitrage, arising from members of the low price group buying at the low price and selling at the high price. If the seller can't prevent arbitrage, arbitrage essentially converts a two-price system to sales at the low price.

Why offer student discounts at the movies? You already know the answer to this – students have lower incomes on average than others, and lower incomes translate into a lower willingness to pay for normal goods. Consequently a discount to a student makes sense from a demand perspective. Arbitrage can be mostly prevented by requiring a student identification card to be presented. Senior citizen discounts are a bit more subtle. Generally seniors aren't poorer than other groups of customers (in the United States, at least). However, seniors have more free time, and thus are able to substitute to matinee showings[77] or drive to more distant locations should those offer discounts. Thus seniors have relatively elastic demand more because of their ability to substitute than because of their income.

Airlines commonly price discriminate, using "Saturday night stay-overs" and other devices. To see that such charges represent price discrimination, consider a passenger who lives in Dallas but needs to spend Monday through Thursday in Los Angeles two weeks in a row. This passenger could buy two round-trip tickets:

Trip One:
First Monday: Dallas → Los Angeles
First Friday: Los Angeles → Dallas

Trip Two:
Second Monday: Dallas → Los Angeles
Second Friday: Los Angeles → Dallas

At the time of this writing, the approximate combined cost of these two flights was US$2,000. In contrast, another way of arranging exactly the same travel is to have two round-trips, one of which originates in Dallas, while the other originates in Los Angeles:

---

[77] Matinee showings are those early in the day, which are usually discounted. These discounts are not price discrimination because a show at noon isn't the same product as a show in the evening.

Trip One:
First Monday: Dallas → Los Angeles
Second Friday: Los Angeles → Dallas

Trip Two:
First Friday: Los Angeles → Dallas
Second Monday: Dallas → Los Angeles

This pair of round trips involves exactly the same travel as the first pair, but costs less than $500 for both (at the time of this writing). The difference is that the second pair involves staying over Saturday night for both legs, and that leads to a major discount for most U.S. airlines. (American Airlines quoted the fares.)

How can airlines price discriminate? There are two major groups of customers: business travelers and leisure travelers. Business travelers have the higher willingness to pay overall, and the nature of their trips tends to be that they come home for the weekend. In contrast, a leisure traveler will usually want to be away for a weekend, so a weekend stay-over is an indicator of a leisure traveler. It doesn't work perfectly as an indicator – some business travelers must be away for the weekend – but it is sufficiently correlated with leisure travel that it is profitable for the airline to price discriminate.

These examples illustrate an important distinction. Senior citizen and student discounts are based on the identity of the buyer, and qualifying for the discount requires showing an identity card. In contrast, airline price discrimination is not based on the identity of the buyer but on the choices by the buyer. The former is known as *direct price discrimination*, while the latter is known as *indirect price discrimination*.[78]

Two common examples of indirect price discrimination are coupons and quantity discounts. Coupons offer discounts for products and are especially common in grocery stores, where they are usually provided in a newspaper section available free at the front of the store. Coupons discriminate on the basis of the cost of time. It takes time to find the coupons for the products one is interested in buying, and thus those with a high value of time won't find it worthwhile spending twenty minutes to save $5 (effectively a $15 per hour return), while those with a low value of time will find that return worthwhile. Since those with a low value of time tend to be more price sensitive (more elastic demand), coupons offer a discount available to all but used primarily by customers with a more elastic demand, and thus increase the profits of the seller.

Quantity discounts are discounts for buying more. Thus, the large size of milk, laundry detergent and other items often cost less per unit than smaller sizes, and the difference is greater than the savings on packaging costs. In some cases, the larger sizes entail greater packaging costs; some manufacturers "band together" individual units, incurring additional costs to create a larger size which is then discounted. Thus, the "twenty-four pack" of paper towels sells for less per roll than the individual rolls; such large volumes appeal primarily to large families, who are more price-sensitive on average.

---

[78] The older and incoherent language for these concepts called direct price discrimination "third degree price discrimination," while indirect price discrimination was called second degree price discrimination. In the older language, first degree price discrimination meant perfect third degree price discrimination.

6.5.5 Welfare Effects

Is price discrimination a good thing, or a bad thing? It turns out that there is no definitive answer to this question. Instead, it depends on circumstances. We illustrate this conclusion with a pair of exercises.

6.5.5.1 (Exercise)   Let marginal cost be zero for all quantities. Suppose there are two equal-sized groups of customers, group 1 with demand $q(p)=12-p$, group 2 with demand $q(p)=8-p$. Show that a non-discriminating monopolist charges a price of 5 and the discriminating monopolist charges group 1 the price 6 and group 2 the price 4. Then calculate the gains from trade, with discrimination and without, and show that price discrimination reduces the gains from trade.

This exercise illustrates a much more general proposition: if a price-discriminating monopolist produces less than a non-discriminating monopolist, then price discrimination reduced welfare. This proposition has an elementary proof. Consider the price discriminating monopolist's sales, and then allow arbitrage. The arbitrage increases the gains from trade, since every transaction has gains from trade. Arbitrage, however, leads to a common price like that charged by a non-discriminating monopolist. Thus, the only way price discrimination can increase welfare is if it leads a seller to sell more output than she would otherwise. This is possible, as the next exercise shows.

6.5.5.2 (Exercise)   Let marginal cost be zero for all quantities. Suppose there are two equal-sized groups of customers, group 1 with demand $q(p)=12-p$, group 2 with demand $q(p)=4-p$. Show that a non-discriminating monopolist charges a price of 6 and the discriminating monopolist charges group 1 the price 6 and group 2 the price 2. Then calculate the gains from trade, with discrimination and without, and show that price discrimination increases the gains from trade.

In this exercise, we see that price discrimination that brings in a new group of customers may increase the gains from trade. Indeed, this example involves a Pareto improvement: the seller and group 2 are better off, and group 1 no worse off, than without price discrimination. (A Pareto improvement requires that no one is worse off and at least one person is better off.)

Whether price discrimination increases the gains from trade overall depends on circumstances. However, it is worth remembering that people with lower incomes tend to have more elastic demand, and thus get lower prices under price discrimination than absent price discrimination. Consequently, a ban on price discrimination tends to hurt the poor and benefit the rich no matter what the overall effect.

6.5.6 Two-Part Pricing

A common form of price discrimination is known as *two-part pricing*. Two-part pricing usually involves a fixed charge and a marginal charge, and thus offers an ability for a seller to capture a portion of the consumer surplus. For example, electricity often comes with a fixed price per month and then a price per kilowatt-hour, which is two-part pricing. Similarly, long distance and cellular telephone companies charge a fixed fee per month, with a fixed number of "included" minutes, and a price per minute for additional minutes. Such contracts really involve three parts rather than two-parts, but are similar in spirit.

From the seller's perspective, the ideal two-part price is to charge marginal cost plus a fixed charge equal to the customer's consumer surplus, or perhaps a penny less. By setting price equal to marginal cost, the seller maximizes the gains from trade. By setting the fixed fee equal to consumer surplus, the seller captures the entire gains from trade. This is illustrated in Figure 6-21.

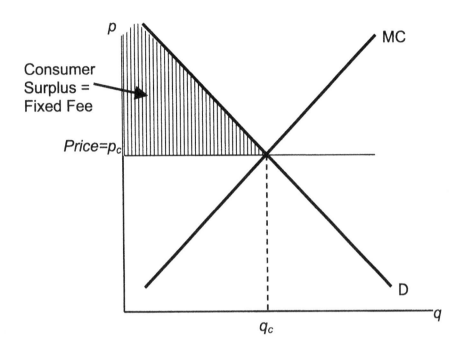

Figure 6-21: Two-Part Pricing

6.5.7 Natural Monopoly

A natural monopoly arises when a single firm can efficiently serve the entire market because average costs are lower with one firm than with two firms. An example is illustrated in Figure 6-22. In this case, the average total cost of a single firm is lower than if two firms operate, splitting the output between them. The monopolist would like to price at p_m, which maximizes profits.[79]

---

[79] The monopoly price may or may not be *sustainable*. A monopoly price is not sustainable if it would lead to entry, thereby undercutting the monopoly. The feasibility of entry, in turn, depends on whether the costs of entering are not recoverable ("*sunk*"), and how rapidly entry can occur. If the monopoly price is not sustainable, the monopoly may engage in *limit pricing*, which is jargon for pricing to deter (limit) entry.

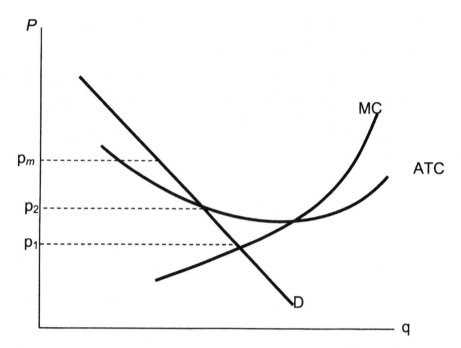

Figure 6-22: Natural Monopoly

Historically, the United States and other nations have regulated natural monopolies like those found in electricity, telephony and water service. An immediate problem with regulation is that the efficient price, that is, the price that maximizes the gains from trade, requires a subsidy from outside the industry. We see the need for a subsidy in Figure 6-22 because the price that maximizes the gains from trade is p_1, which sets the demand (marginal value) equal to the marginal cost. At this price, however, the average total cost exceeds the price, so that a firm with such a regulated price would lose money. There are two alternatives. The product could be subsidized, and subsidies are used with postal service and passenger rail in the United States, and historically for many more products in Canada and Europe including airlines and airplane manufacture. Alternatively, regulation could be imposed that aims to limit the price to p_2, the lowest break-even price. This is the more common strategy in the United States.

There are two strategies toward limiting the price: *price-cap regulation*, which directly imposes a maximum price, and *rate of return regulation*, that limits the profitability of firms. Both of these approaches induce some inefficiency of production. In both cases, an increase in average cost may translate into additional profits for the firm, causing regulated firms to engage in unnecessary activities.

6.5.8 Peak Load Pricing

Fluctuations in demand often require holding capacity which is used only a fraction of the time. Hotels have off-seasons when most rooms are empty. Electric power plants are designed to handle peak demand, usually hot summer days, with some of the capacity standing idle on other days. Demand for trans-Atlantic airline flights is much higher in the summer than the rest of the year. All of these examples have the similarity that an amount of capacity – hotel space, airplane seats, electric generation capacity – will be used over and over, which means it is used in both high demand and low demand states. How should pricing be accomplished when demand fluctuates? This can be thought of as a question of how to allocate the cost of capacity across several time periods when demand systematically fluctuates.

Consider a firm that experiences two kinds of costs – a capacity cost and a marginal cost. How should capacity be priced? This issue is applicable to a wide variety of industries, including pipelines, airlines, telephone networks, construction, electricity, highways, and the internet.

The basic peak-load pricing problem, pioneered by Marcel Boiteux (1922 –), considers two periods. The firm's profits are given by

$$\pi = p_1 q_1 + p_2 q_2 - \beta \max\{q_1, q_2\} - mc(q_1 + q_2).$$

Setting price equal to marginal costs is not sustainable, because a firm selling with price equal to marginal cost would not earn a return on the capacity, and thus would lose money and go out of business. Consequently, a capacity charge is necessary. The question of peak load pricing is how the capacity charge should be allocated. This question is not trivial because some of the capacity is used in both periods.

For the sake of simplicity, we will assume demands are independent, that is, q_1 is independent of p_2 and vice versa. This assumption is often unrealistic, and generalizing it actually doesn't complicate the problem too much. The primary complication is in computing the social welfare when demands are functions of two prices. Independence is a convenient starting point.

Social welfare is

$$W = \int_0^{q_1} p_1(x)dx + \int_0^{q_2} p_2(x)dx - \beta \max\{q_1, q_2\} - mc(q_1 + q_2).$$

The Ramsey problem is to maximize W subject to a minimum profit condition. A technique for accomplishing this maximization is to instead maximize

$$L = W + \lambda \pi.$$

By varying λ, we vary the importance of profits to the maximization problem, which will increase the profit level in the solution as λ increases. Thus, the correct solution to the constrained maximization problem is the outcome of the maximization of L, for some value of λ.

A useful notation is 1_A, which is known as the *characteristic function of the set A*. This is a function which is 1 when A is true, and zero otherwise. Using this notation, the first order condition for the maximization of L is:

$$0 = \frac{\partial L}{\partial q_1} = p_1(q_q) - \beta 1_{q_1 \geq q_2} - mc + \lambda \left(p_1(q_q) + q_1 p_1{}'(q_1) - \beta 1_{q_1 \geq q_2} - mc \right)$$

or,

$$\frac{p_1(q_1) - \beta 1_{q_1 \geq q_2} - mc}{p_1} = \frac{\lambda}{\lambda + 1} \frac{1}{\varepsilon_1}$$

where $1_{q_1 \geq q_2}$ is the characteristic function of the event $q_1 \geq q_2$.

Similarly,

$$\frac{p_2(q_2) - \beta 1_{q_1 \leq q_2} - mc}{p_2} = \frac{\lambda}{\lambda + 1} \frac{1}{\varepsilon_2}$$

Note as before that $\lambda \to \infty$ yields the monopoly solution.

There are two potential types of solution. Let the demand for good 1 exceed the demand for good 2. Either $q_1 > q_2$, or the two are equal.

Case 1: $q_1 > q_2$.

$$\frac{p_1(q_1) - \beta - mc}{p_1} = \frac{\lambda}{\lambda + 1} \frac{1}{\varepsilon_1} \quad \text{and} \quad \frac{p_2(q_2) - mc}{p_2} = \frac{\lambda}{\lambda + 1} \frac{1}{\varepsilon_2}.$$

In case 1, with all of the capacity charge allocated to good 1, quantity for good 1 still exceeds quantity for good 2. Thus, the peak period for good 1 is an extreme peak. In contrast, case 2 arises when assigning the capacity charge to good 1 would reverse the peak – assigning all of the capacity charge to good 1 would make period 2 the peak.

Case 2: $q_1 = q_2$.

The profit equation can be written

$p_1(q) - mc + p_2(q) - mc = \beta$

This equation determines q, and prices are determined from demand.

The major conclusion from peak load pricing is that either the entire cost of capacity is allocated to the peak period, or there is no peak period in the sense that the two periods have the same quantity demanded given the prices. That is, either the prices equalize the quantity demanded, or the prices impose the entire cost of capacity only on one peak period.

Moreover, the price (or, more properly, the markup over marginal cost) is proportional to the inverse of the elasticity, which is known as Ramsey pricing.

6.6 *Information*

An important advantage of the price system is that it economizes on information. A typical consumer needs to know only the prices of goods and their own personal preferences in order to make a sensible choice of purchases, and manufacturers only need to know the prices of goods in order to decide what to produce. Such economies of information are an advantage over centrally-planned economies, which attempt to direct production and consumption decisions using something other than prices, and centrally-planned economies typically experience chronic shortages and occasional surpluses. Shortages of important inputs to production may have dramatic effects and the shortages aren't remedied by the price of the input rising in a centrally planned economy, and thus often persist for long periods of time.

There are, however, circumstances where the prices are not the only necessary information required for firms and consumers to make good decisions. In such circumstances, information itself can lead to market failures.

6.6.1 Market for Lemons

Nobel laureate George Akerlof (1940 –) examined the market for used cars and considered a situation where the sellers are better informed than the buyers. This is quite reasonable, as sellers have owned the car for a while and are likely to know its quirks and potential problems. Akerlof showed that this differential information may cause the used car market to collapse; that is, the information possessed by sellers of used cars destroys the market.

To understand Akerlof's insight, suppose that the quality of used cars lies on a 0 to 1 scale and that the population of used cars is uniformly distributed on the interval from 0 to 1. In addition, let that quality represent the value a seller places on the car, and suppose buyers put a value that is 50% higher than the seller. Finally, the seller knows the actual quality, while the buyer does not.

Can a buyer and seller trade in such a situation? First, note that trade is a good thing, because the buyer values the car more than the seller. That is, both the buyer and seller know that they should trade. But can they agree on a price? Consider a price p. At this price, any seller who values the car less than p will be willing to trade. But because of our uniform distribution assumption, this means the distribution of qualities of cars offered for trade at price p will be uniform on the interval 0 to p. Consequently, the average quality of these cars will be ½ p, and the buyer values these cars 50% more which yields ¾ p. Thus, the buyer is not willing to pay the price p for the average car offered at price p.

The effect of the informed seller, and uninformed buyer, produces a "lemons" problem. At any given price, all the lemons and only a few of the good cars are offered, and the buyer – not knowing the quality of the car – isn't willing to pay as much as the actual value of a high value car offered for sale. This causes the market to collapse; and only the worthless cars trade at a price around zero. Economists call the differential information an *informational asymmetry*.

In the real world, of course, the market has found partial or imperfect solutions to the *lemons* problem identified by Akerlof. First, buyers can become informed and regularly hire their own mechanic to inspect a car they are considering. Inspections reduce the informational asymmetry but are costly in their own right. Second, intermediaries offer warranties and certification to mitigate the lemons problem. The existence of both of these solutions, which involve costs in their own right, is itself evidence that the lemons problem is a real and significant problem, even though competitive markets find ways to ameliorate the problems.

An important example of the lemons problem is the inventor who creates an idea that is difficult or impossible to patent. Consider an innovation that would reduce the cost of manufacturing computers. The inventor would like to sell it to a computer company, but can't tell the computer company what the innovation entails prior to price negotiations, because then the computer company could just copy the innovation. Similarly, the computer company can't possibly offer a price for the innovation in advance of knowing what the innovation is. As a result, such innovations usually require the inventor to enter the computer manufacturing business, rather than selling to an existing manufacturer, entailing many otherwise unnecessary costs.

6.6.1.1 (Exercise)   In Akerlof's market for lemons model, suppose it is possible to certify cars, verifying that they are better than a particular quality q. Thus, a market for cars "at least as good as q" is possible. What price or prices are possible in this market? [Hint: sellers offer cars only if $q \leq$ quality $\leq p$.] What quality maximizes the expected gains from trade?

6.6.2 Myerson-Satterthwaite Theorem

The lemons problem is a situation where the buyers are relatively uninformed and care about the information held by sellers. Lemons problems are limited to situations where the buyer isn't well-informed and can be mitigated by making information public. In many transactions, the buyer knows the quality of the product, so lemons concerns aren't a significant issue. There can still be a market failure, however, if there are a limited number of buyers and sellers.

Consider the case of one buyer and one seller bargaining over the sale of a good. The buyer knows his own value v for the good, but not the seller's cost. The seller knows her own cost c for the good, but not the buyer's value. The buyer views the seller's cost as uniformly distributed on the interval [0,1], and similarly the seller views the buyer's value as uniformly distributed on [0,1].[80] Can efficient trade take place? Efficient trade requires that trade occurs whenever $v > c$, and the remarkable answer is that it is impossible to arrange efficient trade if the buyer and seller are to trade voluntarily. This

---

[80] The remarkable fact proved by Roger Myerson and Mark Satterthwaite (Efficient Mechanisms for Bilateral Trade, *Journal of Economic Theory*, 28, 1983, 265-281) is that the distributions don't matter; the failure of efficient trade is a fully general property. Philip Reny and Preston McAfee (Correlated Information and Mechanism Design, *Econometrica* 60, No. 2, March 1992, 395-421) show the nature of the distribution of information matters, and Preston McAfee (Efficient Allocation with Continuous Quantities, *Journal of Economic Theory* 53, no. 1, February 1991: 51-74.) showed that continuous quantities can overturn the Myerson-Satterthwaite theorem.

is true even if a third party is used to help arrange trade, provided the third party doesn't subsidize the transaction.

The total gains from trade under efficiency are

$$\int_0^1 \int_0^v v - c \, dc \, dv = \int_0^1 \frac{v^2}{2} dv = \frac{1}{6}.$$

A means of arranging trade, or a *mechanism*, asks the buyer and seller for their value and cost, respectively, and then orders trade if the value exceeds the cost, and dictates a payment p by the buyer to the seller. Buyers need not make honest reports to the mechanism, however, and the mechanisms must be designed to induce the buyer and seller to report honestly to the mechanism, so that efficient trades can be arranged.[81]

Consider a buyer who actually has value v but reports a value r. The buyer trades with the seller if the seller has a cost less than r, which occurs with probability r.

$u(r,v) = vr - E_c p(r, c)$.

The buyer gets the actual value v with probability r, and makes a payment that depends on the buyer's report and the seller's report, but we can take expectations over the seller's report to eliminate it (from the buyer's perspective), and this is denoted $E_c p(r, c)$, which is just the expected payment given the report r. In order for the buyer to choose to be honest, u must be maximized at $r=v$ for every v, for otherwise some buyers would lie and some trades would not be efficiently arranged. Thus, we can conclude[82]

$$\frac{d}{dv} u(v,v) = u_1(v,v) + u_2(v,v) = u_2(v,v) = r \Big|_{r=v} = v.$$

The first equality is just the total derivative of $u(v,v)$, because there are two terms; the second equality because u is maximized over the first argument r at $r=v$, and the first order condition insures $u_1 = 0$. Finally, u_2 is just r, and we are evaluating the derivative at the point $r = v$. A buyer who has a value $v + \Delta$, but who reports v, trades with probability v and makes the payment $E_c p(v, c)$. Such a buyer gets Δv more in utility than the buyer with value v. Thus a Δ increase in value produces an increase in utility of at least Δv, showing that $u(v + \Delta, v + \Delta) \geq u(v,v) + \Delta v$ and hence that $\frac{d}{dv} u(v,v) \geq v$. A similar argument considering a buyer with value v who reports $v + \Delta$ shows that equality occurs.

---

[81] Inducing honesty is without loss of generality. Suppose that the buyer of type v reported the type $z(v)$. Then we can add a stage to the mechanism, where the buyer reports a type, which is converted via the function z to a report, and then that report given to the original mechanism. In the new mechanism, reporting v is tantamount to reporting $z(v)$ to the original mechanism.

[82] We maintain an earlier notation that the subscript refers to a partial derivative, so that if we have a function f, f_1 is the partial derivative of f with respect to the first argument of f.

The value $u(v,v)$ is the gain accruing to a buyer with value v who reports having value v. Since the buyer with value 0 gets zero, the total gain accruing to the average buyer can be computed by integrating by parts

$$\int_0^1 u(v,v)dv = -(1-v)u(v,v)\Big|_{v=0}^1 + \int_0^1 (1-v)\left(\frac{du}{dv}\right)dv = \int_0^1 (1-v)vdv = \frac{1}{6}.$$

In the integration by parts, $dv = d\,-(1-v)$ is used. The remarkable conclusion is that, if the buyer is induced to truthfully reveal the buyer's value, the buyer must obtain the entire gains from trade! This is actually a quite general proposition. If you offer the entire gains from trade to a party, they are induced to maximize the gains from trade. Otherwise, they will want to distort away from maximizing the entire gains from trade, which will result in a failure of efficiency.

The logic with respect to the seller is analogous: the only way to get the seller to report her cost honestly is to offer her the entire gains from trade.

6.6.2.1 (Exercise)   Let $h(r, c)$ be the gains of a seller who has cost c and reports r,

$h(r, c) = p(v, r) - (1-r)c.$

Noting that the highest cost seller ($c=1$) never sells and thus obtains zero profits, show that honesty by the seller implies the expected value of h is $\frac{1}{6}$.

The Myerson-Satterthwaite theorem shows that the gains from trade are insufficient to induce honesty by both parties. (Indeed, they are half the necessary amount!) Thus, any mechanism for arranging trades between the buyer and the seller must suffer some inefficiency. Generally this occurs because buyers act like they value the good less than they do, and sellers act like their costs are higher than they truly are.

It turns out that the worst case scenario is a single buyer and a single seller. As markets get "thick," the per capita losses converge to zero, and markets become efficient. Thus, informational problems of this kind are a "small numbers" issue. However, many markets do in fact have small numbers of buyers or sellers. In such markets, it seems likely that informational problems will be an impediment to efficient trade.

6.6.3 Signaling

An interesting approach to solving informational problems involves *signaling*.[83] Signaling, in economic jargon, means expenditures of time or money whose purpose is to convince others of something. Thus, people signal wealth by wearing Rolex watches, driving expensive cars or sailing in the America's Cup. They signal erudition by tossing out quotes from Kafka or Tacitus into conversations. They signal being chic by wearing the right clothes and listening to cool music. Signaling is also rampant in the animal

---

[83] Signaling was introduced by Nobel laureate Michael Spence in his dissertation, part of which was reprinted in "Job Market Signaling," *Quarterly Journal of Economics* 87, August 1973, 355-74.

world, from peacock feathers to elk battles and the subject of a vibrant and related research program.

A university education serves not just to educate, but also to signal the ability to learn. Businesses often desire employees who are able to adapt to changing circumstances, and who can easily and readily learn new strategies and approaches. Education signals such abilities because it will easier for quick learners to perform well in university. A simple model suffices to illustrate the point. Suppose there are two types of people. Type A has a low cost c_A of learning, and type B has a higher cost c_B of learning. It is difficult to determine from an interview whether someone is type A or not. Type A is worth more to businesses, and the competitive wage w_A (expressed as a present value of lifetime earnings) for type A's is higher than the wage w_B for type B's.

A person can signal that they are a type A by taking a sufficient amount of education. Suppose the person devotes an amount of time x to learning in university, thus incurring the cost $c_A x$. If x is large enough so that

$$w_A - c_A x > w_B > w_A - c_B x,$$

it pays the type A to obtain the education, but not the type B, if education in fact signals that the student is type A. Thus, a level of education x in this case signals a trait (ease of learning) that is valued by business, and it does so by voluntary choice – those with a high cost of learning choose not to obtain the education, even though they could do it. This works as a signal because only type A would voluntarily obtain the education in return for being perceived to be a type A.

There are several interesting aspects to this kind of signaling. First, the education embodied in x need not be valuable in itself; the student could be studying astronomy or ancient Greek, neither of which are very useful in most businesses, but are nevertheless strong signals of the ability to learn. Second, the best subject matter for signaling is that in which the difference in cost between the type desired by employers and the less desirable type is greatest, that is, where $c_B - c_A$ is greatest. Practical knowledge is somewhat unlikely to make this difference great; instead, challenging abstract problem-solving may be a better separator. Clearly, it is desirable to have the subject matter be useful, if it can still do the signaling job. But interpreting long medieval poems could more readily signal the kind of flexible mind desired in management than studying accounting, not because the desirable type is good at it, or that it is useful, but because the less desirable type is so much worse at it.

Third, one interprets signals by asking "what kinds of people would make this choice?" while understanding that the person makes the choice hoping to send the signal. Successful law firms have very fine offices, generally much finer than the offices of their clients. Moreover, there are back rooms at most law firms, where much of the real work is done, that aren't nearly so opulent. The purpose of the expensive offices is to signal success, essentially making the statement that

> "we couldn't afford to waste money on such expensive offices if we weren't very successful. Thus, you should believe we are successful."

The law firm example is similar to the education example. Here, the cost of the expenditures on fancy offices is different for different law firms because more successful firms earn more money and thus value the marginal dollar less. Consequently, more successful firms have a lower cost of a given level of office luxury. What is interesting about signaling is that it is potentially quite wasteful. A student spends four years studying boring poems and dead languages in order to demonstrate a love of learning, and a law firm pays $75,000 for a conference table that it rarely uses and gets no pleasure out of, in order to convince a client that the firm is extremely successful. In both cases, it seems like a less costly solution should be available. The student can take standardized tests, and the law firm could show its win-loss record to the potential client. But standardized tests may measure test-taking skills rather than learning ability, especially if what matters is the learning ability over a long time horizon. Win-loss records can be "massaged," and in the majority of all legal disputes, the case settles and both sides consider themselves "the winner." Consequently, statistics may not be a good indicator of success, and the expensive conference table a better guide.

7 Strategic Behavior

Competitive theory studies price-taking consumers and firms, that is, people who can't individually affect the transaction prices. The assumption that market participants take prices as given is justified only when there are many competing participants. We have also examined monopoly, precisely because a monopoly by definition doesn't have to worry about competitors. Strategic behavior involves the examination of the intermediate case, where there are few enough participants that they take each other into account and their actions individually matter, and where the behavior of any one participant influences choices of the other participants. That is, participants are *strategic* in their choice of action, recognizing that their choice will affect choices made by others.

The right tool for the job of examining strategic behavior in economic circumstances is *game theory*, the study of how people play games. Game theory was pioneered by the mathematical genius John von Neumann (1903-1957). Game theory has also been very influential in the study of military strategy, and indeed the strategy of the cold war between the United States and the U.S.S.R. was guided by game theoretic analyses.[84]

7.1 Games

The theory of games provides a description of games that fits common games like poker or the board game "Monopoly" but will cover many other situations as well. In any game, there is a list of players. Games generally unfold over time; at each moment in time, players have information, possibly incomplete, about the current state of play, and a set of actions they can take. Both information and actions may depend on the history of the game prior to that moment. Finally, players have payoffs, and are assumed to play in such a way as to maximize their expected payoff, taking into account their expectations for the play of others. When the players, their information and available actions, and payoffs have been specified, we have a game.

7.1.1 Matrix Games

The simplest game is called a matrix payoff game with two players. In a matrix payoff game, all actions are chosen simultaneously. It is conventional to describe a matrix payoff game as played by a row player and a column player. The row player chooses a row in a matrix; the column player simultaneously chooses a column. The outcome of the game is a pair of payoffs where the first entry is the payoff of the row player and the second is the payoff of the column player. Table 7-1 provides an example of a "2 × 2" matrix payoff game, the most famous game of all, which is known as the *prisoner's dilemma*.

---

[84] An important reference for game theory is John von Neumann (1903-1957) and Oskar Morgenstern (1902-1977), *Theory of Games and Economic Behavior*, Princeton: Princeton University Press, 1944. Important extensions were introduced by John Nash (1928 –), the mathematician made famous by Sylvia Nasar's delightful book *A Beautiful Mind* (Simon & Schuster, 1998). Finally, applications in the military arena were pioneered by Nobel Laureate Thomas Schelling (1921 –), *The Strategy of Conflict*, Cambridge: Cambridge University Press, 1960.

Table 7-1: The Prisoner's Dilemma

		Column	
		Confess	Don't
Row	Confess	(-10,-10)	(0,-20)
	Don't	(-20,0)	(-1,-1)

In the prisoner's dilemma, two criminals named Row and Column have been apprehended by the police and are being questioned separately. They are jointly guilty of the crime. Each player can choose either to confess or not. If Row confesses, we are in the top row of the matrix (corresponding to the row labeled Confess). Similarly, if Column confesses, the payoff will be in the relevant column. In this case, if only one player confesses, that player goes free and the other serves twenty years in jail. (The entries correspond to the number of years lost to prison. The first entry is always Row's payoff, the second Column's payoff.) Thus, for example, if Column confesses and Row does not, the relevant payoff is the first column and the second row, in reverse color in Table 7-2.

Table 7-2: Solving the Prisoner's Dilemma

Column

Row

If Column confesses and Row does not, Row loses twenty years, and Column loses no years, that is, goes free. This is the payoff (-20,0) in reverse color in Table 7-2. If both confess, they are both convicted and neither goes free, but they only serve ten years each. Finally, if neither confesses, there is a ten percent chance they are convicted anyway (using evidence other than the confession), in which case they average a year lost each.

The prisoner's dilemma is famous partly because it is readily solvable. First, Row has a strict advantage to confessing, no matter what Column is going to do. If Column confesses, Row gets -10 from confessing, -20 from not, and thus is better off from confessing. Similarly, if Column doesn't confess, Row gets 0 from confessing, -1 from not confessing, and is better off confessing. Either way, no matter what Column does, Row should choose to confess.[85] This is called a *dominant strategy*, a strategy that is optimal no matter what the other players do.

The logic is exactly similar for Column: no matter what Row does, Column should choose to confess. That is, Column also has a dominant strategy, to confess. To establish this, first consider what Column's best action is, when Column thinks Row will confess. Then consider Column's best action when Column thinks Row won't confess.

---

[85] If Row and Column are friends are care about each other, that should be included as part of the payoffs. Here, there is no honor or friendship among thieves, and Row and Column only care about what they themselves will get.

Either way, Column gets a higher payoff (lower number of years lost to prison) by confessing.

The presence of a dominant strategy makes the prisoner's dilemma particularly easy to solve. Both players should confess. Note that this gets them ten years each in prison, and thus isn't a very good outcome from their perspective, but there is nothing they can do about it in the context of the game, because for each, the alternative to serving ten years is to serve twenty years. This outcome is referred to as (Confess, Confess), where the first entry is the row player's choice, and the second entry is the column player's choice.

Consider an entry game, played by Microsoft (the row player) and Piuny (the column player), a small start-up company. Both Microsoft and Piuny are considering entering a new market for an online service. The payoff structure is

Table 7-3: An Entry Game

		Piuny	
		Enter	Don't
MS	Enter	(2,-2)	(5,0)
	Don't	(0,5)	(0,0)

In this case, if both companies enter, Microsoft ultimately wins the market, and earns 2, and Piuny loses 2. If either firm has the market to itself, they get 5 and the other firm gets zero. If neither enters, both get zero. Microsoft has a dominant strategy to enter: it gets 2 when Piuny enters, 5 when Piuny doesn't, and in both cases does better than when Microsoft doesn't enter. In contrast, Piuny does not have a dominant strategy: Piuny wants to enter when Microsoft doesn't, and vice-versa. That is, Piuny's optimal strategy depends on Microsoft's action, or, more accurately, Piuny's optimal strategy depends on what Piuny believes Microsoft will do.

Piuny can understand Microsoft's dominant strategy, if it knows the payoffs of Microsoft.[86] Thus, Piuny can conclude that Microsoft is going to enter, and this means that Piuny should not enter. Thus, the *equilibrium* of the game is for MS to enter and Piuny not to enter. This equilibrium is arrived at by the *iterated elimination of dominated strategies*, which sounds like jargon but is actually plain speaking. First, we eliminated Microsoft's *dominated strategy* in favor of its dominant strategy. Microsoft had a dominant strategy to enter, which means the strategy of not entering is dominated by the strategy of entering, so we eliminated the dominated strategy. That leaves a simplified game in which Microsoft enters:

---

[86] It isn't so obvious that one player will know the payoffs of another player, and that often causes players to try to signal that they are going to play a certain way, that is, to demonstrate commitment to a particular advantageous strategy. Such topics are taken up in business strategy and managerial economics.

Table 7-4; Eliminating a Dominated Strategy

		Piuny	
		Enter	Don't
MS	Enter	(2,-2)	(5,0)

In this simplified game, after the elimination of Microsoft's dominated strategy, Piuny also has a dominant strategy: not to enter. Thus, we *iterate* and eliminate dominated strategies again, this time eliminating Piuny's dominated strategies, and wind up with a single outcome: Microsoft enters, and Piuny doesn't. The *iterated elimination of dominated strategies* solves the game.[87]

Here is another game, with three strategies for each player.

Table 7-5: A 3 X 3 Game

		Column		
		Left	Center	Right
Row	Top	(-5,-1)	(2,2)	(3,3)
	Middle	(1,-3)	(1,2)	(1,1)
	Bottom	(0,10)	(0,0)	(0,-10)

The process of iterated elimination of dominated strategies is illustrated by actually eliminating the rows and columns, as follows. A reverse color (white writing on black background) indicates a dominated strategy.

Middle dominates bottom for Row, yielding:

Table 7-6: Eliminating a Dominated Strategy

		Column		
		Left	Center	Right
Row	Top	(-5,-1)	(2,2)	(3,3)
	Middle	(1,-3)	(1,2)	(1,1)
	Bottom	(0,10)	(0,0)	(0,-10)

With bottom eliminated, Left is now dominated for Column by either Center or Right, which eliminates the left column.

---

[87] A strategy may be dominated not by any particular alternate strategy but by a randomization over other strategies, which is an advanced topic not considered here.

Table 7-7: Eliminating Another Dominated Strategy

		Column		
		Left	Center	Right
Row	Top	(-5,-1)	(2,2)	(3,3)
	Middle	(1,-3)	(1,2)	(1,1)
	Bottom	(0,10)	(0,0)	(0,-10)

With Left and Bottom eliminated, Top now dominates Middle for Row.

Table 7-8: Eliminating a Third Dominated Strategy

		Column		
		Left	Center	Right
Row	Top	(-5,-1)	(2,2)	(3,3)
	Middle	(1,-3)	(1,2)	(1,1)
	Bottom	(0,10)	(0,0)	(0,-10)

Finally, Column chooses Right over Center, yielding a unique outcome after the iterated elimination of dominated strategies, which is (Top, Right).

Table 7-9: Game Solved

		Column		
		Left	Center	Right
Row	Top	(-5,-1)	(2,2)	(3,3)
	Middle	(1,-3)	(1,2)	(1,1)
	Bottom	(0,10)	(0,0)	(0,-10)

The iterated elimination of dominated strategies is a useful concept, and when it applies, the predicted outcome is usually quite reasonable. Certainly it has the property that no player has an incentive to change their behavior given the behavior of others. However, there are games where it doesn't apply, and these games require the machinery of a *Nash equilibrium*, named for Nobel laureate John Nash (1928 –).

7.1.2 Nash Equilibrium

In a *Nash equilibrium*, each player chooses the strategy that maximizes their expected payoff, given the strategies employed by others. For matrix payoff games with two players, a Nash equilibrium requires that the row chosen maximizes the row player's payoff, given the column chosen by the column player, and the column, in turn, maximizes the column player's payoff given the row selected by the row player. Let us consider first the prisoner's dilemma, which we have already seen.

Table 7-10: Prisoner's Dilemma Again

		Column	
		Confess	Don't
Row	Confess	(-10,-10)	(0,-20)
	Don't	(-20,0)	(-1,-1)

Given that the row player has chosen to confess, the column player also chooses confession because -10 is better than -20. Similarly, given that the column player chooses confession, the row player chooses confession, because -10 is better than -20. Thus, for both players to confess is a Nash equilibrium. Now let us consider whether any other outcome is a Nash equilibrium. In any outcome, at least one player is not confessing. But that player could get a higher payoff by confessing, so no other outcome could be a Nash equilibrium.

The logic of dominated strategies extends to Nash equilibrium, except possibly for ties. That is, if a strategy is strictly dominated, it can't be part of a Nash equilibrium. On the other hand, if it involves a tied value, a strategy may be dominated but still part of a Nash equilibrium.

The Nash equilibrium is justified as a solution concept for games as follows. First, if the players are playing a Nash equilibrium, no one has an incentive to change their play or re-think their strategy. Thus, the Nash equilibrium has a "steady state" aspect in that no one wants to change their own strategy given the play of others. Second, other potential outcomes don't have that property: if an outcome is not a Nash equilibrium, then at least one player does have an incentive to change what they are doing. Outcomes that aren't Nash equilibria involve mistakes for at least one player. Thus, sophisticated, intelligent players may be able to deduce each other's play, and play a Nash equilibrium

Do people actually play Nash equilibria? This is a controversial topic and mostly beyond the scope of this book, but we'll consider two well-known games: Tic-Tac-Toe (see, e.g. http://www.mcafee.cc/Bin/tictactoe/index.html) and Chess. Tic-Tac-Toe is a relatively simple game, and the equilibrium is a tie. This equilibrium arises because each player has a strategy that prevents the other player from winning, so the outcome is a tie. Young children play Tic-Tac-Toe and eventually learn how to play equilibrium strategies, at which point the game ceases to be very interesting since it just repeats the same outcome. In contrast, it is known that Chess has an equilibrium, but no one knows what it is. Thus, at this point we don't know if the first mover (White) always wins, or the second mover (Black) always wins, or if the outcome is a draw (neither is able to win). Chess is complicated because a strategy must specify what actions to take given the history of actions, and there are a very large number of potential histories of the game thirty or forty moves after the start. So we can be quite confident that people are not (yet) playing Nash equilibria to the game of Chess.

The second most famous game in game theory is *the battle of the sexes*. The battle of the sexes involves a married couple who are going to meet each other after work, but haven't decided where they are meeting. Their options are a baseball game or the ballet.

Both prefer to be with each other, but the man prefers the baseball game and the woman prefers the ballet. This gives payoffs something like this:

Table 7-11: The Battle of the Sexes

		Woman	
		Baseball	Ballet
Man	Baseball	(3,2)	(1,1)
	Ballet	(0,0)	(2,3)

The man would rather that they both go to the baseball game, and the woman that they both go to the ballet. They each get 2 payoff points for being with each other, and an additional point for being at their preferred entertainment. In this game, iterated elimination of dominated strategies eliminates nothing. You can readily verify that there are two Nash equilibria: one in which they both go to the baseball game, and one in which they both go to ballet. The logic is: if the man is going to the baseball game, the woman prefers the 2 points she gets at the baseball game to the single point she would get at the ballet. Similarly, if the woman is going to the baseball game, the man gets three points going there, versus zero at the ballet. Thus, for both to go to the baseball game is a Nash equilibrium. It is straightforward to show that for both to go to the ballet is also a Nash equilibrium, and finally that neither of the other two possibilities, involving not going to the same place, is an equilibrium.

Now consider the game of *matching pennies*. In this game, both the row player and the column player choose heads or tails, and if they match, the row player gets the coins, while if they don't match, the column player gets the coins. The payoffs are provided in the next table.

Table 7-12: Matching Pennies

		Column	
		Heads	Tails
Row	Heads	(1,-1)	(-1,1)
	Tails	(-1,1)	(1,-1)

You can readily verify that none of the four possibilities represents a Nash equilibrium. Any of the four involves one player getting -1; that player can convert -1 to 1 by changing his or her strategy. Thus, whatever the hypothesized equilibrium, one player can do strictly better, contradicting the hypothesis of a Nash equilibrium. In this game, as every child who plays it knows, it pays to be unpredictable, and consequently players need to *randomize*. Random strategies are known as mixed strategies, because the players mix across various actions.

7.1.3 Mixed Strategies

Let us consider the matching pennies game again.

Table 7-13: Matching Pennies Again

		Column	
		Heads	Tails
Row	Heads	(1,-1)	(-1,1)
	Tails	(-1,1)	(1,-1)

Suppose that Row believes Column plays Heads with probability p. Then if Row plays Heads, Row gets 1 with probability p and -1 with probability $(1-p)$, for an expected value of $2p - 1$. Similarly, if Row plays Tails, Row gets -1 with probability p (when Column plays Heads), and 1 with probability $(1-p)$, for an expected value of $1 - 2p$. This is summarized in the next table.

Table 7-14: Mixed Strategy in Matching Pennies

		Column		
		Heads	Tails	
Row	Heads	(1,-1)	(-1,1)	$1p + -1(1-p)=2p-1$
	Tails	(-1,1)	(1,-1)	$-1p + 1(1-p)=1-2p$

If $2p - 1 > 1 - 2p$, then Row is better off on average playing Heads than Tails. Similarly, if $2p - 1 < 1 - 2p$, Row is better off playing Tails than Heads. If, on the other hand, $2p - 1 = 1 - 2p$, then Row gets the same payoff no matter what Row does. In this case Row could play Heads, could play Tails, or could flip a coin and randomize Row's play.

A *mixed strategy Nash equilibrium* involves at least one player playing a randomized strategy, and no player being able to increase their expected payoff by playing an alternate strategy. A Nash equilibrium without randomization is called a *pure strategy Nash equilibrium*.

Note that that randomization requires equality of expected payoffs. If a player is supposed to randomize over strategy A or strategy B, then both of these strategies must produce the same expected payoff. Otherwise, the player would prefer one of them, and wouldn't play the other.

Computing a mixed strategy has one element that often appears confusing. Suppose Row is going to randomize. Then Row's payoffs must be equal, for all strategies Row plays with positive probability. But that equality in Row's payoffs doesn't determine the probabilities with which Row plays the various rows. Instead, that equality in Row's payoffs will determine the probabilities with which Column plays the various columns. The reason is that it is Column's probabilities that determine the expected payoff for Row; if Row is going to randomize, then Column's probabilities must be such that Row is willing to randomize.

Thus, for example, we computed the payoff to Row of playing Heads, which was $2p - 1$, where p was the probability Column played Heads. Similarly, the payoff to Row of playing Tails was $1 - 2p$. Row is willing to randomize if these are equal, which solves for $p = \frac{1}{2}$.

7.1.3.1 (Exercise)   Let q be the probability that Row plays Heads. Show that Column is willing to randomize if, and only if, $q = \frac{1}{2}$. (Hint: First compute Column's expected payoff when Column plays Heads, and then Column's expected payoff when Column plays Tails. These must be equal for Column to randomize.)

Now let's try a somewhat more challenging example, and revisit the battle of the sexes.

Table 7-15: Mixed Strategy in Battle of the Sexes

		Woman	
		Baseball	Ballet
Man	Baseball	(3,2)	(1,1)
	Ballet	(0,0)	(2,3)

This game has two pure strategy Nash equilibria: (Baseball,Baseball) and (Ballet,Ballet). Is there a mixed strategy? To compute a mixed strategy, let the Woman go to the baseball game with probability p, and the Man go to the baseball game with probability q. Table 7-16 contains the computation of the mixed strategy payoffs for each player.

Table 7-16: Full Computation of the Mixed Strategy

		Woman		
		Baseball (p)	Ballet ($1-p$)	Man's E Payoff
Man	Baseball (prob q)	(3,2)	(1,1)	$3p + 1(1-p)=1+2p$
	Ballet (prob $1-q$)	(0,0)	(2,3)	$0p + 2(1-p)=2-2p$
	Woman's E Payoff	$2q + 0(1-q)=2q$	$1q + 3(1-q)=3-2q$	

For example, if the Man (row player) goes to the baseball game, he gets 3 when the Woman goes to the baseball game (probability p) and otherwise gets 1, for an expected payoff of $3p + 1(1-p) = 1 + 2p$. The other calculations are similar but you should definitely run through the logic and verify each calculation.

A mixed strategy in the Battle of the Sexes game requires both parties to randomize (since a pure strategy by either party prevents randomization by the other). The Man's indifference between going to the baseball game and the ballet requires $1+2p = 2 - 2p$, which yields $p = \frac{1}{4}$. That is, the Man will be willing to randomize which event he attends if the Woman is going to the ballet ¾ of the time, and otherwise to the baseball game. This makes the Man indifferent between the two events, because he prefers to be with the Woman, but he also likes to be at the baseball game; to make up for the advantage that the game holds for him, the woman has to be at the ballet more often.

Similarly, in order for the Woman to randomize, the Woman must get equal payoffs from going to the game and going to the ballet, which requires $2q = 3 - 2q$, or $q = \frac{3}{4}$. Thus, the probability that the Man goes to the game is ¾, and he goes to the ballet ¼ of the time. These are independent probabilities, so to get the probability that both go to the game, we multiply the probabilities, which yields $\frac{3}{16}$. The next table fills in the probabilities for all four possible outcomes.

Table 7-17: Mixed Strategy Probabilities

		Woman	
		Baseball	Ballet
Man	Baseball	$\frac{3}{16}$	$\frac{9}{16}$
	Ballet	$\frac{1}{16}$	$\frac{3}{16}$

Note that more than half the time, (Baseball, Ballet) is the outcome of the mixed strategy, and the two people are not together. This lack of coordination is a feature of mixed strategy equilibria generally. The expected payoffs for both players are readily computed as well. The Man's payoff was $1+2p = 2 - 2p$, and since $p = \frac{1}{4}$, the Man obtained 1 ½. A similar calculation shows the Woman's payoff is the same. Thus, both do worse than coordinating on their less preferred outcome. But this mixed strategy Nash equilibrium, undesirable as it may seem, is a Nash equilibrium in the sense that neither party can improve their payoff, given the behavior of the other party.

In the Battle of the sexes, the mixed strategy Nash equilibrium may seem unlikely, and we might expect the couple to coordinate more effectively. Indeed, a simple call on the telephone should rule out the mixed strategy. So let's consider another game related to the Battle of the Sexes, where a failure of coordination makes more sense. This is the game of "Chicken." Chicken is played by two drivers driving toward each other, trying to convince the other to yield, which involves swerving into a ditch. If both swerve into the ditch, we'll call the outcome a draw and both get zero. If one swerves and the other doesn't, the swerver loses and the other wins, and we'll give the winner one point.[88] The only remaining question is what happens when both don't yield, in which case a crash results. In this version, that has been set at four times the loss of swerving, but you can change the game and see what happens.

Table 7-18: Chicken

		Column	
		Swerve	Don't
Row	Swerve	(0,0)	(-1,1)
	Don't	(1,-1)	(-4,-4)

This game has two pure strategy equilibria: (Swerve, Don't) and (Don't, Swerve). In addition, it has a mixed strategy. Suppose Column swerves with probability p. Then

---

[88] Note that adding a constant to a player's payoffs, or multiplying that player's payoffs by a positive constant, doesn't affect the Nash equilibria, pure or mixed. Therefore, we can always let one outcome for each player be zero, and another outcome be one.

Row gets $0p + -1(1-p)$ from swerving, $1p + (-4)(1-p)$ from not swerving, and Row will randomize if these are equal, which requires $p = \frac{3}{4}$. That is, the probability that Column swerves, in a mixed strategy equilibrium is ¾. You can verify that the Row player has the same probability by setting the probability that Row swerves equal to q and computing Column's expected payoffs. Thus, the probability of a collision is $\frac{1}{16}$ in the mixed strategy equilibrium.

The mixed strategy equilibrium is more likely in some sense in this game; if the players already knew which player would yield, they wouldn't actually need to play the game. The whole point of the game is to find out who will yield, which means it isn't known in advance, which means the mixed strategy equilibrium is in some sense the more reasonable equilibrium.

Paper, Scissors, Rock is a child's game in which two children simultaneously choose paper (hand held flat), scissors (hand with two fingers protruding to look like scissors) or rock (hand in a fist). The nature of the payoffs is that paper beats rock, rock beats scissors, and scissors beat paper. This game has the structure

Table 7-19: Paper, Scissors, Rock

		Column		
		Paper	Scissors	Rock
Row	Paper	(0,0)	(-1,1)	(1,-1)
	Scissors	(1,-1)	(0,0)	(-1,1)
	Rock	(-1,1)	(1,-1)	(0,0)

7.1.3.2 (Exercise) Show that, in the Paper, Scissors, Rock game, there are no pure strategy equilibria. Show that playing all three actions with equal likelihood is a mixed strategy equilibrium.

7.1.3.3 (Exercise) Find all equilibria of the following games:

1

		Column	
		Left	Right
Row	Up	(3,2)	(11,1)
	Down	(4,5)	(8,0)

2

		Column	
		Left	Right
Row	Up	(3,3)	(0,0)
	Down	(4,5)	(8,0)

3

Row	Column	Left	Right
	Up	(0,3)	(3,0)
	Down	(4,0)	(0,4)

4

Row	Column	Left	Right
	Up	(7,2)	(0,9)
	Down	(8,7)	(8,8)

5

Row	Column	Left	Right
	Up	(1,1)	(2,4)
	Down	(4,1)	(3,2)

6

Row	Column	Left	Right
	Up	(4,2)	(2,3)
	Down	(3,8)	(1,5)

7.1.4 Examples

Our first example concerns public goods. In this game, each player can either contribute, or not. For example, two roommates can either clean their apartment, or not. If they both clean, the apartment is nice. If one cleans, that roommate does all the work and the other gets half of the benefits. Finally, if neither clean, neither is very happy. This suggests payoffs like:

Table 7-20: Cleaning the Apartment

Row	Column	Clean	Don't
	Clean	(10,10)	(0,15)
	Don't	(15,0)	(2,2)

You can verify that this game is similar to the prisoner's dilemma, in that the only Nash equilibrium is the pure strategy in which neither player cleans. This is a game theoretic version of the tragedy of the commons – even though the roommates would both be better off if both cleaned, neither do. As a practical matter, roommates do solve this problem, using strategies that we will investigate when we consider dynamic games.

Table 7-21: Driving on the Right

		Column	
		Left	Right
Row	Left	(1,1)	(0,0)
	Right	(0,0)	(1,1)

The important thing about the side of the road the cars drive on is not that it is the right side but that it is the *same* side. This is captured in the Driving on the Right game above. If both players drive on the same side, then they both get one point, otherwise they get zero. You can readily verify that there are two pure strategy equilibria, (Left,Left) and (Right,Right), and a mixed strategy equilibrium with equal probabilities. Is the mixed strategy reasonable? With automobiles, there is little randomization. On the other hand, people walking down hallways often seem to randomize whether they pass on the left or the right, and sometimes do that little dance where they try to get past each other, one going left and the other going right, then both simultaneously reversing, unable to get out of each other's way. That dance suggests that the mixed strategy equilibrium is not as unreasonable as it seems in the automobile application.[89]

Table 7-22: Bank Location Game

		NYC	
		No Concession	Tax Rebate
LA	No Concession	(30,10)	(10,20)
	Tax Rebate	(20,10)	(20,0)

Consider a foreign bank that is looking to open a main office and a smaller office in the United States. The bank narrows its choice for main office to either New York (NYC) or Los Angeles (LA), and is leaning toward Los Angeles. If neither city does anything, LA will get $30 million in tax revenue and New York ten million. New York, however, could offer a $10 million rebate, which would swing the main office to New York, but now New York would only get a net of $20 M. The discussions are carried on privately with the bank. LA could also offer the concession, which would bring the bank back to LA.

---

[89] Continental Europe drove on the left until about the time of the French revolution. At that time, some individuals began driving on the right as a challenge to royalty who were on the left, essentially playing the game of chicken with the ruling class. Driving on the right became a symbol of disrespect for royalty. The challengers won out, forcing a shift to driving on the right. Besides which side one drives on, another coordination game involves whether one stops or goes on red. In some locales, the tendency for a few extra cars to go as a light changes from green to yellow to red forces those whose light changes to green to wait, and such a progression can lead to the opposite equilibrium, where one goes on red and stops on green. Under Mao Tse-tung, the Chinese considered changing the equilibrium to going on red and stopping on green (because 'red is the color of progress') but wiser heads prevailed and the plan was scrapped.

7.1.4.1 (Exercise)   Verify that the bank location game has no pure strategy equilibria, and that there is a mixed strategy equilibrium where each city offers a rebate with probability ½.

Table 7-23: Political Mudslinging

		Republican	
		Clean	Mud
Dem	Clean	(3,1)	(1,2)
	Mud	(2,1)	(2,0)

On the night before the election, a Democrat is leading the Wisconsin senatorial race. Absent any new developments, the Democrat will win, and the Republican will lose. This is worth 3 to the Democrat, and the Republican, who loses honorably, values this outcome at one. The Republican could decide to run a series of negative advertisements ("throwing mud") against the Democrat, and if so, the Republican wins although loses his honor, which he values at 1, and so only gets 2. If the Democrat runs negative ads, again the Democrat wins, but loses his honor, so only gets 2. These outcomes are represented in the Mudslinging game above.

7.1.4.2 (Exercise)   Show that the only Nash equilibrium is a mixed strategy with equal probabilities of throwing mud and not throwing mud.

7.1.4.3 (Exercise)   Suppose that voters partially forgive a candidate for throwing mud when the rival throws mud, so that the (Mud, Mud) outcome has payoff (2.5,.5). How does the equilibrium change?

You have probably had the experience of trying to avoid encountering someone, who we will call Rocky. In this instance, Rocky is actually trying to find you. The situation is that it is Saturday night and you are choosing which party, of two possible parties, to attend. You like party 1 better, and if Rocky goes to the other party, you get 20. If Rocky attends party 1, you are going to be uncomfortable and get 5. Similarly, Party 2 is worth 15, unless Rocky attends, in which case it is worth 0. Rocky likes Party 2 better (these different preferences may be part of the reason you are avoiding him) but he is trying to see you. So he values Party 2 at 10, party 1 at 5 and your presence at the party he attends is worth 10. These values are reflected in the following table.

Table 7-24: Avoiding Rocky

		Rocky	
		Party 1	Party 2
You	Party 1	(5,15)	(20,10)
	Party 2	(15,5)	(0,20)

7.1.4.4 (Exercise)   (i) Show there are no pure strategy Nash equilibria in this game. (ii) Find the mixed strategy Nash equilibria. (iii) Show that the probability you encounter Rocky is $\frac{7}{12}$.

Our final example involves two firms competing for customers. These firms can either price high or low. The most money is made if they both price high, but if one prices low, it can take most of the business away from the rival. If they both price low, they make modest profits. This description is reflected in the following table:

Table 7-25: Price Cutting Game

		Firm 2	
		High	Low
Firm 1	High	(15,15)	(0,25)
	Low	(25,0)	(5,5)

7.1.4.5 (Exercise)   Show that the firms have a dominant strategy to price low, so that the only Nash equilibrium is (Low, Low).

7.1.5 Two Period Games

So far, we have considered only games that are played simultaneously. Several of these games, notably the price cutting and apartment cleaning games, are actually played over and over again. Other games, like the bank location game, may only be played once but nevertheless are played over time. Recall the bank location game:

Table 7-26; Bank Location Revisited

		NYC	
		No Concession	Tax Rebate
LA	No Concession	(30,10)	(10,20)
	Tax Rebate	(20,10)	(20,0)

If neither city offered a rebate, then LA won the bidding. So suppose instead of the simultaneous move game, that first New York decided whether to offer a rebate, and then LA could decide to offer a rebate. This sequential structure leads to a game that looks like Figure 7-1:

In this game, NYC makes the first move, and chooses Rebate (to the left) or No Rebate (to the right). If NYC chooses Rebate, LA can then choose Rebate or None. Similarly, if NYC chooses No Rebate, LA can choose Rebate or None. The payoffs (using the standard of (LA, NYC) ordering) are written below the choices.

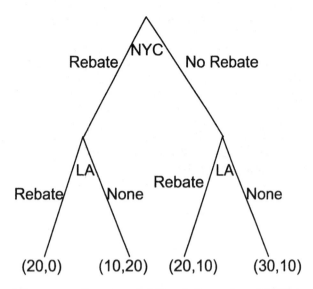

Figure 7-1 Sequential Bank Location (NYC payoff listed first)

What NYC would like to do depends on what NYC believes LA will do. What should NYC believe about LA? (Boy does that rhetorical question suggest a lot of facetious answers.) The natural belief is that LA will do what is in LA's best interest. This idea – that each stage of a game is played in a maximizing way – is called *subgame perfection*.

7.1.6 Subgame Perfection

Subgame perfection requires each player to act in its best interest, independent of the history of the game.[90] This seems very sensible and in most contexts it is sensible. In some settings, it may be implausible. Even if I see a player make a particular mistake three times in a row, subgame perfection requires that I must continue to believe that player will not make the mistake again. Subgame perfection may be implausible in some circumstances, especially when it pays to be considered somewhat crazy.

In the example, subgame perfection requires LA to offer a rebate when NYC does (since LA gets 20 by rebating versus 10), and not when NYC doesn't. This is illustrated in the game using arrows to indicate LA's choices. In addition, the actions that LA won't choose have been re-colored in a light grey in Figure 7-2.

Once LA's subgame perfect choices are taken into account, NYC is presented with the choice of offering a rebate, in which case it gets 0, or not offering a rebate, in which case it gets 10. Clearly the optimal choice for NYC is to offer no rebate, in which case LA doesn't either, and the result is 30 for LA, and 10 for NYC.

Dynamic games are generally "solved backward" in this way. That is, first establish what the last player does, then figure out based on the last player's expected behavior, what the penultimate player does, and so on.

---

[90] Subgame perfection was introduced by Nobel laureate Reinhart Selten (1930 –).

Figure 7-2: Subgame Perfection

We'll consider one more application of subgame perfection. Suppose, in the game "Avoiding Rocky," Rocky is actually stalking you, and can condition his choice on your choice. Then you might as well go to the party you like best, because Rocky is going to follow you wherever you go. This is represented in Figure 7-3.

Figure 7-3: Can't Avoid Rocky

Since Rocky's optimal choice eliminates your best outcomes, you make the best of a bad situation by choosing Party 1. Here, Rocky has a *second mover advantage*: Rocky's ability to condition on your choice meant he does better than he would do in a simultaneous game.

7.1.6.1 (Exercise)   Formulate the battle of the sexes as a sequential game, letting the woman choose first. (This situation could arise if the woman can leave a message for the man about where she has gone.) Show that there is only one subgame perfect equilibrium, and that the woman enjoys a first-mover advantage over the man, and she gets her most preferred outcome.

7.1.7 Supergames

Some situations, like the pricing game or the apartment-cleaning game, are played over and over. Such situations are best modeled as a *supergame*.[91] A supergame is a game played over and over again without end, where the players discount the future. The game played each time is known as a *stage game*. Generally supergames are played in times 1, 2, 3, ...

Cooperation may be possible in supergames, if the future is important enough. Consider the pricing game introduced above.

Table 7-27: Price Cutting, Revisited

		Firm 2	
		High	Low
Firm 1	High	(15,15)	(0,25)
	Low	(25,0)	(5,5)

The dominant strategy equilibrium to this game is (Low, Low). It is clearly a subgame perfect equilibrium for the players to just play (Low, Low) over and over again, because if that is what Firm 1 thinks Firm 2 is doing, Firm 1 does best by pricing Low, and vice versa. But that is not the only equilibrium to the supergame.

Consider the following strategy, called a *grim trigger strategy*. Price high, until you see your rival price low. After your rival has priced low, price low forever. This is called a trigger strategy because an action of the other player (pricing low) triggers a change in behavior. It is a grim strategy because it punishes forever.

If your rival uses a grim trigger strategy, what should you do? Basically, your only choice is when to price low, because once you price low, your rival will price low, and then your best choice is to also price low from then on. Thus, your strategy is to price high up until some point $t - 1$, and then price low from time t on. Your rival will price high through t, and price low from $t + 1$ on. This gives a payoff to you of 15 from period 1 through $t - 1$, 25 in period t, and then 5 in period $t + 1$ on. We can compute the payoff for a discount factor δ.

$$V_t = 15(1 + \delta + \delta^2 + ... + \delta^{t-1}) + 25\delta^t + 5(\delta^{t+1} + \delta^{t+2} + ...)$$

$$= 15\frac{1-\delta^t}{1-\delta} + 25\delta^t + 5\frac{\delta^t}{1-\delta} = \frac{15}{1-\delta} - \frac{\delta^t}{1-\delta}(15 - 25(1-\delta) - 5\delta) = \frac{15}{1-\delta} - \frac{\delta^t}{1-\delta}(-10 + 20\delta).$$

---

[91] The supergame was invented by Robert Aumann (1930 –) in 1959.

If $-10 + 20\delta < 0$, it pays to price low immediately, at $t=0$, because it pays to price low and the earlier the higher the present value. If $-10 + 20\delta > 0$, it pays to wait forever to price low, that is, $t = \infty$. Thus, in particular, the grim trigger strategy is an optimal strategy for a player when the rival is playing the grim trigger strategy if $\delta \geq \frac{1}{2}$. In other words, cooperation in pricing is a subgame perfect equilibrium if the future is important enough, that is, the discount factor δ is high enough.

The logic of this example is that the promise of future cooperation is valuable when the future itself is valuable, and that promise of future cooperation can be used to induce cooperation today. Thus, firm 1 doesn't want to cut price today, because that would lead firm 2 to cut price for the indefinite future. The grim trigger strategy punishes price cutting today with future low profits.

Supergames offer more scope for cooperation than is illustrated in the pricing game. First, more complex behavior is possible. For example, consider the following game:

Table 7-28: A Variation of the Price Cutting Game

		Firm 2	
		High	Low
Firm 1	High	(10,10)	(0,25)
	Low	(25,0)	(5,5)

Here, again, the unique equilibrium in the stage game is (Low, Low). But the difference between this game and the previous game is that the total profits of firms 1 and 2 are higher in either (High, Low) or (Low, High) than in (High, High). One solution is to alternate between (High, Low) and (Low, High). Such alternation can also be supported as an equilibrium, using the grim trigger strategy – that is, if a firm does anything other than what is it supposed to in the alternating solution, the firms instead play (Low, Low) forever.

7.1.7.1 (Exercise)   Consider the game in Table 7-28, and consider a strategy in which firm 1 prices high in odd numbered periods, and low in even numbered periods, while 2 prices high in even numbered periods, low in odd numbered periods. If either deviate from these strategies, both price low from then on. Let δ be the discount factor. Show that these firms have a payoff of $\dfrac{25}{1-\delta^2}$ or $\dfrac{25\delta}{1-\delta^2}$, depending on which period it is. Then show that the alternating strategy is sustainable if $10 + \dfrac{5\delta}{1-\delta} \leq \dfrac{25\delta}{1-\delta^2}$. This, in turn, is equivalent to $\delta \geq \sqrt{6} - 2$.

7.1.8 The Folk Theorem

The folk theorem says that if the value of the future is high enough, any outcome that is *individually rational* can be supported as an equilibrium to the supergame. Individual rationality for a player in this context means that the outcome offers a present value of profits at least as high as that offered in the worst equilibrium in the stage game from that player's perspective. Thus, in the pricing game, the worst equilibrium of the stage game offered each player 5, so an outcome can be supported if it offers each player at least a running average of 5.

The simple logic of the folk theorem is this. First, any infinite repetition of an equilibrium of the stage game is itself a subgame perfect equilibrium. If everyone expects this repetition of the stage game equilibrium, no one can do better than to play their role in the stage game equilibrium every period. Second, any other plan of action can be turned into a subgame perfect equilibrium merely by threatening any agent who deviates from that plan with an infinite repetition of the worst stage game equilibrium from that agent's perspective. That threat is credible because the repetition of the stage game equilibrium is itself a subgame perfect equilibrium. Given such a grim trigger type threat, no one wants to deviate from the intended plan.

The folk theorem is a powerful result, and shows that there are equilibria to supergames that achieve very good outcomes. The kinds of coordination failures we saw in the battle of the sexes, and the failure to cooperate in the prisoner's dilemma, need not arise, and cooperative solutions are possible if the future is sufficiently valuable.

However, it is worth noting some assumptions that have been made in our descriptions of these games, assumptions that matter and are unlikely to be true in practice. First, the players know their own payoffs. Second, they know their rival's payoffs. They possess a complete description of the available strategies and can calculate the consequences of these strategies, not just for themselves, but for their rivals. Third, each player maximizes his or her expected payoff, and they know that their rivals do the same, and they know that their rivals know that everyone maximizes, and so on. The economic language for this is the structure of the game and the player's preferences are *common knowledge*. Few real world games will satisfy these assumptions exactly. Since the success of the grim trigger strategy (and other strategies we haven't discussed) generally depends on such knowledge, informational considerations may cause cooperation to break down. Finally, the folk theorem shows us that there are lots of equilibria to supergames, and provides no guidance on which one will be played. These assumptions can be relaxed, although they may lead to wars on the equilibrium path "by accident," and a need to recover from such wars, so that the grim trigger strategy becomes sub-optimal.

7.2 *Cournot Oligopoly*

The Cournot[92] oligopoly model is the most popular model of imperfect competition. It is a model in which the number of firms matters, and represents one way of thinking about what happens when the world is neither perfectly competitive, nor a monopoly.

In the Cournot model, there are n firms, who choose quantities. We denote a typical firm as firm i and number the firms from $i = 1$ to $i = n$. Firm i chooses a quantity $q_i \geq 0$ to sell and this quantity costs $c_i(q_i)$. The sum of the quantities produced is denoted by Q. The price that emerges from the competition among the firms is $p(Q)$ and this is the same price for each firm. It is probably best to think of the quantity as really

---

[92] Augustus Cournot, 1801-1877.

representing a capacity, and competition in prices by the firms determining a market price given the market capacity.

The profit that a firm i obtains is

$$\pi_i = p(Q)q_i - c_i(q_i).$$

7.2.1 Equilibrium

Each firm chooses q_i to maximize profit. The first order conditions[93] give:

$$0 = \frac{\partial \pi_i}{\partial q_i} = p(Q) + p'(Q)q_i - c_i'(q_i).$$

This equation holds with equality provided $q_i > 0$. A simple thing that can be done with the first order conditions is to rewrite them to obtain the average value of the price-cost margin:

$$\frac{p(Q) - c_i'(q_i)}{p(Q)} = -\frac{p'(Q)q_i}{p(Q)} = -\frac{Qp'(Q)}{p(Q)}\frac{q_i}{Q} = \frac{s_i}{\varepsilon}.$$

Here $s_i = \frac{q_i}{Q}$ is firm i's market share. Multiplying this equation by the market share and summing over all firms $i = 1, \dots , n$ yields

$$\sum_{i=1}^{n} \frac{p(Q) - c_i'(q_i)}{p(Q)} s_i = \frac{1}{\varepsilon}\sum_{i=1}^{n} s_i^2 = \frac{HHI}{\varepsilon},$$

where $HHI = \sum_{i=1}^{n} s_i^2$ is the Hirschman-Herfindahl Index.[94] The HHI has the property that if the firms are identical, so that $s_i = 1/n$ for all i, then the HHI is also $1/n$. For this reason, antitrust economists will sometimes use $1/HHI$ as a proxy for the number of firms, and describe an industry with "2 ½ firms," meaning an HHI of 0.4.[95]

We can draw several inferences from these equations. First, larger firms, those with larger market shares, have a larger deviation from competitive behavior (price equal to marginal cost). Small firms are approximately competitive (price nearly equals marginal cost) while large firms reduce output to keep the price higher, and the amount of the reduction, in price/cost terms, is proportional to market share. Second, the HHI reflects the deviation from perfect competition on average, that is, it gives the average

---

[93] Bear in mind that Q is the sum of the firms' quantities, so that when firm i increases its output slightly, Q goes up by the same amount.
[94] Named for Albert Hirschman (1918 – 1972), who invented it in 1945, and Orris Herfindahl (1915 –), who invented it independently in 1950.
[95] To make matters more confusing, antitrust economists tend to state the HHI using shares in percent, so that the HHI is on a 0 to 10,000 scale.

proportion by which price equal to marginal cost is violated. Third, the equation generalizes the "inverse elasticity result" proved for monopoly, which showed that the price – cost margin was the inverse of the elasticity of demand. The generalization states that the weighted average of the price – cost margins is the HHI over the elasticity of demand.

Since the price – cost margin reflects the deviation from competition, the HHI provides a measure of how large a deviation from competition is present in an industry. A large HHI means the industry "looks like monopoly." In contrast, a small HHI looks like perfect competition, holding constant the elasticity of demand.

The case of a symmetric (identical cost functions) industry is especially enlightening. In this case, the equation for the first order condition can be restated as

$$0 = p(Q) + p'(Q) \frac{Q}{n} - c' \left(\frac{Q}{n} \right)$$

or

$$p(Q) = \frac{\varepsilon n}{\varepsilon n - 1} c' \left(\frac{Q}{n} \right).$$

Thus, in the symmetric model, competition leads to pricing as if demand were more elastic, and indeed is a substitute for elasticity as a determinant of price.

7.2.2 Industry Performance

How does the Cournot industry perform? Let us return to the more general model, that doesn't require identical cost functions. We already have one answer to this question: the average price – cost margin is the HHI divided by the elasticity of demand. Thus, if we have an estimate of the demand elasticity, we know how much the price deviates from the perfect competition benchmark.

The general Cournot industry actually has two sources of inefficiency. First, price is above marginal cost, so there is the dead weight loss associated with unexploited gains from trade. Second, there is the inefficiency associated with different marginal costs. This is inefficient because a re-arrangement of production, keeping total output the same, from the firm with high marginal cost to the firm with low marginal cost, would reduce the cost of production. That is, not only is too little output produced, but what output is produced is inefficiently produced, unless the firms are identical.

To assess the productive inefficiency, we let c_1' be the lowest marginal cost. The average deviation from the lowest marginal cost, then, is

$$\chi = \sum_{i=1}^{n} s_i (c_i' - c_1') = \sum_{i=1}^{n} s_i (p - c_1' - (p - c_i')) = p - c_1' - \sum_{i=1}^{n} s_i (p - c_i')$$

$$= p - c_1' - p \sum_{i=1}^{n} s_i \frac{(p - c_i')}{p} = p - c_1' - \frac{p}{\varepsilon} \sum_{i=1}^{n} s_i^2 = p - c_1' - \frac{p}{\varepsilon} HHI.$$

Thus, while a large HHI means a large deviation from price equal to marginal cost and hence a large level of monopoly power (holding constant the elasticity of demand), a large HHI also tends to indicate greater productive efficiency, that is, less output produced by high cost producers. Intuitively, a monopoly produces efficiently, even if it has a greater reduction in total output than other industry structures.

There are a number of caveats worth mentioning in the assessment of industry performance. First, the analysis has held constant the elasticity of demand, which could easily fail to be correct in an application. Second, fixed costs have not been considered. An industry with large economies of scale, relative to demand, must have very few firms to perform efficiently and small numbers should not necessarily indicate the market performs poorly even if price – cost margins are high. Third, it could be that entry determines the number of firms, and that the firms have no long-run market power, just short-run market power. Thus, entry and fixed costs could lead the firms to have approximately zero profits, in spite of price above marginal cost.

7.2.2.1 (Exercise)   Suppose the inverse demand curve is $p(Q) = 1 - Q$, and that there are n Cournot firms, each with constant marginal cost c, selling in the market.

(i) Show that the Cournot equilibrium quantity and price are $Q = \dfrac{n(1-c)}{n+1}$ and

$p(Q) = \dfrac{1 + nc}{n+1}$. (ii) Show each firm's gross profits are $\left(\dfrac{1-c}{n+1}\right)^2$.

Continuing with 7.2.2.1 (Exercise), suppose there is a fixed cost F to become a firm. The number of firms n should be such that firms are able to cover their fixed costs, but add one more and they can't. This gives us a condition determining the number of firms n:

$$\left(\frac{1-c}{n+1}\right)^2 \geq F \geq \left(\frac{1-c}{n+2}\right)^2.$$

Thus, each firm's net profits are $\left(\dfrac{1-c}{n+1}\right)^2 - F \leq \left(\dfrac{1-c}{n+1}\right)^2 - \left(\dfrac{1-c}{n+2}\right)^2 = \dfrac{(2n+3)(1-c)^2}{(n+1)^2(n+2)^2}$.

Note that the monopoly profits π_m are $\frac{1}{4} (1-c)^2$. Thus, with free entry, net profits are less than $\dfrac{(2n+3)4}{(n+1)^2(n+2)^2} \pi_m$, and industry net profits are less than $\dfrac{n(2n+3)4}{(n+1)^2(n+2)^2} \pi_m$.

Table 7-29 shows the performance of the constant cost, linear demand Cournot industry, when fixed costs are taken into account, and when they aren't. With two firms, gross industry profits are 8/9ths of the monopoly profits, not substantially different from monopoly. But when fixed costs sufficient to insure that only two firms enter are considered, the industry profits are at most 39% of the monopoly profits. This number – 39% -- is large because fixed costs could be "relatively" low, so that the third firm is just deterred from entering. That still leaves the two firms with significant profits, even though the third firm can't profitably enter. As the number of firms rises, gross industry profits fall slowly toward zero. The net industry profits, on the other hand, fall dramatically rapidly to zero. With ten firms, the gross profits are still about a third of the monopoly level, but the net profits are only at most 5% of the monopoly level.

Table 7-29: Industry Profits as a Fraction of Monopoly Profits

Number of Firms	Gross Industry Profits (%)	Net Industry Profits (%)
2	88.9	39.0
3	75.0	27.0
4	64.0	19.6
5	55.6	14.7
10	33.1	5.3
15	23.4	2.7
20	18.1	1.6

The Cournot model gives a useful model of imperfect competition, a model that readily permits assessing the deviation from perfect competition. The Cournot model embodies two kinds of inefficiency: the exercise of monopoly power, and technical inefficiency in production. In settings involving entry and fixed costs, care must be taken in applying the Cournot model.

7.3 Search and Price Dispersion

Decades ago, economists used to make a big deal about the "Law of One Price," which states that identical goods sell at the same price. The argument in favor of the law of one price is theoretical. Well-informed consumers will buy identical goods from the lowest price seller. Consequently, the only seller to make any sales is the low-price seller. This kind of consumer behavior forces all sellers to sell at the same price.

There are few markets where the law of one price is actually observed to hold. Organized exchanges, like stock, bond and commodity markets, will satisfy the law of one price. In addition, gas stations across the street from each other will often offer identical prices, but often is not always.

Many economists considered that the internet would force prices of standardized goods – DVD players, digital cameras, MP3 players – to a uniform, and uniformly low, price. However, this has not occurred. Moreover, it probably can't occur, in the sense that pure price competition would put the firms out of business, and hence can't represent equilibrium behavior.

There are many markets where prices appear unpredictable to consumers. The price of airline tickets is notorious for unpredictability. The price of milk, soft drinks, paper towels and canned tuna varies 50% or more depending on whether the store has an advertised sale of the item or not. Prices of goods sold on the internet varies substantially from day to day.[96] Such variation is known as *price dispersion* by economists. It is different from price discrimination, in that price dispersion entails a given store quoting the same price to all customers; the variation is across stores, while price discrimination is across customers.

Why are prices so unpredictable?

7.3.1 Simplest Theory

To understand price dispersion, we divide consumers into two types: shoppers and loyal customers. Loyal customers won't pay more than a price p_m for the good, but they only consult a particular store; if that store has the good for less than the price p_m, the loyal customer buys, and otherwise not. In contrast, the shoppers buy only from the store offering the lowest price; shoppers are informed about the prices offered by all stores. We let the proportion of shoppers be s. The loyal customers are allocated to the other stores equally, so that, if there are n stores, each store gets a fraction $(1 - s)/n$ of the customers. Let the marginal cost of the good be c, and assume $c < p_m$. Both kinds of customers buy only one unit.

For the purposes of this analysis, we will assume that prices can be chosen from the continuum. This makes the analysis more straightforward, but there is an alternate version of the analysis (not developed here) that makes the more reasonable assumption of prices that are an integer number of pennies.

First note that there is no pure strategy equilibrium. To see this, consider the lowest price p charged by any firm. If that price is c, the firm makes no money, so would do better by raising its price to p_m and selling only to the loyal customers. Thus, the lowest price p exceeds c. If there is a tie at p, it pays to break the tie by charging a billionth of a cent less than p, and thereby capturing all the shoppers rather than sharing them with the other firm charging p. So there can't be a tie.

But no tie at p means the next lowest firm is charging something strictly greater than p, which means the lowest price firm can increase price somewhat and not suffer any loss of sales. This contradicts profit maximization for that firm. The conclusion is that firms must randomize and no pure strategy equilibrium exists.

But how do they randomize? We are going to look for a distribution of prices. Each firm will choose a price from the continuous distribution F, where $F(x)$ is the probability the firm charges a price less than x. What must F look like? We use the logic of mixed strategies: the firm must get the same profits for all prices that might actually be charged under the mixed strategy, for otherwise it would not be willing to randomize.

A firm that charges price $p \leq p_m$ always sells to its captive customers. In addition, it sells to the shoppers if the other firms have higher prices, which occurs with probability $(1 - F(p))^{n-1}$. Thus, the firm's profits are

---

[96] It is often very challenging to assess internet prices because of variation in shipping charges.

$$\pi(p) = (p-c)\left(\frac{1-s}{n} + s(1-F(p))^{n-1}\right).$$

On each sale, the firm earns $p - c$. The firm always sells to its loyal customers, and in addition captures the shoppers if the other firms price higher. Since no firm will exceed p_m, the profits must be the same as the level arising from charging p_m, and this gives

$$\pi(p) = (p-c)\left(\frac{1-s}{n} + s(1-F(p))^{n-1}\right) = (p_m - c)\frac{1-s}{n}.$$

This equation is readily solved for F:

$$F(p) = \left(1 - \frac{(p_m - p)(1-s)}{s(p-c)n}\right)^{\frac{1}{n-1}}.$$

The lower bound of prices arises at the point L where $F(L)=0$, or

$$L = c + \frac{(p_m - c)\dfrac{1-s}{n}}{\dfrac{1-s}{n} + s}.$$

These two equations provide a continuous distribution of prices charged by each firm which is an equilibrium to the pricing game. That is, each firm randomizes over the interval $[L, p_m]$, according to the continuous distribution F. Any price in the interval $[L, p_m]$ produces the same profits for each firm, so the firms are willing to randomize over this interval.

The loyal customers get a price chosen randomly from F, so we immediately see that the shoppers make life better for the loyal customers, pushing average price down. (An increase in s directly increases F, which means prices fall – recall that F gives the probability that prices are below a given level, so an increase in F is an increase in the probability of low prices.)

Similarly loyal customers make life worse for shoppers, increasing prices on average to shoppers. The distribution of prices facing shoppers is actually the distribution of the minimum price. Since all firms charge a price exceeding p with probability $(1 - F(p))^n$, at least one charges a price less than p with probability $1 - (1 - F(p))^n$, and this is the distribution of prices facing shoppers. That is, the distribution of prices charged to shoppers is

$$1-(1-F(p))^n = 1 - \left(\frac{(p_m - p)(1-s)}{s(p-c)n}\right)^{\frac{n}{n-1}}.$$

7.3.2 Industry Performance

How does a price dispersed industry perform? First, average industry profits are

$$n\pi(p) = (p_m - c)(1 - s).$$

An interesting aspect of this equation is that it doesn't depend on the number of firms, only on the number of loyal customers. Essentially, the industry profits are the same that it would earn as if the shoppers paid marginal cost and the loyal customers paid the monopoly price, although that isn't what happens in the industry, except in the limit as the number of firms goes to infinity. Note that this formula for industry profits does not work for a monopoly. In order to capture monopoly, one must set $s=0$, because shoppers have no alternative under monopoly.

Figure 7-4: Expected Prices in Search Equilibrium

As the number of firms gets large, the price charged by any one firm converges to the monopoly price p_m. However, the lowest price offered by any firm actually converges to c, marginal cost. Thus, in the limit as the number of firms get large, shoppers obtain price equal to marginal cost and loyal firms pay the monopoly price.

The average price charged to shoppers and non-shoppers is a complicated object, so we consider the case where there are n firms, $s = \frac{1}{2}$, $p_m = 1$ and $c = 0$. Then the expected prices for shoppers and loyal customers are given in Figure 7-4, letting the number of firms vary. Thus, with many firms, most of the gains created by the shoppers flow to shoppers. In contrast, with few firms, a significant fraction of the gains created by shoppers goes instead to the loyal customers.

Similarly, we can examine the average prices for loyal customers and shoppers when the proportion of shoppers varies. Increasing the proportion of shoppers has two effects. First, it makes low prices more attractive, thus encouraging price competition, because capturing the shoppers is more valuable. Second, it lowers industry profits, because the set of loyal customers is reduced. Figure 7-5 plots the average price for loyal customers and shoppers, as the proportion of shoppers ranges from zero to one, when there are five firms, $p_m = 1$ and $c = 0$.

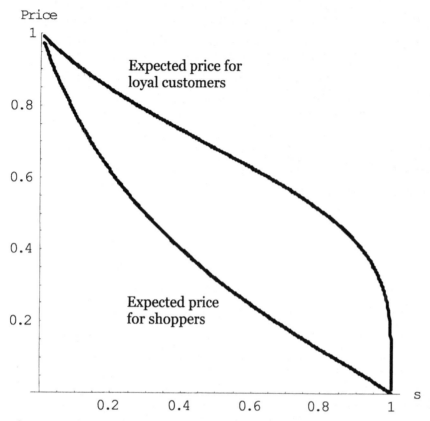

Figure 7-5: Expected Prices (s=Proportion of Shoppers)

People who are price-sensitive and shop around convey a positive externality on other buyers by encouraging price competition. Similarly, people who are less price sensitive and don't shop around convey a negative externality on the other buyers. In markets with dispersed information about the best prices, where some buyers are informed and some are not, randomized prices are a natural outcome. That is, randomization of prices, and the failure of the law of one price, is just a reflection of the different willingness or ability to *search* on the part of consumers.

This difference in the willingness to search could arise simply because search is itself costly. That is, the shoppers could be determined by their choice to shop, in such a way that the cost of shopping just balances the expected gains from searching. The proportion of shoppers may adjust endogenously to insure that the gains from searching exactly equal the costs of searching. In this way, a cost of shopping is translated into a randomized price equilibrium in which there is a benefit from shopping and all consumers get the same total cost of purchase on average.

7.4 *Hotelling Model*

Breakfast cereals range from indigestible, unprocessed whole grains to cereals that are almost entirely sugar with only the odd molecule or two of grain. Such cereals are hardly good substitutes for each other. Yet similar cereals are viewed by consumers as good substitutes, and the standard model of this kind of situation is the Hotelling model.[97] Hotelling was the first to use a line segment to represent both the product that is sold and the preferences of the consumers who are buying the products. In the Hotelling model, there is a line, and preferences of each consumer is represented by a point on this line. The same line is used to represent products. For example, movie customers are differentiated by age, and we can represent moviegoers by their ages. Movies, too, are designed to be enjoyed by particular ages. Thus a "pre-teen" movie is unlikely to appeal very much to a six year old or to a nineteen year old, while a Disney movie appeals to a six year old, but less to a fifteen year old. That is, movies have a target age, and customers have ages, and these are graphed on the same line.

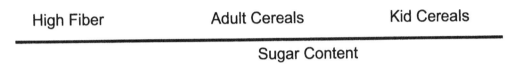

Figure 7-6: Hotelling Model for Breakfast Cereals

Breakfast cereal is a classic application of the Hotelling line, and this application is illustrated in Figure 7-6. Breakfast cereals are primarily distinguished by their sugar content, which ranges on the Hotelling line from low on the left to high on the right. Similarly, the preferences of consumers also fall on the same line. Each consumer has a "most desired point," and prefers cereals closer to that point than those at more distant points.

7.4.1 Types of Differentiation

There are two main types of differentiation, each of which can be modeled using the Hotelling line. These types are quality and variety. Quality refers to a situation where consumers agree what product is better; the disagreement among consumers concerns whether higher quality is worth the cost. In automobiles, faster acceleration, better braking, higher gas mileage, more cargo capacity, more legroom, and greater durability are all good things. In computers, faster processing, brighter screens, higher resolution screens, lower heat, greater durability, more megabytes of RAM and more gigabytes of hard drive space are all good things. In contrast, varieties are the elements about which there is not widespread agreement. Colors and shapes are usually varietal rather than quality differentiators. Some people like almond colored appliances, others choose white, with blue a distant third. Food flavors are varieties, and while the quality of ingredients is a quality differentiator, the type of food is usually a varietal differentiator. Differences in music would primarily be varietal.

Quality is often called *vertical differentiation*, while variety is *horizontal differentiation.*

---

[97] Hotelling Theory is named for Harold Hotelling, 1895-1973.

7.4.2 The Standard Model

The standard Hotelling model fits two ice cream vendors on a beach. The vendors sell the identical product, and moreover they can choose to locate wherever they wish. For the time being, suppose the price they charge for ice cream is fixed at $1. Potential customers are also spread randomly along the beach.

We let the beach span an interval from 0 to 1. People desiring ice cream will walk to the closest vendor, since the price is the same. Thus, if one vendor locates at x and the other at y, and $x < y$, those located between 0 and ½ $(x + y)$ go to the left vendor, while the rest go to the right vendor. This is illustrated in Figure 7-7.

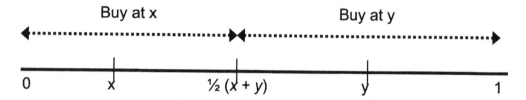

Figure 7-7: Sharing the Hotelling Market

Note that the vendor at x sells more by moving toward y, and vice versa. Such logic forces profit maximizing vendors to both locate in the middle! The one on the left sells to everyone left of ½, while the one on the right sells to the rest. Neither can capture more of the market, so equilibrium locations have been found. (To complete the description of an equilibrium, we need to let the two "share" a point and still have one on the right side, one on the left side of that point.)

This solution is commonly used as an explanation of why U.S. political parties often seem very similar to each other – they have met in the middle in the process of chasing the most voters. Political parties can't directly buy votes, so the "price" is fixed; the only thing parties can do is locate their platform close to voters' preferred platform, on a scale of "left" to "right." But the same logic that a party can grab the middle, without losing the ends, by moving closer to the other party will tend to force the parties to share the same "middle of the road" platform.

7.4.2.1 (Exercise)   Suppose there are four ice cream vendors on the beach, and customers are distributed uniformly. Show that it is a Nash equilibrium for two to locate at ¼, and two at ¾.

The model with constant prices is unrealistic for the study of the behavior of firms. Moreover, the two-firm model on the beach is complicated to solve and has the undesirable property that it matters significantly whether the number of firms is odd or even. As a result, we will consider a Hotelling model on a circle, and let the firms choose their prices.

7.4.3 The Circle Model

In this model, there are n firms evenly spaced around the circle whose circumference is one. Thus, the distance between any firm and each of its closest neighbors is $1/n$.

Consumers care about two things: how distant the firm they buy from is, and how much they pay for the good, and they minimize the sum of the price paid and t times the distance between the consumer's location (also on the circle) and the firm. Each consumer's preference is uniformly distributed around the circle. The locations of firms are illustrated in Figure 7-8.

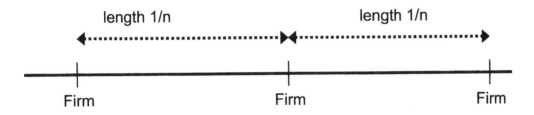

Figure 7-8: A Segment of the Circle Model

We conjecture a Nash equilibrium in which all firms charge the price p. To identify p, we look for what p must be to make any one firm choose to charge p, given that the others all charge p. So suppose the firm in the middle of Figure 7-8 charges an alternate price r, but every other firm charges p. A consumer who is x units away from the firm pays the price $r + tx$ from buying at the firm, or $p + t(1/n - x)$ from buying from the rival. The consumer is just indifferent between the nearby firms if these are equal, that is,

$$r + tx^* = p + t(1/n - x^*)$$

where x^* is the location of the consumer who is indifferent.

$$x^* = \frac{p + t/n - r}{2t} = \frac{1}{2n} + \frac{p - r}{2t}.$$

Thus, consumers who are closer than x^* to the firm charging r buy from that firm, and consumers who are further away than x^* buy from the alternative firm. Demand for the firm charging r is twice x^* (because the firm sells to both sides), so profits are price minus marginal cost times two x^*, that is,

$$(r - c)2x^* = (r - c)\left(\frac{1}{n} + \frac{p - r}{t}\right).$$

The first order condition[98] for profit maximization is

$$0 = \frac{\partial}{\partial r}(r - c)\left(\frac{1}{n} + \frac{p - r}{t}\right) = \left(\frac{1}{n} + \frac{p - r}{t}\right) - \frac{r - c}{t}.$$

---

[98] Since profit is quadratic in r, we will find a global maximum.

We could solve the first order condition for r. But remember that the concern is when is p a Nash equilibrium price? The price p is an equilibrium price if the firm wants to choose $r = p$. Thus, we can conclude that p is a Nash equilibrium price when

$$p = c + \frac{t}{n}.$$

This value of p insures that a firm facing rivals who charge p also chooses to charge p. Thus, in the Hotelling model, price exceeds marginal cost by an amount equal to the value of the average distance between the firms, since the average distance is $1/n$ and the value to a consumer of traveling that distance is t. The profit level of each firm is $\frac{t}{n^2}$, so industry profits are $\frac{t}{n}$.

How many firms will enter the market? Suppose the fixed cost is F. We are going to take a slightly unusual approach and assume that the number of firms can adjust in a continuous fashion, in which case the number of firms is determined by the zero profit condition $F = \frac{t}{n^2}$, or $n = \sqrt{t/F}$.

What is the socially efficient number of firms? The socially efficient number of firms minimizes the total costs, which are the sum of the transportation costs and the fixed costs. With n firms, the average distance a consumer travels is

$$n \int_{-1/2n}^{1/2n} |x| \, dx = 2n \int_{0}^{1/2n} x \, dx = n \left(\frac{1}{2n} \right)^2 = \frac{1}{4n}.$$

Thus, the socially efficient number of firms minimizes the transport costs plus the entry costs $\frac{t}{4n} + nF$. This occurs at $n = \frac{1}{2}\sqrt{t/F}$. The socially efficient number of firms is half the level that enter with free entry!

Too many firms enter in the Hotelling circle model. This extra entry arises because efficient entry is determined by the cost of entry and the average distance of consumers, while prices are determined by the marginal distance of consumers, or the distance of the marginal consumer. That is, competing firms' prices are determined by the most distant customer, and that leads to prices that are too high relative to the efficient level; free entry then drives net profits to zero only by excess entry.

The Hotelling model is sometimes used to justify an assertion that firms will advertise too much, or engage in too much R&D, as a means of differentiating themselves and creating profits.

7.5 Agency Theory

An *agent* is a person who works for, or on behalf of, another. Thus, an employee is an agent of a company. But agency extends beyond employee relationships. Independent contractors are also agents. Advertising firms, lawyers and accountants are agents of their clients. The CEO of a company is an agent of the board of directors of the company. A grocery store is an agent of the manufacturer of corn chips sold in the store. Thus, the agency relationship extends beyond the employee into many different economic relationships. The entity – person or corporation – on whose behalf an agent works is called a *principal*.

Agency theory is the study of incentives provided to agents. Incentives are an issue because agents need not have the same interests and goals as the principal. Employees spend billions of hours every year browsing the web, emailing friends, and playing computer games while they are supposedly working. Attorneys hired to defend a corporation in a lawsuit have an incentive not to settle, to keep the billing flowing. (Such behavior would violate the attorneys' ethics requirements.) Automobile repair shops have been known to use cheap or used replacement parts and bill for new, high quality parts. These are all examples of a conflict in the incentives of the agent and the goals of the principal.

Agency theory focuses on the cost of providing incentives. When you rent a car, an agency relationship is created. Even though a car rental company is called an agency, it is most useful to look at the renter as the agent, because it is the renter's behavior that is an issue. The company would like the agent to treat the car as if it were their own car. The renter, in contrast, knows it isn't their own car, and often drives accordingly.

> "[T]here's a lot of debate on this subject---about what kind of car handles best. Some say a front-engined car; some say a rear-engined car. I say a *rented* car. Nothing handles better than a rented car. You can go faster, turn corners sharper, and put the transmission into reverse while going forward at a higher rate of speed in a rented car than in any other kind." [99]

How can the car rental company insure that you don't put their car into reverse while going forward at a high rate of speed? They could monitor your behavior, perhaps by putting a company representative in the car with you. That would be a very expensive and unpleasant solution to the problem of incentives. Instead, the company uses outcomes – if damage is done, the driver has to pay for it. That is also an imperfect solution, because some drivers who abuse the cars get off scot-free and others who don't abuse the car still have cars that break down, and are then mired in paperwork while they try to prove their good behavior. That is, a rule that penalizes drivers based on outcomes imposes risk on the drivers. Modern technology is improving monitoring with GPS tracking.

---

[99] P. J. O'Rourke, Republican Party Reptile, Atlantic Monthly Press, 1987.

7.5.1 Simple Model

To model the cost of provision of incentives, we consider an agent like a door-to-door encyclopedia salesperson. The agent will visit houses, and sell encyclopedias to some proportion of the households; the more work the agent does, the more sales that are made. We let x represent the average dollar value of sales for a given level of effort; x is a choice the agent makes. However, x will come with risk to the agent, which we model using the variance σ^2.

The firm will pay the agent a share s of the money generated by the sales. In addition, the firm will pay the agent a salary y, which is fixed independently of sales. This scheme – a combination of salary and commission – covers many different situations. Real estate agents receive a mix of salary and commission. Authors receive an advance and a royalty, which works like a salary and commission.

The monetary compensation of the agent is $sx + y$. In addition, the agent has a cost of effort, which we take to be $\dfrac{x^2}{2a}$. Here a represents the ability of the agent: more able agents, who have a higher value of a, have a lower cost of effort. Finally, there is a cost of risk. The actual risk imposed on the agent is proportional to the degree they share in the proceeds; if s is small, the agent faces almost no monetary risk, while if s is high, most of the risk is imposed on the agent. We use the "linear cost of risk" model developed earlier, to impose a cost of risk which is $s\lambda\sigma^2$. Here, σ^2 is the variance of the monetary risk, λ defines the agent's attitude or cost of risk, and s is the share of the risk imposed on the agent. This results in a payoff to the agent of

$$u = sx + y - \frac{x^2}{2a} - s\lambda\sigma^2.$$

The first two terms, $sx + y$, are the payments made to the agent. The next term is the cost of generating that level of x. The final term is the cost of risk imposed on the agent by the contract.

The agency game works as follows. First, the principal offers a contract, which involves a commission s and a salary y. The agent can either accept or reject the contract and accepts if he obtains at least u_0 units of utility, the value of his next best offer. Then the agent decides how much effort to expend, that is, the agent chooses x.

As with all subgame perfect equilibria, we work backwards to first figure out what x an agent would choose. Because our assumptions make u quadratic in x, this is a straightforward exercise, and we conclude $x = sa$. This can be embedded into u, and we obtain the agent's optimized utility, u^*, is

$$u^* = s^2 a + y - \frac{(sa)^2}{2a} - s\lambda\sigma^2 = y + \tfrac{1}{2}s^2 a - s\lambda\sigma^2.$$

Incentive Compensation: A Percentage of What?

Most companies compensate their sales force based on the revenue generated. However, maximizing revenue need not be the same thing as maximizing profit, which is generally the goal of the company. In what follows, Steve Bisset discusses the difference.

"Many years ago I was CEO of a company called Megatest, founded by Howard Marshall and myself in 1975. Around 1987 we were selling test systems in the $1M+ price range. Every Monday morning we would have a meeting with sales management and product marketing, mediated by myself. Individual salesmen came in to make their cases for how they just had to have a huge discount, else they would lose a particular sale. The meeting was part circus, with great performances, and part dogfight.

"I could visualize the sales guys spending their time in the car or the shower using their substantial creative powers to dream up good justifications for their next plea for a huge discount. They knew that if we were willing to bleed enough we could usually win the sale. I wanted to solve both the resultant profitability problem and the problem of the unpleasant meeting.

"Commissions were traditionally a percentage of bookings (net of discount), with part held back until cash was received. The percentage increased after a salesman met his individual quota for the quarter (the performances at quota-setting time to sandbag the quota were even more impressive). The fact that a discount reduced commission did not affect a salesman's behavior, because the difference in commission was small. Better to buy the order by giving a big discount and then move on quickly to the next sale.

"Salesmen are "coin operated", and will figure out how to maximize their total commission. Most salesmen I have met are quite good at math. Further, they have learned to "watch the hips, not the lips" – in other words, they judge management intentions by actions rather than words. They reason – and I agree with them – that if management really wanted them to maximize margins rather than revenues, then they would pay them more if they maximize margins.

"We decided to try a new scheme, against some howling from the sales department. We set a base "cost" for each product, approximately representing the incremental cost to manufacture and support the product. Then we offered commission on the amount that the net sales price exceeded this base cost. The base cost may have been as much as 80% of the list price (it was a very competitive market at the time). Then we increased the commission rate by a factor of about six, so that if the salesman brought in an order at a price near list, then his commission was somewhat higher than before. If he started discounting, his commission dropped sharply. We gave broad discretion to sales management to approve discounts.

"We still had sales guys claiming that a sale was massively strategic and had to be sold at or below cost, and that they needed their commission anyway to justify the effort. In some cases we approved this, but mostly we said that if it's strategic then you'll get your commission on the follow-on sales. While salesmen have a strong preference for immediate cash, they will act so as to maximize income over time, and will think and act strategically if financially rewarded for such.

"The results were that our margins increased significantly. Revenues were increasing too. It's hard to attribute the revenue gain to the new commission plan, given the number of other variables, but I like to think that it was a factor. Now our salesmen spent more of their creative energies devising ways to sell our customers on the value of our products and company, instead of conspiring with sales management as to the best tale of woe to present to marketing at the Monday pricing meeting.

"The Monday meetings became shorter and more pleasant, focused on truly creative ways to make each sale. There certainly were steep discounts given in some cases, but they reflected the competitive situation and future sales potential at each account much more accurately."

(Source: private correspondence, quotation permission received)

The agent won't accept employment unless $u^* \geq u_0$, the reservation utility. The principal can minimize the cost of employing the agent by setting the salary such that $u^* = u_0$, which results in

$$y = u_0 - \tfrac{1}{2}s^2 a + s\lambda\sigma^2 .$$

Observe that the salary has to be higher, the greater is the risk σ^2. That is, the principal has to cover the cost of risk in the salary term.

7.5.2 Cost of Providing Incentives

The principal obtains profits which are the remainder of the value after paying the agent, and minus the salary:

$$\begin{aligned} \pi &= (1-s)x - y \\ &= (1-s)sa - (u_0 - \tfrac{1}{2}s^2 a + s\lambda\sigma^2) \\ &= sa - u_0 - \tfrac{1}{2}s^2 a - s\lambda\sigma^2 . \end{aligned}$$

Note that the principal gets the entire output $x = sa$ minus all the costs – the reservation utility of the agent u_0, the cost of providing effort, and the risk cost on the agent. That is, the principal obtains the full gains from trade – the value of production minus the total cost of production. However, the fact that the principal obtains the full gains from trade doesn't mean the principal induces the agent to work extremely hard, because there is no mechanism for the principal to induce the agent to work hard without imposing more risk on the agent, and this risk is costly to the principal. Agents are induced to work hard by tying their pay to their performance, and such a link necessarily imposes risk on the agent, and risk is costly.[100]

We take the principal to be risk neutral. This is reasonable when the principal is "economically large" relative to the agent, so that the risks faced by the agent are small to the principal. For example, the risks associated with any one car are small to a car rental company. The principal who maximizes expected profits chooses s to maximize π, which yields

$$s = 1 - \frac{\lambda}{a}\sigma^2 .$$

This formula is interesting for several reasons. First, if the agent is neutral to risk, which means $\lambda = 0$, then s is 1. That is, the agent gets 100% of the marginal return to effort, and the principal just collects a lump sum. This is reminiscent of some tenancy contracts used by landlords and peasants; the peasant paid a lump sum for the right to farm the land and then kept all of the crops grown. Since these peasants were unlikely to be risk neutral, while the landlord was relatively neutral to risk, such a contract was

---

[100] There is a technical requirement that the principal's return π must be positive, for otherwise the principal would rather not contract at all. This amounts to an assumption that u_0 is not too large. Moreover, if s comes out less than zero, the model falls apart, and in this case, the actual solution is $s=0$.

unlikely to be optimal. The contract with $s=1$ is known as "selling the agency" since the principal sells the agency to the agent for a lump sum payment. (Here, y will generally be negative – the principal gets a payment rather than paying a salary.) The more common contract, however, had the landowner and the tenant farmer share the proceeds of farming, which gives rise to the name *sharecropper*.

Second, more risk or more risk aversion on the part of the agent decreases the share of the proceeds accruing to the agent. Thus, when the cost of risk or the amount of risk is high, the best contract imposes less risk on the agent. Total output sa falls as the risk costs rise.

Third, more able agents (higher a) get higher commissions. That is, the principal imposes more risk on the more able agent because the returns to imposition of risk – in the form of higher output – are greater, and thus worth the cost in terms of added risk.

Most real estate agencies operate on a mix of salary and commission, with commissions paid to agents averaging about 50%. The agency RE/MAX, however, pays commissions close to 100%, collecting a fixed monthly fee that covers agency expenses from the agents. RE/MAX claims that their formula is appropriate for better agents. The theory developed suggests that more able agents should obtain higher commissions. But in addition, RE/MAX's formula also tends to attract more able agents, since able agents earn a higher wage under the high commission formula. (There is a potential downside to the RE/MAX formula, that it discourages agency-wide cooperation.)

7.5.3 Selection of Agent

Consider what contracts attract what kinds of agents. For a fixed salary y and commission s, the agent's utility, optimizing over x, is

$$u^* = y + \tfrac{1}{2}s^2 a - s\lambda\sigma^2 .$$

The agent's utility is increasing in a and decreasing in λ. Thus, more able agents get higher utility, and less risk averse agents get higher utility.

How do the terms of the contract affect the pool of applicants? Let us suppose two contracts are offered, one with a salary y_1 and commission s_1, the other with salary y_2 and commission s_2. We suppose $y_2 < y_1$ and $s_2 > s_1$. What kind of agent prefers contract 2, the high commission, low salary contract, over contract 1?

$$y_2 + \tfrac{1}{2}s_2^2 a - s_2\lambda\sigma^2 \geq y_1 + \tfrac{1}{2}s_1^2 a - s_1\lambda\sigma^2 ,$$

or, equivalently,

$$\tfrac{1}{2}a\!\left(s_2^2 - s_1^2\right) - (s_2 - s_1)\lambda\sigma^2 \geq y_1 - y_2 .$$

Thus, agents with high ability a or low level of risk aversion λ prefers the high commission, low salary contract. A company that puts more of the compensation in the form of commission tends to attract more able agents, and agents less averse to risk.

The former is a desirable feature of the incentive scheme, since more able agents produce more. The latter, the attraction of less risk averse agents, may or may not be desirable but is probably neutral overall.

One important consideration is that agents who overestimate their ability will react the same as people who have higher ability. Thus, the contract equally attracts those with high ability and those who overestimate their ability.

Agency theory provides a characterization of the cost of providing incentives. The source of the cost is the link between incentives and risk. Incentives link pay and performance; when performance is subject to random fluctuations, linking pay and performance also links pay and the random fluctuations. Thus the provision of incentives necessarily imposes risk on the agent, and if the agent is risk averse, this is costly.

In addition, the extent to which pay is linked to performance will tend to affect the type of agent who is willing to work for the principal. Thus, a principal must not only consider the incentive to work hard created by the commission and salary structure, but also the type of agent who would choose to accept such a contract.

7.5.4 Multi-tasking

Multi-tasking refers to performing several activities simultaneously. All of us multi-task. We study while drinking a caffeinated beverage; we think about things in the shower; we talk all too much on cell phones and eat French fries while driving. In the context of employees, an individual employee will be assigned a variety of tasks and responsibilities, and the employee must divide their time and efforts among the tasks. Incentives provided to the employee must direct not only the total efforts of the employee, but also the allocation of time and effort across activities. An important aspect of multi-tasking is the interaction of incentives provided to employees, and the effects of changes in one incentive on the behavior of the employee over many different dimensions. In this section, we will establish conditions under which the problem of an employer disaggregates, that is to say, the incentives on each individual task can be set independently of the incentives applied to the others.

This section is relatively challenging and involves a number of pieces. To simplify the presentation, some of the pieces are set aside as claims.

To begin the analysis, we consider a person who has n tasks or jobs. For convenience we will index these activities with the natural numbers 1, 2, ... , n. The level of activity, which may also be thought of as an action, in task i will be denoted by x_i. It will prove convenient to denote the vector of actions by $\mathbf{x} = (x_1, \ldots, x_n)$. We suppose the agent bears a cost $c(\mathbf{x})$ of undertaking the vector of actions $\mathbf{x}$. We make four assumptions on c:

- c is increasing in each x_i,
- c has a continuous second derivative
- c is strictly convex, and

- c is homogeneous[101] of degree r.

For example, if there are two tasks ($n=2$), then all four of these assumptions are met by the cost function $c(x_1, x_2) = x_1^2 + x_2^2 + \frac{1}{2}x_1 x_2$. This function is increasing in x_1 and x_2, has continuous derivatives, is strictly convex (more about this below) and is homogeneous of degree 2.

It is assumed that c is increasing to identify the activities as costly. Continuity of derivatives is used for convenience. Convexity of c will insure that a solution to the first order conditions is actually an optimum for the employee. Formally, it means that for any vectors $\mathbf{x} \neq \mathbf{y}$ and scalar α between zero and one ($0 \leq \alpha \leq 1$),

$$\alpha c(\mathbf{x}) + (1-\alpha)c(\mathbf{y}) \geq c(\alpha \mathbf{x} + (1-\alpha)\mathbf{y}).$$

One way of interpreting this requirement is that it is less costly to do the average of two things than the average of the costs of the things. Intuitively, convexity requires that doing a medium thing is less costly than the average of two extremes. This is plausible when extremes tend to be very costly. It also means the set of vectors which cost less than a fixed amount, $\{\mathbf{x} \mid c(\mathbf{x}) \leq b\}$, is a convex set. Thus, if two points cost less than a given budget, the line segment connecting them does, too. Convexity of the cost function insures that the agent's optimization problem is concave, and thus that the first order-conditions describe a maximum. When the inequality is strict for α satisfying $0 < \alpha < 1$, we refer to convexity as *strict convexity*.

The assumption of homogeneity dictates that scale works in a particularly simple manner. Scaling up activities increases costs at a fixed rate r. Homogeneity has very strong implications that are probably unreasonable in many settings. Nevertheless, homogeneity leads to an elegant and useful theory, as we shall see. Recall the definition of a homogeneous function: c is homogeneous of degree r means that for any $\lambda > 0$,

$$c(\lambda \mathbf{x}) = \lambda^r c(\mathbf{x}).$$

Claim: strict convexity implies that $r > 1$.

> Proof of Claim: Fix any $\mathbf{x}$ and consider the two points $\mathbf{x}$ and $\lambda \mathbf{x}$. By convexity, for $0 < \alpha < 1$,
>
> $$(\alpha + (1-\alpha)\lambda^r)c(\mathbf{x}) = \alpha c(\mathbf{x}) + (1-\alpha)c(\lambda \mathbf{x})$$
> $$> c(\alpha \mathbf{x} + (1-\alpha)\lambda \mathbf{x})) = (\alpha + (1-\alpha)\lambda)^r c(\mathbf{x})$$
>
> which implies $(\alpha + (1-\alpha)\lambda^r) > (\alpha + (1-\alpha)\lambda)^r$.

> Define a function k which is the left hand side minus the right hand side:

---

[101] Homogeneous functions were defined in 4.1.8.3 (Exercise).

$k(\alpha) = \alpha + (1-\alpha)\lambda^r - (\alpha + (1-\alpha)\lambda)^r$. Note that $k(0)=k(1)=0$. Moreover, $k''(\alpha) = -r(r-1)(\alpha + (1-\alpha)\lambda)^{r-2}(1-\lambda)^2$. It is readily checked that if a convex function of one variable is twice differentiable, then the second derivative is greater than zero. If $r \leq 1$, $k''(\alpha) \geq 0$, implying that k is convex, and hence, if $0 < \alpha < 1$,

$$k(\alpha) = k((1-\alpha)0 + \alpha 1) \leq (1-\alpha)k(0) + \alpha k(1) = 0.$$

Similarly, if $r > 1$, k is concave and $k(\alpha) > 0$. This completes the proof, showing that $r \leq 1$ is not compatible with the strict convexity of c.

How should our person behave? Consider linear incentives, which are also known as piece rates. With piece rates, the employee gets a payment p_i for each unit of x_i produced. The person then chooses **x** to maximize

$$u = \sum_{i=1}^{n} p_i x_i - c(\mathbf{x}) = \mathbf{p} \bullet \mathbf{x} - c(\mathbf{x}).$$

Here $\bullet$ is the dot product, which is the sum of the products of the components.

The agent chooses **x** to maximize u, resulting in n first order conditions

$$\frac{\partial u}{\partial x_i} = p_i - \frac{\partial c(\mathbf{x})}{\partial x_i} = p_i - c_i(\mathbf{x}),$$

where c_i is the partial derivative of c with respect to the ith argument x_i. This first order condition can be expressed more compactly as

$$0 = \mathbf{p} - c'(\mathbf{x})$$

where $c'(\mathbf{x})$ is the vector of partial derivatives of c. Convexity of c insures that any solution to this problem is a global utility maximum, since the function u is concave, and strict convexity insures that there is at most one solution to the first order conditions.[102]

One very useful implication of homogeneity is that incentives scale. Homogeneity has the effect of turning a very complicated optimization problem into a problem that is readily solved, thanks to this very scaling.

Claim: If all incentives rise by a scalar factor α, then **x** rises by $\alpha^{\frac{1}{r-1}}$.

---

[102] This description is slightly inadequate, because we haven't considered boundary conditions. Often a requirement like $x_i \geq 0$ is also needed. In this case, the first order conditions may not hold with equality for those choices where $x_i = 0$ is optimal.

Proof of Claim: Note that differentiating $c(\lambda \mathbf{x}) = \lambda^r c(\mathbf{x})$ with respect to x_i yields $\lambda c_i(\lambda \mathbf{x}) = \lambda^r c_i(\mathbf{x})$, and thus $c'(\lambda \mathbf{x}) = \lambda^{r-1} c'(\mathbf{x})$. That is, if c is homogeneous of degree r, c' is homogeneous of degree $r-1$. Consequently, if $0 = \mathbf{p} - c'(\mathbf{x})$, $0 = \alpha \mathbf{p} - c'(\alpha^{\frac{1}{r-1}} \mathbf{x})$. Thus, if the incentives are scaled up by α, the efforts rise by the scalar factor $\alpha^{\frac{1}{r-1}}$.

Now consider an employer with an agent engaging in n activities. The employer values the ith activity at v_i, and thus wishes to maximize

$$\pi = \sum_{i=1}^{n}(v_i - p_i)x_i = \sum_{i=1}^{n}(v_i - c_i(\mathbf{x}))x_i \, .$$

This equation embodies a standard trick in agency theory. Think of the principal (employer) not as choosing the incentives $\mathbf{p}$, but instead as choosing the effort levels $\mathbf{x}$, with the incentives as a constraint. That is, the principal can be thought of choosing $\mathbf{x}$ and then choosing the $\mathbf{p}$ that implements this $\mathbf{x}$. The principal's expected profit is readily differentiated with respect to each x_j, yielding

$$0 = v_j - c_j(\mathbf{x}) - \sum_{i=1}^{n} c_{ij}(\mathbf{x}))x_i \, .$$

However, since $c_j(\mathbf{x})$ is homogeneous of degree $r-1$,

$$\sum_{i=1}^{n} c_{ij}(\mathbf{x}))x_i = \frac{d}{d\lambda}c_j(\lambda \mathbf{x})\Big|_{\lambda=1} = \frac{d}{d\lambda}\lambda^{r-1}c_j(\mathbf{x})\Big|_{\lambda=1} = (r-1)c_j(\mathbf{x}),$$

and thus $0 = v_j - c_j(\mathbf{x}) - \sum_{i=1}^{n} c_{ij}(\mathbf{x}))x_i = v_j - rc_j(\mathbf{x})$.

This expression proves the main result of this section. Under the maintained hypotheses (convexity and homogeneity), an employer of a multi-tasking agent uses incentives which are a constant proportion of value, that is,

$$p_j = \frac{v_j}{r},$$

where r is the degree of homogeneity of the agent's costs. Recalling that $r>1$, the principal uses a *sharing rule*, sharing a fixed proportion of value with the agent.

When agents have a homogeneous cost function, the principal has a very simple optimal incentive scheme, requiring quite limited knowledge of the agent's cost function (just the degree of homogeneity). Moreover, the incentive scheme works through a somewhat surprising mechanism. Note that if the value of one activity, say activity 1, rises, p_1 rises and all the other payment rates stay constant. The agent responds by increasing x_1, but the other activities may rise or fall depending on how complementary they are to activity 1. Overall, the agent's substitution across activities given the new incentive level on activity 1 implements the desired effort levels on other activities. The remarkable implication of homogeneity is that, although the principal desires different effort levels for all activities, only the incentive on activity 1 must change!

7.5.5 Multi-tasking without Homogeneity

In the previous section we saw, for example, that if the agent has quadratic costs, the principal pays the agent half the value of each activity. Moreover, the more rapidly costs rise in scale, the lower the payments to the agent.

This remarkable theorem has several limitations. The requirement of homogeneity is itself an important limitation, although this assumption is reasonable in some settings. More serious is the assumption that *all* of the incentives are set optimally *for the employer*. Suppose, instead, that one of the incentives is set "too high," at least from the employer's perspective. This might arise if, for example, the agent acquired all the benefits of one of the activities. An increase in the power of one incentive will then tend to "spill over" to the other actions, increasing for complements and decreasing for substitutes. When the efforts are substitutes, an increase in the power of one incentive will cause others to optimally rise, to compensate for the reduced supply of efforts of that type.[103]

We can illustrate the effects of cost functions that aren't homogeneous in a relatively straightforward way. Suppose the cost depends on the sum of the squared activity levels:

$$c(\mathbf{x}) = g\left(\sum_{i=1}^{n} x_i^2\right) = g(\mathbf{x} \bullet \mathbf{x}).$$

This is a situation where vector notation (dot-products) dramatically simplifies the expressions. You may find it useful to work through the notation on a separate sheet, or in the margin, using summation notation to verify each step. At the moment, we won't be concerned with the exact specification of g, but instead use the first order conditions to characterize the solution.

The agent maximizes

$$u = \mathbf{p} \bullet \mathbf{x} - g(\mathbf{x} \bullet \mathbf{x}).$$

---

[103] Multi-tasking, and agency theory more generally, is a rich theory with many implications not discussed here. For a challenging and important analysis, see Bengt Holmstrom and Paul Milgrom, "The Firm as an Incentive System," *American Economic Review*, Vol. 84, No. 4 (Sep., 1994), pp. 972-991.

This gives a first order condition

$$0 = \mathbf{p} - 2g'(\mathbf{x} \bullet \mathbf{x})\mathbf{x}$$

It turns out that a sufficient condition for this equation to characterize the agent's utility maximization is that g is both increasing and convex (increasing second derivative).

This is a particularly simple expression, because the vector of efforts, $\mathbf{x}$, points in the same direction as the incentive payments $\mathbf{p}$. The scalar that gives the overall effort levels, however, is not necessarily a constant, as occurs with homogeneous cost functions. Indeed, we can readily see that $\mathbf{x} \bullet \mathbf{x}$ is the solution to

$$\mathbf{p} \bullet \mathbf{p} = (2g'(\mathbf{x} \bullet \mathbf{x}))^2 (\mathbf{x} \bullet \mathbf{x}).$$

Because $\mathbf{x} \bullet \mathbf{x}$ is a number, it is worth introducing notation for it: $S = \mathbf{x} \bullet \mathbf{x}$. Then S is the solution to

$$\mathbf{p} \bullet \mathbf{p} = 4S(g'(S))^2 .$$

The principal or employer chooses $\mathbf{p}$ to maximize

$$\pi = \mathbf{v} \bullet \mathbf{x} - \mathbf{p} \bullet \mathbf{x} = \mathbf{v} \bullet \mathbf{x} - 2g'(\mathbf{x} \bullet \mathbf{x})(\mathbf{x} \bullet \mathbf{x}).$$

This gives the first order condition

$$0 = \mathbf{v} - 4\big(g'(\mathbf{x} \bullet \mathbf{x}) + (\mathbf{x} \bullet \mathbf{x})g''(\mathbf{x} \bullet \mathbf{x})\big)\mathbf{x}.$$

Thus, the principal's choice of $\mathbf{p}$ is such that $\mathbf{x}$ is proportional to $\mathbf{v}$, with constant of proportionality $g'(\mathbf{x} \bullet \mathbf{x}) + \mathbf{x} \bullet \mathbf{x}g''(\mathbf{x} \bullet \mathbf{x})$. Using the same trick (dotting each side of the first order condition $\mathbf{v} = 4\big(g'(\mathbf{x} \bullet \mathbf{x}) + \mathbf{x} \bullet \mathbf{x}g''(\mathbf{x} \bullet \mathbf{x})\big)\mathbf{x}$ with itself), we obtain:

$$\mathbf{v} \bullet \mathbf{v} = 16\big(g'(S^*) + S * g''(S^*)\big)^2 S *,$$

which gives the level of $\mathbf{x} \bullet \mathbf{x} = S^*$ induced by the principal. Given S^*, $\mathbf{p}$ is given by

$$\mathbf{p} = 2g'(\mathbf{x} \bullet \mathbf{x})\mathbf{x} = 2g'(S^*)\frac{\mathbf{v}}{4(g'(S^*) + S * g''(S^*))} = \frac{1}{2}\left(\frac{1}{1 + \dfrac{S * g''(S^*)}{g'(S^*)}} \right)\mathbf{v}.$$

Note that this expression gives the right answer when costs are homogeneous. In this case, $g(S)$ must be in the form $S^{r/2}$, and the formula gives

$$\mathbf{p} = \frac{1}{2}\left(\frac{1}{1+r-1}\right)\mathbf{v} = \frac{\mathbf{v}}{r}$$

as we already established.

The natural assumption to impose on the function g is that $(g'(S) + Sg''(S))^2 S$ is an increasing function of S. This assumption implies that as the value of effort rises, the total effort also rises.

Suppose $\dfrac{Sg''(S)}{g'(S)}$ is increasing in S. Then an increase in v_i increases S, decreasing p_j for $j \neq i$. That is, when one item becomes more valuable, the incentives on the others are reduced. Moreover, since $\mathbf{p} \bullet \mathbf{p} = 4S(g'(S))^2$, an increase in S only occurs if $\mathbf{p} \bullet \mathbf{p}$ increases.

These equations together imply that an increase in any one v_i increases the total effort (as measured by $S^* = \mathbf{x} \bullet \mathbf{x}$), increases the total incentives as measured by $\mathbf{p} \bullet \mathbf{p}$, and decreases the incentives on all activities other than activity i. In contrast, if $\dfrac{Sg''(S)}{g'(S)}$ is a decreasing function of S, then an increase in any one v_i causes *all* the incentives to rise. Intuitively, the increase in v_i directly causes p_i to rise, since x_i is more valuable. This causes the agent to substitute toward activity i. This causes the relative cost of total activity to fall (since $\dfrac{Sg''(S)}{g'(S)}$ decreases), which induces a desire to increase the other activity levels, which is accomplished by increase in the incentives on the other activities.

This conclusion generalizes readily and powerfully. Suppose that $c(\mathbf{x}) = g(h(\mathbf{x}))$, where h is homogeneous of degree r and g is increasing. In the case just considered, $h(\mathbf{x}) = \mathbf{x} \bullet \mathbf{x}$. Then the same conclusion, that the sign of $\dfrac{dp_i}{dv_j}$ is determined by the derivative of $\dfrac{Sg''(S)}{g'(S)}$, holds. In the generalization, S now stands for $h(\mathbf{x})$.

7.6 *Auctions*

When we think of auctions, we tend to think of movies where people scratch their ear and accidentally purchase a Faberge egg, like the one pictured at left.[104] However, stock exchanges, bond markets and commodities markets are organized as auctions, too, and because of such exchanges, auctions are the most common means of establishing prices. Auctions are one of the oldest transactions means recorded in human history, and were used by the Babylonians. The word *auction* comes from the Latin *auctio*, meaning *to increase*.

Auctions have been used to sell a large variety of things. Internet auction house eBay is most famous for weird items that have been auctioned (e.g. one person's attempt to sell their soul), but in addition, many of the purchases of the U.S. government are made by auction. The U.S. purchases everything from fighter aircraft to French fries by auction, and the U.S. government is the world's largest purchaser of French fries. In addition, corporations are occasionally sold by auction.

Items that are usually sold by auction include prize bulls, tobacco, used cars, race horses, coins, stamps, antiques, and fine art.

Information plays a significant role in bidding in auctions. The two major extremes in information, which lead to distinct theories, are *private values*, which means bidders know their own value, and *common values*, in which bidders don't know their own value, but have some indication or signal about the value. In the private values situation, a bidder may be outbid by another bidder, but doesn't learn anything from another bidder's willingness to pay. The case of private values arises when the good being sold has a quality apparent to all bidders, no hidden attributes, and no possibility of resale. In contrast, the case of common values arises when bidders don't know the value of the item for sale, but that value is common to all. The quintessential example is an off-shore oil lease. No one knows for sure how much oil can be extracted from an off-shore lease, and companies have estimates of the amount of oil. The estimates are closely guarded because rivals could learn from them. Similarly, when antiques dealers bid on an antique, the value they place on it is primarily the resale value. Knowing rivals' estimates of the resale value would influence the value each bidder placed on the item.

The private values environment is unrealistic in most settings, because items for sale usually have some element of common value. However, some situations approximate the private values environment and these are the most readily understood.

7.6.1 English Auction

An English auction is the common auction form used for selling antiques, art, used cars and cattle. The auctioneer starts low, and calls out prices until no bidder is willing to bid higher than the current high price. The most common procedure is for a low price to

---

[104] Photo courtesy of Paris Jewelers, 107 East Ridgewood Ave. Ridgewood, New Jersey 07450.

be called out, and a bidder accept it. A higher price is called out, and a different bidder accepts it. When several accept simultaneously, the auctioneer accepts the first one spotted. This process continues until a price is called out that no one accepts. At that point the auction ends, and the highest bidder wins.

In a private values setting, a very simple bidding strategy is optimal for bidders: a bidder should keep bidding until the price exceeds the value a bidder places on it, at which point the bidder should stop. That is, bidders should drop out of the bidding when the price exceeds their value, because at that point, winning entails a loss. Every bidder should be willing to continue to bid and not let the item sell to someone else if the price is less than their value. If you have a value v and another bidder is about to win at a price $p_a < v$, you might as well accept a price p_b between the two, $p_a < p_b < v$, since a purchase at this price would provide profits. This strategy is a dominant strategy for each private values bidder, because no matter what strategy other bidders adopt, bidding up to value is the strategy that maximizes the profits of a bidder.

The presence of a dominant strategy makes it straightforward to bid in the private values environment. In addition, it makes an analysis of the outcome of the English auction relatively simple.

Most auctioneers use a somewhat flexible system of *bid increments*. A bid increment is the difference between successive price requests. The theory is simplest when the bid increment, which we will denote as Δ, is very small. In this case, the bidder with the highest value will win, and the price will be no more than the second-highest value, but at least the second-highest value minus Δ, since if the price was less than this level, the bidder with the second-highest value would submit another bid. If we denote the second-highest value with the somewhat obscure (but standard) notation $v_{(2)}$, the final price p satisfies

$$v_{(2)} - \Delta \le p \le v_{(2)}.$$

As the bid increment gets small, this nails down the price. The conclusion is that, when bid increments are small and bidders have private values, the bidder with the highest value wins the bidding at a price equal to the second-highest value. The notation for the highest value is $v_{(1)}$, and thus the seller obtains $v_{(2)}$, and the winning bidder obtains profits of $v_{(1)} - v_{(2)}$.

7.6.2 Sealed-bid Auction

In a sealed-bid auction, each bidder submits a bid in an envelope. These are opened simultaneously, and the highest bidder wins the item and pays his or her bid. Sealed-bid auctions are used to sell off-shore oil leases, and used by governments to purchase a wide variety of items. In a purchase situation, known often as a *tender*, the lowest bidder wins and is paid the bid.

The analysis of the sealed-bid auction is more challenging because the bidders don't have a dominant strategy. Indeed, the best bid depends on what the other bidders are bidding. The bidder with the highest value would like to bid a penny more than the next highest bidder's bid, whatever that might be.

To pursue an analysis of the sealed-bid auction, we are going to make a variety of simplifying assumptions. These assumptions aren't necessary to the analysis but are made to simplify the mathematical presentation.

We suppose there are n bidders, and label the bidders $1,...,n$. Bidder i has a private value v_i which is a draw from the uniform distribution on the interval $[0,1]$. That is, if $0 \le a \le b \le 1$, the probability that bidder i's value is in the interval $[a, b]$ is $b - a$. An important attribute of this assumption is *symmetry* – the bidders all have the same distribution. In addition, the formulation has assumed *independence* – the value one bidder places on the object for sale is statistically independent from the value placed by others. In addition, each bidder knows their own value, but doesn't know the other bidders' values. Each bidder is assumed to bid in such a way as to maximize expected profit, and we will look for a Nash equilibrium of the bidding game. Bidders are permitted to submit any bid not less than zero.

To find an equilibrium, it is helpful to restrict attention to linear rules, in which a bidder bids a proportion of their value. Thus, we suppose each bidder bids λv when their value is v, and examine under what conditions this is in fact Nash equilibrium behavior. We have an equilibrium if, when all other bidders bid λv when their value is v, the remaining bidder will, too.

So fix a bidder and suppose that bidder's value is v_i. What bid should the bidder choose? A bid of b wins the bidding if all other bidders bid less than b. Since the other bidders, by hypothesis, bid λv when their value is v, our bidder wins when $b \ge \lambda v_j$ for each other bidder j. This occurs when $\dfrac{b}{\lambda} \ge v_j$ for each other bidder j, and this in turn occurs with probability $\dfrac{b}{\lambda}$.[105] Thus, our bidder with value v_i who bids b wins with probability $\left(\dfrac{b}{\lambda}\right)^{n-1}$, since the bidder must beat all n-1 other bidders. That creates expected profits for the bidder of

$$\pi = (v_i - b)\left(\frac{b}{\lambda}\right)^{n-1}.$$

The bidder chooses b to maximize expected profits. The first order condition requires

$$0 = -\left(\frac{b}{\lambda}\right)^{n-1} + (v_i - b)(n-1)\frac{b^{n-2}}{\lambda^{n-1}}.$$

The first order condition solves for

$$b = \frac{n-1}{n}v.$$

_____

[105] If $b > \lambda$, then in fact the probability is one. You can show that no bidder would ever bid more than λ.

But this is a linear rule! Thus, if $\lambda = \dfrac{n-1}{n}$, we have a Nash equilibrium.

The nature of this equilibrium is that each bidder bids a fraction $\lambda = \dfrac{n-1}{n}$ of their value, and the highest value bidder wins at a price equal to that fraction of their value.

In some cases, the sealed-bid auction produces *regret*. Regret means that a bidder wishes she had bid differently. Recall our notation for values: $v_{(1)}$ is the highest value and $v_{(2)}$ is the second-highest value. Since the price in a sealed-bid auction is $\dfrac{n-1}{n}v_{(1)}$, the second-highest bidder will regret her bid when $v_{(2)} > \dfrac{n-1}{n}v_{(1)}$. In this case, the bidder with the second-highest value could have bid higher and won, if the bidder had known the winning bidder's bid. In contrast, the English auction is regret-free, in that the price rises to the point that the bidder with the second-highest value won't pay.

How do the two auctions compare in prices? It turns out that statistical independence of private values implies *revenue equivalence*, which means the two auctions produce the same prices on average. Given the highest value $v_{(1)}$, the second-highest value has distribution $\left(\dfrac{v_{(2)}}{v_{(1)}}\right)^{n-1}$, since this is the probability that all n-1 other bidders have values less than $v_{(2)}$. But this gives an expected value of $v_{(2)}$ of

$$Ev_{(2)} = \int_0^{v_{(1)}} v_{(2)}(n-1)\frac{v_{(2)}^{n-2}}{v_{(1)}^{n-1}}dv_{(2)} = \frac{n-1}{n}v_{(1)}.$$

Thus, the average price paid in the sealed-bid auction is the same as the average price in the English auction.

7.6.3 Dutch Auction

The Dutch auction is like an English auction, except that prices start high and are successively dropped until a bidder accepts the going price, at which point the auction ends. The Dutch auction is so named because it is used to sell cut flowers in Holland, in the enormous flower auctions.

A strategy in a Dutch auction is a price at which the bidder bids. Each bidder watches the price decline, until such a point that either the bidder bids, or a rival bids, and the auction ends. Note that a bidder could revise their bid in the course of the auction, but there isn't any point. For example, suppose the price starts at $1,000, and a bidder decides to bid when the price reaches $400. Once the price gets to $450, the bidder could decide to revise and wait until $350. However, no new information has become available and there is no reason to revise. In order for the price to reach the original planned bid of $400, it had to reach $450, meaning that no one bid prior to a price of $450. In order for a bid of $400 to wins, the price had to reach $450; if the price reaching $450 means that a bid of $350 is optimal, than the original bid of $400 wasn't optimal.[106]

What is interesting about the Dutch auction is that it has exactly the same possible strategies and outcomes as the sealed-bid auction. In both cases, a strategy for a bidder is a bid, no bidder sees the others' bids until after their own bid is formulated, and the winning bidder is the one with the highest bid. This is called *strategic equivalence.* Both games – the Dutch auction and the sealed-bid auction – offer identical strategies to the bidders, and given the strategies chosen by all bidders, produce the same payoff. Such games should produce the same outcomes.

The strategic equivalence of the Dutch auction and the sealed-bid auction is a very general result, which doesn't depend on the nature of the values of the bidders (private versus common) or the distribution of information (independent versus correlated). Indeed, the prediction that the two games should produce the same outcome doesn't even depend on risk aversion, although that is more challenging to demonstrate.

7.6.4 Vickrey Auction

The strategic equivalence of the Dutch and sealed-bid auction suggests another fact: there may be more than one way of implementing a given kind of auction. Such logic led Nobel laureate William Vickrey (1914-1996) to design what has become known as the *Vickrey* auction, which is a "second-price sealed-bid" auction. This auction is most familiar because it is the foundation of eBay's auction design. The Vickrey auction is a sealed-bid auction, but with a twist: the high bidder wins, but pays the second-highest bid. This is why the Vickrey auction is called a second-price auction: the price is not the highest bid, but the second-highest bid.

The Vickrey auction underlies the eBay outcome because when a bidder submits a bid in the eBay auction, the current "going" price is not the highest bid, but the second-highest bid, plus a bid increment. Thus, up to the granularity of the bid increment, the basic eBay auction is a Vickrey auction run over time.

As in the English auction, bidders with private values in a Vickrey auction have a dominant strategy. Fix a bidder, with value v, and let p be the highest bid of the other bidders. If the bidder bids b, the bidder earns profits of

$$\begin{cases} 0 & \text{if } b < p \\ \\ v - p & \text{if } b > p \end{cases}.$$

---

[106] Of course, a bidder who thinks losing is likely may wait for a lower price to formulate the bid, a consideration ignored here. In addition, because the Dutch auction unfolds over time, bidders who discount the future will bid slightly higher in a Dutch auction as a way of speeding it along, another small effect that is ignored for simplicity.

It is profitable for the bidder to win if $v > p$, and lose if $v < p$. To win when $v > p$, and lose if $v < p$, can be assured by bidding v. Essentially, there is no gain to bidding less than your value, because your bid doesn't affect the price, only the likelihood of winning. Bidding less than value causes the bidder to lose when the highest rival bid falls between the bid and the value, which is a circumstance that the bidder would like to win. Similarly, bidding more than value only creates a chance of winning when the price is higher than the bidder's value, in which case the bidder would prefer to lose.

Thus, bidders in a Vickrey auction have a dominant strategy to bid their value. This produces the same outcome as the English auction, however, because the payment made is the second-highest value, which was the price in the English auction. Thus, the Vickrey auction is a sealed-bid implementation of the English auction when bidders have private values, producing the same outcome, which is that the highest value bidder wins, but pays the second-highest value.

Because the Vickrey auction induces bidders to bid their value, it is said to be *demand revealing*. Unlike the English auction, in which the bidding stops when the price reaches the second-highest value and thus doesn't reveal the highest value, the Vickrey auction reveals the highest value. In a controlled, laboratory setting, demand revelation is useful, especially when the goal is to identify buyer values. Despite its theoretical niceties, the Vickrey auction can be politically disastrous. Indeed, New Zealand sold radio spectrum with the Vickrey auction on the basis of advice by a naïve economist, and the Vickrey auction created a political nightmare when a nationwide cellular license received a high bid of $110 million, and a second-highest bid of $11 million. The political problem was that the demand revelation showed that the government received only about 10% of the value of the license, making the public quite irate and dominating news coverage at the time.[107] Some smaller licenses sold for tenths of a percent of the highest bid.

In a private values setting, the Vickrey auction, or the English auction, are much easier on bidders than a regular sealed-bid auction, because of the dominant strategy. The sealed-bid auction requires bidders to forecast their rivals' likely bids, and produces the risks of either bidding more than necessary, or losing the bidding. Thus, the regular sealed-bid auction has undesirable properties. Moreover, bidders in the sealed-bid auction have an incentive to bribe the auctioneer to reveal the best bid by rivals, because that is useful information in formulating a bid. Such (illegal) bribery occurs from time to time in government contracting.

On the other hand, the regular sealed-bid auction has an advantage over the other two that it makes price-fixing more difficult. A bidder can cheat on a conspiracy and not be detected until after the current auction is complete.

Another disadvantage of the sealed-bid auction is that it is easier to make certain kinds of bidding errors. In the U.S. PCS auctions, in which rights to use the radio spectrum

---

[107] The Vickrey auction generally produces higher prices than regular sealed-bid auctions if bidders are symmetric (share the same distribution of values), but is a poor choice of auction format when bidders are not symmetric. Since the incumbent telephone company was expected to have a higher value than others, the Vickrey auction was a poor choice for that reason as well.

for cellular phones was sold for around $20 billion, one bidder, intending to bid $200,000, inadvertently bid $200,000,000. Such an error isn't possible in an English auction, because prices rise at a measured pace. Such errors have little consequence in a Vickrey auction, since getting the price wrong by an order of magnitude requires two bidders to make such errors.

7.6.5 Winner's Curse

> "I paid too much for it, but it's worth it."
> -Sam Goldwyn

The analysis so far has been conducted under the restrictive assumption of private values. In most contexts, bidders are not sure of the actual value of the item being sold, and information held by others is relevant to the valuation of the item. If I estimate an antique to be worth $5,000, but no one else is willing to bid more than $1,000, I might revise my estimate of the value down. This revision leads bidders to learn from the auction itself what the item is worth.

The early bidders in the sale of oil lease rights in the Gulf of Mexico (the outer continental shelf) were often observed to pay more than the rights were worth. This phenomenon came to be known as the *winner's curse*. The winner's curse is the fact that *the bidder who most overestimates the value of the object wins the bidding*. Naïve bidders, who don't adjust for the winner's curse, will tend to lose money because they only win the bidding when they've bid too high.

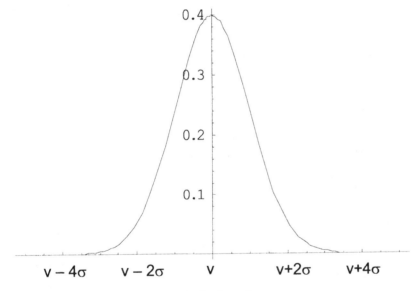

Figure 7-9: Normally Distributed Estimates

Auctions, by their nature, select optimistic bidders. Consider the case of an oil lease (right to drill for and pump oil) that has an unknown value v. Different bidders will obtain different estimates of the value, and we may view these estimates as draws from a normal distribution illustrated in Figure 7-9. The estimates are correct on average, which is represented by the fact that the distribution is centered on the true value v. Thus a randomly chosen bidder will have an estimate that is too high as often as it is too low, and the average estimate of a randomly selected bidder will be correct. However, the winner of an auction will tend to be bidder with the highest estimate, not a randomly chosen bidder. The highest of five bidders will have an estimate that is too large 97% of the time. The only way the highest estimate is not too large is if all the estimates are below the true value. With ten bidders, the highest estimate is larger than the true value with probability 99.9%, because the odds that all the estimates are less than the true value is $(1/2)^{10} = 0.1\%$. This phenomenon – that auctions tend to select the bidder with the highest estimate, and the highest estimate is larger than the true value most of the time – is characteristic of the winner's curse.

A savvy bidder corrects for the winner's curse. Such a correction is actually quite straightforward when a few facts are available, and here a simplified presentation is given. Suppose there are n bidders for a common value good, and the bidders receive normally distributed estimates that are correct on average. Let σ be the standard deviation of the estimates.[108] Finally, suppose that no prior information is given about the likely value of the good.

In this case, it is a straightforward matter to compute a correction for the winner's curse. Because the winning bidder will generally be the bidder with the highest estimate of value, the winner's curse correction should be the expected amount by which the highest value exceeds the average value. This can be looked up in a table for the normal distribution. The values are given for selected numbers n in Table 7-30. This shows, as a function of the number of bidders, how much each bidder should reduce their estimate of value to correct for the fact that auctions select optimistic bidders. The units are standard deviations.

Table 7-30: Winner's Curse Correction

n	1	2	3	4	5	10	15
WCC (σ)	0	.56	.85	1.03	1.16	1.54	1.74

n	20	25	50	100	500	1000	10,000
WCC (σ)	1.87	1.97	2.25	2.51	3.04	3.24	3.85

For example, with one bidder, there is no correction, since it was supposed that the estimates are right on average. With two bidders, the winner's curse correction is the amount that the higher of two will be above the mean, which turns out to be 0.56σ, a little more than half a standard deviation. This is the amount which should be subtracted from the estimate to insure that, when the bidder wins, the estimated value is on average correct. With four bidders, the highest is a bit over a whole standard deviation. As is apparent from the table, the winner's curse correction increases relatively slowly after ten or fifteen bidders. With a million bidders, it is 4.86σ.

---

[108] The standard deviation is a measure of the dispersion of the distribution, and is the square root of the average of the square of the difference of the random value and its mean. The estimates are also assumed to be independently distributed around the true value. Note that estimating the mean adds an additional layer of complexity.

The standard deviation σ measures how much randomness or noise there is in the estimates. It is a measure of the average difference between the true value and the estimated value, and thus the average level of error. Oil companies know from their history of estimation how much error arises in the company estimates. Thus, they can correct their estimates to account for the winner's curse using their historical inaccuracies.

Bidders who are imperfectly informed about the value of an item for sale are subject to losses arising from the way auctions select the winning bidder. The winning bidder is usually the bidder with the highest estimate, and that estimate is too high on average. The difference between the highest estimate and the average estimate is known as the winner's curse correction. The size of the winner's curse correction is larger the more bidders there are but tends to grow slowly beyond a dozen or so bidders.

If the bidders have the same information on a common value item, they will generally not earn profits on it. Indeed, there is a general principle that it is the privacy of information, rather than the accuracy of information, that leads to profits. Bidders earn profits on the information that they hold that is not available to others. Information held by others will be built into the bid price and therefore not lead to profits.

7.6.6 Linkage

The U.S. Department of the Interior, when selling off-shore oil leases, not only takes an upfront payment (the winning bid) but also takes 1/6 of the oil that is eventually pumped. Such a royalty scheme links the payment made to the outcome, and in a way, shares risk, since the payment is higher when there is more oil. Similarly, a book contract provides an author with an upfront payment and a royalty. Many U.S. Department of Defense purchases of major weapons systems involve cost-sharing, where the payments made pick up a portion of the cost. Purchases of ships, for example, generally involve 50% to 70% cost sharing, which means the DOD pays a portion of cost overruns. The contract for U.S. television broadcast rights for the summer Olympics in Seoul, South Korea, involved payments that depended on the size of the U.S. audience.

Royalties, cost-sharing and contingent payments generally link the actual payment to the actual value, which is unknown at the time of the auction. Linkage shares risk, which is a topic already considered in Section 7.5. But linkage does something else, too. Linkage reduces the importance of estimates in the auction, replacing the estimates with actual values. That is, the price a bidder pays for an object, when fully linked to the true value, is just the true value. Thus, linkage reduces the importance of estimation in the auction by taking the price out of the bidder's hands, at least partially.

The *linkage principle*[109] states that, in auctions where bidders are buyers, the expected price rises the more the price is linked to the actual value. (In a parallel fashion, the expected price in an auction where bidders are selling falls.) Thus, linking price to value generally improves the performance of auctions. While this is a mathematically deep result, an extreme case is straightforward to understand. Suppose the government is purchasing by auction a contract for delivery of 10,000 gallons of gasoline each week for

---

[109] The linkage principle, and much of modern auction theory, was developed by Paul Milgrom (1948 –).

the next year. Suppliers face risk in the form of gasoline prices; if the government buys at a fixed price, the suppliers' bids will build in a cushion to compensate for the risk, and for the winner's curse. In addition, because their estimates of future oil prices will generally vary, they will earn profits based on their private information about the value. In contrast, if the government buys only delivery and then pays for the cost of the gasoline, whatever it might be, any profits that the bidders earned based on their ability to estimate gasoline prices evaporates. The overall profit level of bidders falls, and the overall cost of the gasoline supply can fall. Of course, paying the cost of the gasoline reduces the incentive of the supplier to shop around for the best price, and that agency incentive effect must be balanced against the reduction in bidder profits from the auction to select a supplier.

7.6.7 Auction Design

We saw above that the English auction tends to reduce regret relative to sealed-bid auctions, and that the linkage principle suggests tying payments to value where possible. These are examples of auction design, in which auctions are designed to satisfy objectives of the auction designer. Proper auction design should match the rules of the auction to the circumstances of the bidders and the goal of the seller. Some of the principles of auction design include:

- Impose an appropriate reserve price or minimum bid
- Use ascending price (English) auctions rather than sealed-bid
- Reveal information about the value of the item
- Conceal information about the extent of competition
- Handicap bidders with a known advantage

However, many of these precepts change if the seller is facing a cartel. For example, it is easier for bidders to collude in a sealed-bid auction than in an English auction; and reserve prices should be made relatively high.

Reserve prices (minimum bid) have several effects. They tend to force marginal bidders to bid a bit higher, which increases bids of all bidders, reducing bidder profits. However, reserve prices also lead to a failure to sell on occasion, and the optimal reserve trades off this failure to sell against the higher prices. In addition, reserve prices may reduce the incentive of bidders to investigate the sale, reducing participation, which is an additional negative consideration for a high reserve price.

Ascending price auctions like the English auction have several advantages. Such auctions reduce the complexity of the bidder's problem, because bidder's can stretch their calculations out over time, and because bidders can react to the behavior of others and not plan for every contingency in advance. In addition, because bidders in an English auction can see the behavior of others, there is a linkage created – the price paid by the winning bidder is influenced not just by that bidder's information but also by the information held by others, tending to drive up the price, which is an advantage for the seller.

One caveat to the selection of the English auction is that risk aversion doesn't affect the outcome in the private values case. In contrast, in a sealed-bid auction, risk aversion works to the advantage of the seller, because bidders bid a little bit higher than they would have otherwise, to reduce the risk of losing. Thus, in the private values case, risk averse bidders will bid higher in the sealed-bid auction than in the English auction.

When considering the revelation of information, there is always an issue of lying and misleading. In the long-run, lying and misleading is found out, and thus the standard approach is to ignore the possibility of lying. Making misleading statements is, in the long-run, the same thing as silence, since those who repeatedly lie or mislead are eventually discovered, and then not believed. Thus, in the long-run, a repeat seller has a choice of being truthful or silent. Because of the linkage principle, the policy of revealing truthful information about the value of the good for sale dominates the policy of concealing information, because the revelation of information links the payment to the actual outcome.

In contrast, revealing information about the extent of competition may not increase the prices. Consider the case where occasionally there are three bidders, and sometimes only one. If the extent of competition is concealed, bidders will bid without knowing the extent of competition. If the bidders are risk neutral, it turns out that the revelation doesn't matter and the outcomes are the same on average. If, in contrast, bidders are risk averse, the concealment of information tends to increase the bid prices, because the risk created by the uncertainty about the extent of competition works to the advantage of the seller. Of course, it may be difficult to conceal the extent of competition in the English auction, suggesting a sealed-bid auction instead.

Bidders with a large, known advantage have several deleterious effects. For example, incumbent telephone companies generally are willing to pay more for spectrum in their areas than outsiders are. Advantaged bidders discourage participation of others, since the others are likely to lose. This can result in a bidder with an advantage facing no competition and picking up the good cheaply. Second, rivals don't present much competition to the advantaged bidder, even if the rivals do participate. Consequently, when a bidder has a large advantage over rivals, it is advantageous to handicap the advantaged bidder, favoring the rivals. This handicapping encourages participation and levels the playing field, forcing the advantaged bidder to bid more competitively to win.

A common means of favoring disadvantaged bidders is by the use of bidder credits. For example, with a 20% bidder credit for disadvantaged bidders, a disadvantaged bidder only has to pay 80% of the face amount of the bid. This lets such a bidder bid 25% more (since a $100 payment corresponds to a $125 bid) than they would have otherwise, which makes the bidder a more formidable competitor. Generally, the ideal bidder credit is less than the actual advantage of the advantaged bidder.

Auction design is an exciting development in applied industrial organization, in which economic theory and experience is used to improve the performance of markets. The U.S. Federal Communications Commissions auctions of spectrum, were the first major instance of auction design in an important practical setting, and the auction design was credited with increasing the revenue raised by the government substantially.

7.7 Antitrust

In somewhat archaic language, a trust was a group of firms acting in concert, which is now known as a cartel. The antitrust laws made such trusts illegal, and were intended to protect competition. In the United States, these laws are enforced by the Department of Justice's Antitrust Division, and by the Federal Trade Commission. The United States began passing laws during a time when some European nations were actually passing laws forcing firms to join industry cartels. By and large, however, the rest of the world has since copied the U.S. antitrust laws in one version or another.

7.7.1 Sherman Act

The Sherman Act, passed in 1890, is the first significant piece of antitrust legislation. It has two main requirements:

> *Section 1. Trusts, etc., in restraint of trade illegal; penalty*
> Every contract, combination in the form of trust or otherwise, or conspiracy, in restraint of trade or commerce among the several States, or with foreign nations, is declared to be illegal. Every person who shall make any contract or engage in any combination or conspiracy hereby declared to be illegal shall be deemed guilty of a felony, and, on conviction thereof, shall be punished by fine not exceeding $10,000,000 if a corporation, or, if any other person, $350,000, or by imprisonment not exceeding three years, or by both said punishments, in the discretion of the court.

> *Section 2. Monopolizing trade a felony; penalty*
> Every person who shall monopolize, or attempt to monopolize, or combine or conspire with any other person or persons, to monopolize any part of the trade or commerce among the several States, or with foreign nations, shall be deemed guilty of a felony, and, on conviction thereof, shall be punished by fine not exceeding $10,000,000 if a corporation, or, if any other person, $350,000, or by imprisonment not exceeding three years, or by both said punishments, in the discretion of the court.[110]

The phrase "in restraint of trade" is challenging to interpret. Early enforcement of the Sherman Act followed the "Peckham Rule," named for noted Justice Rufus Peckham, which interpreted the Sherman Act to prohibit contracts that reduced output or raised prices, while permitting contracts that would increase output or lower prices.

In one of the most famous antitrust cases ever, the United States sued Standard Oil, which had monopolized the transportation of oil from Pennsylvania to the east coast cities of the United States, in 1911.

The exact meaning of the Sherman Act had not been settled at the time of the Standard Oil case. Indeed, Supreme Court Justice Edward White suggested that, because contracts by their nature set the terms of trade and thus restrain trade to those terms and Section 1 makes contracts restraining trade illegal, one could read the Sherman Act to imply all contracts were illegal. Chief Justice White concluded that, since Congress couldn't have intended to make all contracts illegal, the intent must have been to make unreasonable contracts illegal, and therefore concluded that judicial discretion is necessary in applying the antitrust laws. In addition, Chief Justice White noted that the

---

[110] The current fines were instituted in 1974; the original fines were $5,000, with a maximum imprisonment of one year. The Sherman Act is 15 U.S.C. § 1.

act makes *monopolizing* illegal, but doesn't make having a monopoly illegal. Thus, Chief Justice White interpreted the act to prohibit certain acts leading to monopoly, but not monopoly itself.

The legality of monopoly was further clarified through a series of cases, starting with the 1945 Alcoa case, in which the United States sued to break up the aluminum monopoly Alcoa. The modern approach involves a *two-part test*. First, does the firm have monopoly power in a market? If not, no monopolization has occurred and there is no issue for the court. Second, if so, did the firm use illegal tactics to extend or maintain that monopoly power? In the language of a later decision, did the firm engage in "the willful acquisition or maintenance of that power as distinguished from growth or development as a consequence of superior product, business acumen or historic accident?" (U.S. v. Grinnell, 1966.)

There are several important points that are widely misunderstood and even misreported in the press. First, the Sherman Act does *not* make having a monopoly illegal. Indeed, three legal ways of obtaining a monopoly – a better product, running a better business, or luck – are spelled out in one decision. It is illegal to leverage that existing monopoly into new products or services, or to engage in anticompetitive tactics to maintain the monopoly. Moreover, you must have monopoly power currently to be found guilty of illegal tactics.

When the Department of Justice sued Microsoft over the incorporation of the browser into the operating system and other acts (including contracts with manufacturers prohibiting the installation of Netscape), the allegation was not that Windows was an illegal monopoly. The DOJ alleged Microsoft was trying to use its Windows monopoly to monopolize another market, the internet browser market. Microsoft's defense was two-fold. First, it claimed not to be a monopoly, citing the 5% share of Apple. (Linux had a negligible share at the time.) Second, it alleged a browser was not a separate market but an integrated product necessary for the functioning of the operating system. This defense follows the standard "two-part test."

Microsoft's defense brings up the question of "what is a monopoly?" The simple answer to this question depends on whether there are good substitutes in the minds of consumers – will they substitute to an alternate product in the event of some bad behavior by the seller? By this test, Microsoft had an operating system monopoly in spite of the fact that there was a rival, because for most consumers, Microsoft could increase the price, tie the browser and MP3 player to the operating system, or even disable Word Perfect, and the consumers would not switch to the competing operating system. However, Microsoft's second defense, that the browser wasn't a separate market, is a much more challenging defense to assess.

The Sherman Act provides criminal penalties, which are commonly applied in price-fixing cases, that is, when groups of firms join together and collude to raise prices. Seven executives of General Electric and Westinghouse, who colluded in the late 1950s to set the prices of electrical turbines, spent several years in jail each, and there was over $100 million in fines. In addition, Archer Daniels Midland executives went to jail after their 1996 conviction for fixing the price of lysine, which approximately doubled the price of this common additive to animal feed. When highway contractors are convicted of bid-rigging, generally the conviction is under the Sherman Act, for monopolizing their market.

7.7.2 Clayton Act

Critics of the Sherman Act, including famous "trust-buster" and President Teddy Roosevelt, felt the ambiguity of the Sherman Act was an impediment to its use and that the United States needed a more detailed law setting out a list of illegal activities. The Clayton Act, 15 U.S.C. §§ 12-27, was passed in 1914 and it adds detail to the Sherman Act. The same year, the FTC Act was passed, creating the Federal Trade Commission, which has authority to enforce the Clayton Act, as well as engage in other consumer protection activities.

The Clayton Act does not have criminal penalties, but does allow for monetary penalties that are three times as large as the damage created by the illegal behavior. Consequently, a firm, motivated by the possibility of obtaining a large damage award, may sue another firm for infringement of the Clayton Act. A plaintiff must be directly harmed to bring such a suit. Thus, customers who paid higher prices, or firms driven out of business by exclusionary practices are permitted to sue under the Clayton Act. When Archer Daniels Midland raised the price of lysine, pork producers who bought lysine would have standing to sue, while final pork consumers who paid higher prices for pork, but who didn't directly buy lysine, would not.

Highlights of the Clayton Act include:

- Section 2, which prohibits price discrimination that would lessen competition,
- Section 3, which prohibits exclusionary practices that lessen competition, such as tying, exclusive dealing and predatory pricing,
- Section 7, which prohibits share acquisition or merger that would lessen competition or create a monopoly

The language "lessen competition" is generally understood to mean that a significant price increase becomes possible – that is, competition has been harmed if the firms in the industry can successfully increase prices.

Section 2 is also known as 'Robinson-Patman' because of a 1936 amendment by that name. It prohibits price discrimination that lessens competition. Thus, price discrimination to final consumers is legal under the Clayton Act; the only way price discrimination can lessen competition is if one charges different prices to different businesses. The logic of the law was articulated in the 1948 Morton Salt decision, which concluded that lower prices to large chain stores gave an advantage to those stores, thus injuring competition in the grocery market. The discounts in that case were not cost-based, and it is permissible to charge different prices based on costs.

Section 3 rules out practices that lessen competition. A manufacturer who also offers service for the goods it sells may be prohibited from favoring its own service organization. Generally manufacturers may not require the use of the manufacturer's own service. Moreover, an automobile manufacturer can't require the use of replacement parts made by the manufacturer, and many car manufacturers have lost lawsuits on this basis. In an entertaining example, Mercedes prohibited Mercedes dealers from buying Bosch parts directly from Bosch, even though Mercedes itself was selling Bosch parts to the dealers. This practice was ruled illegal because the quality of the parts was the same as Mercedes (indeed, identical), so Mercedes' action lessened competition.

Predatory pricing involves pricing below cost in order to drive a rival out of business. It is relatively difficult for a firm to engage in predation, simply because it only makes sense if, once the rival is eliminated, the predatory firm can then increase its prices and recoup the losses incurred. The problem is that once the prices go up, entry becomes attractive; what keeps other potential entrants away? One answer is reputation: a reputation for a willingness to lose money in order to dominate market could deter potential entrants. Like various rare diseases that happen more often on TV than in the real world (e.g. Tourette's syndrome), predatory pricing probably happens more often in textbooks than in the real world.[111]

The Federal Trade Commission also has authority to regulate mergers that would lessen competition. As a practical matter, the Department of Justice and the Federal Trade Commission divide responsibility for evaluating mergers. In addition, other agencies may also have jurisdiction over mergers and business tactics. The Department of Defense has oversight of defense contractors, using a threat of "we're your only customer." The Federal Communications Commission has statutory authority over telephone and television companies. The Federal Reserve Bank has authority over national and most other banks.

Most states have antitrust laws as well, and can challenge mergers that would affect commerce in the state. In addition, attorneys general of many states may join the Department of Justice or the Federal Trade Commission is suing to block a merger or in other antitrust actions, or sue independently. For example, many states joined the Department of Justice in its lawsuit against Microsoft. Forty-two states jointly sued the major record companies over their "minimum advertised prices" policies, which the states argued resulted in higher compact disc prices. The "MAP" case settlement resulted in a modest payment to compact disc purchasers. The Federal Trade Commission had earlier extracted an agreement to stop the practice.

7.7.3 Price-Fixing

Price-fixing, which is called bid-rigging in a bidding context, involves a group of firms agreeing to increase the prices they charge and restrict competition against each other. The most famous example of price-fixing is probably the "Great Electrical Conspiracy" in which GE and Westinghouse (and a smaller firm, Allis-Chalmers and many others) fixed the prices of turbines used for electricity generation. Generally these turbines were the subject of competitive (or in this case not-so-competitive) bidding, and one way that the companies set the prices was to have a designated winner for each bidding situation, and using a price book to provide identical bids by all companies. An amusing

---

[111] Economists have argued that American Tobacco, Standard Oil and A.T. & T. each engaged in predation in their respective industries.

element of the price-fixing scheme was the means by which the companies identified the winner in any given competition: it used the phase of the moon. The phase of the moon determined the winner and each company knew what to bid based on the phase of the moon. Executives from the companies met often to discuss terms of the price-fixing arrangement, and the Department of Justice acquired a great deal of physical evidence in the process of preparing its 1960 case. Seven executives went to jail and hundreds of millions of dollars in fines were paid.

Most convicted price-fixers are from small firms. The turbine conspiracy and the Archer Daniels Midland lysine conspiracy are unusual. (There is evidence that large vitamins manufacturers conspired in fixing the price of vitamins in many nations of the world.) Far more common conspiracies involve highway and street construction firms, electricians, water and sewer construction companies or other "owner operated" businesses. Price-fixing seems most common when owners are also managers and there are a small number of competitors in a given region.

As a theoretical matter, it should be difficult for a large firm to motivate a manager to engage in price-fixing. The problem is that the firm can't write a contract promising the manager extraordinary returns for successfully fixing prices because such a contract itself would be evidence and moreover implicate higher management. Indeed, Archer Daniels Midland executives paid personal fines of $350,000 as well as each serving two years in jail. Thus, it is difficult to offer a substantial portion of the rewards of price-fixing to managers, in exchange for the personal risks the managers would face from engaging in price-fixing. Most of the gains of price-fixing accrue to shareholders of large companies, while large risks and costs fall on executives. In contrast, for smaller businesses in which the owner is the manager, the risks and rewards are borne by the same person, and thus the personal risk more likely to be justified by the personal return.

We developed earlier a simple theory of cooperation, in which the grim trigger strategy was used to induce cooperation. Let us apply that theory to price-fixing. Suppose that there are n firms, and that they share the monopoly profits π_m equally if they collude. If one firm cheats, that firm can obtain the entire monopoly profits until the others react. This is clearly the most the firm could get from cheating. Once the others react, the collusion breaks down and the firms earn zero profits (the competitive level) from then on. The cartel is feasible if $1/n$ of the monopoly profits forever is better than the whole monopoly profits for a short period of time. Thus, cooperation is sustainable if:

$$\frac{\pi_m}{n(1-\delta)} = \frac{\pi_m}{n}(1+\delta+\delta^2+\ldots) \geq \pi_m.$$

The left hand side gives the profits from cooperating – the present value of the $1/n$ share of the monopoly profits. In contrast, if a firm chooses to cheat, it can take at most the monopoly profits, but only temporarily. How many firms will this sustain? The inequality simplifies to $n \leq \frac{1}{1-\delta}$. Suppose the annual interest rate is 5% and the reaction time is 1 week – that is, a firm that cheats on the cooperative agreement sustains profits for a week, after which time prices fall to the competitive level. In this case, 1-δ is a week's worth of interest (δ is the value of money received in a week) and therefore $\delta = 0.95^{1/52} = .999014$. According to standard theory, the industry with a week-long reaction time should be able to support cooperation with up to a thousand firms!

There are a large variety of reasons why this theory fails to work very well empirically, including that some people are actually honest and don't break the law, but we will focus on one game-theoretic reason here. The cooperative equilibrium is not the only equilibrium, and there are good reasons to think that full cooperation is unlikely to persist. The problem is the prisoner's dilemma itself: generally the first participant to turn in the conspiracy can avoid jail. Thus, if one member of a cartel is uncertain whether the other members of a price-fixing conspiracy are contacting the Department of Justice, that member may race to the DOJ – the threat of one confession may cause them all to confess in a hurry. A majority of the conspiracies that are prosecuted arise because someone – a member who feels guilty, a disgruntled ex-spouse of a member, or perhaps a member who thinks another member is suffering pangs of conscience – turns them in. Lack of confidence in the other members creates a self-fulfilling prophecy. Moreover, cartel members should lack confidence in the other cartel members who are, after all, criminals.

On average, prosecuted conspiracies were about seven years old when they were caught. Thus, there is about a 15% chance annually of a breakdown of a conspiracy, at least among those that are eventually caught.

7.7.4 Mergers

The U.S. Department of Justice and the Federal Trade Commission share responsibility for evaluating mergers. Firms with more than $50 million in assets are required under the Hart-Scott-Rodino Act to file an intention to merge with the government. The government then has a limited amount of time to either approve the merger or request more information (called a *second request*). Once the firms have complied with the second request, the government again has a limited amount of time before it either approves the merger or sues to block it. The agencies themselves don't stop the merger, but instead sue to block the merger, asking a federal judge to prevent the merger as a violation of one of the antitrust laws. Mergers are distinct from other violations, because they have not yet occurred at the time the lawsuit is brought, so there is no threat of damages or criminal penalties; the only potential penalty imposed on the merging parties is that the proposed merger may be blocked.

Many proposed mergers result in settlements. As part of the settlement associated with GE's purchase of RCA in 1986, a small appliance division was sold to Black & Decker, thereby maintaining competition in the small kitchen appliance market. In the 1999 merger of oil companies Exxon and Mobil, a California refinery, shares in oil pipelines connecting the gulf with the northeast, and thousands of gas stations were sold to other companies. The 1996 merger of Kimberley-Clark and Scott Paper would have resulted in a single company with over 50% of the facial tissue and baby wipes markets, and in both cases divestitures of production capacity and the "Scotties" brand name preserved competition in the markets. Large bank mergers, oil company mergers and other large companies usually present some competitive concerns, and the majority of these cases are solved by divestiture of business units to preserve competition.

A *horizontal merger* is a merger of competitors, such as Exxon and Mobil or two banks located in the same city. In contrast, a *vertical merger* is a merger between an input supplier and input buyer. The attempt by book retailer Barnes and Noble to purchase the intermediary Ingram, a company that buys books from publishers and sells to retailers but didn't directly sell to the public, would have resulted in a vertical merger. Similarly, Disney is a company that sells programs to television stations (among other activities), so its purchase of TV network ABC was a vertical merger. The AOL--Time Warner merger involved several vertical relationships. For example, Time Warner is a large cable company, and cable represents a way for AOL to offer broadband services. In addition, Time Warner is a content provider, and AOL delivers content to internet subscribers.

Vertical mergers raise two related problems: *foreclosure* and *raising rivals' costs*. *Foreclosure* refers to denying access to necessary inputs. Thus, the AOL--Time Warner merger threatened rivals to AOL internet service (like EarthLink) with an inability to offer broadband services to consumers with Time Warner cable. This potentially injures competition in the internet service market, forcing Time Warner customers to use AOL. In addition, by bundling Time Warner content and AOL internet service, users could be forced to purchase AOL internet service in order to have access to Time Warner content. Both of these threaten foreclosure of rivals, and both were resolved to the government's satisfaction by promises that the merged firm would offer equal access to rivals.

Raising rivals' costs is a softer version of foreclosure. Rather than deny access to content, AOL--Time Warner could instead make the content available under disadvantageous terms. For example, American Airlines developed the Sabre computerized reservation system, which was used by about 40% of travel agents. This system charged airlines, rather than travel agents, for bookings. Consequently, American Airlines had a mechanism for increasing the costs of its rivals, by increasing the price of bookings on the Sabre system. The advantage to American was not just increased revenue of the Sabre system but also the hobbling of airline rivals. Similarly, banks offer free use of their own automated teller machines (ATMs), but charge the customers of other banks. Such charges raise the costs of customers of other banks, thus making other banks less attractive, and hence providing an advantage in the competition for bank customers.

The Department of Justice and the Federal Trade Commission periodically issue horizontal merger guidelines, which set out how mergers will be evaluated. This is a three step procedure for each product that the merging companies have in common.

The procedure starts by identifying product markets. To identify a product market, start with a product or products produced by both companies. Then ask if the merged parties can profitably raise price by a *small but significant and non-transitory increase in price*, also known as a "SSNIP," pronounced 'snip.' A SSNIP is often taken to be a 5% price increase, which must prevail for several years. If the companies can profitably increase price by a SSNIP, then they are judged to have monopoly power and consumers will be directly harmed by the merger. (This is known as a *unilateral* effect, because the merging parties can increase price unilaterally after the merger is consummated.) If they can't increase prices, then an additional product has to be added to the group; generally the best substitute is added. Ask whether a hypothetical monopoly seller of these three products can profitably raise price. If so, an antitrust market has been identified; if not, yet another substitute product must be added. The process stops adding products when enough substitutes have been identified which, if controlled by a hypothetical monopoly, would have their prices significantly increased.

The logic of product market definition is that, if a monopoly wouldn't increase price in a meaningful way, that there is no threat to consumers – any price increase won't be large or won't last. The market is defined by the smallest set of products for which consumers can be harmed. The test is also known as the hypothetical monopoly test.

The second step is to identify a geographic market. The process starts with an area in which both companies sell, and asks if the merged company has an incentive to increase price by a SSNIP. If so, that geographic area is a geographic market. If not, it is because of buyers substituting outside the area to buy cheaply, and the area must be expanded. For example, owning all the gas stations on a corner doesn't let one increase price profitably because an increase in price leads to substitution to stations a few blocks away. If one company owned all the stations in a half mile radius, would it be profitable to increase price? Probably not, as there would still be significant substitution to more distant stations. Suppose, instead, that one owned all the stations for a 15 mile radius. Then an increase in price in the center of the area is not going to be thwarted by too much substitution outside the area, and the likely outcome is that prices would be increased by such a hypothetical monopoly. In this case, a geographic market has been identified. Again, parallel to the product market definition, a geographic market is the smallest area in which competitive concerns would be raised by a hypothetical monopoly. In any smaller area, attempts to increase price are defeated by substitution to sellers outside the area.

The product and geographic markets together are known as a *relevant antitrust market*, relevant for the purposes of analyzing the merger.

The third and last step of the procedure is to identify the level of concentration in each relevant antitrust market. The Hirschman-Herfindahl index, or HHI, is used for this purpose. The HHI is the sum of the squared market shares of the firms in the relevant antitrust market, and is justified because it measures the price – cost margin in the Cournot model. Generally in practice the shares in percent are used, which makes the scale range from 0 to 10,000. For example, if one firm has 40%, one 30%, one 20% and the remaining firm 10%, the HHI is

$$40^2 + 30^2 + 20^2 + 10^2 = 3,000.$$

Usually, anything over 1800 is considered "very concentrated," and anything over 1000 is "concentrated."

Suppose firms with shares x and y merge, and nothing in the industry changes besides the combining of those shares. Then the HHI goes up by $(x + y)^2 - x^2 - y^2 = 2xy$. This is referred to as the change in the HHI. The merger guidelines suggest the government will likely challenge mergers with (i) a change of 100 and a concentrated post-merger HHI, or (ii) a change of 50 and a very concentrated post-merger HHI. It is more accurate to understand the merger guidelines to say that the government likely won't challenge unless either (i) or (ii) is met. Even if the post-merger HHI suggests a very concentrated industry, the government is unlikely to challenge is the change in the HHI is less than 50.

Several additional factors affect the government's decision. First, if the firms are already engaging in price discrimination, the government may define quite small geographic markets, and possibly as small as a single customer. Second, if one firm is very small (less than a percent) and the other not too large (less than 35%) the merger may escape scrutiny because the effect on competition is likely small. Third, if one firm is going out of business, the merger may be allowed as a means of keeping the assets in the industry. Such was the case with Greyhound's takeover of Trailways, a merger to monopoly of the only intercity bus companies in the United States.

Antitrust originated in the United States and the United States remains the most vigorous enforcer of antitrust laws. However, the European Union has recently taken a more aggressive antitrust stance and in fact blocked mergers that obtained tentative U.S. approval, such as General Electric and Honeywell.

Antitrust is, in some sense, the applied arm of oligopoly theory. Because real situations are so complex, the application of oligopoly theory to antitrust analysis is often challenging, and we have only scratched the surface of many of the more subtle issues of law and economics in this text. For example, intellectual property, patents and standards all have their own distinct antitrust issues.

8 Index

8.1 List of Figures

8.2 Index

Entrepreneur, 2-17, 2-18, 4-85, 4-86, 4-87, 4-88, 4-89, 4-91, 4-92, 4-93, 4-97
Entry, 3-64, 4-102, 6-211, 6-241, 7-251, 7-252, 7-253, 7-273, 7-274, 7-282, 7-309
Equilibrium, 2-8, 2-20, 2-21, 2-22, 2-30, 4-93, 4-104, 4-105, 4-107, 4-108, 4-109, 4-110, 4-112, 4-114, 4-133, 5-167, 5-168, 5-169, 5-187, 5-188, 5-189, 5-190, 5-191, 5-192, 5-193, 5-194, 6-197, 6-199, 6-203, 6-205, 6-206, 6-207, 6-211, 6-216, 6-224, 6-225, 6-227, 6-230, 7-253, 7-255, 7-256, 7-257, 7-258, 7-260, 7-261, 7-262, 7-263, 7-264, 7-265, 7-268, 7-269, 7-270, 7-273, 7-274, 7-275, 7-276, 7-278, 7-280, 7-281, 7-282, 7-297, 7-298, 7-311
Exclusive Dealing, 7-308
Expenditure Shares, 5-149
Externality, 4-112, 6-213, 6-214, 6-215, 6-216, 6-217, 6-218, 6-219, 6-220, 6-221, 6-224, 6-225, 6-226, 6-233, 7-278
    Common Resource, 6-216
    Commons, 4-127, 6-216, 6-226, 7-262
    Network, 4-112, 6-233
Extinction, 6-216, 6-223, 6-224, 6-225, 6-226
Exxon-Mobil, 4-81, 7-311, 7-312

F

Factor of Production, 2-40
Factor Price Equalization, 2-40
Factors of Production, 2-38, 2-39
FedEx, 6-232
Firm, 4-79, 4-97, 7-265, 7-268, 7-269, 7-270, 7-292
    Competitive, 4-97, 4-98, 4-104
    Corporation, 1-5, 4-79, 4-80, 4-81, 7-283, 7-306
    Non-Profit, 4-80
    Partnership, 4-79, 4-80
    Proprietorship, 4-79, 4-80
Fixed-Proportions, 4-83
Fluctuations, 3-77, 3-78, 7-288
Ford, 1-1
Foreclosure, 1-2, 7-312
Free Market, 6-195, 6-207
Free-Rider, 6-228, 6-229

G

Gains from Trade, 2-10, 2-22, 2-37, 2-39, 4-131, 6-198, 6-201, 6-202, 6-203, 6-205, 6-206, 6-221, 6-240, 6-241, 6-242, 6-246, 6-247, 6-248, 7-272, 7-286
Game Theory, 7-251, 7-256
    Battle of the Sexes, 7-256, 7-259, 7-267, 7-270
    Common Knowledge, 7-270
    Elimination of Dominated Strategies, 7-253, 7-254, 7-255, 7-257
    Folk Theorem, 7-269, 7-270

Grim Trigger Strategy, 7-268, 7-269, 7-270, 7-310
    Mixed Strategy, 7-258, 7-259, 7-260, 7-261, 7-263, 7-264, 7-265, 7-275
    Pure Strategy, 7-258, 7-259, 7-260, 7-261, 7-262, 7-263, 7-264, 7-265, 7-275
    Second-Mover Advantage, 7-267
    Strategic Behavior, 7-251
    Subgame Perfection, 7-266, 7-267, 7-268, 7-269, 7-270, 7-284
Gasoline, 1-2, 2-8, 2-11, 2-16, 2-24, 2-26, 4-81, 4-108, 4-109, 5-178, 6-195, 6-218, 7-303
General Electric, 7-309, 7-311
General Equilibrium, 5-188, 5-189
    Welfare Theorems, 5-188
General Motors, 4-81
    Chevrolet, 2-28
Goldwyn, Samuel, 7-301
Government, 1-1, 1-2, 1-5, 3-48, 3-56, 3-58, 3-59, 3-65, 3-66, 3-67, 3-68, 3-69, 3-70, 3-71, 3-72, 4-80, 4-114, 4-115, 5-160, 5-171, 5-177, 6-195, 6-197, 6-198, 6-199, 6-200, 6-202, 6-210, 6-211, 6-213, 6-218, 6-219, 6-220, 6-232, 6-237, 7-295, 7-296, 7-300, 7-303, 7-305, 7-311, 7-312, 7-314
Greyhound, 7-314
Gross Domestic Product, 3-56, 3-58, 3-59, 3-61, 3-65, 3-66, 3-67, 3-70, 3-71, 3-72, 3-73, 3-74, 3-75

H

Holmstrom, Bengt, 7-292
Homo Economicus, 1-5
Homogeneity, 6-231, 7-289, 7-290, 7-291, 7-292
Homogeneous Function, 4-104, 7-289, 7-291, 7-294
Hotelling Model, 7-279, 7-280, 7-282
Hotelling, Harold, 7-279
Hypothesis, 5-152, 6-221, 7-257, 7-297
Hysteresis, 2-26

I

IBM, 4-101
Identification, 6-238
Income, 1-3, 2-11, 2-13, 3-50, 3-51, 3-52, 3-53, 3-54, 3-55, 3-56, 3-58, 3-59, 3-64, 3-71, 3-72, 3-73, 4-105, 5-139, 5-143, 5-150, 5-152, 5-154, 5-155, 5-156, 5-158, 5-160, 5-161, 5-163, 5-164, 5-169, 5-171, 5-172, 5-173, 6-195, 6-203, 6-238
Income Effect, 5-152, 5-156, 5-158, 5-163, 5-171
Indifference Curve, 5-143, 5-144, 5-145, 5-146, 5-147
Inferior Good, 2-11, 5-155, 5-156, 5-157
Information, 2-23, 3-56, 3-57, 4-101, 4-120, 6-245, 6-246, 7-251, 7-278, 7-295, 7-298, 7-299, 7-300, 7-301, 7-302, 7-303, 7-304, 7-305, 7-311

V

W